INSIDE OUTER S...

Lives of STARS

Chana Stiefel

rourke
Educational Media

rourkeeducationalmedia.com

Scan for Related Titles and Teacher Resources

Teaching Focus:

Phonics: Rhyming Words- Listen to these words: star, far. What part of the words sound the same? What part of the words sound different? Can you think of other words that rhyme with star and far?

Before Reading:

Building Academic Vocabulary and Background Knowledge

Before reading a book, it is important to set the stage for your child or student by using pre-reading strategies. This will help them develop their vocabulary, increase their reading comprehension, and make connections across the curriculum.

1. Read the title and look at the cover. *Let's make predictions about what this book will be about.*
2. Take a picture walk by talking about the pictures/photographs in the book. Implant the vocabulary as you take the picture walk. Be sure to talk about the text features such as headings, Table of Contents, glossary, bolded words, captions, charts/diagrams, or Index.
3. Have students read the first page of text with you then have students read the remaining text.
4. Strategy Talk – use to assist students while reading.
   - Get your mouth ready
   - Look at the picture
   - Think…does it make sense
   - Think…does it look right
   - Think…does it sound right
   - Chunk it – by looking for a part you know
5. Read it again.
6. After reading the book complete the activities below.

Content Area Vocabulary
Use glossary words in a sentence.

black hole
constellations
galaxy
gravity
nebulae
supernova

After Reading:

Comprehension and Extension Activity

After reading the book, work on the following questions with your child or students in order to check their level of reading comprehension and content mastery.

1. *Which star is nearest to planet Earth?* (Text to self connection)
2. *What causes a black hole?* (Asking questions)
3. *What is a galaxy?* (Summarize)
4. *What colors are stars and what does each color mean?* (Summarize)

Extension Activity

A black hole swallows everything that gets pulled into its gravitational pull. To illustrate this you will need a stretchy black material such as tights, nylon, or mesh, a round deep container, a heavy round object and pennies. Stretch the black material over the container, like you are making a drum, but do not make it very tight. Secure the material to the container. Now place the heavy round object in the middle. This is the supernova collapsing. What happens to the black material? What happened to the object? Now place a penny on the slope of the black material. What happens to the penny? How does gravity work in a black hole?

Table of Contents

Starry Night

On a clear night, you can see thousands of stars. Where do these twinkling lights come from? What makes them glow? Will they shine forever?

Stars are not living things. Yet, they do have a life cycle. Stars are born. They shine for millions of years. Then they die. Blast off to see the exciting lives of stars.

Stars are giant, fiery balls of gas. Inside a star, the pull of **gravity** squeezes the gas into a tight ball. The ball heats up. A huge amount of energy is released. It's a burst of starlight!

Stars make their own light. Planets do not. The planets in our solar system shine like stars because they reflect the light of the Sun.

Stars are born inside giant clouds of dust and gas. These clouds are called **nebulae**. Each nebula gives birth to millions of stars.

Newborn stars light up nebulae like a car's headlights shining through fog.

Our Star: The Sun

Our Sun is our nearest star. It was born about 4.6 billion years ago. The Sun is the center of our solar system. Earth and seven other planets travel around the Sun.

SUN

About 1.3 million Earths could fit inside the Sun.

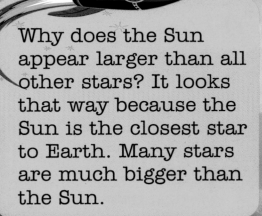

Why does the Sun appear larger than all other stars? It looks that way because the Sun is the closest star to Earth. Many stars are much bigger than the Sun.

The Sun gives us light and keeps us warm. It makes plants grow. It controls our weather. Our Sun makes life on Earth possible.

Hot Stuff

Stars are giant power plants. They spend their lives making energy. They give off light and heat.

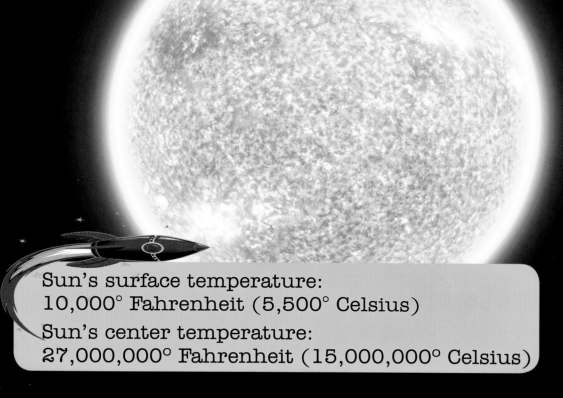

Sun's surface temperature:
10,000° Fahrenheit (5,500° Celsius)

Sun's center temperature:
27,000,000° Fahrenheit (15,000,000° Celsius)

Stars have different colors, depending on their temperature. The hottest stars are blue. Red stars are the coolest. Yellow stars, like our Sun, are in between.

Far, Far, Away

Stars look like small points of light. That is because they are very far away. The Sun is 93 million miles (150 million kilometers) from Earth. The next star is about 25 trillion miles (40 trillion kilometers) away.

How long would it take to travel from the Sun to the next star? At the speed of today's spacecraft, it would take more than 200,000 years!

Long ago, people saw patterns in the stars. These are called **constellations**. You can see shapes of animals, warriors, and more.

A **galaxy** is a huge group of stars. The universe may have as many as 100 billion galaxies. Each galaxy is home to billions of stars. Our galaxy is called the Milky Way.

The Milky Way gets its name from the milky, white disk of stars that stretches across the sky.

The *Hubble Space Telescope* was launched in 1990. *Hubble* sends us amazing photos of stars.

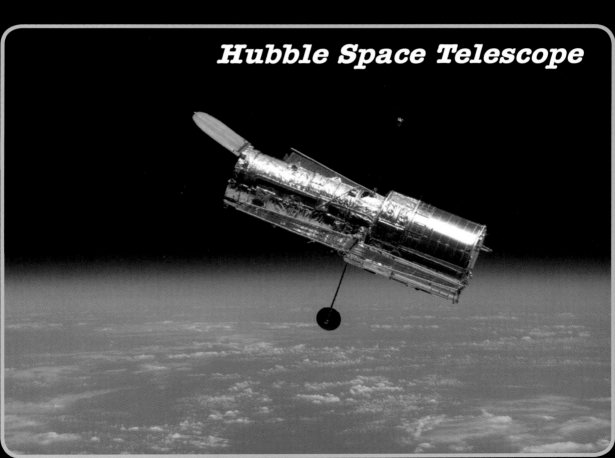

Hubble Space Telescope

How Long Do Stars Shine?

Like cars, stars die when they run out of fuel. Some stars shine for a few million years. Other stars last for trillions of years. Our Sun will shine for about 10 billion years.

When stars die, they change. Some stars puff out and expand. They are called red giants.

Then they cool off. They shrink and become white dwarfs. The Sun will become a white dwarf one day.

White dwarfs are very dense, or thick. If you could scoop up a teaspoon of matter from a white dwarf, it would weigh about the same as an elephant weighs on Earth.

Other stars will explode. They form super stars called supernovae.

Sometimes a **supernova** collapses. It pulls inward and shrinks into a tiny point. Its gravity is the strongest in the universe. This extreme gravity zone is a **black hole.**

Black Hole
Cygnus X-1

A Blue Star

The gravitational pull of a black hole is so strong it pulls material from other space objects towards it. In this drawing , the red and orange is material being pulled from a blue star toward Cygnus X-1.

Scientists continue to discover new facts about the lives of stars. Now when you look up at the stars, you will see them in a whole new light.

Photo Glossary

black hole (BLAK hole): An area of extreme gravity in space is called a black hole.

constellations (kahn-stuh-LAY-shuhns): A pattern of stars is called a constellation.

galaxy (GAL-uhk-see): A group of stars held together by gravity form a galaxy.

gravity (GRAV-uh-tee): The force that presses down on objects, keeping them from floating into space.

nebulae (NEB-yuh-luh): A cloud of gas and dust in space where stars are born is a nebulae.

supernova (soo-pur-NOH-vuh): At the end of a stars life it explodes in a supernovae or super star.

Index

Websites

http://pbskids.org/cyberchase/math-games/star-gazing/
http://www.kidsastronomy.com/astroskymap/
http://hubblesite.org/

Meet The Author!
www.meetREMauthors.com

About the Author

Chana Stiefel has written more than 20 books for kids. She has a Master's degree in Science and Environmental Reporting from New York University. Chana loves to visit the Hayden Planetarium in New York City. You can see her work at www.chanastiefel.com.

www.rourkeeducationalmedia.com

PHOTO CREDITS: Cover and title page © mironov; p4-5 © Traveller Marti p6–7 © francesco de marco, page 7 © janez volmajer; page 9 © Vadim Sadovski; page 10 © Orla, page 11 © djgis; page 12 © Aphelleon, page 13 ©AstroStar; page 15 © Beaniebeagle; page 16 and page 17 courtesy of NASA; page 19 courtesy of NASA and ESA; Page 20 NASA/CXC/M. Weiss; page 21 AJP; page 22 top to bottom © NASA/CXC/M.Weiss, Beaniebeagle, eso1042f ©ESO/P. Grosbøl www.eso.org/public/images/ eso1042f/; page 23 top to bottom © Asier Romero, Vadim Sadovski, NASA and ESA.

Edited by Jill Sherman

Cover design and Interior design: Nicola Stratford   nicolastratford.com

Library of Congress PCN Data

Lives of Stars / Chana Stiefel
(Inside Outer Space)
ISBN 978-1-62717-733-7 (hard cover)
ISBN 978-1-62717-855-6 (soft cover)
ISBN 978-1-62717-967-6 (e-Book)
Library of Congress Control Number: 2014935659

Rourke Educational Media
Printed in the United States of America, North Mankato, Minnesota

Also Available as:
ROURKE'S e-Books

BLIND OBEDIENCE
AND DENIAL

The Nuremberg Defendants

ANDREW SANGSTER

CASEMATE

Philadelphia & Oxford

Published in the United States of America and Great Britain in 2022 by
CASEMATE PUBLISHERS
1950 Lawrence Road, Havertown, PA 19083, USA
and
The Old Music Hall, 106–108 Cowley Road, Oxford OX4 1JE, UK

Copyright 2022 © Andrew Sangster

Hardback Edition: ISBN 978-1-63624-178-4
Digital Edition: ISBN 978-1-63624-179-1

A CIP record for this book is available from the British Library

Printed and bound in the United Kingdom by TJ Books

Typeset in India by Lapiz Digital Services, Chennai.

For a complete list of Casemate titles, please contact:

CASEMATE PUBLISHERS (US)
Telephone (610) 853-9131
Fax (610) 853-9146
Email: casemate@casematepublishers.com
www.casematepublishers.com

CASEMATE PUBLISHERS (UK)
Telephone (01865) 241249
Email: casemate-uk@casematepublishers.co.uk
www.casematepublishers.co.uk

Cover image (also on page xiii): Second row of defendants, including Göring, Hess, von Ribbentrop, and Keitel, created by Edward Vebell, illustrator and US soldier. (United States Holocaust Memorial Museum Collection, Gift of Sheila C. Johnson)

Contents

Foreword

Andrew Sangster has done a great service to the historical community in his study of the defendants at the Nuremberg Trials. By examining these men, their motivations and stories and legal defences, he is addressing the essential but often evaded subject of morality in history. Given that all nations and their armies commit atrocities in warfare, on what basis could the Allies try their defeated enemies for their crimes? Are present-day historians and their readers in any better position to pass judgement?

Certainly in our own present climate, there is no lack of public appetite for revising the historical record in connection with slavery and taking direct action against memorials to those associated with slavery and racism. Historians, for their part, tend to be reluctant to take on the role of overt moral arbiters. They see their role as recording what happened and why. Dr Sangster, however, is reminding us that all historical actors make moral and immoral choices; at Nuremberg, the victorious Allies took the unusual step of making the leading Nazis accountable for those choices in a court of law.

The Allies were conscious of their own vulnerability to accusations of having also committed atrocities in war. They were motivated in part, however, by their consciousness of the need for more rigorous standards of behaviour in war, particularly given the availability of new weapons of mass destruction. They were also determined that one uniquely egregious crime – the attempted extermination of European Jewry by industrial methods – should not go unrecognised or unpunished.

Politicians and opinion shapers often indulge in the rhetoric of 'learning the lessons of history' in order that such crimes 'should never happen again'. Human beings, however, remain stubbornly true to nature and continue to engage in war on false pretences, to commit atrocities on and off the battlefield, and to turn a blind eye to offences committed by political and strategic partners. What is different in the early 21st century, however, is the continuing erosion of any agreed basis of morality, even among the Western democracies.

At the end of World War II, that ethical basis was still securely to be found in the Bible as an expression of the Judaeo-Christian tradition. In 1946, François de Menthon, the prosecutor representing republican, secular France, could still publicly appeal to 'the Scriptures' as providing an agreed standard for human action. The

Nuremberg judgements could not have been made without an assumption of the inviolable dignity of every human person.

Today, while that tradition retains a residual presence, it is now for most people unconnected to any sense of religious belonging or practice. If the sanctity of human life or of the individual person is no longer an accepted moral norm, what are the chances of survival for a Western civilisation founded on that assumption? This history of the Nuremberg Trials reminds us of the cost of the Nazis' rejection of that standard.

The Revd Canon Dr Peter Doll

Preface

On 17 January 1946, François de Menthon closed the French case at the Nuremberg Trial of Nazi war criminals with these words:

> Who can say: I have a clean conscience; I am without fault? To use different weights and measures is abhorred by God ... If this criminality had been accidental; if Germany had been forced into war, if war crimes had been committed only in the excitement of combat, we might question ourselves in the light of the Scriptures. But the war was prepared and deliberated long in advance, and upon the very last day it would have been easy to avoid it without sacrificing any of the legitimate interests of the German people. The atrocities were perpetrated during the war, not under the influence of a mad passion nor of a warlike anger not of an avenging resentment, but as a result of cold calculation, of perfectly conscious methods, of a pre-existing doctrine.[1]

When these words were re-read years later, many asked why the French prosecutor made no mention of what later became known as the Holocaust.* One suggested reason was that it was more of an Eastern European issue, another that it may have been an embarrassment at Vichy France's anti-Semitic stance, and perhaps this was true for most European nations. Nevertheless, de Menthon's closing words clearly outlined why the trial was taking place. During the war, both sides committed atrocities. Individual soldiers, commanding officers, and governments were behind some appalling decisions from the legal and, above all, the moral perspectives.

The Nazi regime had demonstrably planned not only an aggressive war but ordered the vilest atrocities in living memory. The extermination of Jewish people and many others exposed by films and survivors appeared to come as a disturbing shock to some of the defendants, and most pretended ignorance. But all the evil reflected in the indictments demanded that the Nazi regime had to be held to account, not least in the hope it would never happen again.

The International Military Tribunal (IMT) was an indictment of the Nazi regime with the defendants being selected as senior representatives. This exploration paints

---

*   Marsha Parker, a Jewish friend of the author, pointed out that not all Jewish people appreciate the term Holocaust, which means destruction and annihilation, but which historically may carry various hints of sacrificial offering. The term has a complex etymology, but many Jewish people prefer their own expressions *Shoah* (Catastrophe) and *Yom HaShoah* (Memorial Day). This view demands some sympathy, but as the word Holocaust is now used almost universally for this act of genocide, it will be used in this exploration for easier understanding.

a brief backdrop to the trial but concentrates on the individuals in the dock. This book explores who and what sort of people they were as individuals, and why they had made their decisions to support a regime which brought untold suffering on the world. An estimated 80 per cent of this study is given to the selected culprits – some better known than others, some more infamous in their reputations – and explores how and why they were condemned on the international stage.

There were many complex issues as far as the prosecuting countries were concerned, but four issues tended to dominate the minds of the defendants. The first, especially for the military, was the argument 'you were just as guilty as us', namely the banned *tu quoque* ('you also did the same') argument. This enveloped the second argument that the trial was hypocritical, not least with Joseph Stalin's cohorts sitting in judgement. The third area was 'obeying orders', which also related to the *tu quoque* theme as all sides had obeyed questionable orders.

Perhaps the most critical and difficult issue for the defendants was the fourth area of genocide and mass murder, which every man in the dock tried to distance himself from by arguing that they had 'no idea of what was happening' to 'I was not involved'. There were no *tu quoque* arguments here, and this issue caused more anxiety for the defendants than conspiring to prepare and initiate wars of aggression. Murdering Russian prisoners of war, Slavs, Poles, Roma and Sinti, Jehovah's Witnesses, and homosexuals were evil deeds, but beyond this was the spectre of the Final Solution, the attempted physical annihilation of all European Jews, later called the Holocaust. The defendants could twist and turn and argue on many of the prosecution issues, as Hermann Göring cleverly demonstrated. But when murdering millions of Jews at an industrial level was raised, there was no defence. Many observers of the day in and out of the courtroom realised it was a major issue, though the Russians did not feel Jews constituted a special case, and they were listened to. The defendants realised before most that this issue was beyond any defence they could make, and despite claims to the contrary, every single man in the dock was anti-Semitic to one degree or another. All of them bore some responsibility, and they knew this to be uncomfortably true.

A Personal Confession

Although I am the author of some 15 serious historical works on 20th-century history which is the basis of my doctorate, I have also for over 50 years been a priest with occasional meanderings into the educational world. I regret to say I do not have the strength of mind to be a pacifist, but I am strongly opposed to capital punishment. I can understand why the trial and executions happened, and I remain unsure as to how I would have felt had I lost family members in a concentration camp. I do not believe imprisonment would have created martyrs, as proved by Spandau, but it would have supplied a greater opportunity for exploring the minds of the individuals, and therefore the Nazi regime, which was a phenomenon which must be understood, if only to be aware of the inherent dangers and to avoid any repetition. Having once taken a law degree, my first inclination was to study the law behind the trial, but reams have been written on this aspect by significant scholars, and on many other aspects of the trial. It dawned on me that less attention had been paid to the defendants, who were generally taken for granted. The question arose as to who they were, what they had done, what sort of people they were, their reactions, their thoughts and why they followed this route in life. I started to understand what concerned them most, namely the Final Solution. They were all very human and it is from them that we may learn not only the lessons of history so often neglected, but the dangers of human conduct, which sadly takes time to change.

Introduction

Long before the Romans declared *vae victis* (woe to the conquered), the victors of a war took their revenge by exacting their retribution in the most brutal ways. Times changed as civilisation appeared to develop, and after the Napoleonic Wars, the victors arranged a peace settlement which gave some sense of stability to Europe during the 19th century. However, following the Great War (1914–18), the Treaty of Versailles, with its reparation demands, restrictions, guilt clauses, and heavy-handedness, created 'among Germans a near universal agreement that such treatment was unjust and intolerable making the Versailles Treaty perhaps the only political issue around which there was widespread agreement in Weimar Germany'.[1]

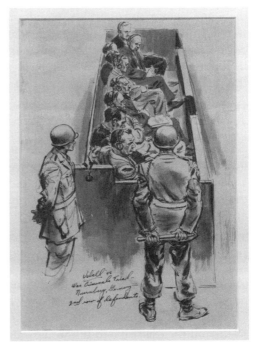

Most Germans regarded the reparations with anger since they were based on the manifestly false premise, namely 'the assertion written into the Versailles Treaty (Article 231) that Germany alone had been responsible for the war'.[2] The treatment of Germany after the war fuelled a rancorous nationalism, but 'apart from the ostracism and humiliation of Germany, which in spite of the servitudes imposed by the Treaty settlements, remained the most powerful nation in Europe'.[3] The Versailles Treaty's financial reparations for Germany were just about possible but not manageable politically, and this was true of nearly every aspect of the Treaty: Germany was politically unstable and the Versailles Treaty made it more so.[4] It helped create the well-known breeding ground for the rise of the Nazi Party (NSDAP) in Germany which eventuated in World War II.

When the 1939–45 conflict finished, the Nuremberg Trial promptly started, accompanied by the first shadows of the emerging Cold War. Much has been written about the Nuremberg International Military Tribunal and the subsequent trials (known as the SNP) as to why and how they took place, accounts of the makeup and personnel, the legalities, the proceedings, and verdicts with many general implications and consequences.

This study concentrates on the initial major trial against major German war criminals, with its focus on the *defendants, who they were and why they were judged*. This exploration is a brief and hopefully readable study, intended to try and understand the significance of the trial, give an understanding of the Nazi regime the defendants served, and look at each of the defendants from every conceivable angle. Their position and contributions within the regime are aired, the documents relating to their responses during the pre-trial interrogations and interviews are considered where they offer insights, what the psychiatrists and psychologists observed, their mutual conversations as a group when they agreed and when they divided into groups. This is followed by their observations as the Allied prosecutors outlined their cases, their own defences, and summations, as well as the views of the prosecutors.

Before arriving at the individual defendants, there will be a brief survey of the debate over the projected trial as it evolved, the intentions of the prosecution, the way the defendants were selected, the indictments, and finally an introduction to the two major issues of 'obeying orders' and 'genocide', which dominated the minds of the defendants more than any other issue.

Debate over the Projected Trial

The question must be asked as to why the 1945–46 Nuremberg Trial was deemed necessary, how they decided on those who were to be prosecuted, and the basis for that prosecution and what it hoped to achieve. Germany was defeated in May 1945, and the trials started in the autumn of the same year, demanding answers to what these selected German leaders had done while under the spell of Adolf Hitler. There had been efforts in the past to define war crimes, dating back to the early 19th century by Francis Lieber who had fought against Napoleon for the Prussians then moved to America. He set out what was called the *Lieber Code*, and this was followed by a series of well-known Geneva Conventions, but World War II surpassed everything in matters of immoral intentions and acts, thereby demanding a hope for a wider international legal basis.

During the Great War there had been massacres and brutality, not helped by false propaganda, but the second war demanded greater reflection of the distinctions between illegal action in military terms and especially against civilians, as well as the responsibility of the political leaders, and with a resolute determination that there had to be changes. The 1939–45 conflict had been deeply acrimonious, with widespread carnage, destruction, and a new legal language of crimes against humanity, genocide, and conspiracy for making war was generated as the trials took place.*

The Allies were themselves at first divided on whether there should be a trial in the first place, with the British being the most obdurate about such a process. Winston Churchill often referred to the Nazis as the 'Hitler gang' referring to them as 'outlaws'. His initial thinking was to hold kangaroo courts and shoot the perpetrators, estimating about 50 to 100 people, which almost amounted to authorised lynching. He even had the support of Lord Simon, the Lord Chancellor, even though the laws appertaining to 'outlaws' had been abolished in English law in 1938.[5] Anthony Eden, then Foreign Secretary, expressed the opinion that the Nazi war-machine was beyond the scope of normal judicial process, and even the then Archbishop of York William Temple also stated that the major protagonists should be killed.[6] The British believed that any procedure should involve the main perpetrators, and lesser criminals should be dealt with by those countries where the offences had taken place.

During the first years of the war there had been early speculative discussion on a proposed trial and condemnation of German Nazi behaviour, despite the belief among many that the Versailles Treaty had been a major contributory factor leading to the 1939–45 conflict. Churchill's secretary, John Colville, in his personal illegal diary in September 1939, thinking Germany would soon be defeated, wrote that the 'guilt clause' and other problems created by the Versailles Treaty should not be repeated, and thereby allow Germans to regain a sense of normality.[7]

There was a precedent for a trial because Article 228 of the Versailles Treaty opened this door. In 1920 the German ambassador had been given a list of nearly 900 'criminal' Germans headed by the Kaiser, Field Marshals Paul von Hindenburg and Erich Ludendorff, Admiral Alfred von Tirpitz, and others wanted for trial in various countries. It did not work as anticipated with the Kaiser retiring to a private domestic life in the Netherlands, and Hindenburg soon became the second president of the Weimar Republic.† There was German public resentment at this demand for a trial, and compromise after compromise was reached, eventuating in the Germans holding the trials (Leipzig, 23 May 1921). The Allies withdrew, and of the some 900 prosecuted there were only 13 convictions; it was regarded as a humiliating time for the Allies. This effort was not only politically aggravating but 'a farce legally, and a fiasco in terms of doing justice', and discouraged any repetition.[8] Twenty years later, this memory remained prominent in British diplomatic and political circles

---

* Terms such as 'genocide' and 'Holocaust' were not in common usage as later. The Polish jurist Raphael Lemkin coined the expression 'genocide' in 1944, and it was adopted by a UN Convention in 1948, although referred to before then from time to time.

† The Kaiser died in his residence at Doorn in 1941.

acting as a warning not to be repeated. Adding to the complexity of the problem was the question that hitherto there had been no previous action or legal basis on the way in which another country treated its own inhabitants, but now there was an emerging issue emanating from Germany with its persecution of the Jews. There was no antecedent judicial process for dealing with this scenario. It was different from established war crimes associated with the manner an enemy treated its prisoners of war and enemy civilians, and the British Foreign Office remained somewhat detached from the problem.

Sir Robert Vansittart, a senior British diplomat who was well known for his visceral hatred of the Nazis, raised the issue (26 February 1940) and pointed out that there was a vast difference between isolated cases of atrocity and a 'deliberate attempt to exterminate a whole nation'.[9] In 1940 the Poles also demanded some form of retribution and international condemnation of Nazi action. Even Churchill hinted to Parliament between 1940–41 demands for active justice. Questions were asked in parliament whether records of behaviour and individuals were being kept. There were concerns raised about executions of hostages in France, and the Jewish massacre at Babi Yar, Ukraine, in September 1941 was known about. It has been purported by Bower that 'Anthony Eden was hopelessly prejudiced against Jews', and the Foreign Office remained somewhat detached.[10] By 1942 there was gathering news of atrocities against British prisoners of war (especially in Japan), and information about the massacre at Lidice, Czechoslovakia, 9 June 1942, following Reinhard Heydrich's assassination. On 10 August 1943, the British Foreign Office received a telegram from the British consul-general in Geneva with information from a Gerhard Riegner (later Secretary of the World Jewish Congress 1965–83), which basically revealed the full horror of the Holocaust. However, many found it difficult to believe, especially after the false rumours and propaganda of the Great War.

In October 1942, the Russian foreign minister, Vyacheslav Molotov, had suggested the Nazi hub of offenders should be held to account, which was regarded as the first suggestion for a Nuremberg-type trial. A month later, Ivan Maisky, the Soviet Ambassador to Britain, sent a note to Eden suggesting an international tribunal should be established. This proposal may have reflected the show-trials of the 1930s during which Stalin had eliminated any possible opponents to his leadership and where guilt was presumed before the proceedings started.

The question of some form of recrimination was increasing, and in late 1943 at the Tehran Conference, Stalin proposed executing some 50,000 to 100,000 German staff officers. US President Franklin D. Roosevelt, probably in repartee, suggested 49,000, not helped by Roosevelt's son unofficially announcing the American Army would support it. Churchill took this seriously or misunderstood the banter and left the room. He was opposed to executing soldiers who had fought for their country, and he probably saw this as a political action by Stalin, knowing about the barbarity of the unmentionable Katyń massacre.* Considerable convincing was necessary for Churchill to accept that a trial was necessary. Initially, the Americans had found the rumours of such atrocities taking place under German occupation difficult to believe, but after they engaged in the war, American opinion was less divided, although Henry Morgenthau (the American Secretary to the Treasury during the Roosevelt administration, who later wanted Germany reduced to agricultural status) tended to agree with Churchill over the shooting of the ringleaders. On the other hand, the powerful figure of Henry Stimson, the secretary of war, demanded that the due process of American law should be upheld and had Roosevelt's support. Stimson proposed an international tribunal following Molotov's proposal that the main charge should be waging war with premeditated brutality. It was argued by the American establishment that it was axiomatic that some form of international military tribunal be created. However, at the Yalta Conference in February 1945, Churchill returned to his theme of summary execution of the Nazi ringleaders, which puzzled the Americans. It has been suggested that it was not just rank revenge by the British, but more a concern that a public trial using the technicalities of the confusing legal systems might get out of hand. It was well known that Hitler's trial after the Munich *Putsch* had played to his advantage, and there were concerns that in a public trial the enemy might grasp the headlines and offer various forms of justification. There was no desire to give Nazism the opportunity to debate international law, challenge the Versailles Treaty, and all in public view. There was also the impression that the head of a state could not be put on trial, which the leading American prosecutor Robert Jackson regarded as an ancient hangover from the days of the Divine Right of Kings. As a matter of curiosity, the Japanese Emperor was not placed in a courtroom by American demand. It was soon apparent that the central issue reflected the popular feeling that no one wanted the major defendants acquitted.

There were tensions between the British and Americans over the necessity of the trial and its nature, but when news of the Malmedy massacre arrived, American determination strengthened because of public uproar.† There were further question marks as it became known that the Russians were already holding on-the-spot trials for culprits found in occupied territory as well as their own citizens who were accused of co-operating with the enemy. The first such prosecution had been as early

---

*   The Katyń massacre, where Polish officers, clergy, teachers and potential leaders were killed, was a Soviet and not a Nazi crime which was suspected to be the case in 1945–46, but it took decades after Stalin's death to be admitted. It was not until 1992 when President Yeltsin released Stalin's written order of 5 March 1940. The danger at Nuremberg was the *tu quoque* argument of 'you also', which would cause deep embarrassment as would Britain's possible invasion of Norway.

†   The Malmedy massacre occurred on 17 December 1944, when the Germans attempted their push through the Ardennes (Battle of the Bulge). Many American prisoners were murdered by German SS troops in this incident.

as July 1943 at Krasnodar, Russia, with larger public trials at Kharkov, Ukraine; the Americans and British were concerned at the possibility of the show-trial taking root. Consequently America, the dominant partner, pushed on regardless of British views, and Justice Robert Jackson, Roosevelt's former Attorney-General, was selected as the prosecution counsel, backed by the Vice-President Harry S. Truman, who constantly insisted on judicial process. Churchill appeared adamant, and Eden argued that with the dictators now dead, a trial was unnecessary. Churchill eventually changed his views, probably because he was unprepared to suffer any political ramifications by opposing the fellow Allies, and it was agreed the French would participate. By March 1945, the British were 'resigned to the fact that they had no choice but to accept the American initiative while trying to limit the damage as best they could'.[11] The tensions persisted and when the Americans had liberated Buchenwald concentration camp (4 April 1945), they invited the press and made what they had discovered totally public. On the other hand, when the British liberated Belsen concentration camp (15 April 1945), journalists were forbidden (although a filmed recording was made), and later this lack of action was justified by claiming that the inmates were not British, and those countries whose victims were in the camp were responsible for the prosecution. Given the circumstances of those days, I find it somewhat strange.

The process of establishing the nature of the trial was no easy task, with initial problems over which form of legal system to use: whether the Anglo-American Common Law process whereby the defendants could testify but make no formal final speech, or the French and Russian Civil Law in which they could not testify but could make a final speech of defence. Common Law relied on the adversarial systems where prosecution and defence fight it out, and the continental Civil Law tended to be more 'inquisitorial'. After the trial, the defendant Hans Fritzsche would understandably complain that the trial was a duel between 'two unequally matched opponents' in which part of their game was 'to destroy confidence in the witness and his evidence', which was alien to the continental system. Fritzsche wrote the British seemed to be the best at cross-examination.[12] An arrangement was made merging the systems which was somewhat unique but appeared workable. The USA provided a huge team of judges, lawyers, researchers, translators, guards, medical men, psychologists and psychiatrists, amongst others, compared to the other nations, with the French having the smallest contingent.* The Soviets appointed Major-General Iona Timofeevich Nikitchenko as their key judge, the French, Professor Henri Donnedieu de Vabres, the Americans, Francis Biddle, and the British, Colonel Sir Geoffrey Lawrence, Lord Justice, who was also appointed President of the Tribunal, all with nominated seconds. The prosecution leaders were Attorney General Sir Hartley Shawcross (UK), Justice Robert Jackson (USA), Lieutenant-General Roman

---

* The American team was in the region of some 200, the British about 34, the Russian and French even fewer.

Rudenko (USSR), and François de Menthon (France), though he was replaced by Auguste Champetier de Ribes.

The general framework was decided, but the whereabouts of the trial also had to be agreed with the Russians, who were insisting on Berlin, and tended to keep themselves isolated from the other legal teams. The Anglo-Americans looked at Munich, Luxembourg, Leipzig, and eventually the American General Lucius Clay suggested Nuremberg. This city was strongly associated with the rise of Nazism, had been their major centre, especially for rallies, was associated with the infamous Race Laws, and the spacious Palace of Justice was one of the few places that had survived the bombing raids. The Russians eventually agreed so long as Berlin was recognised as the official home of the Tribunal authorities.

Colonel Murray Bernays, a lawyer in civilian life and a soldier working in the American War Department, had claimed 'that a trial would have enormous advantages over mere political condemnation—such as had followed the end of the previous war', and he was considered correct in his thinking.[13] Despite the initial British objections, the trial was finally agreed under the terms of the London Charter which started the discussion in Church House, London on 26 June and was agreed and signed on 8 August 1945. Many have expressed doubts then and since about the trials and the principles they established, but they were 'clothed with judicial precedent and United Nations recognition', and as an international legal force remain important and will be referred to again in the closing chapters.[14] It might also be noted that by 1945 the official and public attitudes were changing. The renunciation of war in the 1928 Kellogg–Briand treaty signed by many nations had virtually passed by without notice, but the perceived evil of the Nazi regime had no comparison either in Imperial Germany or elsewhere in the Western world, and there was an urge to condemn the Nazi perpetrators in the hope it could not happen again.* Those who had assisted Hitler by 1945 were almost household names, and it was deemed necessary that something had to be done about this cabal of murderous leaders.

Intentions and Indictments

Given the extreme passions at the end of the war, few people expected those on trial to avoid execution, including many of the defendants who anticipated a death sentence. There were even approaches made by volunteers to assist in the executions. The German public was naturally divided, uncertain as to what was happening, but for many the visceral hatred of these men was evident, especially from people who had suffered under Nazi occupation. It was also true for many Germans, but there was a degree of indifference among the general population given the circumstances

---

* Later in the trial, it would be argued that the Kellogg–Briand Pact had failed to achieve full legal force.

of living in bombed cellars with serious shortage of foods. As the trial progressed, interest became less and less among the Nuremberg residents, and one reporter noted that the local newspaper (*Nürnberger Nachrichten*) had to be 'prodded' to show more interest.[15]

Some defendants, such as economist Hjalmar Schacht, were confident of acquittal; Hans Frank may have hoped his Christian faith revival would come to his rescue; others, once they read the indictments, were less certain. Göring believed he would be tried again and again by various nations, placed under public scrutiny, and executed. The Allied prosecutors tended to feel the same way, with the Russians determined they should all die. Among the main concerns was that the trial would not create martyrs or opportunities for possible neo-Nazi memorial events.

As the various legal minds came together, they realised the outcome of the trial should not be regarded as mere punishment. Various strands of thinking started to emerge, not least the international stage and the need for better standards of behaviour in the way countries in the future should conduct themselves, with a definite hint of morality underpinning the proceedings. It was also regarded as a way of divorcing the German public from the Nazi regime by demonstrating its sheer evil, educating them away from any disposition towards any form of totalitarianism. The trial, it was hoped, would display the history of Nazism in such a way as to make it repugnant to the current and future generations. It was meant by some to be a means to educate the German public about the evils of the regime, which was echoed in the de-Nazifying tribunals held in the following months.

The intentions of those involved in the discussions varied from sheer revenge to a cleansing education, as the different moral, legal, and national motives wavered between the various intellects of those involved in the prosecution. Whether this would work will be left to the closing pages of this exploration and to the reader, but first it is critical to understand the nature of the indictments.

After considerable debate, the Allies agreed on four distinct indictments. The first was participation in a common plan or conspiracy for the accomplishment of a crime against peace. Secondly, planning, initiating and waging wars of aggression and other crimes against peace. Thirdly, participating in war crimes, and finally, crimes against humanity.

There could be no doubt that many countries, including the Americans, British, French and Russians, could be deemed guilty of the first and second clauses. The Russian attack on Finland was within the time sphere of consideration, as was their co-operation with the Nazi regime occupying Poland and the Baltic states. The Soviets were also guilty of the last clause, with the Katyń massacre already widely known but not brought up in this context. There is no doubt that at the local level, many from all sides could be held as criminals within the duress of war. In some small battle scenarios barely mentioned in history, a local conflict could lead to deep loathing and an intense desire for revenge which was exacted against the enemy;

the call for 'no prisoners' was internationally common across the globe. However, as outlined by the French in their opening address, it was understood that in the heat of battle criminal acts were wrong, but they fell into a different category from such acts when ordered by the government or regime of the day.

It could be argued that the use of submarines torpedoing unprotected civilian ships was criminal, but all sides were guilty. Many Germans believed the carpet or strategic bombing of civilian areas victimised them, and without moving into the moral complexities of these arguments, it was quietly agreed that this aspect of the war would be side-lined, as Katyń was placed on a concealed shelf.

There was little question that Nazi behaviour, led by Hitler, had reduced Europe and much of the globe into a state of 'total war', occupying several countries, accompanied by massacres, ill-treatment of prisoners of war, torture, and above all, the extermination processes had taken mankind back beyond the most barbaric times of known human history. Despite the barbarity on all sides, the Nazi regime was decidedly immoral. It was decided by those planning and preparing for the trial that it should be emphasised that the Nazi leaders had formulated their criminal enterprise before September 1939 and, as Jackson told President Truman in June 1945, it involved 'acts which have been regarded as criminal since the time of Cain'.[16] This legal argument included the system of terror and the racist theme of Aryan superiority. The Jewish preferred the use of the word 'genocide', referring to the destruction of a nation or race, but it took time for this critical word to be accepted.* The preferred term by many people on the committee was 'crimes against humanity', which carried huge significance and which, alongside the word genocide, has now become part of everyday language both in English and other languages.

The nature of a *conspiracy charge* was another question, introduced to bind the various and complex prosecution elements. It was conceived by Colonel Murray Bernays and adopted by the American War Department in November 1944 as being critical for demonstrating the criminality of Nazi leadership, and it was very much an American input. This conspiracy theory 'overrode all foreseeable appeals by the SS and Gestapo agents that they had only obeyed German law', which was important

---

*   As news of the *Endlösung*, 'Final Solution', percolated through to London and Washington, it was treated with scepticism and caution, not helped by the false propaganda from the previous war. The Jewish lobbyists were failing to make an impact. Many Allied troops on later entering the concentration camps frequently said, 'Now I know why we were fighting', and the criticism was often voiced that many of the perpetrators escaped because insufficient attention was given to the deeds and who committed them. It was difficult to believe, and the tasks involved needed 'the skills of policemen and detectives, not panels of lawyers and politicians'. See Tom Bower, *Blind Eye to Murder* (London: Warner Books, 1995), 48. Social anti-Semitism abounded in the West but not the biological-racist variation. Before the war, Britain had accepted Jewish children for safekeeping but were nervous about opening Palestine as a refuge because of the tension with Arabs.

as 'obeying orders' was foreseen as a common defence.[17] However, the theme of 'conspiracy' had its critics at the time and since, not helped by the well-known love of 'conspiracy theories'. One argument was the legal violation of making an action illegal once it had been committed and applying that law retroactively, and it was novel to French, Russian, and German law. War itself was not deemed illegal, despite the Kellogg–Briand treaty signed in Paris for outlawing war as a means of settling international disputes in 1928. The sense of collective guilt by belonging to '*x*' organisation had little precedent in British or American law and many were suspicious of the risks of postulating guilt through association.* Perhaps one of the more lucid explanations was provided by American prosecutor Telford Taylor during a presentation in court when he said:

> It is an innocent and respectable business to be a locksmith; but it's nonetheless a crime if the locksmith turns his talents to picking the locks of neighbours and looting their homes. And that is the nature of the charge under counts One and Two against the defendants and the General Staff and High Command group.[18]

This was a telling analogy which covered many aspects of the trial. The Soviets were concerned, and sent a team of advisors under a Colonel Likhachev to keep their past hidden or at least out of the headlines. All these various legal issues demanded a burden of proof which was difficult within the time limits, not only as to who was responsible for specific acts but finding legal evidence of a conspiracy. This task was not helped by the many languages involved. The trial used four languages, English, German, Russian, and sometimes French. There was also Polish, Dutch, and others, with all the photographs showing everyone wearing headphones with a mass of translators. It also demanded teams of researchers, with German speakers wading through reams of documents, interviews, interrogations, and finding witnesses. This was especially true for making a case on 'conspiracy', which was more an assertion than an easily identifiable action, where evidence might prove difficult to demonstrate. The ideal documents were evasive from the point of view of legal demands, but the important 'Hossbach Memorandum' which recorded Hitler's conference of 5 November 1937, eventually came to light, clearly indicating his aggressive ambitions; this 'document destroyed any possible doubt concerning the Nazis' premeditation of their crimes against peace', but it remained questionable evidence.[19] Tellingly, the protocol of the Molotov–Ribbentrop Pact of 22 August 1939 which outlined the Soviet–Nazi occupation of Poland was found, but for diplomatic reasons was not allowed to surface, as later the bombing raids were not raised to avoid *tu quoque* arguments. Jackson had the foresight to see the value of

---

* In 1940 Congress had passed the Smith Act by which it was a felony to belong to any group wanting to overthrow the American government, but had been passed over by the President's veto.

documentation as witnesses could lie or be evasive, whereas a document stood at its moment in time as undeniable evidence.[20]

For John Doe, or the man on the Clapham omnibus, it must have appeared a simple case of convicting an enemy who had started an aggressive war, during which crimes of the grossest conceivable nature had been committed by a barbaric regime. The fact that Stalin had initially worked in tandem with the enemy and had instituted a similar administration in his domain was cast aside as Russia had been a major factor in defeating the Nazi regime. From the international legal perspective, it was not that straightforward; most people had the desire for retribution, and the need to stop this reoccurring.

Churchill had thought at first when selecting the defendants that it should include Japanese and Italian war criminals. Japan was considered a separate issue by the Americans and Russians, but in the initial drawing up of proposed names there were eight Italians – these were eventually dropped with a suggestion that some might need further investigation. Italy had surrendered in 1943, the Allies had occupied the south and central areas, and there had been serious reprisals against Italians by the Germans, classifying that country as a victim of Nazi aggression. There was also a determination by the Anglo-Americans to bring Italy into the democratic family of nations, so *Axis* criminality soon became *German* criminality for the focus of the intended trial. Italy's conquest of Ethiopia had involved gas and was brutal, their attack on their client state of Albania and later Greece were 'crimes against peace', but Nazi Germany was deemed to have been the prime cause and perpetrators of criminal activity. The focus on Nazi Germany was about the only area in which the British and Russians agreed, with the British not forgetting Russia's 1939 agreement with Hitler over occupying Poland, and the Russians unforgiving about the British intrusion into the Russian Revolution. The Russians even accused Britain of seeking peace by having Rudolf Hess in their islands, but he had arrived unexpectedly and was evidently mentally unbalanced. The Americans appeared somewhat ignorant of this divisive atmosphere and were often accused of not knowing enough about the European background. The vexed question of how one selected the chief perpetrators was a problem not least because of a high degree of ignorance about the Nazi form of government and command.

Selecting the Defendants

The critical issue was defining the central figures for individual prosecution. Thousands had carried out criminal acts, but which were described as local and should be judged at that level. These were individuals who had organised massacres, killing prisoners of war and civilians, but they felt justified by the Nazi regime who had demanded such actions; higher command was the focus of the proposed trial. All captured German prisoners had been put through an interview process, identified by physical features to find not only the minor criminals but the major ones – such as Heinrich Himmler trying to pass through as a foot soldier. The selection task was not straightforward as some were prisoners of the Americans, British, Russians, and French, all treating them as personal prizes.

The United Nations was formed in May 1945 and the War Crimes Commission (UNWCC) established in 1943. The initial list, started as early as 1944, omitted Hitler for some extraordinary reason, but the Soviets were understandably quick to correct this omission. Göring's name was appended later, even though he was supposedly Hitler's successor. Benito Mussolini had been on the list until he was killed by Italian partisans. Not long after, Hitler committed suicide. It could not be an arbitrary list and the selection took time and thought. The original list was huge, reduced to just over 30, was altered again, changed several times, and only 14 from the original list arrived at the trial. The British narrowed the list down to Hitler, Himmler, Göring, Joseph Goebbels, and Joachim von Ribbentrop, asking the others who they wanted to add. Hitler and Goebbels killed themselves, and Himmler committed suicide on 23 May 1945 as a prisoner of the British. The inclusion of military officers was frequently raised, and in 1944 'Eden rejected the inclusion of further officers on the grounds that it would be impossible to know where to draw the line; for the same reason, no industrialist was included on the list'.[21] The Americans disagreed with this omission, as did Clement Atlee, Labour leader and member of the War Cabinet, who also wanted some German generals indicted.

It was not simply that the industrialists had supported a corrupt regime or had been pragmatic capitalists making the most of the situation, but Siemens had cheap labour from Auschwitz, Buchenwald, and Ravensbrück, and BMW drew labour from Dachau. The famous I G Farben works even built its own concentration camp near Auschwitz. Zyklon B, the gas used for killing occupants of the camps, had to be financed and produced by industrialists, even if they did not personally release its deadly elements down the funnel. They provided the tool and could not pretend that they did not know what it was used for. This was the matter of collective guilt seized upon by Colonel Murray Bernays. He proposed that whole organisations working for the Nazi regime could be prosecuted through a named representative. This way, he argued, organisations such as the Gestapo, the SS, industrialists, and bankers could be prosecuted through a leading defendant.

Many questioned this procedure both legally, morally, and in practicable results. Others saw the collective guilt as a means of attacking the entire Nazi organisation. One defendant taken into American custody was Hjalmar Schacht who 'admitted after the war that it had always been his intention to raise money for rearmament (armaments second to none), knowing that Hitler intended to declare war on Russia'.[22] Schacht was a pragmatic banker, but he was not a dedicated Nazi (he later ended up in a concentration camp). He was supported by other bankers such as Karl Blessing, a dedicated Nazi who visited the concentration camps. He also had the support of Hermann Abs, a German banker, known pre-war internationally as was Schacht, and both had good connections in England. Many regarded Abs as a figure who could help restore Germany in the years to come. Collective guilt was an ambiguous policy but difficult to fulfil, especially as Germany would need restoration in the years to come.

There was considerable wrangling over who to put on trial, the Russians wanting a hundred on the list, the British much fewer. Finally, the prosecution entered indictments against 24 major war criminals and various organisations, namely the leadership of the Nazi Party, the Reich Cabinet, the Gestapo, the SA, the SS, SD, the General Staff, and High Command. If the organisations were found guilty, then this would imply that the German High Command was responsible for their crimes. The defendants stood as individuals for the part they played and as an indicator of the collective guilt for the regime they represented. There were mistakes made over well-known industrialist Gustav Krupp who had been seriously ill, and it should have been Alfried Krupp who ran the heavy industry conglomerate Krupp AG, or even Bertha Krupp (who the French were after), and confusion seemed to reign. Airey Neave (a British soldier famous for escaping Colditz, and later an MP assassinated by the IRA), who had been set the task of investigating the Krupp family, pointed out that Gustav Krupp survived until 1950 (although he was in a state of constant illness and deterioration), but more pertinently pointed out that more than 70,000 forced labourers, including women and children, had suffered in the Krupp industries.[23]

The final selection, in alphabetical order, was:

> **Martin Bormann**, as successor to Hess as Nazi Party Secretary 1941–45. He never attended the trial as he was believed dead, which was finally confirmed many years after the war.
>
> **Karl Dönitz**, admiral and Hitler's hapless successor (1945), charged on the vexatious issue of submarine warfare 1935–45.
>
> **Hans Frank**, Reich Law Leader and Governor-General of the Eastern General Government 1933–45.
>
> **Wilhelm Frick**, Reich Minister of the Interior 1933–43, Reich Protector of Bohemia and Moravia 1943–45, who helped compose the Nuremberg Laws.
>
> **Hans Fritzsche**, Nazi propaganda radio commentator, often seen as Goebbels's proxy 1933–45.
>
> **Walther Funk**, Minister of Economics, who succeeded Schacht as head of the *Reichsbank*, 1938–45.
>
> **Hermann Göring**, *Reichsmarschall* (second after Hitler) of the *Luftwaffe*, economics overseer, original head of the Gestapo 1933–45.
>
> **Rudolf Hess**, Hitler's deputy in the early days 1933–41.
>
> **Alfred Jodl**, Keitel's second in the OKW, who signed orders for the execution of Allied commandos and Soviet commissars 1939–45.

Ernst Kaltenbrunner, highest-ranked SS leader, Chief of the RSHA, which included SD (security service), the Gestapo, the Kripo (criminal police), and the overall command of *Einsatzgruppen*. The real head of the Gestapo was Heinrich Mueller who was missing, but Kaltenbrunner was taken as the representative because he was available, 1943–45.

Wilhelm Keitel, Head of OKW, who signed orders for illegal executions, 1938–45.

Gustav Krupp, major industrialist, who had a stroke in 1939, stopped work, and was never prosecuted.

Robert Ley, Head of the German Labour Front, who committed suicide during the trial, 1933–45.

Constantin von Neurath, Minister of Foreign Affairs 1932–38, and later Protector of Bohemia and Moravia 1939–43, who resigned following disputes with Hitler.

Franz von Papen, Chancellor of Germany in 1932, Vice-Chancellor under Hitler 1933–34, Ambassador to Austria 1934–38, and to Turkey 1939–44.

Erich Raeder, Commander of the *Kriegsmarine* 1928–43.

Joachim von Ribbentrop, Ambassador to Britain 1936–38 then Minister of Foreign Affairs 1938–45.

Alfred Rosenberg, racial ideologist, and Minister of Eastern Occupied Territories 1941–45.

Fritz Sauckel, *Gauleiter* of Thuringia 1927–45, responsible for Nazi slave labour.

Hjalmar Schacht, President of the *Reichsbank* 1923–30 and Economics Minister 1934–37; later imprisoned in a concentration camp.

Baldur von Schirach, head of the Hitler Youth 1931–40 and later *Gauleiter* in Vienna 1940–45.

Arthur Seyss-Inquart, instrumental in the *Anschluss*, deputy to Hans Frank in Poland, later *Reichskommissar* to the Netherlands, 1940–45.

Albert Speer, Hitler's architect, and Minister of Armaments 1942–45; notorious for using slave labour.

Julius Streicher, *Gauleiter* of Franconia 1922–40, who produced the infamous anti-Semitic paper *Der Stürmer*.

When the trial opened on 20 November 1945, dressed as they were the defendants appeared like a motley crew, almost nondescript. As the trial progressed, the individuals, their internal divisive grouping, and their idiosyncrasies became more evident. Kaltenbrunner was missing because he was receiving medical treatment for a cerebral haemorrhage. Bormann was also absent – it was hoped that he would appear, as his death had not been confirmed at that point. As the defendants emerged as individuals, Telford Taylor later described them from their postures and attitudes.

He described Göring as the ringmaster but expressive and attentive, with Keitel and Jodl looking trim and sitting straight-shouldered with Jodl scowling. He decided that Streicher and Kaltenbrunner were the 'most repellent', with Funk equally unappetising, Schacht looking angry with Dönitz, and Frank wearing dark glasses.[24]

In this strange but formidable list, it had been hoped to cover the entire Nazi fabric, from militarism, to business, economy, financing, general criminality, but disagreement remained prominent. It was made more complicated because the defendants stood in the dock for personal conduct and to represent their various organisations and affiliations. It was known and proved to be a massive task for a single trial examining signed decrees, letters, command orders, ideologies, witnesses, films of evidence, as they attempted to cover the entire era of Nazi rule. The matter of charges had been outlined but their substance needed defining. The defendants had been selected, and interviews and interrogations were utilised to try and establish a realistic picture of the Nazi framework, which was a bewildering structure, all within a narrow timeline, giving the proceedings a sense of panic.

Two Critical Issues

Aufträge sind Aufträge: Orders are Orders

Without becoming overly involved in jurisprudential questions of law and justice, this was an area of concern. It is assumed by most people that the law must have something of a principled basis, but the moral fabric of one society may differ vastly from another. In times past, some societies expected wives who outlived their husbands to be burnt alongside their deceased partners; the Church had once thought it expedient to torture individuals to save their eternal souls, and to this day there are cultural, religious, and major differences between legal systems across the world. Some countries such as China and America execute criminals, while many others have removed capital punishment from the statute book. Worldwide, there are differences in legal systems, penal systems, and national laws. The concept of international law was not new, but was weak, hardly universal, and many hoped the IMT would be a major step forward to provide some form of remedy.

As noted, the common law approach of the Anglo-Americans had managed to accommodate itself alongside the French and Russian civic-type code systems. But it was not German law, and there was the inherent danger of retroactive law – making a deed illegal after it had been committed in a country where it was not deemed wrong or even immoral. The moral repugnance by the Western powers was immense, yet they included Stalin's Soviet Russia with the well-known show-trials of the 1930s, the Katyń massacre, later emerging rumours of their prison camps (the Gulags), and many other acts of aggression which were little different from that of Hitler's regime. France, Britain, and America had reputations of invading other lands and occupying them as their possessions.

Nevertheless, the vexatious question remained as to how one could prosecute a defendant both as an individual and representing a group when they were controlled and ordered by an immoral regime (many of which exist to this day) giving them little choice. Should it be just the policy directors and lawmakers, or the soldier and the policeman who carried out their instructions? There was the genuine concern that it would be difficult to prove that anyone was guilty apart from a dead dictator.

Robert Jackson, lead American prosecutor, fought with this using the analogy of a firing squad – if a person volunteers, he becomes a participant, as those who volunteered to join the SS and Gestapo and similar organisations became willingly involved in the crime. It was a clever analogy but assumed a person could volunteer and not be obligated to participate in a firing squad.

Because of these decisions, the Soviets suddenly had to change their military regulations, claiming that if an order were criminal the participant was guilty, but it never became part of Soviet law. There were hurried changes of policy over other matters such as hostage taking and reprisal. All sides in the heat of conflict were aware of moments when illegal or immoral orders were given and carried out by all sides, but Nuremberg was looking at a national policy with international implications.

The defendants rapidly fastened onto this conundrum of obeying orders which soldiers on both sides of the divide were expected to follow without question. As the British historian Richard Overy later pointed out, if obeying orders worked as a defence, it could lead to a post-war scenario where victims could find themselves living next door to those who had killed, or those who out of 'self-interest or political naïveté allowed them to tolerate without protest a regime whose actions were manifestly criminal'.[1] Many defendants utilised defences based on amnesia, forgetfulness, outright denial, while others – during this and subsequent trials, international and local – fastened onto the defence of obeying orders given under due process of their national leadership. The conspiracy charges were meant to cover this aspect of law, but joining an organisation was not necessarily voluntary. For example, ordinary German policemen found themselves transferred to the Gestapo and even to execution squads.[2] Men like Sauckel, Ley, Frick, and Kaltenbrunner also argued they were mere agents of a system and not responsible for the immoral behaviour of others down the chain of command.

The debate about whether responsibility to individual combatants has continued to this date. On 30 January 1972, there occurred the Bogside Massacre or Bloody Sunday in Northern Ireland, and enquiry followed enquiry as to whether individual British soldiers were responsible or had the command come from higher quarters, reflecting a badly handled situation.

The question of morality during conflict will never be easy to resolve, but such were the widespread atrocities of the Nazi regime, it was decided that obeying orders could not be allowed as a defence. It was a condemnation of organised governmental murder and pulling a trigger on a command was not deemed a defence. The prosecution intended to exhibit the evil of the Nazi regime, which would come clearly to the fore later in the trial with the impact of the extermination and concentration camps. Nevertheless, the differences between right and wrong – generally a straightforward process – proved a difficult exercise among the defendants. Hans Frank would admit he had willingly served an evil regime, and expressed regret, but with the proviso he personally had done nothing wrong. The major military figures of Keitel, Jodl, Raeder, and Dönitz, among others, constantly fell back on the Prussian tradition of following orders, as would many military men across the world.

Genocide

This issue of obeying orders and the responsibility of giving such instructions resting on a government's directives, reached an almost psychological crescendo over the question of the regime's demands for the elimination of an entire race, in what has become known as the Holocaust. This issue also involved Slavs, Roma and Sinti, Russian prisoners of war, the mentally handicapped, homosexuals, Jehovah's Witnesses, and many other minorities vilified by the Nazis. In the courtroom, it would become almost explosive, but it would not be until the 1961 trial of SS-*Obersturmbannführer* Otto Adolf Eichmann in Israel that the full impact of the nature of the Holocaust would receive serious study, public realisation, and historical pursuit.

Since then, serious studies and books have exploded over the Holocaust issue. Some historians regard the Holocaust as having its origins in Hitler's personal drive; others, often called 'functionalists', look to the state and the power-structures of Nazism. This writer discerns a mixture of both, but whether it was Hitler himself or the state, the outcome was the same – the crime was committed. What is known is that the growth of severe anti-Semitism grew during the 1930s, but from 1941 the so-called 'Final Solution' started with personal death squads on the Eastern Front. This policy rapidly advanced to the industrial-scale extermination camps, using the infamous Zyklon B, which had been developed in the 1920s as a pesticide by the German Jewish scientist Fritz Haber.[3]

During the preliminary stages of the IMT in late 1945, relatively little was known about precise figures and the number of extermination camps, and it would take time for the enormity of this crime to be fully understood. To this day, people are still stunned with the knowledge that there were over a thousand such camps, including subcamps, with some existing for only a short duration. To a man, the defendants denied all knowledge, the bogeyman of which all the defendants claimed ignorance, but which preoccupied their conversations and defences. The Soviets regarded the 'Jewish issue' as only an element of the murderous activities of the Nazi regime who had also gassed Russian prisoners of war. This attitude was met with some sympathy because the Soviets of all the combatant nations had lost by far the greatest number of soldiers and civilians.

The main culprits behind the extermination programme, which had its early start with the T4 process of eliminating the mentally handicapped, were Himmler and Hitler, both now dead, and Heinrich Müller (Gestapo chief) and Adolf Eichmann, who were both missing.* Men like Rosenberg and Frank who were responsible for the eastern occupied areas where these atrocities took place denied any knowledge, as did Ribbentrop. All the defendants argued ignorance of these events, holding firm to this defence of not knowing. Ribbentrop was confronted with evidence that he had mentioned the policy when speaking to King Boris III of Bulgaria and Admiral Horthy of Hungary, and it was clear that Mussolini and his foreign minister and son-in-law Galeazzo Ciano knew of the Nazi intentions, but Ribbentrop persisted in denial. When other figures who had been involved in the field of combat where the mass murder of Jews and Russian Commissars had been carried out were questioned, they were always elusive. The SS General Karl Wolff, much favoured by the Americans for his role in arranging the surrender in Italy, when questioned as an acknowledged key SS figure said he had heard of the camps, but nothing since 1939. He suggested that Hitler and Himmler had made a personal vow of silence, but evidence in the trial would unfold the number of senior Nazi leaders who had visited the death camps. It was as if the defendants and many others recognised that the genocidal policy was the one singular area where there was a sense of guilt because it was unquestionably morally corrupt, and they had to distance themselves from the evident consequences. At nearly every level of command, the normal response was to blame Himmler much more than Hitler and to be surprised at the presented evidence.

Wherever possible, prisoners were secretly recorded in their conversations to try to understand what had happened and the personal views of those involved. It has been argued on reasonable grounds that the chief perpetrators tried to conceal their deeds from the wider public, but with thousands of camps across Europe, major roundups, and transports, it was impossible to hide what was happening. There were no written orders, and the language of liquidation was concealed by its own coded language; even at the time, the phrase 'Final Solution' could have referred to many things. It was the infamous Auschwitz commander Rudolf Höss who openly stated that 'Final Solution' was their reference to the extermination of Jews, and the witness Dieter Wisliceny who in conversation with Eichmann recalled that the expression meant 'the biological annihilation of the Jewish race'.[4] Many claimed they thought it was only sterilisation and deportation which was itself morally corrupt and far from harmless. The threads started to come together, and although during the war the information had started to leak through to the democracies, they found it difficult to believe possible, and it took the exposure of the camps after the German defeat to disclose the reality.

---

* The Euthanasia Decree was known as *Aktion T4*, the *T4* standing for the office address of *Tiergartenstraße 4* of the Chancellery Department at that time. This prompts a reminder of Hannah Arendt's reference to 'the banality of evil'.

Men like Funk had visited the camps, his banks had received stolen gold and money, and Speer had demanded concentration camp labour forces. It would take years of research to uncover much of the truth about what they knew, and some questions remain about how much the German public and the defendants knew about the precise horrific details. Julius Streicher (who produced the anti-Semitic paper *Der Stürmer*), despite his visceral hatred of the Jews, denied any knowledge of the Final Solution. While it was true that he probably had little to do with the camps, his years of bombarding the population with his images of rat-Jews indicated his vitriolic anti-Semitism and he never showed any signs of remorse. When he was confronted by his use of the word 'exterminate' in his papers, he evaded the question by claiming he was calling for their deportation only. Such was his stance, a psychiatric report was called for, even by the Russians, but it was decided that he was fit enough to stand trial.

Trying to gain information and admission of knowledge from the defendants seemed an impossible task. An apparent breakthrough came when it was decided to interview junior officers and officials lower down the Nazi food-chain. Although these witnesses were much more open about the atrocities, there remained a high degree of uncertainty about the level of knowledge between the individual defendants, who claimed to be remote from the deeds within the camps. Among the minor figures was Wisliceny, who was interrogated several times. He had been a deputy for Eichmann with responsibilities in Greece and Slovakia. He explained that 'since 1942, by order of Himmler, Jews were only valued as workers. All other Jews who were not used in that capacity were to be executed'.[5] Over a series of interrogations of Wisliceny, the Auschwitz commandant Rudolf Höss, and his officer Otto Moll, and by bugged conversations, the enormity of the crime was slowly revealed. The so-called inspections of those deemed fit enough to work to death, the gassing of the children, the older victims, and the frail, all so well known today, was exposed. The interrogators moved with their questions from country to country where the Jewish roundups had occurred, demanding answers about the crematoria, and those involved. The interviewers must have felt psychologically if not physically sick on hearing the details.

It was a matter of establishing from whom the initial commands for the Final Solution emanated. Generally, it was pinpointed to the opening months of Operation *Barbarossa* (the German invasion of Russia in June 1941) when a directive had ordered the killing of Jews and Soviet Commissars. Task forces (*Einsatzgruppen*) were detailed to follow frontline forces to exterminate these two above elements.

On 31 July 1941, Göring had given Heydrich an order to establish a plan for the 'total solution to the Jewish question' in all the newly occupied areas. Later, Eichmann admitted that Heydrich had told him that Hitler had ordered that Jews in German territories were to be exterminated. Eichmann's trial in 1961 confirmed what many at Nuremberg had worked out but found difficult to believe. There were mixed accusations raising the usual name of Himmler, but also Heydrich and Göring, and the existence of the *Einsatzgruppen* and their acceptance by the military clearly indicated the orders came from the highest level within the Reich. The numbers involved from the occupied countries remains a confusing conundrum. Anti-Semitism was rife across Europe, and embarrassingly it is now accepted that Vichy France, without German prompting, deported Jewish people to Drancy ready for deportation to the east. Despite French prime minister Pierre Laval's argument that they were going to work on farms, most seemed to know the reasons for their deportation.

In the Nuremberg Trial itself, they needed the minor officials and were fortunate that Kaltenbrunner asked for Rudolf Höss as a witness. Höss was a gift to the prosecution as the information was admitted into the proceedings confirming that Himmler had ordered the extermination facilities.

During the trial proceedings, various witnesses testified under oath, one a Frenchman called Maurice Lampe, who described his arrival at Mauthausen where an SS officer greeted them with the words 'Germany needs your arms. You are, therefore, going to work, but I want to tell you that never again will you see your families. Who enters this camp, will leave it only by the chimney of the crematorium'.[6] A female witness described Auschwitz, exposed the medical experiments, the use of human skin for decorative purposes, and as she left the witness-box, she was observed constantly glaring at Göring. Throughout the trial, the brutality of the camps was raised, especially the medical experiments, notably when restrained prisoners were shot in the thigh with aconite nitrate bullets to see how long they would take to die.[7]

Much later, political philosopher and author Hannah Arendt wrote: 'For these crimes, and the extent to which any one of the many criminals was close to or remote from the actual killer of the victim means nothing, as far as the measure of his responsibility is concerned'.[8] Several conclusions may be drawn from this comment, not least that any individual in an evil setting is potentially able to do evil things. The question Arendt posed was whether Eichmann was simply a bad apple, or was the entire apple-barrel bad? If an apple-barrel is bad, it would explain why the apples were rotten.

This is a question which many consider impossible to answer with total satisfaction. The historian Christopher Browning made a study of why ordinary people can suddenly become totally immoral. He explored the German Police Battalion 101, which carried out brutal murders of Jews in Poland during World War II.[9] These men came mainly from Hamburg and non-military backgrounds, the German equivalent of the ubiquitous American John Doe and the Englishman on the Clapham omnibus; they were just ordinary people who committed massacre after massacre. Such was their 'ordinariness' that their actions beg the unsettling question of how we would have reacted in the same situation. Browning and other historians have tried to clarify that if German soldiers or policemen refused to participate, they were not shot but were in fact treated quite leniently, yet the overwhelming majority still participated in these bloodbaths. Browning argued that war created its own high tension and provided a medium for such barbarity. For Browning, the behaviour was explained by the environment of total war changing ordinary men into killers. A clash between the historians Daniel Goldhagen and Browning is of some interest. Goldhagen in his book *Hitler's Willing Executioners* treated the perpetrators as 'responsible agents who made choices', whereas Browning based his reasons more on psycho-sociological theories, founded upon 'the assumption of inclinations and propensies common to human nature but not excluding cultural influences'.[10] This insoluble problem in explaining what turns an ordinary man into a mass-killer will never be easy to explain; namely, why John Doe simply obeyed orders to murder.

The psychologist Stanley Milgram in his well-known experiments with electric shocks tried to demonstrate that ordinary people could inflict powerful electric charges on others, simply because an authoritative figure in charge of the experiment informed them it was correct to follow orders.[11] These individuals were seemingly turned into the puppets of their controllers. This was the spectre of the Nuremberg Trials, with the old argument of 'obeying orders'. Milgram tested how far an individual would go; would he inflict pain simply because he was ordered to? This would appear to indicate that if a person is trained or by nature inclined to follow orders, personal freedom of choice is diminished, and personal responsibility is reduced.

The word Holocaust was not widely used until well after the trials, as the Russians insisted that it was not only Jews the Nazis were attempting to eliminate but Slavs and many others. There was a lack of focus to a certain extent with one historian wondering whether 'the anti-Semitic tendencies of both the Soviet and French states played in glossing over at times the institutional nature of the persecution'.[12] It was not until the 1960s that the full glare of historical focus examined the repercussions of the Holocaust. Nevertheless, the sheer barbarity was evident in the Nuremberg Trial, and these issues may have been privately discussed behind closed doors at Nuremberg, but to this day there are no conclusive answers to human conduct. At Nuremberg, the prosecutors appeared totally convinced of the individual and collective guilt of most of the defendants, who to a man denied any knowledge of the camps, and had to be grilled during interviews, interrogations, and during the proceedings to prove otherwise.

Procedures

The defendants had been kept in various Allied prisons, including a large American one at Mondorf-les-Bains, known by the name of the 'Ashcan'. The British had a smaller one at Kransberg Castle (outside Frankfurt am Main) named the 'Dustbin'. It was less strict than the Ashcan, where a tough-minded Colonel Burton Andrus was in charge.* The names of the camps projected the sense of sheer contempt. However, the British camp was more like a normal prisoner-of-war camp where the prisoners were allowed the freedom to walk and talk, watch shows, and listen to the radio, whereas in the Ashcan food was limited, heavily guarded with the threat of shooting, and the prisoners were kept in small unpleasant cells with no pillows allowed. The Americans held the defendants who were deemed to be the most serious cases, and when the British diplomat Sir Ivone Kirkpatrick visited he 'found the inhabitants repellent … and thought the efforts to prevent the prisoners from committing suicide were misplaced. It will save us a great deal of trouble he wrote to Eden' if they all committed suicide.[1] The prisoners were not physically abused, but life was uncomfortable, intentionally demeaning, and they were placed under psychological pressure and threatened with the unveiled threat of being handed to the Russians. If any of the guards had seen the concentration camps, and most by this time had heard of these centres of hell, this attitude would not have seemed unreasonable to them. The prisoners were permitted to speak among themselves because their conversations were bugged and recorded.

There were many emerging problems, not least reliable translators, and experienced or trained interrogators. Lawyers and even policemen were confounded by the

---

* Andrus was described as 'a meticulous, go-by-the-book regular officer, stocky and pompous, usually seen under a bright green helmet liner and carrying a riding crop'. Taylor Telford, *The Anatomy of the Nuremberg Trials: A Personal Memoir* (New York: Alfred Knopf, 1992), 230. In *Time* magazine, he was portrayed as 'a plump little figure looking like an inflated pouter pigeon', see *Time* Magazine, 28 October 1946. Some of these comments were unfair, and at times he indicated genuine humane concern for his captives; in their end days, he allowed them more freedom to socialise, allowing card games and families to visit.

problem, especially in dealing with the horrors of the extermination camps. At Kensington Palace in London, there had been the 'London Cage', where a Colonel Scotland and his staff held senior German prisoners and often extracted information by the guile of befriending the prisoners.[2] Later, when Field Marshal Albert Kesselring was interned in the Cage prior to his trial in Italy, the guile seemed almost absent, because from Scotland's own account and that of Kesselring's memoirs, they became good friends. In Nuremberg, a vastly different type of interrogator was necessary.

Various bodies were established with different aims setting out on fact-finding missions, and given the speed of events, and the anticipated death sentences, there was a sense of urgency to discover the facts. There were demands to discover scientific progress, information about the war economy, intelligence, military planning, and needed insights into the Nazi state and a historical survey from an operational level. There was a demand to examine the personal and corporate psychology of the culprits, which received less support but was critical in understanding those involved. The Americans, who handled the bulk of this task, worked assiduously at the interrogation, especially knowing that time was short. A Colonel John Harlan Amen was selected to run the Interrogation Division which involved ceaseless paper-trails as recorded documents were analysed, compared, substantiated, and placed in the appropriate folders. Oral testimony was critical and needed verifying. During August 1945, the various prisoners started to be taken to Nuremberg, but not as an entire body for pragmatic reasons of space and building requirements.

Many of the prisoners remained in ignorance of their destination and whether they were to be part of the projected trial. The list was not published until the end of August when men like Schacht and Speer discovered they were on the list. Schacht, who had been at Kransberg Castle, was first sent to what was called the 'Cage' at Oberürsel, which was also an interrogation centre. Hess was flown in from Britain, and eventually the French handed in Neurath. The Soviets brought in Raeder and Fritzsche, where it transpired that the latter had suffered from typical Russian interrogation and therefore agreed with anything they said. Twice they had threatened to shoot Fritzsche, he later claimed, by putting a pistol to his head.[3] Both looked in good health because prior to the move they had been well fed. Raeder, who had been ill, had almost been well treated, even having been allowed the company of his wife. The interrogation teams were given the Grand Hotel, which soon became the social centre for the Allied personnel working in Nuremberg. Even the Russians, housed elsewhere and who were expected to keep their distance, enjoyed some evenings there.

The defendants were kept in small cells, a heavy door with a small grill as an observation point, supplied with a bed, table, Bible, chair, and toilet, all of which could be seen by the guard on duty. They were allowed a brief exercise outside the heavily guarded prison two at a time for quarter of an hour per day. Colonel Andrus was the epitome of strictness, deemed by some to be overbearing, and the guards were not supposed to talk to the prisoners and to ensure silence. Andrus, under instruction, collected as many German-speaking American soldiers as possible, who by pretending ignorance could eavesdrop on any conversations. Prisoners were allowed books and writing material, one shower a week, and one set of clothes but nothing which could be utilised as a noose or a means of suicide. Some of the prisoners remained stoical, some became depressed, and a few were in a near state of collapse. Ribbentrop was such a person and caused some concern that he was potentially suicidal, but he used this during many interrogations to be evasive, while Kaltenbrunner was ill and had to first receive medical attention. Others suffered deep anxiety such as Robert Ley and Hans Frank, while Julius Streicher was regarded as mentally unstable. Walther Funk, who had been the economics minister, always looked depressed, probably because he simply could not understand why he was there, and he knew his fellow culprits despised him for his homosexuality and love of alcohol. Depression was the significant factor which many observers associated with a sense of guilt, but as is widely known, this is not necessarily always true.

The interviews and interrogations continued at a pace, with notes kept, correlated, with some interviews being stressful. Some were more gentlemanly, and it was generally agreed that the best approach was being 'matter of fact'. Translation was often a problem, although some defendants had a general smattering of English, and a few spoke it well and were prepared to use their language skills (a General Walther Warlimont gave English lessons to some inmates). The ex-diplomat Neurath was also an excellent English speaker.* The Russians were noted for their swift interrogations, sometimes less than an hour when others were normally two hours in length. The Russians probably felt somewhat hampered because they could not deploy their Lubyanka techniques, known to be extremely brutal, and some defendants had many interviews spread over weeks.

Documents and information not destroyed in the bombing in Berlin, Munich, Nuremberg, and Dresden started to emerge and were consumed by the various Allied teams, the Americans being the most prodigious. These were necessary not only as evidence but because there was a great deal of ignorance about the Nazi activities, plans, and even knowledge about significant people over the last 10 years. Trying to extract the truth from the interviews was a difficult task as it always is with any accused person. Some interrogators were better than others, and some of the defendants, such as Ribbentrop mentioned earlier, were totally evasive. Amnesia, obeying orders, not knowing the full picture, and ignorance were often the ploys used by the defendants, sometimes to the annoyance of the interviewer. Some were more intelligent than others, and when an intelligence test was applied, Streicher had the lowest score and Schacht, not surprisingly, the highest. There were absentees from the trial as with the suicides of Hitler, Goebbels, and Himmler, the last being

---

*   General Walimont had been Jodl's deputy as Chief of Operations.

the most detested and feared even among fellow Nazis. Martin Bormann was dead, but there was no identifiable body, so he was tried and condemned to death in his absence. If he were eventually found, he could be executed without a further trial. Rumours of his whereabouts sprang up everywhere which demanded exhaustive enquiries, but some road workers found his body in 1972, which was confirmed by his dental records, and in 1999 finally confirmed by DNA.

There was at this stage a deep ignorance of the defeated foe. The Germans had proved to be a formidable enemy, backed by a strong professional military tradition, their weapons had often been superior (which also prompted creating specialist investigative teams to examine), but there were many areas of the Nazi regime, not least the nature of Hitler and his dictatorship, which remained obscure to the Allies, now searching in the rubble and the holding camps trying to understand the intentions and conduct of their enemies. It would take decades of historical research to paint much of the picture, but the Nuremberg Trial was a start to this massive process. World War II had claimed an estimated 50 to 60 million lives, and the uncertainty of this final number indicates not just the confusion but the enormity of a conflict which no one wanted repeated. As such, the necessity for information and insight became critical, trying to understand the nature of conduct both at the highest level and its ramifications down to those lowest depths of command, namely those who had justified their heinous acts at a local level as stemming from their leaders. Perhaps caused by immediate post-war confusion, the huge logistics of prisoners, ignorance of who was who and what had happened, possibly a degree of indifference, many major and minor criminals escaped. Some remained free and were never caught, some attracted publicity such as Eichmann, and there would be further trials over the following years, international and local, and even into the 21st century. The Nuremberg Trial was just the start of a process of understanding, not that this was its first intention, because the victors at this stage only needed the knowledge to provide evidence for prosecution. However, whether intentional or not, the trials opened the first pages of comprehending 'what the hell happened'.

The questions over the defendants' lawyers were settled, and they were all to be Germans. Göring claimed he did not need a lawyer, just an interpreter, but he accepted Dr Otto Stahmer; Streicher thought they were all Jews, but the military men and the older conservative elements carefully selected their lawyers from their own social class. The defence lawyers came together and challenged the juristic foundations of the trial, but it was denied. The military defence lawyers suggested a united front, but it was turned down by their clients on the sensible grounds that it might hint at an organisation. When the trial opened, the packed spectators were expecting to see the giants of the Nazi regime, but there were no medals, decorations, proud uniforms but a selection of tired-looking sallow men showing their age.

Outline of Proceedings

From the historical perspective, there are many elements of interest. First, there were the extensive notes taken during the interviews and interrogations, then the psychologists and psychiatrists with their reports, which later with the trial notes, the witnesses, and the available verifiable evidence, provided many insights into the defendants. The pre-trial interrogators and interviewers were more interested in some defendants than others, with men like Göring, Speer, and others holding their interest. Because Göring was Hitler's number two, he was the main subject of interest and involved the most time and anxiety, and this is reflected in this exploration. The same interest applied to the psychiatrists and psychologists who were curious about the overbearing Göring, the mindset of Streicher, the apparent openness of Speer, and at the end of the list those who did not attract their attention or who had remained aloof from conversations and visitors such as men like Raeder, his military colleagues, and the angry Schacht.

Nearly every involved person who was there has left some form of memoir, some more discerning than others. Airey Neave served the indictments, some defendants treating it as if he was pronouncing a death sentence. Neave's observations were incisive, as were those of some of the more observant journalists. The reactions on receiving the indictments were revealing, and Neave found himself in trouble when they appeared in the *Stars and Stripes*. However, it transpired it was a leak from some of Andrus's staff.[4]

Prosecution Present their Cases, 20 November 1945

The trial started with the arrival of the defendants who looked different: 'there had been a quite a metamorphosis. Attired in rather shabby clothes, slumped in their seats fidgeting nervously, they no longer resembled the arrogant leaders of old'.[5] The trial, which was to last 284 days, started with the four prosecuting countries outlining their cases against the Nazi regime, with some brilliant opening introductions by Jackson and the French leader François de Menthon. It was clear from the start that Jackson was somewhat bitter about the defendants, noting that 'merely as individuals their fate is of little consequence to the world ... what makes this inquest significant is that these prisoners represent sinister influences that will lurk in the world long after their bodies have returned to dust'.[6] In the lunch room and private conversations, the observations by the defendants on the four nations presenting their cases led to some interesting insights.

First Witness for Defence, 8 March 1946

This was followed by the listed individuals taking the stand in their own defence, using witnesses to further their causes. The defence witnesses often had a difficult time as the prosecution had armed itself with thousands of documents carrying signatures and affidavits which often proved overwhelming for both witnesses and defendants. Not all opted to take the stand, and cross-examination followed which proved disturbing to the Germans unaccustomed to this legal system, where even the credibility of their witnesses was challenged. The defendants' conversations about one another's performance and defence methods provides some unique perceptions into their personalities.

Final Statements of the Defence, 4 July 1946

The final part of the individual trials concluded on 4 July with the final statements or summations for the defence. This was accompanied by the prosecution's conclusions which are briefly surveyed because they often reflected the defence and prosecution of the previous months. Perhaps the curious part of this process was Jackson's cynical if not sarcastic statements about some of the individuals. His comments were harsh and stressed his contempt for them but amusing many in the court and making the defendants angry.

Prosecuting Criminal Organisations, 30 July 1946

At the end of July, the trial looked at the broader prosecution of the organisations which had been indicted. The defendants had a break as the Tribunal studied the complex nature of the first count of conspiracy and whether various Nazi organisations could be convicted, which mainly arose from American demands.* It was a major issue potentially involving millions of Germans and was vexatious; it could take a whole volume to study this aspect alone. The question of new law, retrospective law, and many other legal issues dominated the minds of the judges and took to the end of August 1946. To do this justice would take many volumes, and much historical study and literature has been spawned over the years, but this is a brief survey of the defendants, their significance, who they were as people, and they remain the point of this study.

Last Statements of the Defendants, 31 August 1946

There then followed an opportunity for the defendants to offer their final statements which were required to be short in duration and was followed by the verdicts and sentencings. On 31 August, the defendants were permitted to make their own personal statements which were often revealing, the 21 men having sat through months of proceedings, discussions, inter-reactions, hearing witnesses, watching films, and listening to many points of view. They were only allowed a short time which annoyed some of them, and the court adjourned on 1 September.

---

*   The organisations were: the leadership Corps of the Nazi Party, the Gestapo and SD, the SS, the SA, the Reich Cabinet, and the General Staff and High Command of the German Armed Forces.

Verdicts and Sentencing, 30 September–1 October

During this time of anxious waiting, a newly appointed psychiatrist had drawn attention to the level of tension among the defendants. Colonel Andrus relaxed some of the restrictions and he permitted more mixing, and they were even provided with playing cards. Some wives were permitted to visit which pleased some, and a few avoided such emotional visits.

The discussions within the judge's confines over the individual judgements were sometimes fraught, with the Russians demanding all to be executed; the French were of a similar disposition. There were debates over hanging, decapitation, shooting, and convincing the Russians that an affirmative decision needed three votes, but the agreed Charter stipulations were clear. Some judgements, such as for Göring, Keitel, and Ribbentrop, were passed very quickly, some like for Streicher perhaps too quickly. Hess's state of mind caused some discussion, Dönitz, Schacht, and Jodl caused major discussions, and at one time there was nearly deadlock over Speer with the British and Americans inclined in his favour against the Russians and French.

By 1 October, the judges were ready to present their findings on the individual defendants. Fritzsche later recorded that there was an element of surprise that the news photographers had been removed, seeing it as a show of tact.[7] The defendants were surprised that on hearing the judgements regarding organisations, the Reich Cabinet, the SA, and the General Staff of the Armed Forces were not declared criminal, and only certain higher echelons of the Nazi Party leadership Corps. The SS, SD, and Gestapo were guilty, which supported Fritzsche's later claim that the Tribunal *should* have listened to the prosecution, as he believed the prosecution held a more realistic view.

The three who were acquitted, Schacht, Papen, and Fritzsche, were offered liberty but chose to stay in new cells as there were rumours the Bavarian police were after them. The verdicts were announced which, as in all serious cases, meant the atmosphere was tense. Those who were going to prison were moved to the floor above, while the 11 condemned to death remained in their cells. Some made appeals against the sentences involving some strange machinations on the outside of the prison but were rejected. The 11 condemned to die were treated more harshly, handcuffed while out of their cells, and any talks with families had the military police in attendance. On 12 October, they were notified that was to be their last meeting.

One striking note was that when the sentences were pronounced on the individual defendants, most of the onlookers were surprised at the sense of dignity most of them demonstrated.

Executions, 16 October 1946

The condemned sat and waited for 16 October when they were to be hanged in the early hours, their corpses burned, and their ashes scattered to the winds. It was reminiscent of Dr Samuel Johnson's observation that 'when a man knows he is to be hanged in a fortnight, it concentrates his mind wonderfully'. The waiting must have made the previous months of their incarceration and the trial feel like good times.

Under German law, the deceased's remains should be given to their families for burial, but a Military Government directive overrode this custom, and after some wrangling it was eventually agreed the disguised bodies should be burned in a local crematorium with much of this discussion taking place during the trial, but outside the formalities of the courtroom. Many, including Major Airey Neave, believed they were cremated at Dachau concentration camp, others refer to an east Munich crematorium, but there is still no substantive evidence and it is perhaps not important.

Those defendants to be executed were hanged on 16 October 1946 by Master Sergeant John C. Woods, who had previous experience and was assisted by two other GIs. There have been many lurid accounts of the occasion, and suggestions that because they deployed a short drop rather than a long drop death was not so quickly administered. Witnesses were limited and there has been much speculation, but the procedures started at 1.11 a.m. and were finished by 2.45 a.m. Given that 10 were executed one by one having walked from their cells, unleashed from handcuffs, re-leashed with thongs, and allowed to say a few words, raises some doubts about the more appalling speculations. Nevertheless, death by hanging is a squalid affair, as are all planned deaths. The details of the execution may be of interest to some but all we need to know is that they happened. The same lack of information exists in what happened to their bodies. Out of fear that their resting places might become shrines, the location of the final dispersion of their ashes is unknown (probably in the tributary of the river Isar, southern Germany), and remains unnecessary knowledge.

The Defendants

The initial paragraphs of the following main part of the text will give a brief outline of the main aspects of each defendant's involvement with the Nazi regime and some personal background. The second input, where it is available, is to study some of the insights into these figures gleaned from pre-trial interviews and interrogations. The third section consists of observations made by the psychiatrists and psychologists who, in this writer's opinion, give the most telling insights.[*] Also informative are the recorded conversation, debates, and tensions between the defendants. However, the central survey of this exploration is to seek an overall picture of the individual defendants who stood as the 'Major German War Criminals' at Nuremberg to try and understand who they were. They were all well known at the time, but as in any

---

[*] The psychiatrist has a medical degree and a psychologist a degree in psychology, but both are concerned with human reactions and behaviour. The two main figures used are Goldensohn who had a friendly approach which the defendants seemed to appreciate while Gilbert tended to be more direct.

human scenario, some were better known than others either because of their roles, their reputations, historical work since, and for the few who survived the executioner, their own accounts and explanations.

To achieve this, each defendant is looked at separately from the various possible angles known to be secure. The only consistent pattern which emerges with these different defendants is their sense of self-justification, denial of the knowledge, shifting of blame, and an attempt at rationalising what happened.

Having surveyed the general background, this exploration now turns to its central theme and deals not so much with the trials from the legal perspective, but with the views and reactions of the defendants revealing as far as is possible who they were. This is assisted by the various reports of those involved with them at a personal level, and then how they reacted during the proceedings. As noted above, the various cases were first presented by the four Allied prosecutors, and during these moments the defendants' reactions to seeing films and listening to witnesses regarding the murders at concentration camps and elsewhere is informative. The films of the suffering in the camps were shocking, as were the personal witnesses, such as Marie Vaillant-Courturier, and the discovery that soap had been made from human fat.[8] There were also eye-opening moments for the defendants when many discovered that resistance to the Nazi regime included such figures as Admiral Wilhelm Canaris, head of the *Abwehr*, and the references to the Hossbach Memorandum, which was a summary of a meeting between Hitler and his military and foreign office regarding his expansionist plans. Their reactions to these and other pieces of evidence proved to be highly relevant.

This is followed by the individual trials and the question in writing this section was the order in which they should be explored. The military men (Keitel, Jodl, Dönitz, Raeder) fall into one category, the older conservatives of the early period (Schacht, Neurath, Papen) into another. Many patterns are discernible, but it made sense to explore them in the order of their trial placements as their post-trial conversations then make more sense.

As far as the prosecutors were concerned, the major defendant was Göring because of the major role he had played with Hitler, almost regarded as the 'stand-in' for the deceased dictator. Next came Hess for his early position of power, and then Ribbentrop because of his prominent position as foreign minister, and thereafter each as he came from the dock to stand trial. Bormann was still missing and, although on the list, not worth pursuing in this study. Robert Ley committed suicide before his trial so there are only some brief notes on him.

Hermann Göring 1893–1946

Göring in his Days of Power. (Photographer unknown, Bundesarchiv 102-15607; Licence CC-BY-SA 3.0)

Background

Hermann Göring had his first biography written by an Erich Gritzbach in 1938 which naturally paints a vastly different picture of the Göring as viewed post-war. The well-known diplomat and spy R. H. Bruce Lockhart wrote a preface in which he stated that 'in the minds of the average Englishman General Göring is probably fixed as a cross between a brutal tyrant and a festive Falstaff with a private wardrobe as large as that of the late marquess of Anglesey'.[1] Bruce Lockhart added that 'by the youth of his own country he is regarded as a greater figure than any of the generals of the Great War'.[2] It was now the classic case of 'how the mighty have fallen'.

In the Great War, Göring had been an infantryman, but soon became a fighter-plane ace, and the last commander of the *Jagdgeschwader*, a fighter wing once led by Manfred von Richthofen. He was highly decorated and claimed 22 Allied aircraft as his victims. Post World War I, he was an early member of the Nazi Party, and while with Hitler at the Munich *Putsch* was wounded which started his addiction to morphine. He fled abroad for safety having been saved by an elderly Jewish couple. On his return, he was elected to the Reichstag and by 1932 was its president. Following Hitler's elevation to chancellor in 1933, he was named as minister without portfolio, and as a cabinet minister created the Gestapo in Prussia which he eventually handed over to Himmler. With his control over Prussia, he rapidly became the second most important figure in the regime and was appointed to head the *Luftwaffe*. He was also made plenipotentiary for the Economic Four-Year Plan in 1936. Despite many studies of Göring and the *Luftwaffe*, he was more relevant in the regime's history for his economic involvements. Men of more economic common sense such as Schacht wanted to build up Germany's economy. But Göring, as always, obediently and willingly followed Hitler's demand for the Four-Year Plan, and with sheer incompetence and too much responsibility, Göring turned to the policy of autarky, which was intended to put every economic effort into preparing for war. Göring was not a businessman, not an economist, made poor appointments, and it was soon apparent that Germany's economic autarky policy was in total turmoil. Despite being a fundamentally lazy person, he took on too much responsibility. He often claimed that he wanted peace and for a time he was even believed, but Göring had 'strong opinions about the timing of war, but there can be no doubt that he prepared for war and expected it to come'.[3] It was also noted that although he always obeyed Hitler, according to the anti-Nazi resister Carl Goerdeler, the mayor of Leipzig, he had less influence on Hitler than Himmler, Ribbentrop, and Goebbels.[4]

In September 1939, he was designated as Hitler's successor, and in 1940 was named *Reichsmarschall*. Thereafter, although remaining powerful, he was more in the background enjoying a life of luxury, buying or stealing art, which for many was a point of quiet derision. Near the end of the war, when he picked up the rumour that Hitler was planning to commit suicide, he asked permission to assume leadership, infuriating Hitler which led to his dismissal with orders for his arrest by the SS. Later, he was refused any governmental post by Dönitz.[*] He surrendered to the Americans and was being wined and dined by them; they were pleased to have caught such a notable figure. Göring was moved to Zell am See in Austria to the HQs of Robert J. Stack, commander of the 36th Infantry Division, and then to

---

[*]   Göring's claim that Bormann had been behind Hitler's fury was probably justified, see Alan Bullock, *Hitler: A Study in Tyranny* (London: Penguins Books, 1962), 787.

Kitzbühel, the temporary base of the American Seventh Army.* News of his capture spread as did the criticisms that he was being too royally entertained. He even met General Carl Spaatz of the USAAF and shared champagne. He shared a pleasant evening with his captors, even playing his accordion leaving it as a gift, but after holding a press conference with champagne flowing, complaints followed, and he was soon under house arrest in a dingy apartment.

Later, he was angry being kept in a place named the Ashcan, and Andrus was perplexed at his 16 personally marked suitcases and the number of drugs he brought with him. Göring often referred to Andrus as the 'fire-brigade colonel'. Ironically, he was correct about Andrus given that the fire-brigade is an emergency unit, because Andrus talked to the medical people and Göring was gradually weaned off his addiction, recovering much of his old health and mental ability. Much has been made of his drug addiction, which were medically based drugs stemming from his *Putsch* injury, but he had become dependent on them.

His sense of self-importance was not helped by a visit in June 1945 from Sir Ivone Kirkpatrick, who met Göring and renewed their acquaintance. They spent about two hours together and talked about the war. They covered many subjects including Göring's belief that his proposed strategy of invading Gibraltar through Spain would have been more successful than Hitler's attack on Russia. Kirkpatrick found Göring to be holding up better than Ribbentrop who was in a state of mental collapse.

Göring, along with Hess and Ribbentrop, were often seen as the main defendants and the subject of some ridicule, Göring being portrayed as the 'back-slapping air marshal', Hess as the 'mad Messerschmitt pilot', and Ribbentrop as the 'champagne vendor'.[5] There was a degree of fun in these jibes, but when the films of the concentration camps and massacres were shown, they were no longer regarded as 'Jerry the old enemy' but vicious, hate-filled criminals. The impression that Göring was the jovial military man was shattered and any idea that he had some humane elements were dashed. The irony is that while many accepted Göring's criminal activities, and his looting was scorned, he was still Hitler's number two with all the implications.

Interrogations

Because Hermann Göring held the highest rank as *Reichsmarschall*, and until the final months of the Reich had been Hitler's intended successor, he was of the most interest to the Allies of all the defendants because he was standing in the place of Hitler. The British suggested he should have his own trial which did not happen, but his role in the Nazi regime made him the most significant of all the defendants. Unlike many

---

*   On his unusual uniform, Göring wore a white armband to signify he had surrendered, see James Lucas, *Last Days of the Reich: The Collapse of Nazi Germany, May 1945* (London: Arms and Armour Press, 1986), 217.

others, he made no attempt to flee or hide, but he walked into American arms and expected to be treated as the head of Germany albeit defeated. Having been at the centre of a frank news conference assembly until the embargo was placed on such activities, the last thing the Allies needed was a charm offensive by Göring. When he eventually joined the other defendants, he tried to rally, bully, and cajole them under his assumed leadership.

His background as a soldier turned airman during the Great War had drawn Hitler to him, especially as Göring was furious at the defeat and the impositions of the Versailles Treaty. In terms of the conspiracy charges, he was there from the start, involved in the aggressive war charges (the *Luftwaffe* bombing was set aside in view of the Allied massive attacks), and he was intimately involved in most decision making, especially the *Anschluss* takeover of Austria. He was already well known for 'looting' art across Europe and his involvement in persecuting the Jews. He had always been flamboyant, arrogant, a showman, but he was also a shrewd political animal and when he chose, he could appear humorous and even good-natured, making himself companionable even to his captors. Even his guards who often referred to him as the 'fat-stuff' found him difficult to dislike despite his status in the hated regime and his dominance over the other captives. Airey Neave disliked Göring, but even he acknowledged that 'set alongside his miserable companions he was the only man he met at Nuremberg who might have been capable of governing Germany'.[6] The prison psychiatrist Dr Douglas Kelly found him clever and charming, intelligent, and persuasive.

He was moved to the Ashcan where Andrus had noted the suitcases full of drugs which were confiscated. Andrus put him on a diet, which improved his health and allowed him to become intellectually more responsive. He started to become dominant among the other inmates, and even the Russian team appeared to be taken in by his charm. There was no doubting his seniority, his knowledge of the military and political Nazi regime, giving him a status he relished. He was able to provide insight into many incidents, operations, and discussions of the past which had often remained speculative. His views on the air-war were sought, and his acknowledgement that the American long-range fighters had caused the most serious problems was of interest. Speer had been able to give a sound economic assessment and Göring was able to fill in many military details.

His interrogations did not start until late August 1945, and such was his importance that Colonel Amen, Head of Investigation teams, conducted his interviews, trying to ensure every aspect of Hitler and the regime were thoroughly explored. It transpired that Göring was willing to be interviewed, was frank with a sense of pride in most of his answers (perhaps too much so in terms of his defence), claiming he was always involved in major decisions which enhanced the arguments for the 'conspiracy' charges. He was as always proud of himself making sense of the maxim that 'pride comes before a fall' (Proverbs 16, v.18). When challenged about the

Reichstag fire, over which he had been considered a likely culprit, he flatly denied it on the grounds that he had already started the destruction of the Communist Party. He could have added he had some valuable art-tapestries lost in the fire which, had he initiated the blaze, he would have removed first. He was forthcoming about most of his participation, seeing nothing wrong with what had happened, simply claiming, 'it was a matter of war'. Göring was less forthright on the matter of exterminating Jewish people, even though it was known that he had been a major component authorising the Final Solution. He was interesting on Hitler's views concerning Britain, believing the British would not fight a continental war, and would soon reach some form of agreement with Germany, and did not want a two-front war which he considered the cause of Germany's final defeat. Many had regarded Göring as a man who was a trifle more moderate, and his various biographers often point out that he opposed Ribbentrop and his desire to fight Britain and France. Under interrogation, he never once felt Germany was wrong in its expansionist policies. His view, as often quoted, was that the 'victors will always judge the vanquished', and he remained defiant throughout the proceedings, trying to rally the other defendants behind him even though it often resulted in petty squabbling.

He had lived the life of luxury, entertaining people in his country mansion of Karinhall (named after his first wife who died), growing corpulent and enjoyed changing uniforms at any opportunity. Galeazzo Ciano wrote in his diary that Göring reminded him of Al Capone, and that Göring was obsessed with jewellery. He was closely questioned over his reputation for looting art, arguing that wherever he went offers were made and art dealers always sought him out because of his love of the subject. Rosenberg had also been collecting for Hitler's plan for a Reich museum in Linz (Austria) for major pieces, with Göring arguing that his intention was that not all the treasures should go south, almost suggesting a sense of 'selflessness'.* He denied confiscating art works and explained that some of the treasures from Monte Cassino Abbey and Naples had been pillaged but not authorised by him. A few of these treasures had come into his possession brought to him by one of 'his divisions', and he claimed this was somewhat embarrassing. He was correct about the Abbey's treasures as Field Marshal Albert Kesselring had organised their safe conduct to the Vatican. However, through the misadventures of war, some found their way into Göring's hands. After the war, it was estimated that his collection was valued at some two hundred million US dollars. It was not only fine art but jewels, furniture, and any historical artefacts of importance or beauty. It was often observed that Göring when he was anxious would stroke or caress a valuable jewel as if it brought him some form of comfort like a rosary or worry-beads. In his post-war interrogations, he was examined by Colonel Amen as to some valuable jewels taken from a Jewish

---

* A special snatch squad, the *Einsatzstab Rosenberg*, had been set up to seize the cultural treasures of those countries occupied by the Germans.

lady on a particular occasion. He agreed he remembered them but brushed it aside on the grounds they were taken as she was fleeing the country and they landed up in his hands. He purported that 'it was merely an accident'.[7] He had received the assistance of a Berlin art dealer called Walter Andreas Hofer and developed a particular taste for Rubens and Dutch painters of the 17th century. As with Hitler, he despised some modern art but unlike Hitler realised it was of economic value abroad. He always claimed before and after the war he was collecting these pieces to have a national collection for Europe at Karinhall. He also used the expertise of a Dr Bruno Lohse who was in the *Luftwaffe* but whose layman's skill was as an Art historian. The biographer Leonard Mosley makes the interesting point that Lohse was not in the *Luftwaffe* but was given a uniform and rank by Göring to give him freedom of movement.[8] During the last months of the war and post-war, art works and treasures were crossing Europe in all directions, either as a matter of theft or seeking safety from the increasing bombing raids.

After the war, the Allies themselves had to establish their own taskforce to track down the art, furniture, and countless valuables hidden in salt mines, tunnels, basements, and to this day many remain lost or hidden.* These taskforces were sometimes known as the 'Monuments Men' and one of their leaders, James Rorimer (former curator at the Cloisters Museum in New York), was so concerned about the final whereabouts of so many famous works of art that he had been the one who requested that Göring be interrogated over this problem.[9] When they did find one cache of Göring's at Berchtesgaden, Hitler's holiday home in Bavaria, it was a curator's nightmare as over a thousand different treasures lay scattered in their hiding places.† Despite his frankness and excuses, no one had any doubt that among his various travesties he was a major thief, stealing from an occupied country's collections and from individual victims, especially the possessions of Jewish people. It was clear from Speer's interviews that Hitler was unhappy about Göring's propensity for art theft, but he said nothing as he also took art from across Europe for display in Linz and elsewhere, not as a private collector like Göring, but for public display. Göring considered himself as the 'savant and great patron of art, music, and the theatre'.[10]

Göring was questioned during his interviews regarding the growth of the *Luftwaffe*, admitting that under Speer the production rates improved, although he could not

---

* On 28 February 2012, a warrant was given to the police to search the residence of a Cornelius Gurlitt where they found a treasure trove of 121 framed and 1,285 unframed artworks valued at more than a billion US dollars. The work was stolen during the war years mainly from Jewish homes. Göring was not alone in this diabolical series of thefts.

† In the end days, there was a scramble between East and West to find all the treasures. The Americans had their MFA & A (Monuments, Fine Arts and Archives) who found much of Göring's treasure in Berchtesgaden; many were still in crates and in railway sidings, see John Toland, *The Last 100 Days: The Tumultuous and Controversial Story of the Final Days of World War II in Europe* (New York: The Modern Library, 1996), 561.

recall everything. However, he revealed surprising details with a reasonable grasp of the overall situation, including the other areas of *Luftwaffe* responsibility beyond aircraft, such as flak, ground crews, troops, supplies, and the need for dispersing production and the problems it had created. This was a surprise to the interrogators who had been told he was out of touch and living in his own grand luxurious world. He spoke realistically about technical issues and the problems of pilot supply when their planes were brought down over enemy territory, and the issues of training inexperienced pilots too quickly. The interrogators were especially interested in the ME-262, the jet fighter-bomber known to the Germans as the *Schwalbe* (Swallow), both in its production and use. He admitted that Hitler had been the one who demanded that the jetfighters be used as bombers. They found Göring frank and to the point, admitting that the American development of long-distance fighters had been a problem for the Germans, though not admitting that initially he believed that these fighters had been blown over German territory by strong winds. He also agreed with Speer's observation that an Allied bombing attack on electrical generation plants was what they feared most.

He was closely questioned on his role during the *Anschluss*, admitting that he played a major part, noting that it was the Führer's wish which he fully supported, and claiming with little substance that they were worried about the tenuous Little Entente (agreement between Czechoslovakia, Yugoslavia, and Romania). He admitted that he had spent much of his youth in Austria as did his brother Albert (who voted against the German occupation). He was asked about whether Hitler was dead and assured his interrogators he was, and when asked about Bormann, he 'threw his hands in the air and said, "I hope he is frying in hell, but I don't know"'.[11]

There is no question that during the interviews Göring never tried to sidestep an issue except notably for the Final Solution; otherwise he was frank and often amenable. There were few signs of regret, and for him there was no crime committed: they had simply lost a war. Another interesting factor emerged in Göring's interviews, namely that while nearly all the defendants relied on the defence of obeying orders over which they had no choice, Göring occasionally accepted that he had issued orders which he expected to be obeyed.

When questioned about Hitler's intentions, he made it abundantly clear that Hitler had from the earliest of days looked towards expansion in the east, and being so intimately involved with the dictator, immediately placed himself within the charge of waging aggressive war.

Medical Mental Observations

Historian Leon Goldensohn began his notes on Göring as being 'up and down – cheerful usually, on other occasions definitely glum, chin in hand – childlike in his attitudes, always playing to the public', then adding 'he can turn on a smile and turn it off like a faucet'.[12] Göring told Goldensohn that he had not wanted war with Britain, and the English were known to be Germans as could be proved through their royalty. He had also persuaded Hitler not to invade Sweden. He remained totally loyal to the Führer, even though he and Hitler had different tastes in art.

Goldensohn made a point of trying to probe Göring's views on Jewish people about which he always proved evasive. He asked Göring if the Germans had resented the Jews because of their influence. It was a clever way of opening the issue as Göring quickly agreed they had too much control in the cinemas, operas, and theatres, in which Göring always had a deep interest. He claimed that it was at Nuremberg he first heard of Eichmann's name and the rumours of thousands being killed, but he regarded it as mere enemy propaganda. He knew they were ordered out of Germany and sent to Poland but denied any knowledge of the extermination plans. He argued that the difference between Jew and German was too great to make co-existence possible, and he blamed this on the grounds that they had been shut out of economic activity by men like Schacht, suggesting otherwise they could have remained. He disliked Schacht and took this opportunity to shift the blame onto a personal enemy. He criticised Goebbels whom he also disliked, stating he had used anti-Semitism to increase his personal power and said Himmler spoke less on the subject than Goebbels. Göring concluded by claiming he had never been anti-Semitic, and that it had 'played no part in my life'. He further alleged that when some Jews had asked for his help, he had responded, saying he had recommended that Jews with Iron Crosses from World War I should be exempted from persecution or pogrom. He said as second in the regime he had to assume responsibility, but not for the 'ungentlemanly acts and the atrocities which I believe Goebbels and Himmler committed'. He was no fanatic, and these orders should not have been obeyed. He was of course lying.

Even in these casual conversations he always remained loyal to Hitler, calling him a 'great leader' which explained, he said, why the expression 'my Führer' was so widespread. But Hitler had been betrayed by people like Goebbels. He told Goldensohn the people called him Hermann because he was closer to their hearts than Hitler (he thought), but he always subscribed to Hitler's leadership. He also confirmed his believe in the oath of fealty which Germans held dear. It was clear Göring disliked Goebbels, and he was nervous about Himmler to whom he had once given the wings insignia as a gift to stop an investigation into his behaviour.

He was interesting with his views on other defendants. He was dismissive of Hess as being 'off-balance', Schacht (with whom he clashed) heaping blame on him, referred to Dönitz as a 'little admiral', thought Funk and Fritzsche as unnecessary defendants, and Ribbentrop a weak echo of Hitler. He believed that Ribbentrop, Frick, Rosenberg, Seyss-Inquart, and himself were the only people worth prosecuting; the others were 'mere followers'. He considered the trial a sheer mockery, that England had started the war, and that Edward VIII had abdicated not because of Wallis

Simpson but because he foresaw war with Germany. He stated that prosecuting the High Command and the charge of conspiracy was a nonsense, always remaining convinced he was correct on all accounts, and while remaining undaunted in his support of Hitler, continually refused to accept any responsibility for the plan to annihilate European Jews.

Above all, he evaded any sense of guilt by his well-known and constantly claimed 'justice of the victors'. He was a showman and egotist and when he sat the intelligence test was told he was near the top, and therefore thought the test was better than the German ones.

Reactions during the Trial

When Neave presented him with the indictment, Göring was 53 and had lost weight, and Neave's first impression was that of 'meeting a dissolute Roman emperor'.[13] During the trials, Göring spent considerable energy trying to maintain his sense of leadership, cracking jokes, deriding what was happening, and ensuring he was the centre of attention. One reporter observed that Göring's co-defendants seemed dominated by him, 'just as they were when they were all free. By his superior supply of theatrical energy, fancy clothes, and interest in the proceedings, and by his air of participation' Göring maintained his position of prisoner No.1, always sitting in the most prominent place.[14]

Speer later expressed the view that although Göring had some reservations about the regime, he was in favour of whitewashing Hitler and using the trial to create his own legend.[15] Göring would never let go of the idea of his historical importance in the years to come, with Speer writing that 'Göring wants to ride into Valhalla with a large retinue ... but he defended himself more stubbornly than the rest of us did'.[16] This was written years later but it was somewhat perceptive.

On Thursday 29 November 1945, he had enjoyed listening to replays of his telephone conversations regarding his directing the *Anschluss*, and Ribbentrop and Hess had joined in the hilarity as they read the transcripts. This abruptly ceased when a documentary film of the concentration camps was shown. American psychologist Gustave Gilbert and others watched the reactions of the defendants closely as the film revealed the barbarity. Most of them were shocked, some like Frank and Funk had tears, Keitel 'mopped his brow', Ribbentrop 'closed his eyes', and Fritzsche appeared in agony. Hess claimed he could not believe what he was watching only to be instructed by Göring 'to keep quiet'. Gilbert noted that Göring's 'cockiness had gone'. In the cells that evening, Gilbert visited many and found Göring upset, claiming he had been enjoying the day over the *Anschluss* until they showed the film and 'it spoiled everything'.[17] Göring liked nothing which distracted from his self-perceived importance. The atrocity films had a major impact on every single person in the court, and at the end of the trials, Shawcross concentrated their minds on what they had seen, noting one scene showing 'families undressing, kissing farewell, stepping into a pit where a thousand bodies lay covered in blood, while the soldier who was to shoot them finished his cigarette'.[18]

The next day, when the witness Major General Erwin Lahousen claimed that senior leaders of the *Abwehr* had been part of the resistance, Göring could hardly contain himself, and at lunchtime referred to Lahousen as 'That traitor! That's one we forgot on the 20 July'. When told that Hess had found his memory, Göring roared with laughter at what he considered to be Hess having had a joke at the court's expense. He soon tired of finding it amusing once he realised that Hess had suddenly become the centre of attention and not himself. Göring was obsessed with his self-perceived role of being the leader. Frank described the time during an exercise in the yard when Göring had stopped and stared at him until he fell into place and walked behind him, as was the usual German condition when being with a senior officer. Despite the setbacks, Göring lost no time with his cynicism, commenting on 'Negro officers', wondering whether they could command white troops, and returned to the belief that Hess may have found his memory, but 'he was not normal'.

A few days later, Göring was reflecting on the concentration camp film, explaining to Gilbert that the figures had to be exaggerated, and he could not believe them, putting it down as enemy propaganda. He enjoyed watching the films about the rise to power of the NSDAP and Hitler's popularity, telling Gilbert that the films indicated they were preparing for war, and he was happy to acknowledge that saying:

> When they said I was playing with war by building up the Luftwaffe, I just told them that I certainly wasn't running a girls' finishing school. I joined the Party precisely because it was revolutionary, not because of the ideological stuff … and the thing that pleased me was that the Nazi Party was the only one that had the guts to say, 'to hell with the Versailles while the others were crawling and appeasing'.

There is no question that of all the defendants, Göring was the most robust and least repentant. He also had many notes taken of his conversations because he enjoyed talking, mainly about himself, and in many ways, he was standing in for Hitler's absence.

He tried to explain to Gilbert on a pre-Christmas visit that he had tried to avoid war with Britain and the way he had used a Swedish intermediary called Birger Dahlerus.* He also admitted that when the People's Court which followed the 20 July 1944 Plot had been raised, it had disgusted him, and the way Hitler

---

*   Birger Dahlerus was at first trusted by the British with his many international contacts, but they soon discovered his wife was a German national who owned considerable Germany property, that Göring had assisted in gaining a marriage permit for Dahlerus, and that Dahlerus had acted as guardian to Göring's stepson from his first marriage which would have compromised the trust had it been known.

had turned against him during the last two years of the war, even ordering his execution in the end days. After discussing the Ernst Röhm purge in the Night of the Long Knives (30 June 1934), Gilbert wrote that once his jovial mask fell away, 'the ruthless-gangster side of his personality stood clearly revealed'.[19]

When asked during the Christmas recess whether he thought the time would come when the endless conflict and hatred would cease, Göring promptly responded in the negative, claiming there 'were too many people in the world' and continued with his favourite theme that the Russian colossus remained the problem for the future. He also returned to another habitual personal issue that his main concern was not dying, but his reputation in history about which he always expressed self-assurance, and that one day he would have statues representing his greatness.

He later raised the Munich crisis meeting, pointing out that Neville Chamberlain and Édouard Daladier were not at all interested in the fate of Czechoslovakia, making the whole meeting a 'cut-and-dried affair'. However, he was furious at the witness SS functionary Otto Ohlendorf's disclosure of massacres, and he soon turned this conversation with Gilbert by arguing that the case against the General Staff was weak, and had he taken over from Hitler he would have disposed, one way or another, of Bormann, trying to indicate he was a civilised and reasonable person.*

His anger returned on Monday 7 January 1946 when the issue of the Nazi response to partisan warfare was raised, and Nazi witnesses gave testimony to obeying orders. At the canteen lunch that day, he caused a degree of hilarity with his jokes even among those serving the tables, until Gilbert pointed out that 'war would be a great joke if so many people didn't die', which caused the laughter to stop. When in the afternoon the witness Bach-Zelewski gave more evidence of atrocities, Göring could hardly contain his anger, and Bach-Zelewski caused Jodl to explode as well.† For many years after the war, it was often believed that the *Wehrmacht* fought a clean war and that the SS had carried out the atrocities, but Bach-Zelewski openly admitted that *Wehrmacht* officers and men knew about the barbarities.[20]

On Saturday 2 February, Göring was pondering the soon anticipated Russian prosecution and expressing the view they would be 'especially hard on him' because he had always persecuted the communists. He told Gilbert 'they'll never forgive me for that' and 'he laughed with the malicious glee of a little boy who had put a tack on teacher's chair'. The interview stopped as Göring heard the chapel bell, explaining he only went 'to get out of the damn cell'.‡ He was not forgotten by the French prosecution who in winding up their prosecution referred to his looting of French

---

* Otto Ohlendorf, the chief of the SD who commanded *Einsatzgruppe* D in southern Russia; see Bullock, *Hitler*, 702.

† Erich von dem Bach-Zelewski was a high-ranking SS officer responsible for Nazi security warfare, checking behind the lines for opposition, which involved him in civilian activities. He also led the brutal suppression of the Warsaw uprising.

‡ For one reason or another, most attended chapel except for Hess, Rosenberg, and Streicher.

art treasure with Fritzsche telling Gilbert that Göring often sold 'the stuff he stole'. Göring's moral sensibility was negligible, but 'he displayed more open anxiety over revelations about his corruption and ostentation than over Nazi policy'.[21]

When the Russian prosecution started on Friday 8 February, Göring was beside himself with anger, bellowing at the other defendants about Russian atrocities. When they tried to calm or ignore him, he called them 'chicken-hearted little boys', and it was apparent that he still held sway over many of them. Göring became even more agitated a few days later as General Friedrich von Paulus (who had surrendered at Stalingrad) took the stand and the military defendants argued between themselves and their counsels about their responses, referring to Paulus as a traitor and a 'dirty pig'. The civilian defendants tended to have a more sympathetic attitude, seeing Paulus more as a tragedy, especially Speer, Fritzsche, and Schirach.

On Friday 15 February, Göring's overpowering bullyboy tactics were becoming so pronounced that it was decided to limit his influence by returning him to solitary confinement except in court, making many of the others furious. Göring was isolated and had to eat his lunch on his own in another room, giving Gilbert the feeling that Göring felt like 'a rejected child', who explained that his 'joking and horseplay' was only to provide some relief to the proceedings. Göring admitted that there were times when he wished he had taken a different route in life, which Gilbert noted reflected a similar theme to the one he had written to his wife on 29 October 1945.

Göring was furious when placed in a small room by himself, with Gilbert cunningly drawing up a plan as to who joined who in the remaining rooms. He placed Speer and Fritzsche with Funk and Schirach in the hope the latter two could be weaned away from Göring's influence. In another room, he placed the 'elders' of Schacht, Papen, and Neurath in the hope they would influence their fourth member Dönitz. In the third room, Frank, Seyss-Inquart, Keitel, and Sauckel, knowing there would be little communication, Jodl, Frick, Kaltenbrunner, and Rosenberg shared a table, and finally Raeder, Streicher, Hess, and Ribbentrop, hoping they would neutralise or defuse one another.

The removal of Göring into splendid isolation was clever, as in Speer's words he had been 'exercising a kind of moral terror among the defendants'. By mid-February, Göring was trying to strike the 'pose of the misunderstood humanitarian' who had seen 'the realities of war since 1914' and was prepared to die a martyr, always with an eye to his proposed place in history.

On Wednesday 6 March, Churchill's speech in America about the 'Iron Curtain' was hitting the headlines and causing excitement among the defendants, perhaps hoping it would lead to dissension with the Russians in Nuremberg.* The Churchillian speech 'exploded over the Allied courthouse in wrecked Nuremberg like

---

*   Churchill had delivered this speech the day before in Fulton, Missouri, and created headlines. It was Goebbels, though, who had first used the expression 'Iron Curtain'.

a large postwar bombshell' and at a time when the Western Allies and Soviets were becoming more suspicious of one another.[22] Papen said Churchill was outspoken, but Göring took full advantage claiming 'I told you so', implying the real danger was communism. This speech by Churchill sent a thrill through the defendants who felt they had been vindicated by Churchill having listened to thousands of documents condemning them.

As noted, those guards who were closest to the major defendants spoke German without letting the captives know this fact. One overheard Göring say to his defence counsel not to mention something because 'thank God that hasn't come to light yet'. It was little wonder that at times Gilbert was somewhat cynical. It was clear that as far as he could tell, the world for Göring still revolved around him. Later, during his individual trial, Göring almost boasted at his performance, admiring his own efforts and claiming the Russian prosecutor Rudenko was nervous about taking him on. He accused the Catholic clergy of being homosexuals and grooming young ordinands, throwing in quips about nuns being the 'brides of Christ', and in Gilbert's views Göring was more concerned about his German sense of loyalty and how he would go down in history as a national hero.

Gilbert went to see Göring's wife and found her furious at how Hitler had her family and husband arrested and threatened with execution, but also seemingly critical of Göring's obsession with the German sense of total loyalty, describing it as fanatical. When Gilbert spoke to Göring about this conversation, Göring claimed he did not think the Führer had sent the order for his arrest, and that it was probably Bormann. Later, Göring's wife was interviewed by a journalist with the ensuing headlines that Frau Göring called 'Hermann too faithful to Hitler', which Göring dismissed as 'that's all right, she is a woman'. If Göring had anything in his favour, it was his faithfulness to his two wives.

Like many others, Göring could not understand how millions of Jews could be murdered within the time frames, but Gilbert had interviewed Rudolf Höss who had run Auschwitz. Höss had explained to Gilbert, and later in the proceedings to the court, how the gassing of thousands could be done quickly, and the bodies disposed of. When Gilbert passed this frank information on to Göring, it became clear that it had a depressing effect on him who could no longer protest about propaganda. Göring asked who gave this man the orders and Gilbert told him Himmler, under a *Führerbefehl* (Führer Order), 'just another German being loyal to Hitler', and Gilbert challenged him on the subject of 'blind obedience without conscience'.[23]

Göring's Trial

Göring was the first and the most vital case for the prosecution as he epitomised the totality of the Nazi regime. He had been second to Hitler, involved from the start, established the Gestapo, chief of the *Luftwaffe*, deeply immersed in the national economy, the Röhm purge, *Kristallnacht*, the Reichstag fire, and if the 'conspiracy theory were to be proved, then Göring's part in it had to be established beyond any reasonable doubt. If he were not a conspirator, no one was'.[24]

On Friday 8 March 1946, Göring took to the stand to defend himself. Among his witnesses was his adjutant Karl-Heinrich Bodenschatz whose evidence Jackson tore apart. This witness read out his prepared answers from written notes, and when asked how he knew a particular meeting had taken place, he explained that Göring's counsel Dr Stahmer had told him, which caused amused eruptions in the courtroom.

Erhard Milch, who had been the second ranking officer in the *Luftwaffe*, appeared and could not offer much except by explaining that the *Luftwaffe* was a defensive organisation, Göring was against the war, and knew nothing of the atrocities. When Jackson, armed with documents, questioned him, it was not easy for Milch because he was also involved in forced labour and had ordered the hanging of Russian officers. Milch described Dachau concentration camp as a clean and well-run place, and his evident lies were all too easily exposed. At one point, he said it was so well-run it had its own 'slaughterhouse', which 'produced a spate of hysterical laugher in court which the bench instantly silenced'.[25] He was cumbersome in his replies and fell easily into the cross-examination traps, a legal system he had not experienced before. The same experience fell to Colonel Bernd von Brauchitsch, Göring's old adjutant, who denied everything, and this policy of being in the dark continued with other minor witnesses.

Göring's supposed star witness was the Swedish engineer and businessman Birger Dahlerus mentioned above but whose information alienated some of the other defendants. However, the British prosecutor Sir David Maxwell Fyfe skilfully demonstrated, after cross-examining Dahlerus, that the Swede had been misled, and there was a general feeling that Göring, who was fuming in his seat at his defence, appeared 'washed-up'. Dahlerus had just written a book about his efforts (*The Last Attempt*) and had been reluctant to stand as a witness, and this experience would have confirmed his doubts. He had been astonished to hear at the trial that while he thought he was negotiating peace talks with the British, the Nazi regime were fixing dates to invade Poland. Maxwell Fyfe succeeded in turning Göring's Dahlerus into a prosecution witness.

Few of these witnesses were of value, but Göring's best hope was Field Marshal Kesselring, who repeated the defensive nature of the *Luftwaffe* and painted the bombing of Rotterdam and Warsaw as legitimate bombing targets. Kesselring underlined this making it difficult for the prosecution who had used strategic bombing to a greater extent; had Göring been standing only as head of the *Luftwaffe*, he would have been on safer ground. Kesselring pointed out that the defensive nature was clear from the fact the Germans had no heavyweight four-engine bombers like the Allies, causing Jackson to drop the issue in hand and return to the Jewish persecution over which Kesselring denied any knowledge. Overall, Kesselring transpired to be Göring's most plausible witness, though Maxwell Fyfe attacked him over the Rotterdam bombing. Laternser, Kesselring's defence lawyer, later returned to this using the *tu quoque* defence, which was not allowed, but, as in the later Dönitz case, was somewhat pertinent and embarrassing.

When Göring had taken to the witness box and was examined by most of the other lawyers, Göring was 'lucid and impressive, and his description and explanation of how and why things happened during the rise of Nazism and the life of the Third Reich was interesting and at times fascinating'.[26] One reporter on hearing Göring speak described him as 'a brain without a conscience' which, given the overall evidence about Göring, was incisive.[27] However, even those defendants who had little taste for Göring thought he was good, reminding them of the Göring of earlier days, even drawing appreciative comments from Judge Norman Birkett in his notes. Many had despised Göring, knowing him as 'fatty Hermann', especially during his decline and self-indulgence in the later war years. But the limited diet and weaning off his medical drug addiction found him in the witness box untidy but trimmer, and mentally alert to such a degree that it raised some surprise and even admiration. He was determined to enter the history books as a German hero and for a moment this seemed plausible. He adopted a candid tone and addressed the court on his various roles in the Nazi leadership, his economic Four-Year Plan, and the *Luftwaffe*. He even admitted he encouraged the black-market in occupied countries as it was inevitable as he argued, and it could be seen in Germany under Allied occupation. He took the opportunity to taunt his opponents, pointing out that when Hitler as head of state assumed the head of the military and demanded an allegiance oath, it was the same formula in America. He fully accepted his responsibilities and argued plausibly as to why Germany had to rearm and the circumstances of the post-Versailles Treaty days. He admitted he was always consulted but claimed he had no knowledge of the killing of Royal Air Force (RAF) prisoners of war (Stalag Luft III), and when he had heard of the incidents, he claimed he had argued with Hitler that the British might respond against their German prisoners.[*]/[†] When it came to civilian war crimes, his economic powers, the camps, he was more elusive but still presented a better picture than most people had anticipated. He also side-stepped the Röhm purge, the Reichstag fire, and only saw the concentration camps as a form of 'protective custody' using Himmler as the excuse. He started to push the bounds of credibility further, claiming Yugoslavia was attacked because they were mobilising, and that in Poland and the Netherlands only military targets were bombed.

---

[*]   The Lieber Code mentioned above recognised the rights of prisoners to escape and is in the 1929 Geneva Convention.

[†]   On 24 March 1944 76 RAF officers escaped from Sagan camp of which 20 were soon re-captured and returned. Three reached Sweden, three remain missing, and some 50 were executed on Hitler's orders.

He even took the opportunity of defending some of the other defendants by denigrating the roles they played and exalting himself. He explained Keitel could not make decisions, that Ribbentrop was not respected enough to be taken seriously, and it was he and not Papen who helped the Nazi Party to power. It was over 12 hours of evidence well presented, impressing Schirach and even some of the more hostile defendants, demonstrating that the 'old Göring' was back in harness. Generally, the other defendants, even his critics, thought he conducted the first part about the early days well. In the 'elders' room', Schacht, Papen, and Neurath enjoyed hearing Göring's witnesses slowly dismantled, but the nature of this Anglo-American form of cross-examination made them somewhat nervous. Dönitz and Schacht agreed the best way was to avoid notes and answer spontaneously. On the matter of Jews, Göring pushed it aside as merely a matter of excluding Jewry from politics, not least because they opposed National Socialism.[28]

There followed the now well-known duel between Göring and Jackson in the cross-examination during which Göring seemed to have an advantage, answering Jackson's questions with a frankness which developed into a word duel, with Göring gaining some control, and Jackson becoming noticeably irritated as he almost played into Göring's hands. Göring appeared almost breezy during the exchange. When Jackson asked Göring if he was aware that he was the one person who could explain the purposes of the Nazis, Göring answered 'I am perfectly aware of that', as if bothering to explain himself to a minor official was beneath him.[29] As Telford Taylor noted, 'his handling of the questions soon created the impression that the defendant was dialectically superior to the prosecutor'.[30] One reporter wrote that Jackson 'had a transatlantic prepossession that a rogue who had held high office would be a solemn and not a jolly rogue, and was disconcerted by his impudence'.[31] Jackson was failing, and some commentators claim he never recovered from this public debacle. Göring successfully challenged him over language, facts, and some of the documentary evidence. Jackson was not challenging the presumed urbane Göring but an informed and intelligent foe.

When Jackson attempted to stop Göring in his lengthier answers, the presiding Judge Lawrence informed Jackson that the defendant had the right to answer. Jackson's sheer frustration was pushed to the limits when Göring corrected his translation of a German word. A major embarrassment arose over the issue of the early German occupation of the Rhineland with Jackson telling Göring it was all kept secret. Göring promptly responded with 'I do not think I can recall reading beforehand the publication of the mobilisation preparations of the United States'.[32] This cynical reply was clever and brought forward a sense of appreciation from the defendants, and Lawrence, aware of the deep waters in which Jackson was almost floundering, suggested an adjournment for the day. Even on questions relating to the Röhm purge and *Kristallnacht* Göring either denied involvement or was evasive and it was not easy for Jackson to prove otherwise.

The next day, Jackson was on safer ground when he returned to the Jewish persecution and looting art. Documents and recorded conversations relating to Göring and his attitude towards Jews could not be dismissed as mere banter, and Jackson was now damaging Göring. Naturally, Göring tried to deny his predilection for looting art as Jackson produced accumulating evidence to prove otherwise. Göring still managed to gain some upper hand when he was shown an aerial photograph of bomb damage, but with his flying experience was able to demonstrate that it could not have been taken by a plane. Thereafter, he almost proved to be helpful to the prosecution as if his open candour were helping them. Jackson's obvious failure to control or master the cunning Göring for some seemed to threaten the trial, and certainly eventuated in many criticisms and historical comments since.

Göring had not indulged in Nazi propaganda which had been the initial fear of the prosecution. Jackson had appeared wounded, and it was clear that the drug-cleansed and physically leaner Göring was more astute and intelligent than his 1943–45 image had projected. Göring had been highly articulate causing Jackson to lose control of the cross-examination and for some threw the future of the trial into doubt. The attending journalists made much of this clash with the second man of the Third Reich.

Göring found Maxwell Fyfe more difficult to handle as the latter made a nonsense out of Göring's claim he had tried to avoid war. Maxwell Fyfe also had at hand documentation indicating that Göring was not being totally honest over the killing of the RAF prisoners of war, and having investigated the precise timings when Göring claimed to have taken leave, it was 'a textbook example of cross-examination: short, precise questions on facts, winning brief affirmative replies proving Göring must have known of the illegal executions.'[33] Maxwell Fyfe had researched precise timings including Göring's so-called holidays and caught him unawares.[34] This time, the prosecutor was more in the driving seat. Maxwell Fyfe applied extra pressure over Göring's knowledge of *Aktion Kugel* (secret decree), where the prisoners were shot through a so-called measure body-height instrument, but Göring naturally denied any knowledge. Maxwell Fyfe produced a mountain of documentary evidence about violating the neutrality of the Low Countries, and effectively countered Göring's claim that neither he nor Hitler knew anything about Auschwitz. Confronted by calm and methodically presented evidence, Göring's initial impression of candid good will started to evaporate as Maxwell Fyfe played his cat-and-mouse game with superior talent. The Russian prosecutor Rudenko put his emphasis onto forced labour, and the French stated they had little to add.

In terms of court time Göring had consumed 12 days, causing the Tribunal concern and to announce that they would stop other defendants going over the same ground, which had a salutary effect on the proceedings. It later transpired the other defendants had an average of four days. The newspaper pundits had started on their old criticism that a trial would provide a platform for Nazi propaganda.

But the controversy concerning Jackson's prosecution, although a dominant feature of this part of the trial, never blurred the main issue that Göring had been 'up to his neck' in planning an aggressive war, that he had been involved not only in the conspiracy charges but also war-crimes and crimes against humanity, and the international looting of art had added a welcome relish to the prosecution's case. It was summed up by Seyss-Inquart when he said, 'all that talking isn't going to do him any good. They have it all in black and white'.[35] As much as Göring ducked and weaved in the trial, he did not fool or convince anyone that he was innocent. The judges noted that 'this defendant was the planner and prime mover in the military and diplomatic preparation for war which Germany pursued'.[36]

After Taking the Stand

Göring was becoming steadily uncomfortable about being isolated, the feelings against him by the other defendants were evident, and after Höss's testimony on Auschwitz, he was depressed by the disclosure and reality of the Jewish extermination policy. During Frank's trial, it was clear that as early as 1941 and 1942 the liquidation policy had become known, which he alleged he found unbelievable. He told Gilbert that had he known, he would have done something about the matter, indicating for a moment a different attitude. But after 1943, it would have been impossible because of his diminishing position with Hitler. Gilbert did not mention that crossing his mind was that by 1943, Göring was immersed in his drug addiction, luxurious lifestyle, and corruption.[37]

During the Frick trial, when the ex-intelligence agent and Gestapo official Hans Gisevius, who had been in the resistance, had taken the stand as a witness, he referred to Göring's involvement in dirty dealings (Night of the Long Knives, the Blomberg affair, and more), thereby exposing Göring's total involvement. This news delighted some of the defendants and made others angry, and Göring was accused of trying to 'get at' the witness through threats. He even harangued the defendants and their counsels and had to be forcibly put in the elevator to take him from the courtroom. Later, Schacht's testimony concerning Göring upset him, especially allusions to his criminal personality and dressing himself up in a Roman toga emulating a Roman emperor. The diplomat Ulrich von Hassell had noted with great amusement in his diaries that Göring loved dressing up, often in a violet kimono, wearing a golden dagger in the morning, 'and around his plump body was a wide girdle set with many stones'.[38]

During Jodl's trial Göring regained some hope, but was soon disillusioned when Jodl ridiculed politicians whenever there was an opening. Göring warned Gilbert the trials would not change anything, warning him of the Russians, that it was 'only your atom-bomb' which keeps them in check, and that the Americans would make no progress with nationalistic Germany.

After Speer's trial, Göring was livid with rage, although he tried to conceal it from Gilbert until Gilbert challenged him as to why he never questioned Hitler or even replaced him. Göring explained it would have been impossible to do such a thing in war, and although he speculated thousands would have joined him, it would have meant sheer chaos. It was all a matter of German tradition which an American could not understand. Gilbert suggested to Göring that notions were all out of date, but Göring revelled in his self-perceived image of the 'last renaissance figure'. Gilbert observed in his notes that Göring, as the trial was gathering momentum, was 'bothered' by the fact that he had been loyal to a murderer. Göring made the threat he would raise the issue of the Katyń massacre, which had been a point the Allies had tried to stop the Russians raising because of the then already current suspicions it had been ordered by Stalin and was not a Nazi crime.

Summation, Final Statements, and Verdicts

During the discussion time during the summations, the theme of the 'renaissance figure' was returned to again with Dr Stahmer, his counsel, referring to his medieval sense of loyalty which he thought might interest Gilbert as a psychologist. When Gilbert said there was another side to Göring, Stahmer laughed and said that was for the prosecution to outline. Göring was unhappy that during this time the *Stars and Stripes* carried the headlines that 'Göring had plot to hide 50 million dollars', which naturally caused a stir among the defendants, with Göring calling it a dirty trick.

Stahmer had a difficult time presenting Göring's defence because he was deeply entrenched under all the indictments and spent his initial time challenging the disproportionate strength between the prosecution and the defence. Apart from claiming that the Germans could not be prosecuted for the Katyń massacre, there was little he could add to all that had already been said. Others, he argued, would try and shift the blame, or argue obeying orders, denouncing Hitler, or claiming ignorance. Apart from pretending he did not know of the extermination plans, Göring accepted all the questions with a frankness which at times had thrown the prosecution into crosswinds.

When Jackson arrived at the prosecution summation, he started with an overall observation that at least the defendants had been given a fair trial which would not have happened under their regime. He pulled no punches saying:

> The large and varied role of Göring who was half-militarist and half-gangster. He stuck a podgy finger in every pie … He was equally adept at massacring opponents and at framing scandals to get rid of stubborn generals. He built up the Luftwaffe and hurled it at his defenceless neighbours. He was among the foremost in harrying the Jews out of hand.[39]

Airey Neave was not that impressed by the 'podgy finger' joke as it made Göring appear like a 'harmless fat boy'. However, Jackson added a sarcastic note of ridicule, that as the second in command, Göring had pretended he knew nothing of the excesses of the Gestapo, which he had created, and never knew about the extermination programme, although his signature was on many of the decrees which instituted the persecutions of that race.[40] Göring was furious and said that the British Shawcross would be more 'dignified', and while it was true Shawcross did not deploy humour, he was just as contemptuous, accusing the defendants of being murderers. It was the extermination of European Jews which caused Göring the most embarrassment and potential shame, a feeling shared by all the defendants.

Göring was the first to give his final statement and there was an expectancy that he would say something revealing or exceptional. However, he simply tore into the prosecutors as treating the defendants with contempt, and who had for their part sworn an oath to tell the truth and then had been accused of lying. There was no basis for proof of the allegations, stated in his usual robust way by accusing the prosecution as 'treating the defendants and their testimony as completely worthless'.[41]

He concluded by saying he had been solely motivated by his love 'for my people, its happiness, its freedom, and its life. And for all this I call on the Almighty and my German people to witness'.[42] In the canteen, Papen attacked him as being the source of all the problems. During the month of September 1945, as the judges talked, prisoners' wives were permitted to visit. Göring's wife Emmy and their daughter Edda arrived with the other families.

Lawrence read Göring's case, finding him guilty on all four counts, stating there was nothing to be said in mitigation. For Göring was often, indeed almost always, 'the moving force, second only to his leader … the record discloses no excuses for this man'.[43] As Göring came to hear the verdict, it was accompanied by some minor drama as the earphones were not working. They were soon fixed, and he heard he had been sentenced to death. He bowed 'slightly' towards the Tribunal and left for the elevator.

As the lift door opened in the basement, Göring met the acquitted Fritzsche. They were permitted to shake hands as Göring, almost kindly, told him that he was pleased that Fritzsche had been acquitted. He protested loudly at not being allowed the tradition of being shot, and the night before his proposed hanging the guard noted his twitching and it was discovered he had taken a file of cyanide, cheating the hangman. In a note in his cell, he insisted no one had helped, and that he had once hidden a cyanide capsule in a bottle of cream. It was apparent that either he had not been thoroughly searched or someone had secreted it to him. Another hidden capsule was eventually discovered on 19 October 1946. Telford Taylor had some suspicions and named an American soldier, but it remains speculation. This incident resulted in a thorough investigation which never resolved the problem and has since provided hundreds of conspiracy theories to which this study will not add. Several too hasty journalists sent reports of his hanging. Andrus had been obsessed with possible suicides since Ley's death, and later wrote that the cells were regularly searched as well as the prisoners. They had been rummaged for nails, bits of metal, paper clips, and even Keitel had been found with a small piece of sheet metal in his wallet. But 'Göring and Hess were clean'; to the end Göring was cunning.[44] It had one direct ramification for the other defendants; it had been previously agreed they could walk to the gibbet untethered, but for fear of another suicide attempt, they were handcuffed in their cells before they started their last walk.

Final Notes

As a child and young boy, Göring had been spoilt. He had risen to prominence following his reputation as an ace fighter pilot, and he had supported Hitler from the earliest days. Although Hess had been designated as Deputy Führer it was widely understood that Göring would be Hitler's natural successor and had been deeply involved in every aspect of the rise of Nazism. He was the major feature of the trial because Hitler was dead, and he was the last surviving member of the top Nazi leadership.

His sense of self-importance and self-grandeur had been known for many years even by Hitler, but the trial exposed his flaws in depth. His drug addiction, dressing up, his love of jewels and wealth, looting art, and general incompetence had dominated his life during the critical war years. He was more than a festive Falstaff, who could at times appear affable and likeable, despite adamant denials he was one of the instigators of the Holocaust, founder of the Gestapo, an intriguer and plotter looking to his own elevation through the Borgia-type courts of Nazism. He was with some justification found guilty on all four counts. He regarded himself to the last moment as a major figure of the day, a German hero albeit a martyr, the last of the Renaissance men. As Richard Overy wrote: 'The "Iron Man" divorced from his political empire and the apparatus of Nazism was an historical creature of little substance', yet here was the man who thought one day there would be statues of him if not a shrine of the martyr.[45] He may have started the Gestapo, but it was Himmler who made it the infamous structure it became. Had he been charged as chief of the *Luftwaffe* he would probably have escaped a death sentence like Dönitz. In the major task of economics he was lazy and incompetent, but he had helped Hitler and Nazism rise to power, plotted, and intrigued. He may have been affable, at times good company, but he had given Hitler total support in planning aggressive wars and was aware of the atrocities against prisoners of war. Finally, he had played an active part in the planning for the extermination of European Jews despite his denials.

A Russian assassin called Miklashevsky reported to the Soviet authorities that he could assassinate Göring, but they 'rejected this proposal, for Göring's removal seemed more likely to assist the Nazi war effort', which said it all.[46]

Rudolf Hess 1894–1987

Background

Rudolf Hess had been in the infantry in the Great War, serving in the same regiment as Hitler. He was wounded several times and awarded the Iron Cross. He started to fly but he never had any aerial combat experience. Post-war, he studied geopolitics at Munich University, joined the *Freikorps* in 1919, and the Nazi Party in 1920. He was with Hitler at the Munich *Putsch*, served time with him in prison, and helped in the writing of *Mein Kampf* ('My Struggle'), Hitler's mix of autobiography and political manifesto. It has been suggested that it was Hess who added sections to the book on the issue of *Lebensraum*. Hess spent 10 more days in prison than Hitler, but the Nazi Party was re-established and grew, with

Hess meets Anton Mussert, Dutch fascist leader, Seyss-Inquart, right. (*Nationaal Archief Netherlands, Photographer Unknown*)

Hitler naming Hess as his private secretary in 1925. On 15 December 1932 Hess was made chairman of the Party-Political Commission, and on 21 April 1933 was made Deputy Führer.

His influence faded during the latter part of the 1930s, and on the outbreak of war in 1939, Göring was declared as Hitler's official successor and Hess named as second in line. It has been projected by some that his loss of influence may have been a factor in his flight to Britain on 10 May 1941, by which he tried to avoid a second front as Operation *Barbarossa* was being planned, a view held by the Russians who remained highly suspicious of the British and constantly demanded Hess's execution. He had flown to Britain unauthorised with the seeming intention of making peace through the Duke of Hamilton whom he hoped would arrange for him to meet King George VI, indicating a gross ignorance of the British scene. He had tried his hand in diplomatic matters, but as Ribbentrop would argue in his own defence, Hitler was the sole source of authority in these matters. It has also been suggested, but without evidence, that Hitler had an inkling of what Hess planned, but he flew into a rage when it occurred, which Mussolini interpreted as weeping through sadness, explaining that Hess was trying to reach Ireland to stir a revolt. It was a bolt out of the blue for everyone, with Goebbels describing it as 'a tragi-comedy. One doesn't know whether to laugh or cry'.[1]

The bewildered British soon discovered that Hess was mentally unbalanced, and he was examined, interviewed, and imprisoned, with Churchill suggesting his execution in November 1943. There were questions raised as to whether he was mentally fit to stand trial, which Hess later dismissed by claiming his amnesia was a ploy, to the joy of the Russians who were demanding his prosecution. He had twice tried to commit suicide in Britain, first by jumping over some bannisters and later by stabbing himself with a kitchen knife. He was initially kept in Buchanan Castle, a Scottish medical hospital, then the Tower of London, later Mytchett Place near Aldershot, and finally in Maindiff Court, a former hospital at Abergavenny. The British had little idea what to do with their uninvited captive-guest. Many regarded Hess as mad and harmless, and his flight to Britain was popularly seen as seeking peace, making him an object of some pity.

The British journalist Rebecca West thought 'it seemed shameful to put him on trial' and wrote 'he had the classless air characteristic of asylum inmates'.[2] Nevertheless, Hess had been a major part of Hitler's coterie and had assisted Göring in Röhm's death. He was deeply anti-Semitic, signing the Nuremberg Laws, which was a short step to planning the extermination process. Hess was the one defendant who could have offered the most telling insights into the early days of Hitler and the Nazi regime, but while most of the defendants tended to remain loyal to Hitler, Hess claimed he could not even remember him. Once chosen for the trial, the British flew him back to the continent.

Interrogations

Jackson and others raised questions as to whether he was worth including because of his state of mind. He could not have been involved in the major crimes committed from 1941 onwards, but under the conspiracy theory he could be prosecuted for the overall Nazi design or conspiracy of aggressive war, and he had signed the Nuremberg Laws.

This was the theory, but in October 1943, after his suicide attempts, Hess seemed to suffer from total amnesia which ended for a time in February 1945, and then started again. He even admitted the amnesia was deliberate, and when faced with the stress of the Nuremberg Trial the amnesia returned. Speer once described him as 'one of the great cranks of the Third Reich', but he had once played a vital role alongside Hitler in the early days.[3] Because of his close relationship with Hitler in the early days as the Nazi regime grew, he was of considerable interest. Interrogations were followed by interviews, an organised confrontation with Göring and others from his past, including secretaries, and all-round psychologist reports and investigations were carried out, but two mysteries remained unresolved. The first surrounded his intentions for flying to Britain in 1941, and the second as to how far the recurrent amnesia was genuine. Colonel Amen who headed the interrogation teams personally interviewed him and tried every conceivable trick in the book but discovered that Hess was either 'crazy' as Göring described him, or far too clever to be outwitted. Despite the amnesia, he had a quick mind and when he appeared to have slipped up, he immediately found a means to extricate himself. This confirmed what the British had already stated that he was constantly in a paranoid state. When it was suggested that he should receive some form of medical intervention by drugs to settle and soothe him, he point-blank refused; he had arrived in Nuremberg convinced the British had tried to poison him and brought some food to prove he was right.

As noted above, a special interview was arranged with Göring, with Colonel Amen present. Göring asked Hess if he knew him, only to be met by 'Who are you?' Göring persisted, pointing out that they had known one another for years, that he was head of the *Luftwaffe* and Hess had flown one of his planes to Britain, and that Hess had been present when Göring was made *Reichsmarschall*. But Hess would not budge from his 'no-memory' posture. There was a slight change when Hess met his two secretaries, an Ingeborg Sperr and Hildegarde Fath, the guard present observing that there seemed to be some recognition, which Hess persistently denied. There could be little question that Hess was not just stubborn but intelligent in his way of evading direct questions, but his mental stability remained an issue. It was not surprising that post-war he attracted many disturbing conspiracy theories.

Medical Mental Observations

Psychologists from the Allied camps examined him and found remarkably similar results to those of the formal interrogation teams. They all agreed, as the British had long stated, that he was unstable, but this did not exclude him from prosecution. At times, he indicated precise thinking, emotions appeared normal, and it was generally believed he deployed amnesia as his form of defence, but with his mental instability, these phases had become habitual. Even the patient Goldensohn managed only two pages of notes on Hess, which mainly consisted of the fact that Hess could not remember much about his father or mother, or his siblings, and he was more concerned about his health, his diet, and having stomach cramps. There was the suggestion he was suffering from hysterical amnesia which was difficult to prove. This form of mental illness comes in two forms. The first is the failure to remember past events, sometimes called retrograde amnesia, and does not depend on a brain disorder. The second type is the failure to register current events and is rare, usually associated with a pre-existing amnesia of organic origin. They are rare and often rapidly clear up without psychotherapy.

Reactions during the Trial

When Airey Neave served the indictment in Hess's cell, he was shocked by his looks, 'his great dark brows contrasted sharply with his white face. The deep sockets of his blue eyes gave it the look of a skull. I immediately felt sorry for him'.[4] He gave Neave a Nazi salute when he entered according to Andrus, who put an immediate halt to this gesture. He told Neave that above all he did not want to be tried alongside Göring and he would defend himself.*

At the beginning of the trial, to everyone's astonishment, he declared his amnesia had gone and admitted he deployed it as a tactical method. He claimed that 'henceforth my memory will again respond to the outside world. The reasons for simulating loss of memory were of a tactical nature'.[5] This did not last as he sat and read Grimms' *Fairy Tales*, showing no interest in the proceedings. Then it became clear the relapse from amnesia was not total and he soon regressed to a state of neurotic behaviour. The experts eventually decided he had no brain disease, but a form of selective amnesia which was hysterical in type, leading to an emotional neurotic state, explaining his almost total instability in matters of memory recall. The trial continued with Hess seemingly indifferent and a point of annoyance for the legal teams or bemused bafflement for the other defendants, but he was one defendant from whom nothing significant was gained. He may have held the key to the early rise of Nazism, may have been able to supply answers about the early Hitler and his intentions, but nothing of value emerged, even though he had for a time been Hitler's deputy and closest confidant.

During the first day of the trial, it was clear that Hess had no idea what an atom bomb was, and Ribbentrop had to explain to Hess who was clearly living in his own world. On 1 December 1945 Gilbert visited the cells of some of the defendants to inform them that Hess's memory had returned. At first, Göring refused to believe

---

* Airey Neave later became a major campaigner for Hess's release from Spandau, thinking a life sentence for an elderly man was unjust.

it and then roared with laughter at what he decided had been Hess's form of a joke. Gilbert talked to Hess about the issue, reminding him that he had expressed the opinion that Hess might not be playing a game, to which Hess responded that was the reason he had 'opened up'. Later, he tried to explain that by his flight to Britain he had at least tried to bring peace. In a pre-Christmas discussion over racial psychology, Hess admitted that the Nazis had made a mistake in their racial attitudes. Hess worked on his defence during the Christmas recess, asking Gilbert to eat a couple of crackers to see if they gave him headaches as they did with Hess. Gilbert must have left the cell, having eaten the crackers, wondering if Hess would ever change.

In January, Schacht had inferred to Gilbert that Hess was still crazy, and much of Gilbert's time in Hess's cell was spent quietly assessing this situation. Gilbert suggested to Hess that the solitary confinement was not helping to which Hess readily agreed. By the weekend of 19 January Gilbert realised that Hess was again having memory problems, being able to recall only some of the evidence and witnesses during the previous week.

However, when the Russian prosecution started on Friday 8 February 1946, Hess made the gesture of removing his headphones, along with Göring, to indicate the Russian General Rudenko was not worth hearing. Hess later explained he did not want to listen to 'foreigners slandering his country'. During February it became increasingly clear that Hess was suffering again not only from stomach cramps but loss of memory, and this was even noted by the other defendants. Gilbert tried time and time again to prompt him to remember recent events during the proceedings, but it was obviously too difficult, and by the time he arrived at his own trial on Monday 25 March, his mental stability had evidently regressed.

Hess's Trial

Many observers wondered whether Hess was simply mad: 'He was a grotesque figure, gaunt and with angular projections from a baggy, grey tweed suit. Everyone watched with fascination'.[6] His counsel called Dr Alfred Seidl, who was evidently reluctant to represent him, told the *Sunday Express* that Hess refused to go into the witness box and expressed the opinion that he was pessimistic about Hess being able to defend himself.[7] This was a major limitation and Seidl was informed by the Tribunal that professionally he had to offer the defence himself. This pleased Göring and probably his own counsel, who had urged him forward in this policy. Hess's case, because of the unique background, only took a day and a half. It was unusual because of his flight to Britain in 1941 which had shortened his time in terms of war crimes possibilities. Dr Seidl also added that Hess had assumed all responsibility for orders and actions he issued when in post, and he did not want to answer for the internal affairs of the sovereign state of Germany.

Seidl started with long-prepared arguments about the Versailles Treaty which appeared to try to distance the trial proceedings from the charges. Maxwell Fyfe warned the judges that these arguments were detracting from the point of the trial, and that the Versailles Treaty was irrelevant. Historically, the Versailles Treaty was important in the light of subsequent events, but the trial was concerned with the evil horrors perpetrated by the Nazi regime, and the court ruled that Seidl's arguments were irrelevant and inadmissible. Seidl then tried his second argument by raising the disturbing Molotov–Ribbentrop Pact between the Nazis and the Soviets. This introduced a new embarrassment into the proceedings. Apart from the problem of finding a copy of the referenced protocol, it caused friction with the Russians which was undoubtedly part of Seidl's plan. However, it took Hess's case no further than a few jangled nerves.

This was followed by Hess's chosen witnesses, but Seidl only read their affidavits for the court records. His first witness statement was written by Hess's secretary who asserted that his flight to Britain was to establish peace. Then witness Ernst Bohle tried to defend Hess against the charge of creating fifth column forces in other countries, which was easily torn apart by the legal expertise of the British prosecutor Mr Griffith-Jones. Hess's next witness statement from a Karl Stroelin, who had once been Lord Mayor of Stuttgart, was of no consequence, and the rest of the defence consisted of reading documents and arguing over the Versailles Treaty which the court ruled as totally irrelevant. Griffith-Jones and Colonel Amen were well prepared with documentation which thwarted any value the witness statements offered. Seidl then spent time on the reasons for Hess's flight to Britain and the meeting between Hess and Lord Simon which was interesting but of no value to the court or Hess. Seidl made next to no case for Hess but dwelt more on challenging the court's jurisdiction and exposing the sordid side of Allied and Soviet relationships, leaving Hess as a historical remnant whose mental state was the only substantial question. One reporter noted that 'the judges found it repulsive to try a man in such a state'.[8]

There was no cross-examination of Hess, leaving the main charge that Hess was a major player under the conspiracy charge mainly based on his position in the Nazi hierarchy. He had been with Hitler from the start, assisting him in writing *Mein Kampf* on the question of *Lebensraum*, and had been Hitler's constant companion. He had signed the infamous racial Nuremberg Laws and the laws to incorporate Austria and Poland into the Reich. However, Hess had left Germany too early for him to be involved in war crimes and crimes against humanity.

Summation, Final Statements, and Verdicts

Dr Seidl created problems by not providing translations of his German speech for the judges. He again attacked the Versailles Treaty until Lawrence stopped him, eventually telling Seidl he would have to return later when prepared, which he did at the very end following Fritzsche's summation. When Seidl resumed, he hardly mentioned Hess, and instead of arguing that Hess was innocent, he based his argument on insisting the Nazi government's policies and military actions were legal and challenged the policy of criminal organisations by trying to divert attention away from his client. He left Hess the person to the very end of his address by merely pointing out that his flight to Britain was to seek peace. Seidl irritated the Russians by saying that they were participants in aggressive wars and that Russia had joined with Germany against Poland and they should not be sitting in judgement on such matters.

Jackson during the prosecution summation described Hess as a 'zealot succumbing to wanderlust', but who had been a dedicated part of the early Nazi regime.[9] Hess was especially attacked by the Russian Rudenko because they were demanding his execution. For his final statement, Hess started to read from crushed papers stuffed in his pockets. He started to speak with some sense and then descended into seeming nonsense with Göring trying to stop him. Lawrence eventually told him with a sense of gentleness his time was expended. His final words were 'no matter what human beings may do, I shall someday stand before the judgment seat of the Eternal. I shall answer to him, and I know he will judge me innocent'.[10] Hess in the stand appeared to some as 'chilling and unsettling', and his five-page statement 'was nearly always incoherent as it lurched disturbingly from denial of the rights of the accusers to bring charges' to describing Hitler's eyes as cruel.[11]

In the final judgement, it was proposed that Hess was entirely sane at the time when he committed the charges laid against him and was found guilty on the first two counts. The imposed verdict was life imprisonment but to all appearances Hess appeared oblivious and the guards had to turn him round and take him to the lift.

Post-war

In the end, Hess was found guilty on the counts of crimes against peace and conspiracy with other Nazi leaders to commit crimes, but not guilty of war crimes and crimes against humanity. He was sentenced to life imprisonment in Spandau Prison in West Berlin. On 17 August 1987, he managed to hang himself in a gardening summer house and was first buried in secret to avoid any martyrdom by neo-Nazis, but he was later reinterred in a family plot at Wunsiedel, north-east Bavaria, on 17 March 1988, joined by his wife less than 10 years later. His life prompted a myriad of conspiracy theories which were eventually shut down by a convincing DNA confirmation from a living male relative. The only real question was how far he controlled his amnesia and how far he was paranoid, but he left no legacy or insights into the mind of Hitler or the Nazi regime.

Final Notes

There have been many stories, much of it fuelled by the British refusal to release documents, including the well-known conspiracy theory, that Hess had a double. He had often been diagnosed as a psychopath, suffering from hysterical amnesia, but no one considered Hess clinically insane. Many thought the life sentence was too much, as he had not been implicated in the two counts of war crimes and crimes against humanity, his influence within the Nazi Party had diminished, and although an 'odd character', he was not a major player. Many, including Airey Neave, long campaigned for his release, but he became a forgotten remnant of the past wandering around the gardens in Spandau's solitary isolation. It could be argued that he had been trapped in the historical circumstances of Germany in the interbellum years, and though he had undoubtedly supported the rise of Nazism at least he was not involved in massacres and the annihilation of European Jews, albeit he was a traditional anti-Semite.

Joachim von Ribbentrop 1891–1946

Ante Pavelić and Ribbentrop. (Photographer Henkel, Bundesarchiv, 183-2008-0612-500, Licence CC-BY-SA 3.0)

Background

Joachim von Ribbentrop was Hitler's foreign affairs minister from 1938 to 1945 and before that, had been Ambassador to Britain, 1936–38. During the Great War, he served in the 12th Hussars, won the Iron Cross, serving on both the Western and Eastern fronts, was given a commission, and as a first lieutenant staff officer served as a military attaché meeting Franz von Papen while in Turkey. He returned to his pre-war occupation working for the Henkell family who headed a major champagne and wine industry. He married Annelies, daughter of Otto Henkell in July 1920, whom he met at a tennis tournament, and they married very much against the wishes of the Henkell family. It appears from many accounts that she was attracted to him as a young man, but she often disagreed with his views.

Ribbentrop came from the affluent middle class, had lived in Canada and studied in London, and was fluent in both English and French which had impressed Hitler who was ignorant of other languages. He was not born with the title 'von', but it was adopted or even purchased which bemused those who knew the details of the transaction. He first met Hitler in 1932, offering his services as an interpreter and a year later was the Nazi Party's adviser on foreign affairs. He was somewhat obsessed with Hitler and the prestige it brought him. His party number was 1,119,927, but he was socially involved with Hitler who not only attended his wedding, but it was in Ribbentrop's house that the machinations of Hitler becoming chancellor occurred in January 1933.

He set up the 'Ribbentrop Bureau' which was a cluster of amateurs who spoke various languages and provided information from the world's press coverage, and Ribbentrop became Hitler's adviser on foreign policy. In April 1934, he was given his first 'official' appointment as plenipotentiary minister for matters concerning disarmament, and as ambassador extraordinary of the German Reich he helped conclude the Anglo-German Naval Treaty of June 1935. A year later, Himmler who had befriended him, made him an honorary SS major-general, and in 1936 he took up the ambassadorial role in London. When Neurath was dismissed, he became foreign minister in February 1938.

He had been central to several key events, not least the Pact of Steel of May 1939 aligning Italy and Germany, but also the Molotov–Ribbentrop Pact which he considered his greatest achievement. After this so-called triumph, his role and importance diminished. He failed to rally Mussolini to join the war immediately, and he was unsuccessful with Francisco Franco in Spain and Philippe Pétain in France. Thereafter, he was used by Hitler more as a messenger boy, keeping an eye on neutral countries and those allies who might turn against the Nazi regime. After Operation *Barbarossa*, his standing within the hierarchy was minimal, and later substantial evidence was accumulated to indicate that he knew about the plans to exterminate Jewish people.

He was generally one of the most personally disliked figures even by many of his Nazi colleagues, especially as noted by Goebbels in his diary. There is no record of anyone holding Ribbentrop in high esteem in his role, and in his diary, Goebbels exhibits total distaste for the man, complaining about the lengthy letters of abuse Ribbentrop sent him.[1] In his diary, the Italian foreign minister Ciano spent pages disparaging him, and Hassell in his diary described him as giving 'insane leadership' and as becoming totally 'rabid'.[2] He was initially admired by Hitler who sometimes referred to him as the 'second Bismarck'. This remark was noted by many on several occasions when Hitler had been asked about his foreign minister, but his response related not to Ribbentrop's brilliance but because Ribbentrop was totally subservient to Hitler who gave all the necessary directions. Hitler was thereby calling himself the second Bismarck. Undoubtedly, Hitler kept him in post because he did what he was told, but as the war entered its final phases, Hitler started to push him aside. After Hitler's death, Ribbentrop tried to find a new role under Dönitz's brief leadership but was firmly rebuffed. He was finally arrested on 14 June 1945 in Hamburg while trying to hide, one of the last to be netted. As Airey Neave pertinently observed, 'once his leader was dead, his psychological collapse was complete, but he never deserted or denounced Hitler'.[3]

Interrogations

Ribbentrop, like Funk and others, used selective amnesia as a defence. At first, in the early days of his capture Ribbentrop, when questioned in General Dwight D. Eisenhower's headquarters, appeared amenable and easy to communicate with leaving a better impression than he had managed as a diplomat in pre-war years. His defence was basically the same one of obeying orders, that Hitler gave the directions and he simply followed. By the time he arrived in Nuremberg, with the realisation of facing trial as a major war-criminal, he was vastly different from his initial presentation as an amenable captive, and he was soon resorting to forgetfulness and even pretending amnesia. As the ex-salesman of champagne, he had always been deemed by the diplomatic community and even fellow Nazis as an unlikely foreign minister. Both Neurath and Göring suggested he had been selected as Hitler's ideal 'yes-man', with Göring further describing him as 'Germany's Number One parrot'.[4] He even claimed that Hitler never revealed his overall plans to him, denying the charges on war of aggression, and always trying to justify himself through ignorance. It was little wonder that the Americans utilised Galeazzo Ciano's diaries in which the executed Italian foreign minister, who like many hated Ribbentrop, often blazed away at his opposite German number, and in his diary exposed Ribbentrop's aggressive war intentions. Ribbentrop was not the only defendant to plead ignorance and be evasive, but he was the most frustrating one for the prosecution.

Before he went into apparent mental decline, his first interviews appeared helpful in gaining insights into the Nazi regime and its intentions. Although in his diplomatic days he used a translator, at Nuremberg his initial interviews exposed that he could speak excellent English with, as Goldensohn noted, a 'British accent' which should not have surprised him. He believed that Hitler's attack on Russia had been a major error of judgement not least because it reversed his proposed foreign policy. This was assuming that Ribbentrop was an influence because it was generally understood that in nearly all matters Hitler gave the orders and proposed all policies.

He claimed, as did many others, that Operation *Barbarossa* happened because the Russians were building up forces on their western borders and looking towards the Balkans having already taken the Baltic States. Hitler hated the Bolsheviks and all forms of communism, and he had encouraged the Molotov–Ribbentrop Pact as a temporary strategic device prior to invading Poland. It is well known that despite many warnings, Stalin never believed that Hitler would attack Soviet Russia. As Göring had intimated in his interviews, Hitler had from his earliest days looked towards the east for expansion. Ribbentrop explained that the Germans were aware that the Russians were asking for 'offensive rather than defensive' weapons, and they appeared to be producing better quality weapons in some areas. It was merely the deceptive excuse that Operation *Barbarossa* was a preventative war. It was common knowledge that Hitler regarded the Soviet forces as weak, especially after their performance in Finland in November 1938. Ribbentrop described Hitler as obstinate and as a man who once he developed his plans would not deviate. Such was Hitler's gross self-assurance that once he had projected a policy, he assumed he must be right, and nothing could be changed. From his earliest days, Hitler's preoccupation with *Lebensraum* meant expansionist movement towards the east was likely. Ribbentrop had been pleased with his management of a pact with Molotov and disappointed it was cast aside. He even claimed in his interviews that communism and Nazi policy had much in common and a rapprochement was possible, which Hitler had promptly rejected. Ironically, Nazi Germany and the Soviet Union had much in common in so far that Soviet Communism was dominated by Stalin already emerging as a feared dictator. Ribbentrop defied belief by claiming in interview that his rapprochement with the Soviets was an effort to establish peace in Europe.

Ribbentrop claimed, contrary to other sources, that Hitler did not want to invade Britain, and he had been somewhat reluctant to make allies of the Italians because of their previous history in the Great War, and of the Japanese because of their ethnic differences. The reluctance was put aside regarding Japan, according to Ribbentrop, for the sake of neutralising America and keeping that country out of the war. He further claimed that the attack on Pearl Harbor had been a disagreeable surprise, which was far from the truth. The declaration of war against America had been, he claimed, the result of confusion and he had argued against this policy. In his diary, Ciano recorded that when the Japanese attacked Pearl Harbor, the 'day of infamy', Ribbentrop was on the phone to Ciano 'jumping with joy'.[5] Ribbentrop was playing his old diplomatic game of smokescreens and bluff, hoping that he would emerge safely from his current situation. Ciano was also revealing about Ribbentrop, pointing out how he made a mess of his post when ambassador to Britain. Speer claimed they were all surprised at Hitler's support for his foreign minister. Speculatively, it may have stemmed from the surprising Molotov–Ribbentrop Pact, or more probably that Hitler knew Ribbentrop had been overseas and naïvely believed he would therefore make a good diplomat.

Even in the early interviews, before he realised that vagueness and loss of memory were his best defences, he tried to convince his interrogators that he was only aware of some elements of Hitler's foreign policy. He claimed he was against the bombing of London, refused to acknowledge he fell within any of the indictments, was not involved in any criminality, knew nothing about slave labour, the killing of hostages, Russian prisoners of war, Allied airmen, or that Jews were being exterminated. To the sheer annoyance of those interrogating him, he constantly used cautious expressions such as 'possibly' or 'maybe', ensuring he could not be pinned down, and that it was only conjecture. It must have been abundantly clear to all that Ribbentrop was using all his old diplomatic skills to evade execution or prison.

Medical Mental Observations

Goldensohn found him courteous but with an 'air of superficial depression'. When Ribbentrop talked, Goldensohn found it was more like a recital, and he spent endless hours in Ribbentrop's cell preparing his defence. Goldensohn appeared to have two basic themes, the first being as to whether Hitler could have known about the atrocities, and if he did, why he let them continue. Ribbentrop found this difficult to understand saying that Hitler was a 'good man' who never ate meat, and it must have been all Himmler's activities. That Hitler was a good man because he was a vegetarian and never smoked is as ridiculous as the claim that Himmler was inherently kind because he liked butterflies. His second theme was why he was in the cell in the first place.

In his usual conversational style, Goldensohn asked him about the well-publicised time he had greeted the king of England with a Nazi salute, always regarded as a major *faux pas*. In his usual style, Ribbentrop said the king had been gracious about the episode and that it was the usual custom, which Goldensohn challenged. Ribbentrop revealed that it was not until late April 1945 that Hitler thought the war might be lost, which may have been true, but Ribbentrop was no expert concerning the end days, and was probably indicating his own importance, a lifelong characteristic. When asked about Hitler's anti-Semitism, Ribbentrop started to explain that Hitler was suspicious of all the Jews surrounding Roosevelt, stumbling for a moment before announcing Morgenthau, who was Jewish. This line of thinking, apart from being nonsense, was hardly diplomatic given Ribbentrop's circumstances, with Goldensohn noting that 'he is quite an affected fellow, but his affectation is so practiced it is almost natural', and later 'Ribbentrop has the air at times of a ham actor taking the part of the great statesman who has become a little foggy because of all he has undergone in the past few years'.[6] Goldensohn tried to steer the conversations but Ribbentrop would often become evasive, claiming he was hard of hearing or he spoke in the broadest of terms. When asked about Hitler, Ribbentrop described him as a 'great personality', charming, diplomatic, and 'magnetic', but admitted that the trials were revealing he must have had a cruel side, although insisting he had extracted Germany from the post-war 'dirt'. As with all the defendants, Ribbentrop tried to assure his captors that the Jewish extermination plan had come as a great shock to him. Like many other defendants, it was dawning on Ribbentrop that the repugnance felt by the Final Solution with its subsequent ramifications was not going to be ignored. Goldensohn referred to the recently exposed Hans Frank's diary in which Frank had reported the death of a 150,000 Poles to Hitler. Ribbentrop expressed disbelief that Frank could have written this, causing Goldensohn to wonder whether Ribbentrop was less concerned about the deaths of Poles and the ramifications than with the stupidity of putting it into writing.

Ribbentrop spoke of his relationships with Stalin and Molotov, both of whom he liked, and claimed he never knew about the attack on Russia until it happened. Ribbentrop had been proud of his pact with Molotov and did not want the Russian conflict, probably because it was undoing what he considered one of his great achievements. It was at this juncture that he focused on a major part of his own defence claiming, probably with some reality, that Hitler dictated his policies and never discussed them with Ribbentrop, who said Hitler kept the foreign office out of military affairs. If any discussion took place, it was with Himmler and Bormann who were the two most hated personalities onto whom the defendants tried to shift the blame.

Another line of defence Ribbentrop invoked was his physical self, suggesting he was ill, possibly having some disease in his brain, which might explain his inability to recall past events, even having problems recalling the events of the day before. He suggested he may have a tumour and appeared obsessed that he had never had venereal disease which he wrongly assumed was the cause of brain tumours. His defence of amnesia was palpable, and Goldensohn several times examined Ribbentrop and told him he was well. As with the others, he insisted on discussing the problems of the Versailles Treaty which had some foundation, but it was consistently used by most of the defendants in shifting accountability for the previous years onto the Western Allies, predicting that in the years ahead everyone would see the Nuremberg Trials as a 'great mistake'. He claimed that although the attempted Jewish extermination would be a blot on German history, and that Hitler must have lost his sense of proportion, history would judge the previous decades on the fact 'that Germany had really been oppressed and never given a chance'. At one point, he said he assumed the Jewish issue was a 'temporary political' matter which would find its own solution. He then turned his still latent anti-Semitism onto international British and American bankers, assuming they were all Jewish. Goldensohn challenged him on this line of thinking, with Ribbentrop finally giving the impression that he felt obliged to admit Hitler lost his balance thereby giving Ribbentrop the wrong information. He illustrated this loss of balance by turning the issue on the way he was treated by Hitler, often warmly and as a friend, then the next day cold and dismissive, but falling back on the old argument that it was either Hitler or communism, understanding like all the defendants the persisting issues between the communist Soviets and the West.

He was aware that many of his ex-colleagues in the prison regarded him with a high degree of contempt, especially Papen, Neurath, and Göring, and admitted, probably defensively, that he had been 'under Hitler's spell' which some hoped would be part of an excuse for their actions of obeying orders, living in 'a dictator state'. Gilbert regarded him as 'a confused and demoralised opportunist in defeat, without even a consistent argument to maintain a presentable front', asking everyone from the guards to the barber for advice.[7] His efforts were regarded as ridiculous as he would claim he supported the Führer yet always warned the British and French against Hitler; quite how he thought he could be believed is mind-defying.

Reactions during the Trial

When Airey Neave gave Ribbentrop the indictment, he was filled with contempt for the man because he was so full of self-pity, noting as others had that his cell was in a mess and his appearance slovenly. He was 52 but looked older and the arrogance of the past had gone. He did not know any lawyers and begged for help. Neave had anticipated arrogance but found a man wringing his hands in worry causing the Jewish interpreter 'to smirk'. As the journalist and historian William Shirer noted, Ribbentrop 'was shorn of his arrogance and his pompousness, looking pale, bent and beaten'.[8] On the first day, having explained to Hess what was meant by an atom-bomb, Ribbentrop had to leave the courtroom suffering an attack of vertigo and tinnitus. When the Hossbach Memorandum was disclosed (26 November), he told Gilbert he had never heard of it and countered by claiming that none of this would have happened 'if the Allies had given us half a chance on the Versailles issue, you never would have heard of Hitler'.[9]

On a visit to his cell a few days later, Gilbert found Ribbentrop concerned about the mounting evidence against him, especially over some of his anti-Semitic statements. Such was the barbarity of the Final Solution, this was becoming more of a central issue than Ribbentrop's dubious diplomatic efforts. He referred to a time he purported to have inquired into the Majdanek affair (massacre of Jews in Poland) only to be told it had nothing to do with him. He cast the blame on Himmler and Goebbels and how magnetic Hitler's personality was, cleverly claiming that even Daladier and Chamberlain in Munich had been taken in by Hitler's charm. However, at the end of November 1945 when Colonel Amen was questioning the witness Major General Lahousen about an overheard conversation in which Ribbentrop was alleged to have said to Canaris that in Poland 'all farms and dwellings of the Poles should go up in flames, and all Jews be killed', Ribbentrop seemed on the point of collapse.[10]

When on Tuesday 11 December films were shown depicting the rise of Hitler with the parades, crowds, and sense of jubilation, it was noted that Ribbentrop was overcome with emotion, weeping, and explaining it was a reminder of Hitler's 'terrific strength of personality'. Göring said it was so inspiring that even Justice Jackson would want to join the NSDAP. In the afternoon, the film concentrated on the 20 July 1944 Plot, but that evening when Gilbert visited Ribbentrop he was still moved to tears at the sight of Hitler on film.

During the Christmas recess, Ribbentrop spent his time poring over and pondering his defence papers, telling Gilbert that it was confusing with all the different opinions and 'so many angles'. He also explained that the Jews still had their influence, quoting Jewish bankers in New York and then, as if realising his mistake, explained he was not anti-Semitic. He changed the subject to the plea as to why the victors accept the last years as a 'historical tragedy' which was inevitable and had not worked towards a solution. Gilbert responded, asking why the Nazis had not thought of that solution in the first place. Ribbentrop again shifted the blame onto Himmler describing Hitler as 'tender' and that from Himmler's face he could tell that he was not a 'real German'.

When SD chief Ohlendorf described the massacre orders, Ribbentrop described himself as 'speechless', stating there was no defence, and how he had tried to convince his English and French friends how to stop Hitler rising to power.[11] The idea that Ribbentrop had English and French friends understandably caused Gilbert to query his statement. He responded by mentioning a few unknown people he had met in his days as a salesman, indicating how desperate his search was for a near feasible defence.

During the early part of February, when the Russians had placed General Paulus in the dock, Gilbert discussed with Ribbentrop his initial *rapprochement* with Russia causing Ribbentrop to resort to his usual diplomatic gymnastics as he tried to explain the past, causing Gilbert to write in his notes 'the sheer bare-faced hypocrisy of this man is incredible'.[12] He was very different in the lunchtime gatherings where he was influenced by Göring, and followed Rosenberg's line of thinking by arguing that the Americans had slaughtered the indigenous Indians and the British had invented the concentration camp system, agreeing with the views of his stronger defendant companions one moment, and then with his captors the next.

Gilbert was fascinated by the Molotov–Ribbentrop Pact and tried almost on every visit to try and fathom out Ribbentrop's input and plans on that occasion, writing that 'he maintained a pose of social broadmindedness and statesmanship, but there is a hypocrisy implicit in virtually every sentence'.[13] Goebbels and many Nazis had despised Ribbentrop, Ciano, the Italian foreign minister, constantly attacked him in his diaries and papers, and even in prison Gilbert and others found him distasteful in the extreme. He occasionally returned to his previous belligerence, telling Gilbert at the end of February that Russia would eventually win all, Yugoslavia was already in Comintern, Spain was dangerously isolated, and the British and even the Americans could not be able to contain Soviet Communism; he had briefly reverted to his diplomatic stance with his characteristic theme of 'knowing everything' when he was just a blusterer. When news came through in early March about Churchill's 'Iron Curtain' speech, Ribbentrop was almost beside himself with joy as it appeared to make all his predictions about the Russians justified.

However, it was becoming clear that Ribbentrop was floundering, trapped by his work on defence, evasive one moment, full of himself the next, apologetic about the past then justifying it. On Wednesday 13 March, his counsel took Gilbert aside concerned that Ribbentrop was on the verge of a nervous breakdown, causing Gilbert to wonder whether the legal man was 'fishing for the possibility of a plea of insanity'. The next day, Ribbentrop appeared in court in an open-necked shirt without a tie, looking droopy. Gilbert sent for the tie, wondering whether it had reminded Ribbentrop of a potential noose around his neck.

Ribbentrop's Trial

Ribbentrop's defence followed that of Hess's effort on Tuesday 26 March 1946. His counsel a Dr Martin Horn was 'awkward', and according to many did not do a good job and he was not appreciated by the Tribunal. If there were a widespread ignorance of Germany by many in the Allied court it was also true of the Germans about the Allies, and Horn had to have it explained to him that Churchill had not been the 'official leader of His Majesty's loyal opposition' in the 1930s.[14]

Ribbentrop's requests for witnesses typified the man and his defence, and he gave the 'impression he was arranging one of his smart cocktail parties in his London embassy rather than preparing a defence. He wanted to call the Duke of Windsor, the Duke of Buccleuch, Lord Derby, Lady Astor', and his application for Churchill was also turned down along with his request for King George VI with countless others.[15] Other defendants were more realistic in their choices, but many witnesses could not be found because they were keeping themselves below the parapets in the prison camps or hidden in the total confusion of Europe's post-war months. Ribbentrop's entirely unrealistic requests were simply beyond belief.

It was not a difficult case for the prosecution who had demonstrated that Ribbentrop attended many critical meetings which challenged him on the first two charges, and there had been plenty of documentary evidence to indicate not only his connivance on the last two charges, but plenty of evidence with his verbal encouragement and activity, not least his statement that all allied airmen should suffer instant execution.[16] It was soon apparent it was a hopeless case and Ribbentrop appeared so frightened he must have realised the ramifications. Although he spent much time in his cell proclaiming that he liked Jews, there was no escaping the reality with the evidence that he had told Admiral Horthy of Hungary to exterminate the Jews, and he had encouraged anti-Semitic Vichy France to move more quickly in transporting their Jews east. When the French prosecutor Edgar Faure questioned

Ribbentrop whether he had told Horthy that 'the Jews were either to be exterminated or sent to concentration camps and there was no other solution', Ribbentrop answered 'not in those words'.[17] He was always slippery, evasive, forgetful, and to many observers simply lying. His case was hopeless and not helped by his despised personality, and this probably caused him the panic of demanding unrealistic witnesses and prompted him to sack his first counsel Dr Fritz Sauter. As the day of his trial arrived, Ribbentrop tried to evade the moment by claiming he was too ill to take the stand, but after a medical check he was obliged to cooperate.

Dr Horn called his first witness, a Baron Dr Steengracht von Moyland, who had been Ribbentrop's adjutant, then his state-secretary. He basically claimed that Hitler never listened to experts, there was always a wrangling over authority, everyone was at odds with one another, and Ribbentrop had no choice but soldierly obedience. Ribbentrop's approach of blaming Hitler or Himmler in turn created anger among the other defendants, especially the 'elders' who had always regarded Ribbentrop as a self-seeking distasteful adventurer who was no diplomat, and who created too much boredom. As Gilbert had tried during his conversations, the court waited with anticipation for any revelation about the pact between Germany and Russia and the secret protocols regarding Poland. The court recessed twice to discuss whether this delicate question should be asked, and men like Jodl were waiting with eager anticipation because his battle plans clearly indicated such an agreement with the Russians.

If anything could be slightly amusing about this trial, it occurred when one of Ribbentrop's witnesses, Fräulein Margarete Blank, his secretary, agreed she knew of the secret arrangement with the Russians, but then added the bombshell that it had stayed in the envelope. She explained how Ribbentrop suffered if he did not see Hitler on a regular basis, and she was not cross-examined too closely which caused Ribbentrop concern, with his counsel reassuring him there was nothing to worry about.

The witness who caused him the most damage was the interpreter Paul Schmidt who was obliged to admit the truth of his affidavit in which he stated, 'the general objectives of the Nazi leadership ... from the start ... was the "domination of the European continent", and "territorial expansionism" under the policy of *lebensraum*'.[18] It was later made clear from Schmidt's post-war account that he had little regard for Ribbentrop as he noted that Ribbentrop was something of a bully, and 'tried this tactic on Ciano but without success'.[19] Ciano's diaries were among the evidence to illustrate how Ribbentrop had encouraged Italy into aggressive war. Schmidt's evidence was excellent for the prosecution as he helped establish their case. Ribbentrop complained to his counsel that Schmidt knew nothing of the overall policies which begged the question as to why he called him in the first place revealing Ribbentrop's innate incompetence.

The trial continued with long explanations by Ribbentrop over the Versailles Treaty and reading too many documents, with the court instructing him to move along more rapidly. By the time the secret protocol was reached, it was something of an anti-climax, with Ribbentrop instructing his counsel to stop 'coaching' him, which was so typical of Ribbentrop who always assumed he knew best.

On Monday 1 April, Ribbentrop was cross-examined by Maxwell Fyfe, with Ribbentrop using every means at his disposal to evade the questions. He was not helped by his many self-contradictions, irrelevancies, and his reinterpretations of events and documents, which Maxwell Fyfe was only too happy to expose. In the afternoon, Maxwell Fyfe drew ridicule down on Ribbentrop over his claim he had not applied pressure on Emil Hácha, the Czech president from 1938–39, to surrender Czechoslovakia. Despite Ribbentrop quibbling over various documents and events, he could not escape Maxwell Fyfe's analytical and intelligent questions. The next day, the French prosecutor also tied Ribbentrop up by accusing him about his anti-Semitic statements, with Ribbentrop feeling obliged to fall back on the argument that he was obeying Hitler's orders. The cross-examination clearly revealed that Ribbentrop was adept at lying, made mistakes and although tangling himself up time and time again thought highly of himself. Some of his lies when exposed were almost embarrassing. When Ribbentrop had expressed surprise that Himmler had given him an honorary rank in the SS, documents were produced showing Ribbentrop's application to Himmler for this rank and asking for a size-17 SS ring.[20] The same happened with Ribbentrop denying knowledge of the concentration camps when it was demonstrated that he owned six houses, some within easy proximity of the camps. Maxwell Fyfe's cross-examination reduced him to a mental wreck, and the other defendants despised him until he partially redeemed himself in their eyes by stating he was not 'anti-Semitic but I was a faithful follower of Adolf Hitler', which also seemed like a contradiction.[21] Cynically, it could be thought that in this statement he was trying to endear himself to some of the defendants but also avoid incrimination on the Jewish annihilation issue.

During his defence there was hardly another defendant who was not extremely critical of Ribbentrop's efforts, ranging from men like Schacht to Göring, and from Fritzsche to Funk. After the presentation of his defence Ribbentrop was exhausted, and he was not helped by Gilbert reminding him that although the secret protocol with the Russian pact had come to light, he had always denied knowledge of such an agreement. Ribbentrop resorted to attacking the prosecution for 'maligning' his integrity and for 'mudslinging'. It was clear that Ribbentrop was held in low esteem by both the prosecutors and all his fellow defendants. Only Frank described him as 'that poor fish' because he was so 'ignorant and untutored'. Gilbert found him in his cell poorly dressed and his place a total mess of papers and clothes, employing Göring's argument that the rest of the world did not understand the German sense of loyalty, especially Americans. There is a distinct feeling that Ribbentrop felt trapped and was totally lost in himself.

After Taking the Stand

During the Easter weekend, Ribbentrop was visited by Gilbert who found him showing no interest in the other trials but consumed with reading his own cross-examination, and by how unfair the prosecution had been. When challenged by Gilbert on the Jewish issue, Ribbentrop claimed that Hitler only wanted them transported to Madagascar or the east, and like Göring, found it difficult to believe that extermination had been discussed as early as 1940 or 1941. During Streicher's trial, Ribbentrop made the unbelievable claim that 'some of his best friends had been Jews', but he was more interested in what others were saying about him. Such was Ribbentrop's self-seeking that he even suggested to Streicher he could tell the court that he was not a fanatical anti-Semite. Later, in early May, he informed Gilbert that he tackled Hitler on anti-Semitism on the ground that it would incite 'World Jewry' against the Nazis which only served to underline his own inane attitudes towards Jewish people. Again, he claimed he may have worked for an anti-Semitic government, but he was not anti-Semitic. During the Dönitz trial, when the Hossbach Memorandum was raised, Ribbentrop said, 'Yes, if we had objected to it we would have been treated worse than the Jews', underlining the fact he had been well aware of the treatment meted out to Jewish people.[22] Following Jodl's trial Ribbentrop, following another talk with Gilbert who observed that Ribbentrop was isolated in being the last to acknowledge that Hitler had started the war, responded by claiming it was the British who started it by 'not telling the Poles to give in'. As regards the mass murders, he was convinced that Hitler had been talked into this policy.

Papen's trial for some reason encouraged Ribbentrop to convince Gilbert he was also a cultured statesman. The French should thank him for asking Hitler not to bomb Paris, which was a highly dubious claim, and had America listened to him the whole disaster could have been avoided. He concluded with his usual claims that he had really tried hard to divert Hitler from his anti-Semitic measures. For his diplomatic wrangling as an obedient servant to Hitler, it was the Final Solution which quite rightly scared him more than anything else.

Summation, Final Statements, and Verdicts

Ribbentrop was pleased with Dr Horn's summation and that he had explained all foreign policy decisions had been made by Hitler, but he was unhappy that his major work on the anti-Semitic issue had not be included. It was not a 'major work', but rambling excuses trying to distance himself from the extermination plans which he knew about. Generally, it was thought that Ribbentrop was an ungracious client.

Horn had explained that Hitler never discussed policy with Ribbentrop and just gave him instructions which clashed with the charge of planning and conspiracy for war. He made no reference to war crimes and applying pressure on Italy and France to hasten the deportation of their Jewish population. At this stage, it already felt as if the closing arguments were a precis of the trial omitting some of the negative elements. In what Gilbert called the 'youth lunchroom', there was growing amusement over the 'white lambs' in so far that the ex-foreign minister was claiming he was only an 'office boy', Keitel only an 'office manager', and all the anti-Semites were in 'favour of chivalrous solutions'.

During the prosecution summation, Jackson ridiculed Ribbentrop as 'the salesman of deception' who was to pour wine on troubled waters of suspicion by 'preaching the gospel of limited and peaceful intentions', alluding to his champagne sales days, and belittling him.[23] Later, he added that Ribbentrop was foreign minister and yet one who claimed he knew nothing of foreign affairs. Shawcross was equally scathing, and Ribbentrop must have felt the stinging attack as Ciano's Italian diaries had revealed that even Hitler's Axis partner Mussolini had been kept in the dark. Ribbentrop was furious and thought Shawcross made Jackson appear 'charming'.

Ribbentrop's final statement tended to reflect everyone's opinion of him as stupid and unnecessarily angry. He pursued his relentless excuse that his foreign policies had always been determined by Hitler, and he deplored the atrocious crimes he had been made aware of. Again, he said nothing about his instructing occupied countries and Italy to deport their Jews. He claimed the only thing he felt guilty about was that his aspirations in foreign policy had not been successful. At the judgement, the Tribunal found him guilty on all four counts, mentioning the horrific deportation of the French and Hungarian Jews. The verdict was death by hanging. Later in the cells, it was noted that Ribbentrop was understandably in some distress. He made an appeal, as did his counsel and wife, and typically Ribbentrop's letter was eight pages long.

He was the first to be hanged, with his last words being 'God protect Germany. God have mercy on my soul. My final wish is that Germany should recover her unity and that, for the sake of peace, there should be understanding between East and West. I wish peace to the world', whispering, 'I'll see you again' to the Lutheran chaplain Pastor Henry Gerecke.

Final Notes

Kaltenbrunner was hated, Streicher was loathed, but Ribbentrop in the view of the other defendants became a part of this tasteless trio because he was so despised. He was the epitome of servile obedience. The scorn became worse during the trial as it was realised that Ribbentrop was terrified, and his fears were so apparent that many despised him for that alone. Here was a man who in the successful years regarded himself as important if not critical to the European world – thus the selected photograph of him above. Even after his decline following Operation *Barbarossa*, he always regarded himself as an essential element of the Nazi government, but when faced with the agony of the trial's interrogation and the humiliation of the cell he trembled like a frightened schoolboy. He never moved from his lifelong belief that he was right and others wrong. As such, he had left some notes in his cell before he was hanged in which he complained the defendants had been unfairly victimised, and only the victorious powers were standing in judgement; the law as *ex post facto* and the 'conspiracy' charges were unfounded.[24]

He had been a man who grasped at power under Hitler, and his self-importance was widely known and despised even in his days of power. Like a schoolboy bully brought to account by more powerful elements, he collapsed in self-pity to save himself. He was an anti-Semite who knew about and encouraged the extermination of the Jews, yet he had tried to pretend that some of his best friends were Jews. His diplomatic manoeuvring was bad enough but became insignificant in his last-ditch attempt to say that he was not anti-Semitic on the grounds that it had dawned on him that the outside world had found this Nazi policy totally abominable.

Wilhelm Keitel 1892–1946

Background

He was born Wilhelm Bodewin Johan Gustav Keitel and was 63 when he was brought to the Nuremberg Trials. He came from a middle-class farming background and his father made him join the 46th Field Artillery; he would have preferred cavalry but could not afford a horse. In April 1909, he married Lisa Fontaine who came from a wealthy family. During World War I, Keitel was wounded in Flanders, afterwards joined the *Freikorps*, and from 1926 to 1933 he headed the organisational branch of the *Truppenamt*, which was the clandestine German General Staff banned by the Versailles Treaty, busily rebuilding German military strength. From 1935 to 1938 he headed the Armed Forces Office (*Wehrmachtamt*) and was promoted to major general. In February 1938, he was made head of the new OKW and then full general and, having conducted the French armistice at Compiegne on 22 June 1940, was promoted to field marshal.

Wilhelm Keitel. (Bundesarchiv, 183-H30220; Licence CC-BY-SA 3.0)

It was generally believed that Keitel had full knowledge of Hitler's aggressive war plans, knew about population transfer and mass murders, and was aware of the *Einsatzgruppen* activities. There were times when it was more than evident to many witnesses that he was an admirer of Hitler, and he was remembered for declaring the dictator 'the great field commander of all times' on the capitulation of France. Following the 20 July 1944 Plot, he greeted Hitler effusively because he had survived the explosion, and then sat on the Army Court of Honour handing many officers over to the notorious People's Court in which an estimated 5,000 people were executed. In some ways Keitel was similar to Ribbentrop, as they both held their positions because Hitler found them useful in their total subservience. Hitler initially referred to Keitel as von Keitel as he did Kesselring, assuming all generals came from this class. But Hitler once said Keitel was 'obedient as a dog'. On 6 June 1941, Keitel had signed the *Kommissarbefehl* (Commissar Order) for killing Soviet political commissars, accepted the SS reign of terror in Poland, was also responsible for the Night and Fog Decree, and encouraged German civilians to lynch downed pilots. He had ordered that for every German soldier killed in the occupied territories, '50 to 100 communists were to be executed in retaliation ... that a human life in these countries often counts for nothing'.[1]

During the war, many of the enemy regarded Keitel as the major guiding general, not knowing that Hitler had chosen him because he would not argue, even though General Werner von Blomberg was known to have once described him as 'no more than an office manager'. Keitel was anti-Semitic and in 1944 was awarded the Nazi Golden Party Badge of Honour. He was given cynical nicknames by his critics, but he was undoubtedly an ambitious man, though without talent.

Even with Hitler dead, Keitel did not prevent the war continuing, even as the willingness of the soldiers was failing. He delayed the end of hostilities because with the bargaining counters of Denmark, Norway, and Bohemia, he hoped for better negotiation chips, provoking General Gotthard Heinrici to comment that Keitel 'was completely detached from reality'.[2]

On 8 May 1945, Keitel met the representatives of the Allied powers and saluted them with his baton; it was not returned, and he signed Germany's unconditional surrender and was arrested on 13 May. Just prior to his arrest, and evidently knowledgeable of the atrocities, he asserted that the *Wehrmacht* had nothing to do with the SS or SD, which was soon repeated by Jodl and Dönitz. Thus, 'the myth of the good Wehrmacht, which had such currency for decades in postwar Germany, was being forged'.[3]

In his last testament, Hitler denounced the General Staff for their failure, but Keitel was the epitome of the disciplined, obedient Prussian soldier and later Andrus approved of him because his cell was immaculately tidy, unlike Ribbentrop's which was in a perpetual mess.

Interrogations

In his position, Keitel had full knowledge of the plans to invade Poland, and the criminal nature of this episode led to a series of protests by various German officers which Keitel ignored as they became numbed to the atrocities. As such, Field Marshal Wilhelm Keitel was of particular interest for the interrogators in seeking information about the military aspect and the charges of waging aggressive war, and by signing orders which could be identified as incriminating him with the indictment of crimes against humanity. General Heinz Guderian had described Keitel as a 'basically decent character' but overpowered by Hitler's personality.[4] He may have been correct, but a man even in Keitel's position had choices, even if it meant resigning.

The formal interviewer started with the post-Poland invasion, trying to establish Hitler's intentions. Keitel claimed his initial impression was that Hitler had hoped that the western conflict would fade away. He offered the interesting insight that the lack of belligerence by the French and British during the Phoney War seemed to indicate similar thinking on their part. He suggested that had the Allies attacked, 'the Germans would have been torn to shreds', as they were at that moment not sufficiently prepared after the Polish war. After Poland's defeat, many weapons, especially tanks, had to be replaced, and units rebuilt. He also observed that he thought the British Expeditionary Force was greater than it was. He confirmed that the military had preferred the Schlieffen Plan for the invasion of France, but Hitler had disagreed and ordered the well-known attack through Sedan and Luxembourg. He believed the Dunkirk evacuation had been a failure on the grounds that while it saved lives, the Allies' equipment was lost. He indicated part of the German success had been the destruction of the French Air Force which was why the French were soon asking for British RAF support. He also underlined the effective use of the *Luftwaffe* in supporting ground troops, a feature of aerial warfare the Germans used effectively and from which they would later suffer as the Anglo-Americans deployed the same tactics.

Questions followed concerning the attack on Britain, with Keitel expounding on the concerns of crossing the English Channel with the fear of the Royal Navy, the German lack of shipping space and supplies (the Germans had no aircraft carriers), and the need to hold aerial dominance in the critical areas. There was the additional concern of finding the few vital days when the sea would be calm, and the alternative of starving Britain into submission by the U-boat war. The German Navy had constant and serious doubts about Operation *Sea Lion*. Göring as head of the *Luftwaffe* was confident, but Keitel claimed there was the growing concern of Russian troops amassing on the western borders. In terms of Operation *Sea Lion*, there followed the usual method of discussion with Hitler talking to various experts, sometimes in groups, often individually, then he would return with a decision, and discussion ceased.

When it came to discussing the bombing strategy, Keitel pointed out that the British had started the bombing war with their attacks on Berlin, and the Germans had mainly attacked ports and ammunition and armament centres. The latter was called tactical bombing compared to the former strategic bombing, and Keitel was correct in this assessment. Much was made of the German bombing, but the intention had been to hit the ports which is why the London eastern docks suffered so badly. He talked briefly on the proposed economic warfare against Britain but accepted that it was somewhat limited.

When he came to Operation *Barbarossa*, he admitted that an early victory in 1941 would have resolved the matter, but it soon became apparent that with the climatic conditions in Russia it would be a long war. When asked about the initial discussions concerning invading Russia, Keitel said they arose in November 1940. But his political henchmen would have known about Hitler's hatred of communists and insistence on his policy of *Lebensraum* in the east. When questioned, he admitted that the Balkan issue and the Yugoslavian campaign came as something of a surprise, but it was the way that Moscow and Leningrad remained in Russian hands which indicated it could not be a short war. He also pointed out that German soldiers and commanders were not expected to discuss politics, and people like Ribbentrop had to keep to their own areas of influence. Posters were put up in barracks to remind soldiers of this, which again raised the issue of obeying orders.

In discussing the North African campaign, Keitel stated that this was the first time they had realised the strength of the Allied air-force, and how they had suffered from lack of supplies because of the poor performance of their Axis partner Italy. In his diary, Galeazzo Ciano often pointed out that Italian warships were locked in their home ports because of lack of oil. It was equally true that the Royal Navy and the RAF made crossing the Mediterranean a dangerous venture. Keitel also acknowledged that the failure to take Malta was serious, again blaming it on the Italians, but it was Hitler who never gave the necessary orders.

In terms of Normandy D-day, Keitel explained the invasion as being successful because of air superiority. He acknowledged other factors such as holding armoured divisions back awaiting commands from the Führer, and the growing weakness of the *Luftwaffe*, yet another witness to their negligence of technical advancement, apart from jet planes which were too late. The Germans had speculated that Normandy would be a good area to invade because of Cherbourg but were concerned by the shortest route across to Calais. Hitler retained command, hindering General von Rundstedt, and somewhat surprisingly Keitel admitted that *Luftwaffe* officers and enlisted men 'were not as courageous and anxious to fight as at the beginning of the war', which given the way events were unfolding was not surprising. He stated that Speer had done well with his war production efforts, but they knew logistically they were outclassed by the Anglo-Americans. None of this was helped by their diminishing oil supplies and other resources, especially after the loss of Romania. Tanks could not travel long distances and placing them in the critical areas had been made difficult by the attack on the transport systems, again mainly carried out by the Allied air-forces. He even admitted that some of the required leadership rested in incompetent hands.

When asked about strategic withdrawal as to why they fought to the bitter end, Keitel explained the policy of keeping the war away from the German homeland, but further admitted the OKW had little say in the matter as the Führer always gave the orders.* Once again, this defendant made it clear that Hitler was the dominant person, and Keitel and his associates were mere flunkies jumping to his orders. Churchill always believed he was an expert on military matters, but he was always kept in check by his Chief of the Imperial General Staff and his associates. Churchill, although he felt restrained, listened to his experts. Keitel was well known for his sycophancy and his name was joined with *Lakai* (lackey) to make 'Lakaitel'. He had other nicknames including *Nickesel* which was a toy donkey which constantly nodded its head. Göring used to claim that Keitel had a 'sergeant's mind in a field marshal's body'. The interrogators managed to extricate considerable information from Keitel about the German side of the war and gained evidence to convict him on all the charges.

Medical Mental Observations

Goldensohn managed his usual friendly conversations with Keitel who seemed to enjoy the company. Keitel's family background was farming which he said he would have preferred, but he explained that family finances precluded this possibility. There is of course the distinct possibility that this preference arose in his mind while sitting in a cell ready to face a court likely to execute him. In another conversation, Keitel explained that to be a Prussian officer was a position held in higher respect than most other professions, which is probably why he was not a farmer. He lost his daughter in 1942 from pneumonia following a bombing raid, lost his youngest son in 1941 on the Russian Front, another son unheard of in the same area of conflict, with only two children surviving. The eldest son was in an American prisoner-of-war camp, and his daughter and wife were living in one of his homes which had not been destroyed. Goldensohn may have thought but never asked that all this family sadness had its origins in Hitler's pursuit of power.

Keitel told Goldensohn he was not a party member (but was not that sure) and had not been involved in party discussions and politics. He explained that he was just a soldier who had served the Kaiser, Friedrich Ebert, Hindenburg, and Hitler over 44 years. Sometimes he said he thought of resigning, but in the end days he said it would have felt more like desertion. He admitted that he was no tactician and had little experience, but he signed the orders passed down by Hitler, with the hint of the usual argument of 'obeying orders'. He said, 'I had no authority. I was field marshal in name only. I had no troops, no authority—only to carry out Hitler's orders … and I had no idea of Hitler's general plans. I was told to confine myself to military matters only'.[5]

---

* The belief that Hitler alone made all the military decisions was widely held and held some substance. See General Siegfried Westphal, *The German Army in the West* (London: Cassell, 1951), 22.

He denied any knowledge of the extermination camps, and claimed he did his best to keep the army free of anti-Semitism. He listed three of Hitler's failures: first his actions against the Church, secondly persecuting the Jews, and finally allowing Himmler and the Gestapo too much power. It was more than obvious that he was aware of the evils perpetrated by his master, especially against Jewish people.

He thought the attack on Russia was reckless and only done because Hitler did not want Russia taking the German oil supplies in Romania. As Keitel spoke, Goldensohn wrote in his notes that 'Keitel is the wooden soldier, the wooden ingratiating smile, yet suffering from the human woes of love of attention, desire for approval'.[6] Goldensohn's description appeared fitting, and perhaps Keitel was Hitler's wooden puppet jumping to his command, but he had a mind, free will, and was now trying to find excuses that as a soldier he had a politician as his senior officer and believed in obeying orders. When Goldensohn asked him why he called Hitler a genius, Keitel explained this was based on the early successes, noting he was a 'simple soldier and nothing convinces a soldier more than success'. Hitler's greatest ability was his power to convince others, and Keitel pointed out that he spoke to military officers in one fashion and to party members in another; this was true enough as it was clear that Hitler knew how to measure his audience. Hitler, he explained, demanded three things from his commanders: first their ability for the position they held, secondly to report truthfully, and finally obedience. It may have reflected Hitler's views, but for Keitel it was his defence, which for many would have been the same as Al Capone's cronies claiming they had no choice but to do as they were told.

Gilbert wrote that the Prussian military-trained field marshal 'was almost obsequious when interviewed', claiming he 'had no more backbone than a jellyfish'.[7] He told Gilbert that the accusations against him were unfair because he was just the 'mouthpiece'. He was, he constantly explained, a Prussian soldier who by tradition obeyed orders. He claimed there were only three things he could do – the first, to refuse orders which meant death, the second, resign, and the third, commit suicide. He claimed he had considered resigning three times. He told Gilbert that it was hard to explain to an American that a Prussian soldier simply could not challenge his commander-in-chief or question his decisions. Keitel would have been shocked had he read the diary of Churchill's senior military commander Lord Alanbrooke who spent much of his time challenging Churchill's views. Keitel added the interesting observation that naval officers were better politically equipped because they had travelled the world.

Reactions during the Trial

Airey Neave amusingly described Keitel on first meeting him as looking like 'a retired colonel from Budleigh Salterton'. He was bemused to see him standing to attention in carpet slippers, reflecting that when he himself had been in a Gestapo prison, he had to stand on a cold floor in bare feet.[8] Neave could not forget that this was the man who had given the order to have British commandoes shot in Bordeaux in the famous 'Cockleshell' heroes incident (Operation *Frankton*, 8 December 1942).

Keitel explained to Gilbert on his pre-Christmas visit that he was 'spiritually' in a bad shape. He had assumed, so he said, that the *Wehrmacht* had not been involved in the atrocities and that it was all the SS. The evidence of the Warsaw ghetto had thrown him off balance because he claimed that he had had no idea of the order for *Wehrmacht* engineers to kill the Jews in their burning and tumbling residences. For years after the war, and despite evidence at the trial, many believed the *Wehrmacht* had fought a clean war to keep West Germany onside during the Cold War, but this was eventually dislodged by the unsettling claims of the German historians Omer Bartov, Atina Grossmann, and others.

Keitel explained he had no choice, and he was not in the Führer's confidence because he was instilled with the belief that he was a soldier and therefore kept out of politics. He had decided that the Nazi effort to attack the Church, the Jews and give unbridled power to the Gestapo had been the main causes of the shame, a theme he repeatedly raised.

During the Christmas recess, Keitel was in a confidential mood with Gilbert and asked to speak to him about matters he did not want repeated, almost treating the psychologist as a priest. He explained that in the failure to occupy Britain, Hitler felt compelled to do something, at first taking Gibraltar (the proposed Operation *Felix*) but Franco was uncooperative. Hitler had the constant fear of Britain starving Germany, and the Russians taking Germany's main oil supplies from Romania. He referred to the North African conflict as Erwin 'Rommel's little shooting match', all of which he used to account for the attack on Russia. His Christmas thinking concluded with his ignorance of Roosevelt's and Chamberlain's pleas for peace, the problems of the Versailles Treaty, and asked Gilbert not to mention all this to Göring because he was likely 'to blow up'. At the end of this session Keitel stood up, snapped to attention, and bowed to Gilbert, thanking him for the visit.

When the SD chief Ohlendorf described the massacre orders (Thursday 3 January 1946), Keitel returned to his theme that he lived in the tradition of obeying orders and that he was a mere mouthpiece and had never held a command post. He thought Speer's admission of trying to kill Hitler was therefore the wrong approach, and how a Prussian officer could be arrested and disgraced if found to be 25 marks in debt, and that Hitler had a painting of Frederick the Great in his office, as if that explained everything for Keitel. He finally admitted that he was suffering 'agony of conscience and self-reproach' more than anyone knew. There is a distinct impression that Keitel was squirming as the evidence mounted.

The argument which Keitel continuously employed was that although he had protested, he had to obey orders. This process of his thinking was underlined by a witness called General Adolf Westhoff who reported that on the execution of the escaped RAF prisoners of war. Keitel thought it a bad thing but having been admonished by Göring with Himmler present, prompted Keitel to warn his officers that this incident must set an example to other prisoners.

Keitel's Trial

During the general presentation of the cases Keitel had suffered implied legal attacks, not least with an affidavit from General Johannes Blaskowitz (well known for his protests to Hitler about Polish atrocities), and General Blomberg who wrote: 'As far as I heard, Keitel did not oppose any of Hitler's measures. He became the willing tool in Hitler's hands for every one of his decisions'.[9] Keitel was especially hurt by Blomberg because his eldest son had married Blomberg's daughter. But it should be recalled that Keitel had been an active component in the assault on Blomberg's reputation and honour.

During Ribbentrop's trial, Keitel had accused Hitler of lying to everyone, a moment of insight and truth he would not have dared state had Göring not been isolated from the group. But on Wednesday 3 April it was Keitel's turn to take the stand, led by his counsel Dr Otto Nelte. He spoke with his back rigid and always addressed himself directly to the judges, turning to the dock and onlookers as if giving an address.

His main argument was that he had simply done his duty for 44 years and had 'acted in good faith and was loyal'. He gave a sense of deeply felt pleading as he explained he had only been the transmitter of Hitler's commands, and was quite openly frank about this situation when questioned by Nelte stating:

> It is correct that there are a large number of orders with which my name is connected, and it must also be admitted that such orders often contain deviations from existing international law … there are a group of directives and orders based not on military inspiration but on an ideological foundation and point of view. In this connection I am thinking of the group of directives which were issued before the campaign against the Soviet Union and also which were issued subsequently.[10]

It was a frank statement which acknowledged blind obedience to Adolf Hitler as head of state. Keitel was dependent on the Prussian military demand of obedience under all circumstances which could not lead to an acquittal. In the words of one historian, his early statement 'I can only say that I was a soldier by inclination and conviction … for more than 44 years without interruption', could have served as his epitaph.[11] The question the court was asking was not about his years of service but what kind of soldier he had been. The blind obedience to carrying out orders was raised by one journalist asking that if a senior commander asked his admirals or generals to 'broil babies' they ought to disobey but Nazi commanders had carried out the orders.[12]

He argued that the decisions were political and therefore nothing to do with him. As a soldier, he always obeyed, ignoring the fact that soldiers are bound by international law and at least a basic sense of morality. His second theme widely used was that he never knew about this fact or that incident, denying any knowledge of the concentration camps or even some of the events in prisoner-of-war camps. His third theme was that the Führer gave the orders which had to be carried out despite the horrific ramifications. His trial took up a whole week, and his examination lasted nearly three days. The themes, repeated to the point of monotony, caused the Tribunal to rethink timing parameters and the dangers of repetition.

He stated that he disapproved of Hitler's attack on Poland, but only from the point of view of lack of preparation. He had misgivings about attacking France and expressed his surprise that the West had not intervened. He would not have been the only military man to have been concerned about the French attack because they had the largest army, but the collapse of France enhanced Hitler's reputation among many. If Keitel had tried to talk to Hitler about his various doubts, he always failed but continued to issue the orders and put his rank and authority behind unlawful and often immoral orders.

His military colleagues and luncheon group (Seyss-Inquart and Frank) made encouraging remarks; Schacht was less impressed. By Friday 5 April, Keitel was having to explain he had general supervision of the prisoner-of-war camps and that he had objected to Hitler handing over the RAF prisoners of war to Himmler. As regards the various attempts on the French generals Weygand's and Giraud's lives, he explained all he had done was transmit the orders, and he had never received any 'loot' which everyone took to be a snipe at Göring.

Later in the process, he admitted that some of the orders were 'regrettable' or even 'illegal' and even at one point admitted that 'Hitler abused his authority'. However, it came to light that Canaris had once objected to the way Russian prisoners of war were treated, and Keitel had written in the margin in his own handwriting that 'these objections arise from the military conception of chivalrous warfare. We are dealing here with the destruction of an ideology, and I therefore approve such measures and I sanction them'.[13] It was not surprising that the Russian Rudenko was short and angry in his cross-examination, forcing Keitel to admit that his orders implied that in the eastern zone life had little value, and the number of hostage-reprisals was simply unjust.[14]

Maxwell Fyfe was more prepared, and Keitel was accused of killing prisoners of war, saboteurs, and their families, and all Keitel could do was admit he had signed the orders but under Hitler's directives. Maxwell Fyfe was especially provocative about the killing of Allied airmen following the escape from Sagan (Stalag Luft III). Keitel continued to argue that Hitler always advanced his own views and 'as far as I am concerned, and as a soldier, loyalty is sacred to me'. Maxwell Fyfe asked if he had ever tried to protest, and Lord Lawrence asked if he had ever put any of his protests into writing and Keitel could only recall one such situation but had no copy.

It was known as with Canaris that when others had protested Keitel always overruled them. Both Maxwell Fyfe and Thomas Dodd, an American prosecutor, forced the issue that Keitel had knowingly given criminal orders, and his only response was that 'I only transmitted them'. He admitted to Gilbert and Goldensohn that Hitler was the real culprit claiming he should be branded the murderer, and his only personal alternative was suicide, but he had hoped to prevent some of the worse things.

Nelte called the witness Hans Heinrich Lammers (Chief of the Reich Chancellery), Keitel's civilian equivalent, in a failed attempt at portraying Keitel's limited authority, but he was cut short when Lawrence pointed out it was mere repetition. The prosecution called General Westhoff, Keitel's subordinate in the prisoner-of-war section of the OKW. This added little to Maxwell Fyfe's presentation of this aspect of the case, but it underlined the unlawful treatment of Russian prisoners. The same happened with the witness Max Wielen (once responsible for the criminal police in Breslau, a region of old Prussia), adding details which further implicated both Keitel and Göring.

None of this augured well for Keitel whose only defence was obeying orders and his sense of loyalty to an immoral head of state. During the war years, Keitel had been regarded as a political general and the main apparatus for military planning and operations. The trial, though, revealed a weak man, often known as the 'office manager', 'filing system', and even 'the typewriter'. Significantly, the main point was that because of his standing in the Nazi regime Keitel had carried influence with other ranks, and he had not protested at illegal and downright immoral orders.

After Taking the Stand

By early May 1946, following a discussion on Jodl's signing the surrender agreement, Keitel was becoming angry that Hitler had killed himself, leaving the rest of them to face the music. He claimed he should have been the one to shoulder the responsibility, but when challenged he still fell back on the argument that Prussian officers followed orders. He had no choice and persisted in this line of defence until the bitter end. In a series of covertly taped conversations between German generals and senior officers, his reputation was no better. General Hans Cramer claimed that Keitel and Jodl 'didn't want to hear the truth', General Wilhelm Ritter von Thoma said that top men like Keitel and Dönitz should have put 'Hitler in a padded cell', and General Georg Neuffer told his friends that 'Keitel had to share the responsibility' and he was always saying, 'Yes my Führer, yes my Führer'.[15] Hassell, in his diary, recorded as early as 1938 that General Walter von Brauchitsch thought the same. He turned up his collar in imitation of Keitel and said: 'I am a soldier, it is my duty to obey'. Keitel's reputation was widespread.[16]

Summation, Final Statements, and Verdicts

Dr Nelte started his defence by criticising the Tribunal for being one-sided with the supply of evidence, and the French for not providing requested documents. He raised the initial argument that despite holding the top military rank, Keitel was legally responsible for the orders he received. He tried to picture Keitel as a tragic figure caught by fate and attempted to move him away from Hitler's crimes. His rhetoric was strong, and he described Keitel as not hearing the 'warning voice of universal conscience'. It was easy to see, as Telford Taylor wrote, that Keitel 'had hitched his own wagon to Hitler's star'. There was a tendency by many of the defence team to spend too much time on history, Versailles, and general themes, and the 'Tribunal President did his best to shepherd them back into their clients' pastures'.[17]

Jackson during the prosecution summation described Keitel as the 'weak and willing tool' who delivered the armed forces to the party as a tool of aggression.[18] He issued orders to the armed forces but had no idea of the results they would have in practice. Jackson later described Keitel as 'an innocent middleman' who regarded himself as a post boy merely transmitting messages. Keitel and all the military group were described by the Russian Rudenko as 'noble-minded simpletons' who simply followed their leader's unlawful orders.

Compared to Ribbentrop who preceded him, in the final statements Keitel was more honest and open. He said it was not his intention to minimise the part he played, and he had acknowledged his actions from his official position. He corrected some errors made in the prosecution's statements and offered a form of confession. He accepted that he would have been proud of a victory (arising from an earlier question posed by the prosecution) and if he had known in advance how it would all work out, he would have preferred death rather than be 'drawn into the net of such pernicious methods'. He admitted he had erred, and he was not able to prevent what he ought to have prevented. What he had to offer as a soldier was loyalty and obedience which was exploited in a way he had failed to recognise – 'that is my fate'. Keitel did not try to shift the blame away from himself and bravely announced his own failings. Keitel found the waiting month of September difficult, and he even refused to meet his wife when permission for such visits had been granted, with Papen behaving along the same lines.

At the judgement, Keitel was found guilty on all four counts with the Tribunal adding there 'was nothing in mitigation'. The verdict was death by hanging, which Keitel as a proud military man abhorred, as shooting was the tradition for soldiers. Behind the judicial scenes, it was later discussed whether Jodl should be shot and then the other military men. There were several changes of mind by the judges, but hanging was finally decided upon as it was the most dishonourable way to be dispatched.

Final Note

The core of a totalitarian system is that it frequently produces an all-powerful and dangerous leadership in the unchallengeable figure of one person, be it Hitler, Stalin, or Franco with whom disagreement can be life or death. Many feared the dangers of contradicting Hitler, just as members of Al Capone's gang would have thought twice about challenging or contradicting him. Fear of Hitler was a feature of life during the Nazi regime, but for men in leading positions, the court implied that top leaders should be challenged if issuing illegal and immoral commands. Churchill had been a formidable character to oppose but in military terms he was surrounded by his own version of the OKW, known as the Chiefs of the Imperial General Staff, mainly led by General Alan Brooke who was well known for challenging many of Churchill's ideas and military policies. Churchill had deliberately surrounded himself with strong men and not 'yes-men' who saw their loyalty involving the need to challenge any proposals which they considered misguided. Hitler deliberately chose flunkies who obeyed his every wish, and when Keitel claimed that 'Loyalty is sacred to me', his opposite numbers in Britain and America would have seen their loyalty as first to their country and its people. During his time in prison, he wrote his memoirs, which read in a somewhat stilted fashion, and in which he claimed on one occasion he threw his briefcase down and walked out of Hitler's room, trying to prove he could stand up to Hitler, which was sheer fantasy.[19] Churchill could become angry and was known to storm out the room when contradicted. There was the possibility of demotion for his advisers, but not execution or disappearance.

The moral question was whether men like Keitel, if they realised the commands were immoral or illegal, had the courage to contradict their leader. It was from the personal safety point of view somewhat hazardous, and it is easy to pontificate from the safety of a warm study in theory. But Keitel (and others) used the Prussian tradition of obeying orders as their safety rope. There was German resistance, but Keitel became the 'filing cabinet', the 'office manager', and put his rank and position above moral issues. He was too weak to oppose Hitler even when he thought the commands were immoral, even reprimanding Canaris for his objections to illegal orders. He had written 'we are dealing here with the destruction of a philosophy; therefore, I approve the measures and sanction them', probably because he was tempted by rank and decorations to desert his own code of honour and may well have feared for his life.[20] On another occasion, when Keitel was informed of the sweeping executions in Poland, he noted it had been decided by the Führer and if the army did not want to help they would have to stand by and accept the SS and Gestapo to do the work.[21] However, it needed someone like Keitel to object, but he stuck rigidly to his argument that 'I believe I can truthfully say that throughout my military career I was brought up, so to speak, in the old traditional concept that one never discussed this question'.[22]

Keitel asked to be shot rather than hanged but this was turned down on the grounds that his activities reflected a more criminal than military career. Before his execution, he received the sacraments, and his final words were a call to 'God to have mercy on the German people'. The trapdoor was small and damaged his face before he fell, showing a bloody corpse in many of the photographs. It is often claimed that the speed of fall was insufficient to break his neck which left Keitel in convulsions for nearly half an hour, though there is no substantive evidence, no more than there is evidence to indicate that Keitel had the will to stand up to Hitler. This defence of obeying orders even when illegal and immoral was widely used, but it could not excuse the barbarity of war crimes and crimes against humanity.

Ernst Kaltenbrunner 1903–46

Kaltenbrunner. (Courtesy of Solomon Bogard, Memorial Museum (USHMM) Washington D. C.)

Background

Ernst Kaltenbrunner was an Austrian who was born near Braunau, upper Austria, which had been Hitler's birthplace. His father had been a lawyer and Kaltenbrunner followed in his footsteps studying law at Graz. He then worked for a year in Salzburg before opening his own law firm in Linz. His face was marked by what looked like duelling scars though many sources indicate they were the result of a less romantic car accident. He joined the Nazi Party in 1930 (number 300,179) and soon after joined the Austrian SS, heading this sector even though it was proscribed. He married a Nazi Party member Elisabeth Eder and had three children; later, he had twins with his long-term mistress, Gisela. He was detained for a short time by the Engelbert Dollfuss administration in a detention camp with other Nazi figures for conspiracy. In 1935 he was jailed for high treason; the charge was dropped, but he lost his licence to practise law.

Following the *Anschluss* in which he played a part, he was appointed the higher SS and police leader (*Hoher SS und Polizeführer*) in Vienna. He assisted in establishing the Mauthausen-Gusen concentration camp near Linz and was promoted to the rank of SS-*Gruppenführer* (lieutenant-general). He succeeded the assassinated Reinhard Heydrich in June 1942, was Chief of the RSHA (Reich Main Security Office) which included control of the Gestapo, Kripo, and SD from January 1943 to the end of the war, and in February 1944 subsumed the *Abwehr* following Canaris's arrest.

There was no question that he was a fanatical follower of Hitler and deeply anti-Semitic. According to many, he was present at the December 1940 meeting when the gassing of Jewish people was discussed, was always kept aware of the concentration camp processes, and he was undoubtedly behind the policy of compulsory castration of homosexuals. In 1943 he conducted an inspection of the Mauthausen concentration camp where he witnessed the various methods of killing people, and rumour had it that he was always keen on studying various means of quick execution. He always denied this, but documentary evidence proved otherwise. Near the end of the war, it was Kaltenbrunner who passed on the orders for the liquidation of men like Dietrich Bonhoeffer, the religious pastor held in captivity, and signed orders for the execution of British and American prisoners of war at Mauthausen.

From the day he took over the RSHA, he was convinced that the head of the *Abwehr*, Canaris, was a traitor. He was correct in so far that Canaris opposed Hitler, and Kaltenbrunner pursued this matter with dedicated hatred, convinced the *Abwehr* was full of sexual perverts. During the end days of the war, he issued orders that police chiefs could use their own discretion on whom they thought fit to kill among foreign workers, especially Russians. He informed Hitler of Himmler's financial deals to send Jews to Switzerland, and he was known to be close to and trusted by Hitler.[1]

He was arrested on 12 May 1945 in a remote cabin in the Austrian mountains by American troops where he was carrying false papers. He was tall, and his face was pockmarked and scarred, and the journalist Rebecca West described him as a 'vicious horse'.[2] Neave, when he met him, described him as 'a giant with massive hands, I felt at once like his victims … there were gaps in his black teeth, and he had huge ears'.[3] Neave and many others, including Kaltenbrunner's co-defendants, found him repulsive. When defeat was evident, Kaltenbrunner suddenly became a humanitarian and Colonel Andrus claimed he was 'sick with fright' and was prone to weeping. The novelist Evelyn Waugh, who attended the trials, thought Kaltenbrunner was the only one who looked like a criminal. As Canaris had once observed, he had cold eyes and 'a murderer's paws'.

Interrogations

Despite the gathering knowledge and evidence of his activities, Kaltenbrunner still argued he was only an administrative agent and had nothing to do with criminal acts. He enveloped his interrogators in extensive arguments about the nature of jurisdiction, trying to explain that as head of the RSHA he had nothing to do with the Gestapo, or mass murders and they were only departments within his administrative building complex. His constant claim became that he was only an administrator.

He missed the early stages of the Nuremberg process because he had two episodes of subarachnoid haemorrhage while in prison but was restored to health in an American hospital, which ironically had once been the Gestapo and SD headquarters. This illness was probably caused by intense anxiety and tension; in everyday language, everyone regarded Kaltenbrunner as a bully and executioner but who was now so scared, he nearly died of fright.

Medical Mental Observations

When Goldensohn conversed with him, he was suspicious of Kaltenbrunner's gentle way of speaking and his 'well-mannered attitudes' and thought he was trying to conceal his ferocious reputation and ruthless past. He explained to Goldensohn 'that I am not the disagreeable, uncouth fellow the public probably thinks because of all the atrocities committed under Himmler's rule, and of which I am totally innocent'.[4] He maintained that he knew nothing about the mass murders because since 1943 he had worked in Berlin away from such areas, and he had only learnt about these events at Nuremberg. He insisted on explaining to Goldensohn in great length the nature of the RSHA, its various offices, the constant changes, and the internal wrangling for power. He claimed that many of the original police had opposed Nazism, fewer of them had voted for Hitler when compared to the general population, and he persisted in trying to paint a picture of himself as a mere functionary despite the obvious importance of his status and office. He explained when the Nazis came to power, some policemen who were not that politically way inclined were replaced, but they were not shot – it was not brutal, just simply 'replaced'.

Part of his personal self-defence was to shift any blame onto Heydrich and Himmler, explaining their tussle for power, implying he was not part of the central hub of influence, but played a 'subordinate role'. Kaltenbrunner spoke of Himmler's passion for power and how he expanded the SS into a major fighting force, and Himmler had probably been relieved that Heydrich had been assassinated because of his supposed subordinate's rise in status. He described the internal Machiavellian machinations between Heydrich, Himmler, and Bormann leaving an assumed portrait of himself as a mere observer of events. These three men were dead (although Bormann was thought at this time to have escaped) which made Kaltenbrunner's efforts somewhat easier. Much of what he said may have had some elements of truth, but by fascinating others with these insights into the dark past he was trying to move the focus of blame away from himself. He added that such was the structure and the influence of the party that there was no room for criticism, offering yet another argument to his defence. He further explained that it had been the 'workers' who had given about 60 per cent to the Nazi support, adding 'you can imagine what happened to a little labourer who suddenly finds himself a leader'.

He explained to Goldensohn that 'it was not possible to talk to Hitler objectively', revealing he had been closer to the throne than he pretended, and he even suggested that Hitler's future aim was to have some form of democracy but based on the leadership principle, which made no sense at all. When Goldensohn asked who was the more sadistic, Kaltenbrunner responded with Himmler, describing him as a 'stingy small person' who was like a schoolmaster gaining pleasure from punishing others, and who was merely a slave to Hitler. Later, he said that people thought he was another Himmler and made him out to be a criminal, but 'I never killed anyone'. As far as is known, Himmler never personally murdered anyone, but such was Himmler's power, his orders had turned him into one of the most infamous evil criminals of all times. However, Goldensohn, who always seemed to befriend the interviewees, never raised this obvious point that Kaltenbrunner may not have personally killed, but he had ordered many executions and deaths.

There followed a discussion over Jodl's defence that the Russian war had been defensive because of the evident build-up of Russian troops along their mutual borders. When Goldensohn expressed surprise, Kaltenbrunner launched into a debate indicating all the perceived reasons as to why the war was preventative rather than aggressive. He claimed that it would not have been an aggressive war because German troops were tied up in the west, to which Goldensohn expressed understandable surprise that France and the Low Countries were occupied, and Britain at that stage stood alone. Kaltenbrunner avoided the question and launched into an attack on the Russians and the danger they presented to world peace, even referring to Churchill and his recent 'Iron Curtain' speech in America. Goldensohn persisted but Kaltenbrunner could only counter by saying the Germans could not accept the war in the west was won until England was finished.

This debate seemed to rattle Kaltenbrunner, who launched into an attack on the trial and on Gilbert whom he claimed 'tortured' the defendants by showing them the American paper the *Stars and Stripes*, which had suggested they would all be executed. He argued that the court process would go on and on until the prosecutors found a reason to have them killed. He returned briefly to the Russian threat, using the case of Turkey's control of the Dardanelles and the Bosporus, which had dictated German foreign policy in Turkey. Goldensohn noted that Kaltenbrunner was becoming 'excited', his face was becoming red in these interchanges, and his 'phrases and sentences were sharper and more clipped than ever'.[5] The session concluded with Kaltenbrunner attacking Canaris as being duplicitous and that he had been ordered to replace Canaris at the *Abwehr* (after the 20 July 1944 Plot) because it was well known that his abilities were better than those of Canaris. The general impression was that Goldensohn had scratched the surface of a man who was pretending he was an innocent bystander, a good and intelligent man according to himself, but who through Goldensohn's clever approach revealed the darker side of the reality of his nature.

Reactions during the Trial

On Monday 10 December 1945, Kaltenbrunner was brought into the courtroom for the first time. Gilbert described 'a coldness swept the prisoner's dock as if a freezing blast had come in through the open door'.[6] Kaltenbrunner was mistaken in thinking he would receive a warm welcome and everyone did their best to ignore his friendly gestures and handshakes. Even his defence lawyer evaded shaking Kaltenbrunner's extended hand. Göring was of course annoyed that the cameras concentrated on Kaltenbrunner and not on himself. Here was the man who had to be associated with the extermination process as head of the RSHA and friendship with him was for some dangerous, for others distasteful.

When on Wednesday 27 February 1946 victims from the concentration camps had given direct evidence of the barbarity, Dönitz announced during the lunch hour that throughout its command the RSHA personnel must have known what was happening. Gilbert sat beside Kaltenbrunner asking him if he knew of the atrocities. He replied by 'whispering' he had no idea, listing Hitler, Himmler, Bormann, Heydrich, and Eichmann among the knowledgeable. He told Gilbert that concentration camps had not been his remit and were nothing to do with him. He was lying and scared, and everyone knew this feature of Kaltenbrunner. He always denied knowing Eichmann but in fact they had been boyhood friends in Linz, Austria, and had worked closely together in the SS; Kaltenbrunner was known by all to be dishonest. Few, if any, believed Kaltenbrunner's claimed ignorance of the extermination policy because at the start of January the witness Alois Hoellreigel, an SS NCO who had been a guard at Mauthausen, stated that Kaltenbrunner and Schirach had visited the camp in 1942 and saw SS officers killing prisoners by pushing them off a cliff.[7]

Kaltenbrunner's Trial

On Thursday 11 April Kaltenbrunner took the stand (his trial lasted just short of three days), assisted by his counsel Dr Kurt Kauffmann, with Kaltenbrunner hoping his newly devised charts of the RSHA would show the Allied perceptions were wrong; he was an administrator and had nothing to do with the mass murders. However, his position had given him control of the Gestapo and the SD with the responsibility for the concentration camps, and he was the most feasible representative of this organisation since Himmler was dead. Göring had initiated the existence of the Gestapo in Prussia, but after some tussling had relinquished it to Himmler. The prosecution was aware that Kaltenbrunner had taken over the whole organisation in 1943, and the indictment was serious with the accrued evidence stacked against him. There were documents and letters with his orders for Allied commandoes to be shot, the initiation of anti-Jewish measures in Denmark, the murder of prisoners and drafting SD personnel into the *Einsatzkommando* units, although he claimed he had never heard of Auschwitz apart from the fact it was an armaments factory.

His defence counsel was orderly and succinct which helped with the timing, but Kaltenbrunner's appearance did not help: 'he was everyone's nightmare of a Gestapo brute' with his scarred and pock-marked face and his gigantic size.[8] He took a similar stance to Keitel, not by denying the crimes but claiming he had no connection with them, even rejecting the claim that he had signed the forms. The *Daily Telegraph* concluded he was the most totally inept Nazi apologist to date.[9]

His defence started with affidavits from two other Gestapo officials testifying that 'Kaltenbrunner was a nice man and not Himmler's number two'. Kaltenbrunner then took the stand explaining his nationalistic motives, admitted he was Hitler's second-in-command as formal head of the RSHA but only responsible for the intelligence agencies, nothing else.

His main line of defence was to try and shift all the responsibility onto Himmler, Heydrich, Müller (head of the Gestapo who disappeared after the war), Eichmann (also vanished for a time), and Oswald Pohl (Chief of SS Economic and Administrative Office), narrowing down his own area of authority. He insisted, vehemently at times, that his signature was either a forgery or typed in by someone else, and when his counsel showed him a document ordering and approving of executions, signed by him, Kaltenbrunner denied all knowledge of the paper. Colonel Amen asked if he denied writing a specific letter to which Kaltenbrunner replied, 'yes', also denying it was his signature, even though it had been signed with *Dein*, a German idiom for intimating a close relationship.[10] It appeared to everyone he was lying and he was impossible to believe. Behind the scenes, even Fritzsche and later Speer were calling him a liar with Schacht asking whether Kaltenbrunner was a senior officer or not. The other defendants were equally as sceptical including Raeder and Dönitz. One journalist noted that Kaltenbrunner's defence had been all too typical; 'it ignores the bad deeds attributed to him and claims for him good deeds no one has ever heard of'.[11]

Otto Ohlendorf had provided testimony that as Chief of the RSHA, Kaltenbrunner had to be involved with the *Einsatzgruppen* activities. Colonel Amen produced more affidavits which basically stated that Kaltenbrunner transmitted orders for executing prisoners of war. All Kaltenbrunner could counter was that the complexity of the chain of command was a slender defence, shifting the blame onto Himmler and other officers. The next morning, documents and papers were presented as evidence which tended to expose Kaltenbrunner that he knew more than he claimed. Kaltenbrunner's signature on some documents made the prosecution case strong, with Kaltenbrunner claiming he may have signed some because he had to sign so many, and sometimes 'not recognising the signature'.

Kaltenbrunner could not wangle his way out of being the head of the RSHA. Colonel Amen had produced evidence that Kaltenbrunner had visited Mauthausen more than once, and a letter which had personal connotations and was not forged containing the following statement: 'The women and children of these Jews who are unable to work, and who are all being kept in readiness for a special action' intimating a clear knowledge of all that was happening to the Jews.[12]

At one stage, under attack, Kaltenbrunner started to lose control, with Judge Birkett writing in his notes on Kaltenbrunner that 'he is a fluent speaker and speaks with great animation … in some matters he is no doubt right … but it is impossible to think of the position occupied by Kaltenbrunner and, at the same time, to believe that he was ignorant of so many matters'.[13]

Kauffmann called the Auschwitz commandant Colonel Höss as a witness which struck many as an extraordinary decision, not least because it was so welcomed by the prosecution. When Höss testified and explained how he and his colleagues had managed to murder millions in a short space of time it led to a gloomy silence, as Höss proudly described his life of murdering helpless Jews and their families as if demonstrating his personal efficiency.[14]

Höss testified that Kaltenbrunner had never visited Auschwitz and all orders had been signed by Herman Müller, but he was challenged by Amen obliging Höss to admit that Müller's signatures were on behalf of the RSHA run by Kaltenbrunner. Höss provided in a very matter-of-fact way the brutality and the numbers of the extermination process. None of this was helpful for Kaltenbrunner nor the other defendants as it cast a deep shadow of shame upon them all as Nazi leaders. The systematic annihilation of Jewish people came as a looming spectre to Kaltenbrunner's door, and he had brought it upon himself in legal terms by producing Höss as a witness. The attempted annihilation of European Jews seemed to put the other indictments at a lesser level. Andrus had once described Kaltenbrunner as coming into his custody 'sick with fear' and it seemed he had good reason. The other defendants found him repulsive, and although many of them offered misleading answers and falsehoods, they were flabbergasted at the number of lies which Kaltenbrunner blatantly told to try and save himself.

Summation, Final Statements, and Verdicts

Dr Kauffmann made the plea for Kaltenbrunner claiming he was not the model of virtue, making no plea for Kaltenbrunner's acquittal, but claiming he had good intentions and although sadly millions had died in the camps, that was Himmler's doing, not his client's. Kaltenbrunner spotted Colonel Amen enjoying that statement, causing Kaltenbrunner to request Gilbert to congratulate Amen on his success and for arranging for him to have such a 'stupid attorney'.

In the prosecution summation, Jackson described Kaltenbrunner as the 'grand inquisitor' who took up the 'bloody mantel of Heydrich' and built up Nazi power on a 'foundation of guiltless corpses'.[15] In his final statement to the Tribunal, Kaltenbrunner indicated signs of anger and repeated his denials and explanations to which few took any heed, and he ended with an ominous warning about the Soviet threat without specifically naming them.

During the month of September, when the judges were working, it was noted that Kaltenbrunner along with a few others were becoming somewhat tense and fraught as the lockdown restrictions were lightened. Kaltenbrunner was eventually found guilty on counts three and four having later taken over from Heydrich, making the first two charges irrelevant. The verdict was later pronounced as death by hanging.

Final Notes

During the individual trials, it was clear that many had lied to avoid conviction, but few did it as profusely as Kaltenbrunner. Here was the man who in taking over from Heydrich had assumed the head role beneath Himmler in the terror apparatus system and pretended he was a mere administrator. He had been seen and photographed at a concentration camp which he had helped establish and yet denied knowing much about the place. When he called the infamous Höss from Auschwitz as a witness, which defied belief that Kaltenbrunner thought it would help him, he brought a cloud down upon himself and all the defendants, especially when Höss described the clinical way they had killed millions of people and disposed of their bodies. Regarding the Holocaust, 'the 1950–59 decade was a period of silence' and would have to wait for the Eichmann trial before it became a serious focus of attention.[16] The Kaltenbrunner case and its evidence and the witness of Höss underlined the sheer evil of the regime which Kaltenbrunner had served as a major figure in the terror apparatus; even the other defendants did not believe him. After Himmler and Heydrich, he had been deeply feared because of his powers but his time in the trial had exposed him as not just a cruel person but fundamentally weak, which reflected many others in this gathering of one-time Nazi leaders.

Alfred Rosenberg 1893–1946

Background

Alfred Rosenberg was regarded as a Nazi theorist and ideologue and held various posts within the Nazi regime. Born on 12 January 1893 in Reval (now Tallinn) in Estonia, he studied engineering in Riga followed by architecture in Moscow, completing his PhD in 1917 when the Russian Revolution started from which he fled in disgust. He married a Hilda Leesmann in 1915 but was divorced in 1923. Two years later, he married Hedwig Kramer and remained married until his death. They had two children: a boy who died as an infant and a daughter, Irene, who was born in 1930.

When he fled Russia, he arrived in Germany as anti-Church, anti-Slavic, and anti-Semitic, writing articles for a Munich newspaper, and known as a person who hated Bolshevism. He joined the Nazi Party in 1919 and, following the Munich *Putsch*

Rosenberg. (Photographer Friedrich Franz Bauer, Bundesarchiv 183-1985-0723-500; Licence CC-BY-SA 3.0)

and Hitler's imprisonment, Rosenberg was appointed as the Nazi Party leader, a post which he held until Hitler's release. He was probably chosen because Hitler would have needed a man who would not seek to take his place. He became the editor of the Nazi newspaper *Völkischer Beobachter*, and in the early stages had some influence over Hitler, somewhat all-pervading to start with, but Hitler soon kept him at arm's length. In 1927 he was made head of the new National Socialist Society for Culture and Learning, but more to the point, he was a Russian speaker and became the Nazi expert on Eastern matters and was named leader of the NSDAP's Foreign Office, and a Reichstag deputy in 1930. In 1933 he visited Britain and laid a wreath with a swastika at the Cenotaph, which a Labour Party candidate threw in the Thames and who was duly fined. In 1934 Hitler placed him in charge of the spiritual and philosophical direction of party members. In 1939 he was asked to set up the Institute for the Investigation of the Jewish Question. Before the outbreak of war, he had been involved with the infamous Norwegian leader and Nazi sympathiser Vidkun Quisling, who had encouraged German interest in Norway before the British could arrive.

He became the titular head of an organisation (*Einsatzstab Rosenberg*) which used his name to purloin paintings, books, and *objets d'art* from the occupied territories for the Nazi regime. As noted, he hated any form of Bolshevism and found Hitler's later agreement with Russia disagreeable, causing Hitler to note that Rosenberg should be ignored politically. However, on 17 July 1941, he was appointed as *Reichsminister* for the occupied Eastern Regions but had little authority, with Goebbels referring to the post as the 'Ministry of Chaos'. It has been claimed by some that he was not keen on genocide and expulsion, preferring to fight communists. However, on 18 November 1941, he spoke at a press conference warning that six million Jews lived in the east, and 'this question can only be solved by a biological extermination of the whole of Jewry in Europe … and to this end it is necessary to force them beyond the Urals or otherwise bring about their eradication'.[1] This singular statement underlined his corrupt thinking more than all his rantings about communism and the churches.

He considered himself a philosopher and historian and wrote the book *The Myth of the Twentieth Century* (1930). It was regarded as the seminal work of Nazi ideology, and in sales terms was only second to *Mein Kampf*. It included racial theories, Aryanism, anti-Semitism, expounded on *Lebensraum*, attacked the Versailles Treaty, and even modern art. This book was mainly unintelligible Nazi belief, and even Hitler did not like the effort. Rosenberg once claimed he was 'sovereign over the judgment of all intellectual institutions' when he was a mere pseudo-intellectual. Sir Robert Vansittart once described him as 'a ponderous lightweight'.[2] As editor of the anti-Semitic paper *Völkischer Beobachter*, he helped shape Nazi thinking about Aryan supremacy, attacked homosexuals as unwanted degenerates, and repeated the theme of his 1920 publication (*Immorality in the Talmud*) identifying Jews with the Anti-Christ, rejecting original sin (because Germans were born noble), and that Christianity enfeebled people. He wrote other minor jumble-filled books, *The Tracks of the Jews through the Ages* and *The Crimes of Freemasonry*, all of which were supposed to outline the so-called Nazi philosophy.

Despite his alleged protest at the murderous conduct, there was still considerable evidence stacked up against him, and when in October 1944 he wrote a letter to Hitler about resigning, it was never answered. He was refused a place in Dönitz's new government and was captured by British soldiers in Flensburg-Mürwik on 19 May 1945.

Interrogations

Rosenberg point-blank refused to accept the evidence which piled up against him regarding the 'Eastern Territories', blaming the conduct of the enemy as the chief cause for his brutal administration, and telling his interrogators that the Versailles Treaty had left Germany in a worse situation. When it came to the question of genocide, especially relating to the Jews (where his area of responsibility in the occupied Eastern Territories had been the major centre for the extermination camps), he admitted to being anti-Semitic but almost unbelievably denied knowledge of the camps, although he had heard that some German soldiers had shot 'some' Jews. Even the so-called Nazi intellectual recognised the shame of the regime's policy through the evidence presented. The prosecution tended to turn towards him as the 'theoretician or philosopher' which has been claimed 'was without any merit whatever'.[3]

Medical Mental Observations

Goldensohn and Gilbert met him for a brief interview with the former noting that 'he greeted us with superficial amiability ... his face is a costume of sobriety and philosophic calm, smiling, understanding, broad vision, and reflective of the true philosopher, who looks on all that is transpiring with critical, but not bitter detachment'.[4] In Goldensohn's inimitable style of writing, he was not describing Rosenberg as he saw him, but as Rosenberg regarded himself. When Gilbert confronted him with material demonstrating that the *Protocols of the Elders of Zion*' had been based on false premises, Rosenberg evaded a direct answer and did not think the facts were that important, and that it all involved a 'dark secret'. He argued the Jews were a nation and they should have stayed in their own place, suggesting the French and British had come up with ideas where they could go to mentioning Alaska or Madagascar, though historians have found such official suggestions difficult to identify except in Germany. Rosenberg claimed Jews 'spat' at German culture, controlled the theatre, publishing, and even the commercial stores. He then claimed that he 'was not a fanatic about Jews, that he once made a speech in which Jews were not mentioned'. For today's reader of this last statement, it must cross the mind as to Goldensohn's and Gilbert's reactions to his boast he had not mentioned Jews on one occasion.

When asked if he thought himself as a philosopher or a historian, he said both, and when asked what he had his degree in, he responded 'architecture' to their pointed question. He then explained how he edited the *Völkischer Beobachter* which was the more educated and intellectual version of *Der Stürmer*. There followed a brief interchange on race and bloodline issues, and he was pressed by the two

---

* The infamous *The Protocols of the Elders of Zion* was published in Russia in 1903 and was long proven to be fake.

Americans as to whether an injured Nazi soldier given Jewish blood or that of a black soldier would change him. He replied, 'That would be a brutal experiment such as was done in the concentration camps', smiling as if 'he had scored a triumph of reasoning'.[5] The conversation swung to communism which invoked him into a vitriolic attack on the system, but modified by arguing that it was up to each country so long as it stayed within their borders. This may have arisen in his mind as he knew totalitarianism was equally distasteful to democratic-based Westerners. Rosenberg turned their talk to the Germans then being evicted from their lands with no intervention by any international body. When asked if this was not an expected reaction by the Poles who had suffered so badly at the hands of the Nazis, he evaded the question and reverted to condemning the Versailles Treaty. In this session, Goldensohn did not ask Rosenberg about his reaction to the genocide in the camps and whether he could pretend it was news to him and be shocked; his anti-Semitism was more than evident.

Reactions during the Trial

During the second day of the trial, the Nazi crimes against Christianity were raised, with Rosenberg demanding that the Russians with their crimes against the churches should be questioned. When on Monday 10 December the planned aggression against Russia was central to the court's activities, Rosenberg told Gilbert over lunch 'just wait – in 20 years you'll have to do the same thing – you can't escape this problem'.[6] In the canteen Göring, overhearing this comment, roared in support of Rosenberg's view. On the weekend of 15–16 December, Gilbert found Rosenberg in his cell pondering the evidence of mass killings. When asked what he 'now' thought of Hitler, he remained uncertain, claiming 'it just ran away with him, we didn't contemplate killing anyone in the beginning', which was a contradiction to his known stated views. He said that as 'he hoped for *Lebensraum* for the Germans, he had only hoped for the same thing for Jews outside Germany'. He explained that the Jewish foreign press had not helped, and along with the murder of Ernst vom Rath had probably forced matters.[*] It is easy to gain the impression the evidence relating to the extermination process was ringing alarm bells in Rosenberg's mind, but only because he realised that he would stand condemned. This was to be a characteristic of most of the defendants.

During the Christmas recess, Rosenberg and Gilbert discussed the *Führerprinzip* as the former tried to rationalise the concept.[†] Rosenberg claimed it was an ideal which

---

[*]   Ernst vom Rath was a German diplomat assassinated in Paris in 1938 by a Polish-Jewish teenager to avenge his parents; the immediate repercussion was *Kristallnacht*, the Night of Broken Glass. As a matter of sheer irony, Rath was being checked by the Gestapo for opposing anti-Semitism.

[†]   *Führerprinzip* was the principle that civilians and soldiers were responsible to their superiors and ultimately to the Führer which implied unquestioning obedience.

had been abused, comparing it to the ideals of the 1789 French Revolution and Martin Luther's 95 theses which had suffered the same consequences. He conceded that the defendants may have been guilty to a certain extent of helping to build a party of such ideals, but the real criminals were Hitler, Himmler, Bormann, and probably Goebbels who were all dead.

When on Tuesday 8 January 1946 the persecution of the Church was raised, Rosenberg at lunch launched an attack both on the Russians and the Church. He returned to his theme that the Russians after their treatment of the Church had no right to sit in judgement. He was probably right in this view but Stalin as a need for national defence had loosened his more severe anti-clericalism to a degree. Rosenberg admitted he was also anti-clerical but the Russians 'had a nerve' to be among the prosecutors on this subject.

Gilbert visited Rosenberg on his birthday (12 January) to see how he was doing and heard that in Rosenberg's opinion National Socialism was not based on racial prejudice, but a simple effort to 'maintain our own racial and national solidarity' and that different cultures did not mix easily nor the different faiths. He launched into a characteristic tangent with an attack on other countries, referring to Britain's opium wars in China, and the difficulty of binding different cultures when Gilbert queried him on this subject.

Rosenberg's Trial

Rosenberg's trial started (Monday 15 April) the day after Höss from Auschwitz had just been cross-examined at the end of Kaltenbrunner's trial. He was unhappy about the timing as it cast a vast shaming shadow across all the defendants and according to Telford Taylor, Rosenberg looked 'less menacing'. His approach was quite different from the other defendants, seemingly pleasant but verbose which infuriated his counsel Dr Alfred Thoma, and which annoyed Justice Lawrence with Rosenberg analysing every question and sentence.

Rosenberg started his defence with his habitual views of his own eccentric philosophy and was frequently instructed to move along with more speed, even by his own counsel with whom Rosenberg became angry. His defence amounted to Rosenberg taking himself as important and with a superior intellect which started by boring everyone with meaningless jumble, most of which made no sense. It was virtually impossible to understand what he was expressing even in written form, and it must have been a nightmare to listen to him.

He claimed that he had been in favour of resolving the Jewish problem by moving them towards Asia where they could establish their own culture, trying to sidestep the issue of extermination, a word which he later dissembled over trying to point out it meant different things. He offered testimony on the *Einsatzstab Rosenberg* which was established in 1940 to seize art works and properties left or taken from

Jews. He made the unbelievable defence of portraying the intention as 'safeguarding abandoned property and protecting it from bomb damage', but then admitted that he wanted the art works to stay in Germany.

In the following session, Rosenberg attempted to defend himself during his role as minister for the Eastern Territories by claiming there was not much that he could do about what was happening around him, and that his philosophy had been taken too literally. He claimed he had unsuccessfully appealed to Hitler for a more humane occupation policy. Dodd cross-examined him, producing Rosenberg-signed documents clearly indicating that he had helped put his philosophy into practice, and this included correspondence between Rosenberg and Bormann making the onslaught against Jews and Slavs abundantly clear. This clearly changed the self-portrait which Rosenberg had presented of himself. He was also provided with the contents of a speech he gave on 20 June 1941 in which he said: 'We see absolutely no reason for any obligation on our part to feed the Russian people with the products of that surplus territory … a very extensive evacuation will be necessary, without any doubts, and it is sure that the future will hold very hard years in store for the Russians'.[7]

During the Russian cross-examination led by Rudenko, Rosenberg tried to obfuscate his answers by complaining about the translation and blaming it all on unruly subordinates. He also quibbled again over the meaning of the German *Ausrottung* (extermination) claiming it had several meanings, but he was not the only intellect in the courtroom and a dictionary clearly outlined it meant eradication or extermination. He pointed out that the term 'extermination' had been used by the British prime minister as he continued to seek refuge in mere semantics.[8] Although not raised in the trial, he had once used the word *Ausmerzung* (eradication) over which semantics could not be deployed as he went on to say 'some six million Jews still live in the East, and this question can only be solved by a biological extermination of the whole of Jewry in Europe'.[9]

He had little choice but to admit he was aware of the nature of the *Einsatzgruppen* activities but argued his only involvement were overheard rumours. The French prosecutor followed demanding answers for the shooting of French Jews and stealing their valuables. Despite his self-perceived opening success, the cross-examination backed by evidence was extremely uncomfortable if not damning.

After Taking the Stand

Those in the 'elder's room' turned their discussion onto the question of Nazi anti-Semitism with Papen criticising Rosenberg's 'pagan philosophy', and Dönitz claiming it had little influence in the navy where few men had read Rosenberg's books and articles. When Gilbert suggested the Nuremberg Laws were the start of vicious anti-Semitism, Neurath agreed claiming he had tried to advise Hitler against the policy. In Rosenberg's cell during the Easter weekend, Gilbert found him displeased with Frank's open confessions, explaining that he was a good speaker but being musical he was 'whacky' as if that explained everything with clarity; thus spoke the so-called philosopher. He then relaunched his attack on other countries' similar misdemeanours, quoting Britain's opium wars, the carpet bombing of Germany and the atom bomb attack on Japan, finishing on the usual appeal regarding the vicious Versailles Treaty and the 'vengeful French'.

In late May, Rosenberg's lawyer Dr Thoma informed Gilbert that he was becoming 'sick' over Rosenberg's hateful attitudes, demanding him to present evidence justifying the persecution of the Jews even though he had denied having any knowledge of the extermination policy.

Summation, Final Statements, and Verdicts

Before the summations, Rosenberg talked with Frick taking the line that the Nuremberg Laws were based purely on the fundamental laws of nature. He claimed he had never hated the Jews and the laws were simply scientific in nature intended to protect German blood, and he rambled on talking of *volk* (people) and breeding livestock.

His counsel approached the summation seemingly convinced of Rosenberg's innocence, stating he only played a minor role in the Norwegian occupation through his acquaintance with Quisling, and that he was an avowed follower of Hitler and an anti-Semite which was not a crime. He then turned to Rosenberg's administration in the east declaring that calling for workers or forced labour did not contravene the 'Rules of Land Warfare'. He argued that although Rosenberg was anti-Semitic, he was not an instigator of the Jewish persecution, but followed Hitler's orders. Rosenberg like Göring refused to attack Hitler or disavow Nazism. Later, Dr Thoma told Gilbert that he found Rosenberg an 'arrogant heathen' and a 'vicious anti-Semite'.

In his summary of Rosenberg, Jackson described him as 'the intellectual high priest of the master race', the party philosopher who had no idea of the violence which his philosophy had incited.[10] In his final statement to the court, Rosenberg who followed Kaltenbrunner also followed his style by going over again what had been argued in the trial. He had little to say about Nazism, never mentioned anyone else, and his only thoughtful words were expressed in his hope for 'a new, mutual understanding among nations, without prejudice, without ill-feeling, and without hatred'.[11]

Despite his efforts to distance himself from past events, Rosenberg was found guilty on all four counts, not least for having full knowledge of the atrocities when in the Occupied Eastern Territories. The verdict was death by hanging, and below in the cells, Rosenberg was angry with the outcome. According to Joseph Kingsbury-Smith working for the International News Service and covering the executions, when asked before he died whether he had anything to say for a last statement, he replied, 'No'.

Final Notes

Most agreed Rosenberg had a decisive role in shaping Nazi ideology, especially his books and articles, always inciting hatred, facilitating the persecution of the churches and above all the Jews. His vitriolic and dangerous racial views were draped in what he regarded as intellectual superiority, but which were not only superficial but downright evil. He may not have stood alongside the killers with a gun in his hands, but he had given them a sense of justification. He had been their self-elevated teacher and had been believed even though his views were totally misguided and evil. The adage that the 'pen is mightier than the sword' implies that the writer can create more damage than swords, and to this day inciting racial hatred remains not only a legal and moral issue, but a pernicious source of ongoing problems. If a person is portrayed as being an intellectual guide, as the Nazis painted Rosenberg, who believed it himself, then the outcome can be as horrific as the Holocaust. Of all the selected photographs of the defendants, the one above portrays Rosenberg as the type of self-assured arrogant person he had been.

Hans Frank 1900–46

Background

Hans Frank became the governor of the remnant of Poland. He was a lawyer and the Nazi Party's legal adviser, and he was happy to blame Hitler and Himmler for the racial policies, but he refused to admit to any role in the process. Frank was born in Karlsruhe where his father Karl was a lawyer. He joined the German Army in the Great War but served no time at the front probably because of his age. After the war he pursued his legal studies, gaining his doctorate in jurisprudence in 1924. He joined the *Freikorps* and qualified as a lawyer. He had been an early member of the Nazi Party and met Anton Drexler, the first party leader. In April 1925 he married Brigitte Herbst, and they had five children, the youngest being Niklas born in 1939 who would one day write disparaging comments about his father.

Hans Frank. (Bundesarchiv, 146-1989-011-13; Licence CC-BY-SA 3.0)

He took part in the Munich *Putsch* of 1923 and rapidly grew in prominence and served as the party's lawyer representing it in over 2,000 cases. On one occasion, an old teacher appealed to him saying, 'No good will come of it. Political movements that begin in the criminal courts will end in the criminal courts', which was visionary.[1] He was well known for his legal work, advised Hitler, and in the autumn of 1930 served as the lawyer at a court-martial in Leipzig of two army officers and three *Reichswehr* officers charged with membership of the NSDAP. Hitler appeared as a witness using the occasion to attack the Weimar Republic; the court case attracted wide publicity and served to draw in many army officers to the party's cause.

In 1930 Frank was elected to the Reichstag and made *Reichsleiter* (second highest rank in the party). In 1933 he was made Minister of Justice for Bavaria, then later the head of the National Socialists Jurists Association, and he founded the Academy of German Law as its first president. He was intelligent, played the piano well, and was educated. He claimed he believed in the rule of law and had protested at the illegal actions of the Gestapo and SD, especially the extrajudicial killings at Dachau and during the Night of the Long Knives, but with little evidence and to no avail, later claiming there was but one jurisdiction, that of the Führer.

Many were surprised when in 1939 he had been made governor-general of the occupied Polish territories, during which time ensued a reign of terror, including forced labour and the construction of four extermination camps. He took over the palace in Krakow and lived a life of luxury as the population starved. In his position, he took it as a right to confiscate property on behalf of the Reich; he also did it for his own fortune. He had fought Himmler over the treatment of the Jews but could be brutal himself; his diaries revealed he had no time for the Jews and had come around to Himmler's way of thinking.

He lost favour with Hitler in 1942 and was stripped of party honours when he suggested a return to constitutional rule in Germany but stayed in his position. He was one of the few to indicate some remorse at the atrocities, but being a lawyer was quick to point out the Allied and especially the Soviet atrocities; he was according to William Shirer the 'typical example of the Nazi intellectual gangster'.[2]

Frank was eventually found by an American patrol at Tegernsee in southern Bavaria and handed over his diary of over 11,000 typed pages. He twice tried to commit suicide and after his arrest he converted to Roman Catholicism, encouraged by the Roman Catholic priest Sixtus O'Connor. As Neave later noted, Frank had converted the burden of guilt and the demand for punishment into religious penitence and mysticism.

Medical Mental Observations

When talking to the various psychiatrists, some indications of his character and personality emerged. When asked about his general health, there followed detailed accounts of a sty on his eyelid, a middle-ear infection, even taking his medical history back to his youth. He spoke some English and was noted for his sudden bursts of laughter, especially at his own witticisms. He was prone to up-and-down mood-swings, often making visitors to his cell feel welcome, with a smile which Goldensohn sometimes described as 'leering'.[3] He was the only defendant to appear before the hang rope with a smile on his face, thanking people for their kind treatment. He had, he admitted, attempted suicide, but his sudden conversion to the Roman

Catholic faith probably halted this inclination, though there is the possibility the attempt may not have been genuine.

He would frequently recall 1942 when Hitler had fallen out with him, though he kept his position in Poland. Being a lawyer, it was his less than subtle way of trying to suggest he was in opposition to the dictator. He suggested that he had wanted to resign on many occasions but had been refused. He appeared to like the Americans (and their tobacco), and this may also have been his way of winning some sympathy, but the psychiatrist Goldensohn thought that he was not being hypocritical or cynical.

He described his marriage as being a mistake, only staying together for the sake of the children. He complained his wife was older than him (she had once been his typist), she did not appreciate sex, and he had later returned to his first girlfriend which relationship he had once broken off to marry his wife. He also later admitted he had had several mistresses. He had wanted to remarry but Hitler was against divorce and stopped him. Goldensohn in later interviews concluded that if anything depressed Frank it was his personal life.

He watched the trial as a lawyer, and like some others showed some appreciation of the American judge Francis Biddle. He was critical of Göring, saying, 'if he had spent more time collecting planes, and less collecting art, we wouldn't be where we are today', and characteristically laughed loudly at his own joke. He then suggested only America could 'stave off' Russia and it would be a good idea for the Pope to move to the USA. Goldensohn turned his attention away from these reflections and asked Frank when he had become anti-Semitic, putting him on the defence. He responded by saying he joined the Nazi Party not out of anti-Semitism but love of Germany, and denied that many Jews were killed in Poland, pointing out that Auschwitz was in Upper Silesia. Frank was unquestionably lying and skilfully changed the conversation back to his mother and sister.

Frank held the view that prosecuting the SS and Gestapo made sense, but not the High Command because they had existed long before the Nazis took power. From the legal perspective, he claimed it made sense to prosecute individuals not whole organisations, an opinion expressed by many since the trial. His opinions on politics and legal systems were kept separate. He expressed the opinion that men like Justices Jackson and Thomas Dodd were more politicians than lawyers. He explained that the first he had ever heard of the Jewish persecution had been at the trials, using the argument others had, namely that it was secret and there was no free press. He rapidly returned to the time he had fallen out with Hitler in 1942, and the way Hitler once in power moved away from the original NSDAP programme which had not included exterminating Jews. It was patently a weak defence. He argued the NSDAP had found its growth through sheer starvation, and he noted that 'paradoxically Hitler had now created still greater hunger'. He was astute enough to forecast that Russia and America would be the major powers of the future, and that the British would not be able to hold their massive empire, based on sheer logistics. He may have been misguided, immoral, but he was undoubtedly quite clever and astute.

He suggested although Hitler was dead, he should still be prosecuted and as his ex-lawyer Frank could defend him. He also noted that one word, 'Auschwitz', was all the prosecution needed, a thought somewhat shared by this writer. He thought such a procedure would combat any legends which might develop around Hitler, but it might just have been that he wanted to stand in a better or safer limelight. He concluded his interviews with Goldensohn saying, 'What a horrible system we had. How blind we were', but it is impossible, with the best will in the world, to believe he was 'blind' to events he had so obviously lived through.

Gilbert often found Frank reading the Bible (having recently converted to the Catholic faith), turning the pages with his little finger having damaged himself by trying to slash his wrists and throat when captured. The interrogators had told Gilbert they had found Frank surly and evasive, calling them 'swine', and Gilbert was therefore surprised 'that in our conversations ... he was all sweetness and light, full of abject remorse, and could curse Hitler with an amazing vehemence and literary facility'.[4] He was fixated with the evil that had been committed, declaring he had missed the Satanic streak in Hitler and that he had been in league with the Devil.

Reactions during the Trial

When Neave met Frank to serve the indictment, he found his cell stank and was full of breadcrumbs, and he looked like 'a sick spaniel', later describing him when he appeared for the trial as looking like an 'off-duty undertaker in a Boris Karloff horror film'. When on Friday 14 December 1945 the razing of Warsaw to the ground and extermination of Jews was on the agenda, Frank's diary was quoted 'that we sentence 1,200,000 Jews to die of hunger ... it is a matter of course that should the Jews not starve to death it would, we hope, result in a speeding up of anti-Jewish measures'. A Major General Stoop had kept a record of obliterating a ghetto in which he recorded the most appalling inhuman behaviour possible: 'I therefore decided to destroy the entire Jewish residential area by setting every block on fire ... a great number of Jews who could not be counted were exterminated by blowing up sewers and dugouts'.[5] This and Frank's diary revealed atrocity after atrocity. Gilbert asked Frank in his cell about these terrible diary notes. Frank blamed it on the days of his 'blind Nazi fanaticism' and that in good faith he had handed his diaries over to the Allies so the truth could be brought to light. At the lunch table next day, Hess and Ribbentrop queried whether Hitler realised 'these things' with Frank responding that it was impossible for him not to know. Göring became involved stating that Hitler was their sovereign and as such could not stand trial and he, Göring, was the chief war criminal. Frank retorted that other sovereigns had stood trial, but such was Göring's outburst, Keitel and Dönitz stood up and left Göring alone at his table.

Later in the evening, Frank expressed the view that they should all tell the truth 'for the German people and the world to know'.

During the Christmas recess, Gilbert continued visiting the defendants and often picked up novel information about their reported conversations with one another. Frank told him that he had just had an argument with Ribbentrop who had claimed the war 'was necessary and inevitable', and that the 'fat one' (Göring) had been furious that he had given his massive diary collection to the Allies, prompting Frank to repeat his belief that the truth had to be told. He explained to Gilbert the comfort he had found by embracing his Christian faith again, explaining that he felt that he, like most men, had some basic evil running through them, a reference to the Christian doctrine of 'original sin'.

Two days later (10 January), the court heard of the charges against Frank, mainly based on his diaries, and later raised during Streicher's speeches. At lunchtime, Frank was pleased how one judge had questioned the context of one of his statements, and Frank also commented on the 'German mania for making complete records'. Gilbert asked him if he was sorry that he had given his diaries to the Allies, which again he denied claiming mankind had to know the truth.

By the weekend of 19 January, Frank was wavering and wondering whether to make his last stand alongside the Nazi leaders and his comrades. Gilbert was surprised and wondered whether Frank's basic lack of integrity was re-emerging, and whether the discovery that he had some Jewish ancestry had anything to do with his enmity towards Hitler, but Frank proved evasive on this issue. By early February, Gilbert watched Frank still wavering as to where he stood and believed that Göring was exercising some influence over him, whom Frank said he found almost charming at times. Frank wondered whether he was personally suffering from a split personality as he fought between the old theme of loyalty to Hitler and telling the truth. On Sunday 10 February, Gilbert had a revealing talk with Frank over these matters, and whether his ambitions were causing him to stumble away from his original views of telling the truth when he had handed over his revealing diaries. Frank believed there was the one evil person Frank, and the alternative was his 'religious ecstasy'. Once Göring had been isolated Frank returned more to his former views, detesting the things he had said and written, but still believing he was not guilty and finishing that conversation about his unhappy married life. Even during the opening of Göring's trial time in early March, Gilbert found Frank so self-absorbed in 'his own abstractions' he was hardly listening and was annoyed at the Russians being there and sitting in judgement.

Frank's Trial

Frank had little chance of avoiding the anti-Semitic issue as one of his speeches in Krakow in 1941 had been read in court: 'We must annihilate the Jews, wherever it is possible, in order to maintain the structure of the Reich as a whole'.[6] Having listened to Rosenberg's defence and the earlier evidence of Höss, Frank took the stand, outlining his early life and how he became the legal adviser for Hitler. When challenged about the Jews, he made a full confession admitting they all knew, and that Germans would be ashamed about this for 1000 years. Possibly noting Göring shaking his head in disgust, he then added that he had never found the time to collect art treasures, though it also applied to Rosenberg still fresh in their memories. He had already handed his extensive diaries over to the Allies and acknowledged the ghettos, the exploitation of slave labour, and 'the stigmatisation of Jews'.

When asked by Dr Seidl about the indictments he faced, he explained that having listened to the trial so far 'I have gained a full insight into all the horrible atrocities which have been committed, I am possessed by a deep sense of guilt', and later on the subject of the camps stated, 'If Adolf Hitler personally has laid that dreadful responsibility on his people, then it is mine too, for we fought against Jewry for years … my own diary bears witness against me'.[7]

Having given it to the Americans, his 43-volume diary had been carefully examined which annoyed some of the other defendants, and it came back to bite him as he tried to hide his past details by claiming he had not perpetrated the atrocities. Dodd read an extract regarding some Polish professors who should be returned to Poland for 'imprisonment or liquidation'. The diaries made it abundantly clear that he was very aware of the forced labour and the horrors of the ghetto; in a careful fashion, Frank admitted his guilt in a way which he hoped would serve him.

There were various evidence-documents available which simply contradicted his defence of being humane; he had written 'this territory in its entirety is booty for the German Reich', and the 'Poles shall be slaves of the Greater German world empire'.[8] Later, he had noted that the German administration had been crowned with success as Jews could not be seen anywhere. He claimed he had tried to resign some 14 times and said he had founded an orchestra, but the Poles and Jews would have preferred personal safety rather than listening to music.

Göring, following his social separation, had lost much of his influence, and Frank's outright confession helped to create deeper divisions among the defendants. Creating a legal defence had been difficult, the documentary evidence was simply vast, and Frank's confession caused more than mere ripples.

After Taking the Stand

Frank found some support and approval from Papen and Seyss-Inquart, but Fritzsche was unhappy that Frank had identified the whole German people with crime, while others were happy with the deliberate attack on Göring's looting of art. Gilbert visited Frank on 19 April and found him in fine fettle because it was Good Friday and Frank felt that his confession on the witness stand had also been his confession before God, and that he 'had paid his bill'. He also explained that he had heard of the death of one of his father's good friends, a Jewish lawyer, which had been the final impetus for him to admit everything.

Despite what he claimed during his trial, Frank was still meandering in his thinking between denouncing Hitler and staying loyal. He accused Papen of being a 'trapped fox' then came back again to Hitler stating that murdering people was so ghastly, the word 'crime' was not strong enough to define the situation, returning to his religious thinking and wondering about divine justice.

Summation, Final Statements, and Verdicts

In Rosenberg's defence, Seidl ensured to let the court know that prior to the war Frank was only involved in legal issues and could have had nothing to do with conspiracy charges. Frank only came to be of interest as governor-general of Poland. Here, the central argument was a repetition of the main defence that this role had little to do with forced labour and the treatment of the Jews. As a lawyer, Seidl skilfully avoided some areas, for everyone notable omissions, because so much incriminatory evidence had been built up against his client.

The prosecution summation by Jackson claimed Frank had solidified Nazi control by 'establishing the new order of authority without law'. Therefore, the will of the party could export its unlawfulness into Poland which he 'governed with the lash of Caesar', robbing the area by claiming its economy.[9] In the prosecution summation, Frank's time in Poland was described as a time when he reigned but did not rule.

Frank's final statement struck a marked contrast to his two predecessors as he derided Hitler for committing suicide and asserted that the German people had turned away from God, which became the core of his message. He later added that Hitler's road was turning away from God, and '1000 years would not suffice to erase the guilt brought upon our people because of Hitler's conduct of the war'. He finally turned his attention to the fact that the Germans were still being persecuted and as to who would judge these crimes. Francis Biddle read Frank's judgement; he had been charged on counts one, three, and four, but acquitted on count one (conspiracy) for insufficient evidence. He was found guilty on counts three and four, very much like Rosenberg when in Poland, and could not evade responsibility for the atrocities. Indeed, Biddle pointed out that the Tribunal realised Frank had been a 'willing and knowing participant'. The verdict was inevitable, and he was condemned to death by hanging. Down in the cells, he remained calm explaining that he 'deserved' the sentence. His final words were 'I am thankful for the kind treatment during my captivity, and I ask God to accept me with mercy'.

Final Notes

While in prison, he wrote his memoirs *Im Angesicht des Galgens* (In the Face of the Gallows). It opened some light on Hitler's background to which Frank had been privy, possibly revealing a Jewish element, but its truth has often been suspected and many scholars have rejected the thesis. His youngest son Niklas Frank, whose godfather was Hitler, in a memoir depicted his father as a craven, cowardly weakling with animal cunning and suggested his father wrote his account out of revenge against Hitler. In 1987 Niklas published a book about his father, *Der Vater: Eine Abrechnung* (*The Father: A Settling of Accounts*), translated into English as *In the Shadow of the Reich*, in which he questioned his father's remorse before he died.[10]

Frank gives the appearance of a man torn apart by his own behaviour, with Hassell recording that he had heard of his 'brutal methods', and yet later recording that Frank was disturbed when Bormann had instructed him from Hitler that Poles were not European but Asiatic, and were to be 'handled as slaves'.[11] Hassell later described him as weak, especially in ecclesiastical matters, but noted that he had disapproved of the massacres following Heydrich's assassination but had been powerless against the SS.[12]

Frank had been called the 'Butcher of Poland' and Niklas questioned the remorse his father exhibited during the trial and his conversion to Christianity, which raises for many a complex question. Was his conversion to Christianity, his admission of guilt along with his denunciation of Hitler a sly way of trying to evince sympathy and avoid the gallows or was it genuine? There is no question that he was guilty under counts three and four and the epithet of being the Butcher of Poland was well-founded. But whether he reformed by renouncing himself and the Nazi regime and turning to the Christian faith can only be speculation as God only knows, literally. There would have been times when the repentant Frank may, like many others, have paused over St Paul's letter to the Romans: 'For the good that I would I do not: but the evil which I would not, that I do'.[13]

Wilhelm Frick 1877–1946

Alexander Mach (Slovak nationalist) with Frick. (Narodowe Archiwum Cyfrowe; Unknown Photographer)

Background

Wilhelm Frick was born in Alsenz, Bavaria, in 1877. His father was a Protestant teacher. Frick studied philology but soon turned to law and joined the Bavarian civil service in 1903, working in the Munich Police Department. He continued in this work as he was declared unfit for service in the Great War. He married Elisabetha Nagel in April 1910, and they had two sons and a daughter. However, the marriage ended in a traumatic divorce in 1934. Immediately after their separation he married a Margarete Schultze-Naumburg, the former wife of a Nazi Reichstag member.

He had been part of the failed Munich *Putsch* and was imprisoned for just over four months, though some sources claim he avoided this by having the sentence suspended. He then returned to his police work. His position and legal skills were used by the Nazi Party, and his power increased rapidly because of the Reichstag Fire Decree and the Enabling Act of 1933. He was responsible for drafting many of the *Gleichshaltung* laws which helped consolidate the Nazi regime, and he assisted in drafting a law appointing the *Reichkommissare* which effectively disempowered the state governments. As minister of the interior under Papen, they had started to abolish civil rights, free assemblies, and there was no longer any privacy by post or telephone.

There were more sinister laws in which he was involved, not least in July 1933 in implementing the Law for the Prevention of Hereditarily Diseased Offspring which included forced sterilisation. On 10 October 1933 he was appointed a *Reichsleiter*, and in May 1934 was appointed Prussian Minister of the Interior, with Göring giving him control over the police in Prussia. After the appointment of Himmler to chief of police in June 1936, although Frick technically remained Himmler's superior, this did not last long as Himmler grew his empire of SS tentacles. In June 1936, Frick was named Chief of the German Police. As a representative in the German Reichstag for Upper Bavaria, he was also a 'party whip'. He was part of Hitler's cabinet, gradually losing his prominence as Himmler rose in power. It was claimed that he protested at Himmler's murders but whether this was based on grounds of morality, or he was at odds with Himmler, for many remains questionable.

In addition to these powers, by 1935 he virtually had total control over local government. In this same year, he drafted laws against Jewish citizens (Law for the Restoration of the Professional Civil Service) and the infamous Nuremberg Laws. There were many other dubious laws for which he was responsible, including draft laws introducing universal military conscription intended to extend to Austria. He was also strongly associated with the euthanasia policy of killing those who were mentally handicapped; his clever bureaucratic skills enabled this policy to flourish for a time. He was part of the machinery which turned Germany into a police state, extending this aspect into the occupied territories.

He had become a prominent member of the NSDAP, served as a Reich Minister of the Interior (1933–43) and in August 1943 was appointed Protector of Bohemia and Moravia, although he later argued he was only an administrative agent. The capital was Prague where Frick used ruthless methods to counter dissent and was one of the last occupied cities to fall at the end of the war.

Frick always claimed that because of his political work in the early stages the Nazi strength in the Reichstag increased. He has been described as the typical bureaucrat, a 'cold fish', the least interesting of all the defendants with psychologists barely visiting him as he stayed in his own world. Frick's lawyer Dr Robert Kempner later described Frick as the 'administrative brain who devised the machinery of state for

Nazism'.[1] He was eventually captured in Munich where he may have originally been heading for Hitler's favourite area of Berchtesgaden which was a magnet for those senior men fleeing.

Interrogations

When one interrogator asked Frick if he was aware that nine million had died in the camps, he suggested the figure was 'too high by two zeros', that it was more likely 90,000 and even that was too high.[2] Various defendants during their interviews and interrogations exhibited this same line of defence. The major defence was abdication of any responsibility by obeying orders, that the government and Hitler was legitimate as chosen by the German people. Others have claimed ignorance of the facts, of which some may have been true in a few cases, but which interrogators naturally found difficult to believe. Some defendants simply denied the indictments, the military claiming their men fought a war while the SS and police carried out atrocities. Frick argued he had done nothing criminal according to the law, and he should be released. He remained obstinate in his denial of having done anything wrong. He was interviewed on 25 September 1945 during which he vehemently protested his total innocence. He claimed he was never informed of the inferred actions and was basically kept in the dark. He argued that Himmler and the SS were by nature totally secretive and administrative personnel such as himself had no idea what was happening. When asked if he was in favour of suppressing the Jews, he claimed not only ignorance but that he had not approved. However, he had co-authored or assisted in the Nuremberg Racial Laws. He protested that it was only in the interest of preserving 'German blood' which was more to do with health and based on science. He argued that the Jews were the same, not allowing mixed marriages within their traditions, and that America also followed this way of thinking. He admitted he had visited a concentration camp in 1937 with Himmler and had found everything in 'good order'. Apart from that, he had not been allowed to show any interest in such institutions, again referring to the demand for secrecy.

The interrogator pursued this matter of ignorance demanding whether he had heard anything else outside of the official agencies. He admitted he had heard of occasional Jews being arrested, but not of the masses being transported. It was, he said, a 'party matter' and all to do with the SS. He was reminded that he had been Minister of the Interior and head of the Order Police, and some 70 to 80 concentration camps had been constructed within his area of responsibility. Again, his only answer to this direct question was SS secrecy, pointing out that even minor officials if they spoke openly could be cast inside the same camps. When pressed again, he resorted to the argument that Germany was not a democracy, there was no free press or free speech, and the veil of official silence stemmed from the top. Frick agreed that 'residents' living close to the camps may have known, only to be countered by his interviewer Henry Sackett who said the waiter at his hotel had heard of these camps from various sources.

Medical Mental Observations

Frick told a psychologist it was his task to change the failing Weimar Republic to a more 'authoritarian way', oblivious that this information could seal his death warrant. Frick was believable only to himself, and at the conclusion of this interview all he wanted to know at his age (69) was what was going to happen, and why he could not be released at once. The psychologist noted he was neither hostile nor friendly, and spoke 'with a clipped, precise speech which has appropriate pauses, and rises and falls, but is apparently quite automatic and practiced'.[3] He was always elusive, and when asked about the Reichstag fire he said he had no answers or thoughts, just rumours. This may have been true and was also a possible defence, namely ignorance, but with his early prominence in the party it was difficult to believe him.

When questioned over his views about Hitler he said the Führer was 'too rash' and that he 'was a genius who lacked self-control'. He admitted he lost Hitler's confidence in 1934 as the Führer surrounded himself with bad advisers such as Himmler, Bormann, Goebbels, and Göring. When asked about Göring he claimed he had never been friendly and accused the others of being criminals. When questioned about his family it was clear it had not been a happy marriage, Frick having been divorced and subsequently married a woman younger than him by nearly 20 years. One son had been killed in the war, and the other had committed suicide at the end of the conflict rather than end up in the hands of the Russians. He gave the appearance of being somewhat cynical but stating he was a realist. When asked about the future, he claimed more war could not be prevented, 'it's the law of nature', and further stated that he was not depressed because these views were all too evidently true.

Reactions during the Trial

Airey Neave observed that he could see in Frick's 'fierce dark eyes the close-cropped, ruthless official, committed without question to the party' and who believed that the Nazi regime had the force of law to be obeyed. Fritzsche had noticed that Frick's wife had somehow managed to manoeuvre herself into the courtroom. She tried to catch Frick's eye by moving her small umbrella, but he was bewildered as if 'bewitched by an apparition'. Someone noticed which meant from that time defendant families were barred from entry.[4]

When visited during the Easter recess, Gilbert found Frick 'less cold and unconcerned than usual' as he prepared his defence. He had decided not to take the stand but would have the one witness, Hans Gisevius. He said he had little to say because he had not seen Hitler since 1937 and never approved of the persecution of the Jews. When Gilbert challenged him on this subject relating to the Nuremberg Laws, he countered by referring to the black and white racial situation in America.

Before his trial Frick, according to Gilbert, appeared 'quite cool' and his witness would 'straighten everything out'. The idea that Gisevius would be the witness was causing a high degree of nervous anticipation for some and excitement for others.

Frick's Trial

Frick's trial opened on Wednesday 24 April 1946 and only lasted two days. He had signed so many decrees and important documents the evidence against him was vast. He appeared to accept the charges against him with only the demand to challenge some of the details, not least his limited powers under the supremacy of Himmler, and questions of some money others suspected he had purloined. Frick called Hans Gisevius as a witness, as did Schact for his trial. Frick had once given the anti-Nazi Gisevius some protection when he had fallen under suspicion, and his evidence in the trial gave Frick some limited protection from the accusation of direct responsibility for police atrocities. He explained that Frick's powers were limited by Himmler, but he then disclosed that Frick had some responsibility for the concentration camps and used this as his 'starter' for a general attack on the Nazi leaders.

Hans Gisevius had been a civil servant who on being transferred to the Gestapo immediately realised that it was illegal and morally wrong, and thereafter worked to uncover the truth and expose Nazism as corrupt. Gisevius is a book in waiting, but wrote one himself called *To The Bitter End*, with a foreword by Allen Dulles, who had worked for the OSS in Switzerland and later became director of the CIA.[5] The Gestapo was soon aware of his activities and, in brief, Canaris saved him by sending him to Switzerland, ostensibly as an agent, where he contacted Allen Dulles of the OSS. Göring was the one who suffered the most from this defence witness who rapidly transpired to be of prosecution value because of his hatred of Nazism. Göring had more reason than most to be concerned as Gisevius exposed his dealings on a variety of issues. He described Göring's role in establishing the Gestapo and announced that the Night of the Long Knives had been a Himmler and Göring *Putsch*. This session concluded with the shattering news that Göring's counsel, Dr Stahmer, according to Schacht's counsel, had been instructed to intimidate the witness to stop him mentioning the General Blomberg affair (when this general had been trapped by purportedly marrying a 'loose woman'). This raised the temperature in the courtroom but surprisingly the Tribunal made no major comment on this attempt by Göring to intimidate a witness. Later, Dr Stahmer was overheard trying to push Göring into some form of explanation as this had discredited him as a lawyer, but Göring was reluctant and preferred the matter to pass by.

In the next session, the Blomberg affair was raised which clearly indicated Göring's hand in this notorious miscarriage of justice. Göring was also shown to have been a main instigator when General von Fritsch was wrongly accused of being a homosexual. Among the defendants it was beginning to look like a raging confrontation between the political and the military. It was clear from this episode of the trial that the Blomberg and Fritsch affairs had all been part of a Nazi effort to strengthen Hitler's dominance and to advance the personal interests of Himmler and especially Göring.

Gisevius was cross-examined by Jackson who had met Gisevius after the war, and who in his cross-examination further implicated Göring in the Reichstag fire, who had blamed the communists. The next day (26 April), the cross-examination continued enabling Gisevius to underline the brutality of the SA which eventuated in the early horror of the concentration camps. None of this valuable witness's evidence or his cross-examination helped Frick, and where Frick may have had some hope, Jackson managed to draw out from Gisevius that Frick had full knowledge of what was happening within the Gestapo. Gisevius also created further damage for both Keitel and Kaltenbrunner. He had created more interest in the courtroom by what he revealed about the other defendants than offering Frick a lifeline; the prosecution had been aware of this potentiality before Frick's case opened. Gisevius, whom Frick had relied upon, did him little good and lowered any remaining morale among the sharply divided defendants. Frick, by refusing to enter the witness box, 'Had done nothing to help himself or his fellow defendants'.[6]

After Taking the Stand

Gilbert decided that Frick's witness Gisevius had exposed Göring and by doing so had done exactly what Frick had anticipated. Frick, because he was a lawyer, explained to Gilbert that it seemed right. This caused Gilbert to write that 'it was ironic to see the promotor of the Nuremberg Laws hiding behind the virtuous cloak of legality while backbiting against the gangsters who beat him at his own opportunistic game'.[7] Perhaps Frick was too clever or too cunning for his own safety.

Summation, Final Statements, and Verdicts

Frick, in liaison with Rosenberg, was taking the line that the Nuremberg Laws were based purely on the fundamental premise of nature which also worked for animals. He claimed he had never hated the Jews and the laws were simply scientific in nature and to protect German blood, talking of *volk* and breeding livestock. This may have struck Frick as a clever ploy to avoid being involved in the massacre of European Jews but using animals as a comparison could not conceal the shameful deeds in which he had been involved. His counsel Dr Otto Pannenbecker was short in his address, and as Frick had not testified it was a simple blow-by-blow summary of his defence.

Jackson described Frick as the minister of the interior who had no idea what went on in his own office, 'the ruthless organiser who helped the Party seize power'.[8] Frick always gave the appearance of being somewhere in the background and his final statement was short stating that he had a clear conscience and had he acted differently it would have been treason and a breach of his oath. 'In fulfilling my legal and moral duties, I believe that I have deserved punishment no more than have tens of thousands of faithful German civil servants'.[9]

The judgement on Frick found him guilty of counts two to four, describing him as 'the chief Nazi administrative specialist and bureaucrat'. In the ensuing verdict, he was condemned to death by hanging. His last words before execution were 'long live eternal Germany'.

Final Notes

Frick had been a bureaucrat in the upper echelons of the Nazi regime administration. His attitudes, and even photographs, suggest he was for a time self-important, probably like many in the world of bureaucracy something of a petty Hitler at the personal level and lethal elsewhere. He used his legal expertise in drawing up some utterly evil legislation and his behaviour in Prague indicated he was not just a legal theorist. His bureaucratic assumption was that he had done nothing wrong according to the law, which is why he would not take the stand, probably along with the knowledge that he would find it impossible to evade questions on his knowledge of the various atrocities in the camps. He was clever and cunning, and when Gilbert asked him why he had called Gisevius, it raised the suspicion he had done so to draw attention to the main perpetrators such as Göring and away from himself, like a boxer's feint blow. If true, it was not a clever move because although much of his trial was taken up by the informative evidence of Gisevius about others, it also locked Frick into the same box. There is no evidence that he killed anyone, but he arranged the legal apparatus for this to happen over a broad spectrum of Nazi German life. In many ways, he was more guilty than the unthinking killing thugs as he was a central part of the structure which seemed to give them authority.

Julius Streicher 1885–1946

Background

Julius Streicher, commonly known as the 'Jew-baiter', and responsible for the rabidly anti-Semitic paper *Der Stürmer*, was born in Fleinhausen, Bavaria, as one of nine children. His father was a teacher in the primary school sector, a profession Julius Streicher pursued. In 1913 he married Kunigunde Roth in Nuremberg and had two sons, but his wife died in 1943 and in 1945, he married his secretary, Adele Tappe.

During the Great War, he was awarded the Iron Cross both first and second class and was made a lieutenant despite having a poor behaviour record. After the war, he returned to teaching and was noted as being seriously anti-Semitic. He always had the tendency to associate Jews and Bolsheviks and was sacked from his teaching post because of his obsessive attacks on the Weimar Republic. In 1921 he left the

Streicher. (Photographer Hoffmann Heinrich, Bundesarchiv 146-1997-011-24; Licence CC-BY-SA 3.0.1)

German Socialist Party (which was similar to the NSDAP in terms of its policies) for the NSDAP, taking with him other members. On a visit to Munich, he met Hitler and stood with him in the front row during the Munich *Putsch*. This endeared him to Hitler who protected him from attacks by the more balanced elements. Along with Hess, he was the only other Nazi mentioned in *Mein Kampf* and was among the few to be waiting for Hitler when he returned to his apartment after leaving prison in 1924.

He started *Der Stürmer* (Stormer, Striker or Attacker) in 1923–24 with his vitriolic attack on Jews, frequently depicting them as sexual predators against German women, with pornographic and revolting cartoons often portraying Jews as rats. It was exclusively an anti-Semitic production and was unbelievably lurid. The historian Richard Evans described it as a paper of screaming headlines, full of sexual innuendo, racist caricatures, with accusations of ritual murders by Jews with pornographic stories of Jewish men seducing German girls.[1] *Der Stürmer* was met with many criticisms and accusations, but Streicher always claimed he based his arguments on race and not religion, as if that was a sound defence, and that his views were political and therefore protected by law. He blamed the Jews for losing the war, creating the depression, unemployment, inflation, ritual murder, white-slave traders, and anything else his repulsive imagination could produce.

In 1937 he commissioned a book entitled *The Jewish Question in the Classroom* and a year later produced *The Poisonous Mushroom* (anti-Semitic). Hitler protected him and helped make *Der Stürmer* popular, increasing its circulation. Hitler also rewarded Streicher by appointing him *Gauleiter* of Nordbayern, a large Bavarian area including Nuremberg. Initially the *Gauleiter* was a mere functionary role, but its power grew to immense proportions under Nazi authority.

In January 1933, he became a member of the Reichstag for Franconia. However, after 1938, his relationship with Hitler deteriorated, being accused of misappropriation of property after *Kristallnacht* and of spreading scandalous stories about Göring, suggesting he was impotent. This was his greatest mistake as it was the enraged Göring who appointed the commission of enquiry into Streicher's finances. It was apparent that Streicher and some of his cronies had benefitted from *Kristallnacht* and at other times at the expense of Jewish victims. It had been Streicher who had ordered the destruction of the Grand Synagogue of Nuremberg as his contribution to *Kristallnacht*, later claiming its architecture 'disfigured' the town.

During February 1940, he was stripped of party offices and removed from his privileges as *Gauleiter* of Franconia for tax evasion. He was permitted, though, to keep the title and continue with publishing *Der Stürmer*, and still managed to retain Hitler's friendship. He had an appalling personal reputation, known to be a sadist and pornographer, and William Shirer could recall him 'striding through the streets of the old town brandishing a whip'.[2] As *Gauleiter* he had given the sense that he 'ruled' and he was a 'blatant sexual pervert, as his jailers were able to observe, and a lifelong Jew-baiter whose speciality lay in linking sex with anti-Semitism', and not even Hitler could defend him.[3]

He was captured at the end of the war in Waidring in Austria. Streicher was sitting on the veranda painting pretending he was someone else, when an American major called by seeking a glass of milk when it eventually dawned on him it was Streicher. When given an IQ test, unsurprisingly he was the lowest of all the defendants, who apart from Ley kept their distance from him, not just to evade his reputation but out of sheer personal distaste.

Streicher's lawyer was Dr Hans Marx who immediately requested a psychiatric examination of his client 'in view of the exceptional nature of the case and of the difficulties of the defence in handling it', and the Russians agreed.[4] Streicher wanted to refuse this action but was overruled, and it was agreed he had a neurotic obsession but was not insane. Rebecca West described him as 'a dirty old man', which 'a sane Germany would have sent to an asylum'.[5]

Both Streicher and Fritzsche were held accountable for what would one day be classified as 'incitement to genocide'. Streicher was among the most disliked defendants, not because of his anti-Semitism, but for his bullying approach, his love of being naked, his personal promiscuous habits, obsessive swearing, and there were major questions about his sanity.

Medical Mental Observations

It was not just the defendants who found him distasteful. Goldensohn, who talked to him in January 1946, wrote:

> He smiles constantly, the smile something between a grimace and a leer, twisting his large, thin-lipped mouth, screwing up his froggy eyes, a caricature of a lecher posing as a man of wisdom. He requires no stimulation to embark on his unique and favourite topic, anti-Semitism, which has been and remains his *raison d'être*. 'I know more about the Jews than the Jews themselves. I've known all along you are Jewish [referring to Gilbert] by your voice'.[6]

Having started the conversation in this vein, Streicher constantly returned to this favourite theme, but claimed he had no personal feelings in the matter and was purely a scientific and psychological student of the subject. He even claimed he admired the way the Jews managed to dominate, pointing to the figure of Christ, the success of the Russian Bolshevik Jews and the Jewish democracy in America. It was little wonder that Goldensohn considered him 'limited', 'generally ignorant, obsessed with maniacal anti-Semitism which served as an outlet for his sexual conflicts'. There followed a debate on circumcision which he saw as a 'diabolical Jewish plot' even though Goldensohn pointed out that it was often done to gentiles for sound medical reasons. Astoundingly, he then explained he had no personal animosity towards the Jews but regarded himself as a 'beacon of truth'. He seemed to be genuine in his belief that he was regarded as a serious thinker and researcher into Judaism.

Streicher, Goldensohn noted, was not a fit man. He had some respiratory infection and possibly some heart problems, but he was always asking for favours such as sweets and chocolate. The most frustrating issue for Goldensohn, though, was his inability to pin Streicher down to discuss any matter in a logical fashion, so he had to give him a free rein with Streicher talking incessantly about Jews and the success of *Der Stürmer*. Goldensohn asked him what had happened in 1940 when he found himself on trial. Streicher explained that he had been put in the same prison he now inhabited because he was supposed to have said something about Göring's children, and he had purchased illegal stocks. But he stated that it had all been a mistake, and because of the charges, he had been obliged to 'live on my estate in Fürth'. When questioned about his general attitude towards religion, he appeared for a moment to be more cautious, concerned that what he said might appear in the newspapers. He then launched into a general attack on religious faith, thinking it absurd that God made the universe, that the immaculate conception was nonsense, and Christ was a Jew. When asked if he felt any guilt about the extermination of the Jews, he laughed and said it was nothing to do with him, adding that he had always proposed they be sent to Madagascar, which had appeared several times in *Der Stürmer*. He also thought that the quoted numbers of millions of Jews were exaggerated and pure propaganda. He then turned his rampant bigotry towards the trial personnel, accusing them of being Jewish, and explaining that the American prosecutor Jackson was a cover for Jacobson. He then went on to explain he had a clear conscience, pointing out that in *Der Stürmer* there was not a word about 'extermination'.

In the June conversation, he complained about the noise made by the guards at night, he wanted different rations, and he asked for his wife's address. Goldensohn explained the dietary commands were beyond his remit and they were the same for everyone. He also complained about the way he had been treated when captured by the Americans in their holding camp at Freising, Bavaria. When Goldensohn questioned him about the trial asking him if he thought it was being conducted in a fair way and whether he felt any of the defendants were guilty, Streicher responded that from the German point of view none were guilty except the mass murderers. He also thought that Göring, despite his clashes with him, was correct in all he was saying in and out of the courtroom. When challenged about the forced labour, Streicher defended the policy and pointed out the barbarity of the Allied bombing mentioning ancient towns like Rothenburg and Dresden. He defended the military command saying they had nothing to do with the extermination process, concluding that most of the population including him had no idea of what was happening in the camps. He added that 'It's perfectly understandable and proper for one to be an anti-Semitic, but to exterminate women and children is so extraordinary it's hard to believe. No defendant here wanted that'.[7]

Gilbert noted that Streicher's own defence counsel wondered whether he had a 'diseased mind', with Gilbert adding that when Streicher was asked to strip for a medical examination a female Russian interpreter turned her back with Streicher making the 'leering' comment 'What's the matter? Are you afraid of seeing something nice?'[8] It was after this examination that the medical people decided he was suffering from a neurotic obsession but was not insane and could stand trial. Gilbert carried out a series of tests (including the IQ test) which indicated a limited mentality, slightly above average intelligence, but with a hysterical personality.

Reactions during the Trial

When Airey Neave gave Streicher the indictment, it would have come as no surprise to the psychiatrists that he immediately expostulated that the judges were all Jews, flinging out his arms in protest. On the first day, Streicher caught Gilbert's attention and explained that he had been sentenced in the same courtroom before, and when asked how often he had been prosecuted, he replied about 13 times. This jollity did not last, as a few days later (21 November) Jackson opened the Jewish issue, tracing it back not just to the Nuremberg Laws, but planned persecutions such as *Kristallnacht* and the pogroms. He quoted Streicher who had complained that Christian teaching had hindered the Führer's radical extermination plans, concluding with the telling line that the real 'complaining party at your bar is civilisation'. In the cell that evening, Streicher made his usual protests that he was not the cause, and then told Gilbert that he could tell three of the judges were Jews. On a pre-Christmas visit, Gilbert found Streicher 'still as unwaveringly fanatic as ever ... completely unaffected by the accumulation of evidence' which was causing such unrest among the other defendants.[9] During the Christmas recess, Streicher remained busy attacking the Christian belief and asked Gilbert about the atom bomb, requesting him to bring him a book on the subject with pictures.

By the end of Friday 18 January 1946, the British had completed their case and the French had opened with an attack on racism. Gilbert went to see how Streicher was coping over the weekend; he had not changed in the slightest, leading Gilbert to write:

> A quarter of an hour with this perverted mind is about all one can stand at one time, and the line never varies; World Jewry and circumcision serve as the channels for projecting his own lascivious thoughts and aggressions into a pornographic anti-Semitism which could get official support only in Hitlerite Germany.[10]

During the Easter recess, Gilbert found Streicher more subdued, speculating that this was caused by the 'cool contempt' with which the other defendants viewed him. He had been impressed by Rosenberg's defence, and for his part he had been out of touch since 1940.

Streicher's Trial

Streicher's case was unusual because given his history, he could hardly come under any of the indictments. There was no evidence that Streicher had actually been involved in any action leading to the death of Jewish people, leaving the question as to whether incitement alone had enough basis for a conviction. Most of the other defendants held some position of authority and Streicher stood alone in the legal sense; even his membership of the Reichstag had given him no status or power. He was no great party man but was known only for his total loyalty to Hitler. This meant that the trial would be of short duration as they were trying a man better known for his financial corruption and sadism but who was a notorious 'Jew-baiter'. However, at Nuremberg, anti-Semitism was not a crime, and there was no evidence he had killed anyone. By 1940 he had been stripped of all offices and apart from his editorial work had lived a private life.

All too typically of Streicher, he started his defence by attacking his own legal counsel Dr Hans Marx for not following his instructions, probably because his counsel did not want to defend anti-Semitism. Marx asked to be relieved after one outburst but was told by Lawrence to continue as Streicher opened his defence 'with a bombastic oration, describing himself as the fate-ordained apostle of anti-Semitism'.[11] He complained about the conditions he suffered as a prisoner, comparing it to Gestapo methods and explained how the Jews seized power in 1918 Germany, and stated he was sad not to have been consulted over the Nuremberg Racial Laws.

There were moments when Streicher gave some well-formulated answers to questions, especially when asked about his relationship with Hitler, saying that 'Adolf Hitler was a little eccentric in every respect, and I believe I can say that friendship between him and other men did not exist – a friendship what could be described as an intimate friendship'.[12] Other times he was warned by the Bench not to be insolent. He persisted in describing Jewish rituals of murder and rape as if they were verifiable which revived doubts about his sanity.[13]

At times, he was like Ribbentrop and could not be pinned down to a direct answer of 'yes or no', but he wanted to expound and explain everything from his point of view. When asked if he preached religious hatred, he explained that in *Der Stürmer* 'I repeatedly stated that for me the Jews are not a religious group but a race, a people', as if that explained everything.[14]

He had admitted to visiting Dachau several times but only to visit non-criminal inmates from his area of Franconia. He maintained he had not been involved in any of the anti-Jewish atrocities, had not been part of *Kristallnacht* planning, and he even explained in the next session that the destruction of the old Nuremberg Synagogue had been based on architectural tastes. He blamed Goebbels for the anti-Jew demonstrations and claimed Himmler and Schirach had given him support when *Der Stürmer* was under threat. It is claimed that Streicher at one time announced that Himmler's looks indicated he was not a true German, emphasising the fanaticism of his beliefs. His cross-examination was less than half a day, and when confronted by a speech he had given, he swiftly countered by claiming he had not preached religious hatred because Judaism was a race, not a religion, and his anti-Semitism was to enlighten, not persecute. When challenged on many of his articles and speeches, the prosecution was met by similar replies from this extreme fanatic. He explained that he had never incited the population but rather 'enlightened them'.[15]

Everyone in the court including the defendants and officials exhibited signs of embarrassment as Streicher held forth. He looked to the other defendants for approval, but they had turned their faces away from him. In the next session, he denied any knowledge of the extermination policy, but he came under extreme pressure during the cross-examination, and Streicher argued that even if he had used the expression 'extermination', it was never meant in the literal sense of the word, what he described as 'literary licence'. Four witnesses were called by Marx, but they added no new insights, and adding to the embarrassment of this trial, his last witness was his wife who described him as a 'nice man'. The prosecution decided not to cross-examine her (or the other witnesses), probably wondering what she had seen in him. The question of what should happen to him at the end of this short trial could not have been clearer, but whether he was legally guilty of crimes, or could be condemned for his extreme anti-Semitism, must have lurked in some minds.

After Taking the Stand

During the Papen trial, as the discussion raged among his fellow defendants, Streicher managed to catch Dönitz's attention telling him it was a mistake to attack great figures like Hitler 'who are brought about by supernatural forces'. Dönitz managed to turn his back on Streicher, which happened most of the time with the defendants who considered him mad and an embarrassment.

Dr Marx was preparing to make his plea for Streicher as a person obsessed with anti-Semitism and not taken seriously by most German people. In a conversation a week later, Streicher expressed the opinion that Hitler had made a mistake by killing so many Jews because this had made a martyr race of them. When Gilbert had asked him what he meant by 'race laws', he started to talk of chromosomes until it dawned on him that Gilbert may have known more than he did. He thus resorted to physical recognition with the eyes, nose, and even the soft bottoms which even the male Jews had with their air of femininity.

Summation, Final Statements, and Verdicts

Streicher's counsel Dr Marx had to prove there was insufficient evidence that his client had incited the killing of Jews and, hopefully, that his attitudes and appearance giving him such unpopularity did not influence the court's decision. He pointed out the small distribution of *Der Stürmer* and only a few articles called for 'extermination' which could have several meanings. It was also clear that Marx had no pleasure in defending his client, who infuriated Streicher by claiming that his client 'had never been taken seriously'.

In the prosecution summation, Streicher was understandably described as a 'venomous vulgarian' and his inciting racial hatred in his publications was noted.[16] Jackson described him as the *Gauleiter* of Franconia 'whose occupation was to pour forth filthy writings about Jews, but who had no idea that anybody would read them'.[17] It was noted that although Streicher appeared to be paying little attention, he was puzzled by Jackson's estimate of murdered Jews, which was not unreasonable as even to this day the truth is unknown; Streicher thought it was closer to four million than six.

Surprisingly, Telford Taylor noted that Streicher's last statement was presented with a sense of dignity and dispatch. He informed the court that the prosecution had failed to prove that the mass killings could be placed at his feet, which he repudiated, pointing out that Hitler had ordered it because he blamed the Jews for the defeat of Germany in 1918. He informed his listeners that he had not committed any crime and 'I look forward to your judgment with a good conscience', and 'do not pronounce a judgment which would imprint the stamp of dishonour upon the forehead of an entire nation'.[18] His wife Adele who had been one of his witnesses came every day despite some rules. A new psychiatrist a Dr Dunn had been brought in by Andrus to see how the defendants were coping during these end days, and he saw no problem with Streicher who 'was bolstered by his lack of sensitivity and imagination and by limitations in intelligence'.[19]

When it came to judgement, Streicher had been indicted on counts one and four but the first was ruled out and he was found guilty on count four. When the verdict was announced that he would be hanged, Streicher's reaction was one of anger, stamping noisily out towards the lift. His last words were reported as 'the Bolsheviks will hang you one day', and he mentioned his second wife Adele's name; it was, according to some, a bungled execution.

Final Notes

People found Streicher unbelievably repugnant. He used to exercise in public stark naked to everyone's embarrassment and used to shout out at night causing defendants to complain until Andrus threatened him. Knowing Streicher's propensities, Andrus once set up an interview with a blond, blue-eyed interpreter which thrilled Streicher, but the man was in fact Jewish, although Streicher described him as a perfect example of German Nordic.[20] There is no doubt that normal people would have found Streicher repulsive and offensive to such a degree that he would have been considered mad or at best mentally unbalanced. He was an obsessive person, but his fixation was not harmless, not stamp-collecting, but a matter of stirring up racial hatred. The question was initially raised by Telford Taylor as to whether he was condemned because of his awful personality and whether it was legally correct.[21] When Telford Taylor later in his study described Streicher's sentence of execution as 'callous', it rings too many bells.[22] Stirring up racial hatred is criminal by many of today's standards, it becomes more questionable when it is felt that the culprit is eccentric, low in intelligence ratings, and possibly mentally unbalanced. What he did was criminal, his views undoubtedly appealed to similar base-type minds, but he would have been better sentenced to a prison with psychiatric help, and he would have made an ideal subject from which studies of the mind could be developed.

Hjalmar Schacht 1877–1970

Background

Hjalmar Horace Greeley Schacht's parents had been Danish citizens living in Schleswig-Holstein. His father had emigrated to America but returned to Germany where Schacht was educated in Germany and France. Curiously, he was named after an American newspaper editor his father had admired, but the name 'Horace Greeley' was not used at Nuremberg possibly because Greeley had once been a presidential candidate. Schacht gained his doctorate at Kiel with a thesis on mercantilism. In 1903 he joined the Dresdner Bank, and on their business travelled to America where he met the well-known banker J. P. Morgan, and the American President Theodore Roosevelt. He became a deputy director of Dresdner Bank and a board member of the German National Bank.

Hjalmar Schacht. (*Bundesarchiv,* 102-1273, Licence CC-BY-SA 3.0)

During the Great War, he was attached to the staff of General von Lumm in occupied Belgium and helped organise the finances for German purchasing. General Lumm dismissed him when it was discovered that Schacht had used the Dresdner Bank against instructions. After the war, he continued to work for Dresdner and applied to be head of the *Reichsbank* but at first was rejected because of General Lumm's dismissal incident. In November 1923, he became the currency commissioner for the Weimar Republic, and in 1926 provided the funds for I G Farben to start its enterprise. He was soon known at the international level and became friendly with

Montagu Norman, Governor of the Bank of England, who became a godfather to one of Schacht's grandchildren.

He was an economist, a banker, centre-right politically, an extreme nationalist, and in 1918 had co-founded the German Democratic Party. His first wife had been so pro-Nazi that she could not tolerate any criticisms of the regime and they parted in 1938. Schacht remarried in 1941 to a woman some 30 years younger and he had two daughters with her.

Under the Weimar Republic, which he detested as a fervent nationalist, he became president of the *Reichsbank* (for two periods 1923–30 and 1933–39) and a strong critic of the Versailles Treaty, especially the reparations. Schacht first met Hitler at Göring's apartments in January 1931 where he and Fritz Thyssen spent an evening listening to Hitler's views.[1] He left the Democratic Party in 1926 and veered towards the NSDAP to help them raise funds because at that time he thought they were heading in the right direction. He never became a party member, but he was made an honorary member with the award of the Golden Party Badge. As a strong nationalist, he wanted to see Germany back in its appropriate standing internationally, and he believed that 'as the powers became more involved in their own economic problems in 1931–32 … a strong government based on a broad national movement could use the existing conditions to regain Germany's sovereignty and equality as a world power'.[2]

Hitler appealed to his nationalistic leanings, and he came to their financial aid in 1932 when the tide appeared to be against the Nazis. He and Gustav Krupp continued to raise contributions for the party. He always dressed as a traditional man of his class, as a banker with high-flying collars which made him stand out in photographs with others in some form of uniform; even later in the Nuremberg prison he would make these collars from white paper.

As the *Reichsbank* president he served under Hitler (1933–39) and was Minister of Economics from August 1934 to November 1937. During the economic crisis (1935–36), he worked with the Price Commissioner Dr Carl Friedrich Goerdeler to support the 'free-market' policy within the regime, urging Hitler to reduce spending on armaments and move away from autarky policies, but in doing so he clashed with Göring. Goerdeler was the Mayor of Leipzig who became an active resistance member against the Nazi movement and who was executed in February 1945.

When Hitler's demand on money for rearmaments escalated, he clashed first with Göring then Hitler, and came into conflict with the party leadership, even though he was regarded as having produced an 'economic miracle' for Germany. Following the events of *Kristallnacht* in November 1938, Schacht publicly made it known he disagreed and suggested other ways to resolve the Jewish issue had to be found. He came to the solution that funds should be made available for emigrating Jews, and their property should be held in a financial trust to assist them. He later wrote a book about this effort entitled *The Magic of Money* (1967). The clash with Hitler and Göring persisted, and in January 1939 he was dismissed as the *Reichsbank*'s president. He remained as minister without portfolio receiving the same salary, probably because Hitler did not want to raise international interest in any clash; he was eventually dismissed in January 1943. He was well known on the international stage and had travelled widely. He always claimed he was not anti-Semitic but appeared to support Hitler's views until it came to extermination.

It has been claimed that Schacht was involved in resistance to Hitler as early as 1938 and was possibly involved in a plot to overthrow the regime if it started a war against Czechoslovakia. Goerdeler led the civilian resistance and had been a colleague and friend of Schacht, Hans Gisevius, and Theodor Strünck to whom he offered one of his properties when Strünck was bombed out. After the 20 July 1944 Plot, because of his acquaintances, Schacht fell under suspicion and was arrested by the Gestapo. It will always be questionable as to how immersed he was in such plots, but it was known that he was one of the few who had suggested Hitler could be replaced by the eldest son of the Crown Prince Wilhelm, which would not have been a democratic future.[3] He was interned in Ravensbrück concentration camp and later at Flossenbürg with men in a similar situation, but unlike many of them, he was not executed (such as Dietrich Bonhoeffer and Theodor Strünck). He was then transported to the Alpine Fortress of Niederdorf in the South Tyrol in the company of such men as French politician Léon Blum, industrialist Kurt Thyssen, German pastor Martin Niemöller, and the last legitimate Austrian chancellor Kurt Schuschnigg, where they were freed on 30 April 1945. He was later re-arrested by the Americans and was furious, and ironically he would be on the same defendant's bench as Kaltenbrunner. One thing that was already clear was he could be charming to people he respected but he did not suffer fools gladly, and later many of his fellow defendants were wary of his sarcastic asides and his dominating presence.

Interrogations

Schacht was not so much a dedicated Nazi but a conservative German who agreed to work with Hitler in the early stages. He was regarded as the economic genius who helped Hitler stabilise the German economy. He argued that he and others of the same disposition were able to operate a moderating influence over the regime. This sounded somewhat spurious to the interrogators because in the early 1930s, many realised that Hitler could not be restrained. As with Papen, Neurath, and the military commanders such as Keitel, and Raeder, who were not official Nazi Party members, but in their various ways, they had been considered to have supported Hitler.

Schacht told interrogators 'you will have to admit that Hitler was a genius, but an evil genius'.[4] Schacht was a staunch nationalist but as early as 1937 he had decided to part company with Hitler over excessive spending on military equipment, and ended up in Dachau concentration camp. As with Robert Ley, his captors asked him to write a report on a future Germany as they speculated on a way ahead for post-war Germany. Intermixed in this report was some of his own thinking about the past and the future. He thought nationalism was good but not when it tried to enforce its supremacy over other nations; it should in his opinion have been a beacon for others. He also added a note that the report was not to indicate any willingness on his part to re-enter public life. He admitted that he had not studied any details or statistics since 1939 and having been 'duped' by Hitler was now intent on the private life.

He pointed out in his various interviews, with some validity, that other countries needed Germany in the light of mutual economic support. Many of his suggestions made sense in light of the 1945 German defeat. After the debilitating Treaty of Versailles, Germany by its sheer size was potentially a major economic player in Europe, as has been proved since the last war. He even made the puzzling suggestion at one point that Germany might be included in the British Empire which he thought might give political and economic stability. He pointed out to his interrogators that his proposals needed to be more than mere theory and must be practical, noting that given the current circumstances German sovereignty would be restricted. He wrote that while the foreign powers might dictate political direction, the economy should be left to a German administration.

He spent time on the complex issues of currency, looking to the gold standard as essential, and the necessity of international economic contracts. He foresaw the need to rebuild German agriculture, the return of proper farming (not just small holders who often just fed themselves) and the artisan, much of this having been lost during the war. He even went so far as to propose that new houses for workers should have small garden plots to grow their own food. He recognised that the post-war years would be difficult with the shortages and would need state control, but it was critical to think about people's diets, and calory intake. He noted that the armament industry had all but destroyed Germany's social fabric and economy and proposed it should be abandoned. He wrote about simplifying the gigantic bureaucratic system the Nazi regime had built up and the necessity for moral education.

He concluded with a revealing passage regarding the passions felt about the war and searching for the guilty parties. He concluded with his main theme, that while not denying the guilt of Hitler and National Socialism, he begged there should not be a repetition of the Treaty of Versailles which had been a major factor in Hitler's popularity. He compared it to post-Napoleonic France when outlawing France had not happened, and peace followed, whereas after 1918 there was continuous unrest in Europe. For many, this was and is a pertinent point. He finished by writing that Germany had much to offer 'the western world'. This report clearly indicated he was a clever man if once misguided by Hitler, or as he expressed 'duped' by the dictator. His observations were thoughtful, sensible, and some of his conclusions were highly astute.

Medical Mental Observations

When Goldensohn met Schacht, he found him the 'same as ever', 'the hail-fellow-well-met, indignant at his being accused as a war criminal', using the word 'frightful' time and time again. There is a distinct sense on reading Goldensohn's notes that he was not so much at ease with Schacht as he had been with some of the other defendants, stating that although Schacht had been Hitler's economic minister, Schacht still referred to him as his archenemy. When Goldensohn intimated that Schacht had continued in Hitler's service as a minister without portfolio, Schacht told him that during this time he had lived on his small farm outside Berlin and done nothing, only being allowed to do this because Hitler knew Schacht had an international reputation; there was probably some truth in this statement. Schacht again informed the unimpressed Goldensohn that he had met Roosevelt (1934 and 1935) and many other American presidents. They talked about the ex-American ambassador William Dodd (no obvious relation to the American prosecutor) and that Schacht had been part of the 20 July 1944 Plot, prompting Goldensohn to note that 'clinically, it is obvious that Schacht has tremendous energy and vitality for a man of his years'.[5] There followed a tussle in the conversation with Goldensohn tackling Schacht over anti-Semitism with Schacht 'bridling' at the suggestion. He pointed out that his only distaste was communism and posed a barbed question that the Americans would repeat their behaviour of 1918 leaving Europe to its own devices, and Russia would dictate what would happen. This would mean, he argued, the loss of private freedoms and enterprise, followed by his favourite exclamation of 'frightful'.

On the question of rearmament, Schacht told Goldensohn he had only helped in so far that Germany needed to rearm itself to the level of its neighbours for a matter of defence, but he had disagreed and clashed with Hitler when he wanted more. He explained that was why he was sacked as president of the *Reichsbank* because he blocked the necessary loans. After his dismissal, Hitler issued a law which obligated the bank to give any credit that he demanded which had led to inflation. Schacht then accused Funk of being a willing servant but adding that he probably had little choice. Goldensohn, as with some other defendants, challenged him as to why he allowed Hitler to use him after his dismissal. Schacht responded raising the Versailles Treaty, pointing out that the Allies not only demanded severe reparations, but closed Germany's overseas banking operations which made the situation financially impossible. He then explained how the various German governments had tried various routes in seeking stability, but generally failed to overcome the economic problems, leaving the choice between Hitler and communism. In the early stages, Hitler had promised freedom, religious safety, national dignity, even though later he betrayed all these promises; nobody, Schacht argued, knew at that time that Hitler was such a 'bad character' and that he would betray the nation.

Schacht argued that he had taken the bank's presidency because it was an independent position, and as the economics minister, he had taken the post under Hindenburg's signature (thereby hinting at respectability) and it was the last time Hindenburg signed any official document. Goldensohn asked if Hitler's nature was beginning to reveal itself, and Schacht replied that as early as 1935 he had started to oppose Hitler, especially over such unlawful matters as the persecution of the churches, the Jews, and the establishment of the Gestapo. When it dawned on Schacht that Hitler was preparing for war, it was then that he retired from the ministerial role which Hitler would only accept if he stayed as minister without portfolio, which was a mere title.

Schacht argued that Hitler was popular because of his early successes and Chamberlain and Daladier had not helped at Munich. Goldensohn again challenged him as to why he had not left the country like the writer Thomas Mann. Schacht argued that Mann had achieved little, and his Jewish friends who had fled to Switzerland and elsewhere had detracted from German culture by their absence, not that they had much choice, admitting that Germany had become an 'atrocious place' to live. Schacht pointed out that he was not being prosecuted under the Jewish issues. When Goldensohn suggested his department of economics had passed some anti-Semitic regulations, Schacht was furious, and it led to a 'cold' end to their meeting.

To ease tensions, the next interview concentrated on Schacht's family, with him declaring that 'my father was very honest from head to toe, and so am I'. Schacht pointed out that on arrival in prison his watch and money had been taken from him without receipt and had now disappeared. At the following interview a month later, Goldensohn found Schacht 'fairly depressed' but 'becoming more grandiose and boastful as we talked'. It was clear that this defendant was not to Goldensohn's liking, and Schacht was depressed because of his wife's impoverishment in terms of food and where she was living. They discussed the trials, with Schacht saying he would have refused to carry out immoral orders and found the thought of taking teeth out of a corpse outrageous. He challenged Goldensohn as to why he always took notes which led to a discussion on psychiatry. Goldensohn asked if Schacht thought the Hitler period had lowered the nation's moral standards which Schacht denied on the grounds that most people did not know of the atrocities. Schacht then criticised the nature of the court and being from his Germanic background, he had little trust in the cross-examination of the adversarial style of Anglo-American legal culture, commenting on the judges with his contempt for the Russians being obvious. Throughout these conversations it was abundantly clear that Schacht was a typical right-wing conservative German of the old school, was not a Nazi, but had raised deep suspicions within Goldensohn who most of the time appeared as a benign, almost friendly, conversationalist.

According to Gilbert, Schacht passionately believed he was the most innocent man among the defendants and had the best mind; his intelligence was proven to a degree when he came top in the IQ test. Gilbert had a degree of sympathy for Schacht bearing in mind that he had spent 10 months in concentration camps, and only discovered the atrocities at Flossenbürg where he could hear people being forced to undress and marched to the woods where they were shot.[6]

He had a violent temper and he was prone to screaming when he was angry which he often was. On one occasion, Colonel Andrus described the time Schacht threw a cup of hot coffee over a photographer taking surprise pictures, for which he lost his coffee ration for a week.[7] On another occasion, Andrus threatened to deprive him of his daily exercise because of his attitude.

Reactions during the Trial

On presenting Schacht with the indictment, Airey Neave found him 'patronising and supercilious … he glared at me through heavy spectacles and took the indictment … he said in haughty English "I will read these documents, but, of course, I expect to be acquitted. I am after all a banker. My son-in-law is a jurist. Please put me in touch with him"'.[8] In the same way, whenever Gilbert visited Schacht, he always found him confident 'and chipper', totally convinced that he had nothing to worry about and hoping that the trial would move along rapidly and be finished. During the Christmas recess, Schacht was still cheerful, telling Gilbert the trial was not meant for him, that he had tried to stop Hitler and he considered 'Göring was a born criminal'. However, he reminded Gilbert that in terms of commerce, German efforts against the Versailles Treaty were not so bad. He looked forward to his release but did not think that Germany would have any more use for bankers.

Following the disclosure by the SS functionary Otto Ohlendorf on Thursday 3 January 1946 describing the orders for exterminating 90,000 Jews, Schacht was in his cell continuously playing his solitaire card game and told Gilbert that 'Kaltenbrunner's goose was now cooked'. He was also surprised at Ohlendorf whom he had always considered as looking 'upright' and informed Gilbert he would not have obeyed such orders. He also commented on Speer's revelation of hoping to kill Hitler, pointing out he had tried to 'remove Hitler' in 1938. He had concluded that Hess was still crazy, and later ridiculed Hess's childish diplomacy in flying to England.

When on 15 February the defendants were returned to solitary confinement, Schacht was furious, explaining that although he did not like talking to criminals such as Göring, Rosenberg, Streicher, and Ribbentrop, he missed the company of decent people like Papen, Neurath, men of his old conservative cultured class. This led Gilbert and Schacht into a discussion about the values of German culture, the Weimar Republic, the disaster of Munich, and the way Schacht was treated, even suggesting he had been shown more respect in the concentration camp; he felt, with some justification, he was innocent, and he should not be there. When on Tuesday 19 February the Russians showed a more horrific film about the atrocities than the Anglo-Americans, Göring pretended not to watch and claimed it was false. Frank was beside himself in mental anguish, and Schacht had also refused to watch the film, pointing out that it was a disgrace not just on the Germans but on all human beings which was probably true. He also argued that it should be the Germans who should track down and punish the guilty.

During Göring's trial, Schacht felt he would never be able to defend himself against the charges, showing perhaps more depth than some of the other defendants. When Gilbert suggested Hitler's cardinal mistake was attacking Russia, Schacht corrected him by stating it was not the attack on Russia but Poland, with which Dönitz agreed. During Hess's trial, when the court ruled the Versailles Treaty arguments as irrelevant, Schacht and Dönitz argued that there would have been no Hitler if there had been no Versailles Treaty, which may have had some foundation historically, but as Gilbert pointed out, it had nothing to do with waging aggressive war and crimes against humanity. The Versailles argument was pertinent and which Rosenberg and Kaltenbrunner supported, but rightly ruled as irrelevant by the court; crimes against humanity of this extreme nature could not be explained by recent history.

He was equally critical of Keitel during his trial, telling his 'group' that he heard of a German officer who refused to massacre some prisoners had been warned, still refused, and was not punished. Schacht explained that this proved it was possible to disobey orders, and Keitel did not have to obey. During the Easter recess, Gilbert found Schacht pleased that to that date the other defendants were exhibiting or to having their criminality revealed. This was especially true when Frick's witness Gisevius exposed Göring's dealings. Although Gisevius played a more important role in Schacht's favour than he did for Frick, Gilbert thought Schacht displayed a sense of nervousness because of the unpleasant glances at him from the military defendants. Later, when the Frick trial was concluding, Schacht told Gilbert it was the end of the 'Hitler legend' and the whole rotten system had been exposed.

Schacht's Trial

Under the initial court arrangements, Funk was supposed to be tried before Schacht, but because Schacht had more to do with the pre-war years, he took the stand first, indicted under counts one and two, basically in assisting the Nazis to power. Schacht was legally intelligent enough to know that being a nationalist, violating treaties, objecting to the Versailles Treaty, and helping a country to rearm were not crimes, and the prosecution had to prove that he had been aware that Hitler was preparing for an aggressive war. He had already received support from Frick's witness, the Nazi resister Gisevius, and he exuded self-confidence in his appearances backed by his articulate and precise answers. The simmering German resistance had such famous names as Admiral Canaris, head of the *Abwehr*, General Hans Oster, Carl Goerdeler, and Schacht had been involved in their company. Gisevius had stated in court that the group were strongly attracted to Schacht 'because of his exceptional personal courage and the fact that he was undoubtedly a man of strong moral courage, and he did not think only of Germany but also the ideals of humanity'.[9] Schacht was totally convinced he would be declared innocent: 'he could have borne on his shield the words of Metternich when looking back at his career: "Error has never crossed my mind"'.[10] His aloof arrogance and disdain for others made him not only formidable but unlikeable; few people warmed to him, but he was clever, cunning, and articulate. He said that in some respects Hitler was a genius 'capable of sudden ideas of which nobody else had thought', but in his next statement called him a 'mass psychologist of really diabolical genius'.[11] He believed Hitler had swindled him because he had promised equal rights but his adherents 'enjoyed privileges before all other citizens'.[12] There was a degree of hypocrisy here because for a time Schacht had enjoyed these so-called privileges.

The prosecution was based on the evidence that although not a member of the Nazi Party, he was committed to them, regarding them as a means of destroying the Weimar Republic. Economically, he had won bankers over to Hitler, arrested the inflation, helped in rearmament, and contested that Schacht had not resigned out of disgust for the Nazi regime but over the dispute with Göring who believed German economics could rely on self-sufficiency and not in foreign trade as Schacht demanded. Schacht was believed to be a man who was able to play for both sides depending on the timing. The British had not been supportive of putting Schacht on trial, but like the Russians, Jackson was eager to convict him, and it has been suggested that Jackson and his team were not that well-versed in Schacht's activities. It must have appeared to many that a man who had stood up to Hitler, who had joined the German resistance, and ended up in concentration camps was an unlikely candidate for a successful prosecution.

Schacht's trial opened at the end of April 1946 with him presenting himself as a nationalist, an idealist, and a democrat, hastily claiming that in the early days Hitler had not appeared so radical, and he believed he could moderate the dictator. He pointed out that *Mein Kampf* clearly indicated Hitler was a poorly educated fanatic, but there had been a degree of truth in his attack on the Versailles Treaty, cleverly pointing out that even at the time the Americans were unhappy with the settlement because Wilson's 14 points had been betrayed. In the next session (Wednesday 1 May), he explained his growing contempt for the Nazis and his attempt to help Germany build up enough armaments only to keep a balance with its immediate neighbours who always posed a threat. This brought a degree of derisory scorn from Göring, accusing Schacht in a loud voice of lying, implying he had told Hitler more arms were necessary, with Ribbentrop supporting Göring. He denied taking part in any plans for aggression and believed in foreign trade as a means of self-determination and international understanding for all nations, and admitted he was a nationalist. In the afternoon session, Schacht indicated his opposition to the anti-Semitic policy and explained he took the oath of loyalty not to Hitler but to the head of state, accusing Hitler of perjury. In the following session, he painted the best possible picture of himself and in leading plots to have Hitler removed.

Jackson started his cross-examination by pursuing the line that Schacht was more enthusiastic about Hitler in the early days than he pretended, quoting speeches he had given and papers he had once prepared. He exhibited photographs of Schacht in the company of Nazi leaders, but this carried little weight as official photographs proliferated in all countries. Jackson referred to the time when Schacht had suggested to Papen that Hitler could be the man 'to save Germany', which Schacht acknowledged, inferring that during that time there was some hope in the emerging figure of Hitler. But there were indications from Jackson's cross-examination that Schacht had done more for the rise of Nazism than he had admitted. It has been noted that Jackson, still smarting from the debacle with Göring, was determined to cross-examine Schacht well, but he was not an economic expert, had probably not done sufficient background work, and time and time again was trapped by Schacht's corrections and superior knowledge, which Schacht enjoyed.

Jackson then embarrassed Schacht by reminding him he had contributed to party funds after receiving the Golden Party Badge from the party. Schacht, though, denied he had been a party member and that the gold swastika badge was the gift of the party. Jackson added that by giving funds, Schacht had encouraged the Nazis to trust him. When asked whether he often wore the badge, Schacht responded in the affirmative because it helped him hire cars and board trains more quickly which drew a few smiles from the listeners. Perhaps they were reflecting on Schacht's earlier claims that Hitler's cohorts had privileges above the ordinary citizen. He was on more delicate ground as Jackson pursued his views of anti-Semitism exposing that Schacht had signed a decree excluding Jews from civil service positions to which Schacht appeared somewhat indifferent. Given what had happened to the Jews, this demanded a clearer response. Jackson referred to a speech Schacht made at Hitler's birthday in 1937 in which he stated, 'we are meeting here to remember with respect and love the man to whom the German people entrusted the control of its destiny … and has won for himself the soul of the German people'.[13] All Schacht could do was ask Jackson whether he was quoting it correctly. Biddle was not impressed with Jackson's cross-examination, writing in his notes that Schacht 'most certainly held his own', though many of the other defendants thought otherwise.

In terms of Schacht as a conspirator against Hitler, Gisevius gave his support, mentioning the time they had uncovered Gestapo bugging devices in Schacht's office. However, he then expressed some reservations that Schacht remained something of a puzzle to the other conspirators, and some, including a later witness called Karl Severing (Social Democratic Minister for the Interior), claimed they would have nothing to do with Schacht during the 20 July 1944 Plot.

In the 3 May session, Jackson continued his cross-examination, drawing out Schacht's views that Göring was a criminal-type personality suffering from egotism. Schacht quoted a time when Göring had dressed in a Roman toga to greet guests, causing Göring to squirm in his seat to everyone's amusement. Jackson pointed out that Schacht may have theoretically objected to the *Anschluss* and occupation of Czechoslovakia, but he had too happily taken control of their banks. Schacht insisted that it had been the invasion of Poland and the west which he regarded as sheer aggression. Schacht presented his case well and coped easily with the cross-examination. A *Daily Telegraph* reporter noted that Schacht had given 'the most consistent and best supported apologia yet submitted'.[14] The defendants noted that there was a turn in the trial as it was now taking on moral issues and received some sympathetic acclaim in the press.

In the defendant's box, there was a general feeling that Schacht had gone too far in his renunciation of Hitler so early in their relationship. Either way, most of the defendants were happy with the way that Jackson appeared to put the aloof Schacht back in his box. However distasteful some may have found Schacht's personality, it had proved to be difficult to find him guilty.

After Taking the Stand

Dönitz, who was no friend of politicians, objected to Schacht's stance as an enemy of the regime from such an early period, and he may have been correct that Schacht implied his opposition to Hitler had started earlier than was the case. In his cell, Schacht asked Gilbert why he could not be released at once. Gilbert responded that he had helped the finances behind the war machine. Schacht sharply pointed out that despite the attacks on his character, he was only being indicted on 'planning for aggressive war' and was pleased he had caused Göring discomfort. One defendant enjoyed telling Gilbert, and no doubt others, that he could recall Schacht's wife wearing a large diamond-studded swastika and asking Hitler for his autograph. Schacht moved in his own circles and this included the company of Hassell, who observed on 1 October 1938 that Schacht was making 'biting attacks' on the regime but his 'political remarks were obscure and contradictory'.[15] Hassell was a shrewd observer of men and the times, which he later paid for with his life. He regarded Schacht as 'self-centred and hence was likely to act precipitately', and by 1941 added the comment that Schacht was 'affected by boundless personal ambition and his unreliable character'.[16] Hassell revealed that Schacht had considered or joined conversations about a coup or some form of resistance, but it was evident that he kept his distance for safety reasons.[17]

Summation, Final Statements, and Verdicts

Generally, the British favoured acquittal, the French and Americans less so, and the Russians wanted him executed. On behalf of Schacht, Dr Rudolf Dix made a somewhat emotional appeal, pointing out that sitting in the same box with Schacht was Kaltenbrunner, the head of the RSHA, and it was Schacht who been a concentration camp inmate. Here was a man, Dix argued, backed by the witness Gisevius, who was among the few to actively oppose Hitler, and unlike other counsels, demanded an acquittal.

In the prosecution summation, Schacht was referred to as the 'façade of starched respectability' who provided the window dressing of early days allowing Hitler to rearm, which inevitably made Schacht angrier than ever.[18] In his final statement, Telford Taylor thought him 'self-righteous, boastful and arrogant', but acknowledged Schacht was painfully right, admitting he had erred politically in not realising soon enough the extent of Hitler's criminal nature, but he was not the only one, and the only way forward was not through violence but 'through the strength of the spirit and morality of actions'.

Schacht had been indicted on the first two counts. The Russians wanted him dead, and Biddle wanted him in prison for life, but how far the counts were justified was questionable, and he was found not guilty and discharged. Schacht was aware of his unpopularity, especially with Jackson, and as the judgement was read out, Schacht turned to face Jackson, but he had only just evaded prison.

Post-war

The police tried to arrest Schacht in Nuremberg, but the Americans intervened, and he was allowed freedom so long as he reported to the police from time to time. Schacht then set off to his wife's home in the British zone, but made a deviation to see a friend via Württemberg and was arrested by the Stuttgart police. He remained there until April 1947 for denazification proceedings and was given eight years. His lawyers demanded an appeal and on 2 September 1948, he was again acquitted. There were further denazification efforts in Lüneburg, with a final acquittal at the end of 1950. Penniless, he wrote a book entitled *Account Settled* and sold 250,000 copies. He travelled to Indonesia to offer economic advice (landing in Tel Aviv where he was not spotted) and in 1952 was invited to Damascus for founding a central bank for Syria. He wrote another book entitled *Confessions of the Old Wizard*, but his reputation was fading.

In 1955 Schacht started a bank in Düsseldorf which he led until 1963 and gave economic and financial advice to heads of states of developing countries. He was a hired consultant for Aristotle Socrates Onassis, the Greek businessman, during the

1950s and he died in Munich on 3 June 1970. Altogether, after his arrest in July 1944, he spent the next four years in 23 prisons, both German and Allied.

Final Notes

Schacht was an arrogant and ambitious type of person and the prison tests had proved he had a high IQ. There seems little doubt that his self-assurance gave him a sense of arrogance. He evidently had many talents, but they were not as impressive as he believed, and wrote his autobiography entitled *Kleine Bekenntnisse* (*Small Confessions*) which caused many to question whether he was telling the truth about his relationship with Hitler. Schacht thought he could keep Hitler tamed as did many other conservative-minded Germans who seriously misjudged both Hitler and the Nazi regime. He had been anti-Semitic but had not descended to the evil level of extermination and the Tribunal was probably correct in acquitting him. Historically, he had been of considerable use to the early rise of Nazism, and his failure had been his inability to understand its reality until it was too late. He had been a link between the old Imperial Germany and Nazi Germany, and his effort to bring down the democratic Weimar Republic was a major error but not part of the indictments.

Walther Funk 1890–1960

Background

Walther Funk was born in East Prussia and came from a commercial family. He studied law and economics at the Humboldt University of Berlin. He joined the infantry during the Great War but was wounded and discharged as unfit in 1916. Thereafter, he started life as a journalist working for the *Berliner Börsenzeitung* ('Berlin Stock Exchange Newspaper') giving him his starting point in economics, and he was evidently a man of some talent. In 1920 he married Luise Schmidt-Sieben and was known to play the piano well. In his early days, he enjoyed card games, and was known for his social enjoyment, which was a stunning contrast to the man in the dock who had lost all his previous confidence. By 1932 he was welcomed by Hindenburg, was known to Nazi official Gregor Strasser, and Hitler appointed him to his government as Reich Press Chief in March 1933, which

Walther Funk (right) meets Franz Hayler (Acting Economic Minister). (Photographer Schwahn, Bundesarchiv 183-J30376, Licence CC-BY-SA 3.0)

had little meaning as Goebbels, the notorious propaganda expert, was rising in power. On 5 February 1938, Funk was appointed as General Plenipotentiary of Economics, replacing Schacht. Between April 1938 and March 1939, he was a director of a Swiss multi-national bank. In January 1939, Hitler appointed him as president of the *Reichsbank*, and in September of 1939, to the six-person war cabinet which never had any real substance or power, although he attended many significant meetings.

During the 1930s, he carried some influence, and often gave the address at Göring's lavish birthday parties. It was Funk who thought of the name *Kristallnacht* to describe the night of violence against the Jews. He was best known as an economist and Nazi official, who after Hitler's disagreement with Schacht became better known as Reich minister for economic affairs between 1938–45, having replaced Schacht as president of the *Reichsbank*. He has often been regarded more as the 'red tape' man with the grand title of the plenipotentiary for the war economy.

He always claimed that despite his titles and positions he held little power in the regime. It was true that as a propaganda man he was dominated by Goebbels, in economic matters by Göring, and over war-resources was subordinate first to construction engineer Fritz Todt then to Speer. However, he admitted that having little choice, he had signed the laws which Aryanised Jewish property, both personal and business, prompting Robert Jackson to call him the 'banker of gold teeth'. Schacht had called him a 'harmless homosexual and an alcoholic, drunk at his own parties'. Age had changed his looks from the young socialite, and Shirer described him as a 'greasy, shifty-eyed, paunchy little man whose face always reminded the writer of a frog'.[1]

Interrogations

As with Ribbentrop, Funk tried to utilise amnesia as a defence, though he was lucid in matters of memory unless there was an implication of criminality. As the evidence against him accumulated, he became somewhat vague, claiming as a general argument he was a minor component in a huge machine. He stated he knew nothing about the concentration camps though there was available evidence that he had visited Dachau in 1943, and he was clearly disturbed by the brutal, revealing evidence from the concentration camps. During the war years, he had written an autobiography entitled *Walther Funk, A Life for the Economy*, which the prosecution used against him. One report described him as a 'tubby homosexual suffering from diabetes, and afflicted with bladder pains', and was obviously frightened and scared of his interrogators.[2]

Medical Mental Observations

When Goldensohn started his psychiatric notes on Funk he wrote, 'Walther Funk is a little fat man, roly-poly in appearance, with an indeterminate air, given to sentimental phrases and platitudes, concerned mainly about his immediate comfort, and absorbed in his genitourinary complaints'.[3] Goldensohn appeared correct in his description as Funk was accustomed to comfort and the high life and was now in a cell desperately caught between proving himself innocent and justifying himself, claiming 'I was only a small man and I had no idea what was going on'. Funk was told that the notetaking was just personal but having lived through the Nazi regime, Funk appeared suspicious that the notes would be used by the prosecution.

Goldensohn, as usual, asked about his family, in which he heard Funk was happy enough but spent most of his youth in a formal boarding school. One brother was a prisoner of the British, and his other brother and only sister had died as children. He described his marriage as happy, but they could not have children, that his wife was not a party member and he wished he had taken her advice and remained a journalist. He described their luxury lifestyle and the looting of his properties by the Russians and Poles. He explained he loved his music, had started life as a journalist, and said he was attracted to the NSDAP because of the failure of the Weimar democratic system. He opposed communism, believing in private enterprise and that the National Socialists could restore economic stability to Germany and prevent a class struggle, expressing the hopes of many Germans.

He felt attracted by Hitler's so-called magnetism but felt the Führer needed help in economic affairs. In the early days of 1933, he was appointed chief of the news service and then Minister of Economics, swiftly pointing out that it was a 'useless position' because Göring was in charge and in 1942 Speer was 'more or less' the economic chief. He also believed that *Lebensraum* was not about conquering other countries but by finding space through trade pacts and the colonies, giving the impression he was squirming to prove his innocence. He also added that he only wanted to resolve the unemployment issue and was opposed to rearmament plans, blaming that on Fritz Todt. He claimed he was never a central figure in the 'inner circle' and was not a politician, stating, 'I was present at cabinet meetings, but I had no voice, was not a member of cabinet', which clashed with the known evidence, though he probably had little influence.

As with Fritzsche, he talked about his Jewish friends in a desperate effort to disassociate himself from the Jewish persecutions, claiming he was not a radical and could not be blamed for not foreseeing what would happen, including going to war. He acknowledged that the prosecution had a case for being part of a criminal government, that ignorance of the law was no defence, and that he had accepted SS gold into the bank, but never knew its origins. As with many others, he indicated that Nazi Germany was a state of secrets, even arguing that as a minister no one would tell him of the atrocities in case he reported them, and friends did not want to involve him. This statement alone revealed he had had some idea of what was happening. Given that he visited Dachau in 1943, these were somewhat tenuous arguments. To push him on this matter, Goldensohn asked him about his friend Otto Ohlendorf who had been associated with the *Einsatzgruppe*, but Funk evaded this by saying they never discussed the Jewish question or even politics. When Goldensohn confronted him with Dodd's evidence that he had been aware of gold dentures and gold spectacles, he found it difficult to answer and weaved the question around to 'my country, right or wrong', reminding

Goldensohn that this expression was British. The fact that gold was deposited in the bank for which he was responsible was raised but he denied knowledge; the bank was huge with many personnel, and it was probably the finance ministry. He may have been telling the truth, but Goldensohn's notes tended to paint a picture of a man ducking and weaving. He later stated that he was as guilty as any German who participated in the regime but the specific charges against him could be rebutted legally.

When questioned about the confiscation of Jewish businesses, he protested that they should have certain economic rights, and the *Kristallnacht* events had made him angry. When he protested to Goebbels, he was met by the reply that it was his fault because Funk should have removed all Jewish businesses by then. He had heard that Jews were encouraged to leave Germany but never a word about extermination. According to Goldensohn, Funk then became absorbed in self-pity as he tried to apologise for being even a minor tool in such events when he could have taken a stand. He protested he had nothing to do with forced labour and in the end days had not encouraged Hitler's scorched earth policy; all that he had done by staying on was because of his support for his nation.

In Funk's argument that he had tried to protect Jewish interests, Goldensohn suggested the anti-Semitic legislation hardly did that, to which Funk was obliged to agree saying that all he could do was hand down 'what had been given from above', thereby utilising, as with so many others, the obeying of orders defence. His main defence though tended to be painting a picture of himself as a minor functionary and suffering from a degree of amnesia. How far he was a serious defendant under the major charges was questionable. He was one of Andrus's least favourite defendants 'always whimpering and whining' and was too weak in personality to face a trial, later crying in the witness box.

Reactions during the Trial

As Neave delivered the indictments, he found Funk sitting on his bed weeping, and at one time sobbing almost beyond control, prompting Neave to describe him as a 'bald nonentity of 55', while Andrus thought him 'incapable of running a gas station'.[4] Funk told Gilbert that he 'conceded that Göring and Schacht were strong types of character, but the rest of us', by which he meant himself, were not made from 'heroic stuff'. He had asked himself, he said, what he would have done had he realised or knew at the time about the atrocities, and then cried. During Göring's trial, Funk tried to explain to Gilbert the necessity for putting Jewish property on a legal basis – the Aryanization policy. But when Gilbert described it as an attempt to give robbery a legal basis, Funk responded, 'I don't justify it in the slightest – the whole policy was wrong – I do not mean that – it was entirely unjustifiable', swaying between his beliefs of the past and the necessity of the present.[5]

After Schacht's defence, Funk explained that 'I used to have a very great respect for Schacht, but I think he has become morally discredited', somewhat agreeing with Frank who thought Schacht had been prone to exaggeration.

Funk's Trial

Many agreed that Funk's case was one of the least difficult and least interesting. As he sat in the witness box on Saturday 4 May he was a symbol of sheer pathos, weeping openly in public. He had been a significant component of the Nazi regime throughout his life, and when he had taken over Schacht's role as Minister of Economics and President of the *Reichsbank*, he had been under the control of Göring. But there was little evidence indicating that he had been involved in violent crime. He brightened up at one time as he described 'the fascinating personality of the Führer' but most of the time he was in his own world of pathos.[6]

His counsel was Dr Sauter, noted for his habit of introducing his questions in court and hinting at what the required answer should be. As with Keitel and Ribbentrop, he based the defence on Funk's limited authority, claiming that he started his Nazi life under the thumb of Goebbels then later Göring. Funk could not avoid even at his level the issue of knowing something about the policy of aggressive war and the general oppression of Jewish people. He had been at the meeting held after *Kristallnacht* to discuss the financial implications and the penalty placed on the Jewish victims for the damage, explaining to the court that 'in this matter I placed the will of the state before my conscience and my inner sense of duty because, after all, I was the servant of the state'.[7] He attempted to defend himself over the Jewish issue claiming he had helped the famous German composer Richard Strauss, but was immediately rebutted by the argument that helping a few Jewish people was irrelevant against the charge that he had signed decrees against Jews as a whole.

The difficult issue for Funk was the question of the bank receiving the gold teeth extracted from corpses. When Dodd asked him when he started to do business with the SS, Funk instantly replied, 'Business with the SS? I have never done that'.[8] There is a possible feeling on reading the original text that Funk had genuinely been caught by surprise. A witness called Emil Puhl had testified that arrangements had been made for this and other confiscated gold. Funk was examined as to how far he was aware of the arrangements which included gold spectacles and rings. Another witness called Thoms explained in detail how they were melted down, and he could see the labels of concentration camps in the supplied boxes. Telford Taylor recalled Funk's sense of panic as Dodd during the cross-examination demonstrated that Funk's bank received stolen gold, including the extracted gold teeth.[9] The Puhl episode caused Funk to shout and claim the affidavit Puhl had produced was untrue. The film showing the gold teeth in the bank was claimed by Puhl to have been done for the benefit of the film, and it was soon apparent to the court that both Puhl and Thoms were more interested in their own safety than that of Funk. Curiously, in the course of Höss's testimony during Kaltenbrunner's trial, Höss had explained they melted down all the gold which was then sent to the SS offices in Berlin.[10]

Dodd's cross-examination was well prepared with evidentiary documentation. He added that in 1942 the Ministry of Economics had looted French assets and Funk's activities were not as harmless as he liked to portray. It struck some that Funk was genuine in his denunciation of anti-Semitism, that *Kristallnacht* although morally repugnant was not a war crime, that Funk's involvement in SS bank deposits was too vague, and the evidence in terms of the indictments was there but somewhat scanty. It could be counter-argued that *Kristallnacht* was a crime against humanity such was the barbarity of that episode. Funk in the witness box had not helped himself against the rather flimsy case, and his witnesses failed him the minute their evidence was presented.

Summation, Final Statements, and Verdicts

Having heard some summation speeches, it appeared to prompt Funk towards a sense of shame regarding the immorality of both the political and military leadership. He felt so depressed he told Gilbert that he was the only person to make him feel like a human being. He admitted his own conscience bothered him when he reflected on the moments that he had signed laws for taking Jewish property, which he considered morally wrong but not necessarily illegal, but wished he had listened to his wife who had suggested he simply retired from politics.

His counsel Dr Sauter announced that his summation would be 'dry and prosaic' which reflected Funk's defence which had, after the cross-examination, left him vulnerable, especially over the issue of extracted gold teeth. But the psychological state of the man made it clear he could not be regarded as a murderer. In the prosecution summation, it was pointed out that Funk had accelerated the pace of rearmament and as the *Reichsbank* president had accepted the SS gold including tooth-fillings, making it the most 'ghoulish collateral in banking history'. It was later added that he was a banker who did not know what was going in and out of his own bank.[11] If true, the gold teeth linked him without question to the extermination programme. As such, the gold-teeth episode was the spanner in the works and obsessed Funk, who in his final statement talked about this, complaining that others had not kept him informed. He acknowledged that he had allowed himself to be deceived too easily, but he considered himself free from criminal guilt.

On the day of judgement, Funk stood facing all four counts, but he was declared guilty only on counts two to four. The Tribunal added that despite holding important offices, he 'was never a dominant figure in the various programmes ... this is a mitigating fact of which the tribunal takes notice' which gave Funk some hope he would not be executed.[12] The hope was fulfilled when his sentence was announced, but he was shaken to be given a life sentence. He considered it too long and down in the cells expressed his anger. He was held in Spandau Prison but was released on 16 May 1957 because of ill-health and died three years later in Düsseldorf from diabetes.

Final Notes

Funk may have held many grand titles but he was obviously a weak character and subservient to superior orders of which there is the occasional hint that he knew them to be immoral. He was anti-Semitic but the reality of the extermination process seemed to have come as a shock, and it is difficult to know how far he was evasive and how much he knew. There remains the issue of the gold teeth in his bank, given that the film may just have been concocted, that the melting of the gold was probably done elsewhere, and if not, whether he as president of the bank would have known this while his witnesses were saving their own necks at his expense. In his memoirs, Fritzsche queried the truth behind the gold teeth saga, and it was later suggested that the objects had been found in the Merkers salt mines.[13]

He was quintessentially the red tape figure of bureaucracy and not a major player, a 'yes-man' and a flunky, and therefore guilty. Nevertheless, he played his part, and the consequences shook him, revealing his weakness of character. Many thought a life sentence was too long, but he was released early on compassionate grounds.

Karl Dönitz 1891–1980

Background

Karl Dönitz began his naval career in the Imperial Navy, starting as an observer with a seaplane squadron, but by 1916 was commander of U-boat 68, sunk by the British near Malta. He was imprisoned where it is claimed he thought of *Rudeltaktik* – pack tactics. During the interbellum years when U-boats were banned, he commanded torpedo boats as part of the *Reichsmarine*, and in 1934 commanded the cruiser *Emden*. In 1916 he married his wife Ingeborg (daughter of the German General Erich Weber) and had two sons and a daughter raised as Protestants; both sons were killed during the 1939–45 conflict.

Dönitz. (UK Government in public domain)

At the start of World War II, he was the senior U-boat officer in the *Kriegsmarine*. It was his planning of the attack on the *Royal Oak* in Scapa Flow in October 1939 which brought him attention and he was promoted from commodore to rear-admiral. He replaced Raeder in January 1943 and was promoted to Grand Admiral. Following Hitler's death, he became head of what had been called the 'Flensburg government' (dissolved by the Allies on 23 May 1945) and ordered Jodl to sign the surrender documents at Reims.

There are varying opinions about Dönitz and his relationship with the Nazi regime, appearing as a passionate admirer of Hitler and his ideology at one glance yet according to some he stood up to Hitler. Dönitz, unlike the army generals, tended to be regarded as non-political, but a survey of the surviving documents makes this questionable. On 12 March 1944, he read a message to the German nation stating, 'what would have become of our country today if the Führer had not united us under National Socialism?'[1] This sounded too optimistic even for March 1942 and being read two years later many could have regarded it as cynical. He tried to conceal any knowledge of the Jewish issue as noted in his interviews, but in October 1943, it was claimed he was at the Posen Conference when Himmler mentioned mass extermination, though he may not have been present at Himmler's session. There was a possibility he was anti-Semitic but there persists that vacuum of uncertainty as to how deep his personal animosity ran. There was some uncertainty about including him on the list of defendants because the British Admiralty found nothing to condemn, and when compared to the army and *Luftwaffe*, 'the German navy came much closer to following the rules of chivalry'.[2]

When the U-boat war turned against Germany in 1943, Dönitz's main preoccupation was fighting the Bolshevik threat and he sent 50,000 sailors to fight on the Eastern Front who had no army experience. It has also been claimed that he tended to associate the alien Bolshevism with Jewry. Jackson was keen on indicting Dönitz on the grounds that he had taken over Hitler's role in the so-called farce of the Flensburg government. In taped conversations between senior German officers, this was also the main point of criticism against Dönitz.[3]

Interrogations

Both at the time and since, Dönitz appearing as a defendant raised many eyebrows among his old enemies because his conduct as an admiral hardly differed from that of his enemy opposite numbers, and his selection as successor to the Führer was an unwelcome surprise to this non-political man. The U-boat war had been deadly, underhand, at times merciless and cruel, yet was exercised in the same way by all belligerents. It is popular even to this day in the film industry to show scenes of U-boats gunning survivors in the water, but there was only one known case of such behaviour.* Various naval historians have uncovered many incidents where U-boat commanders went to extreme lengths to assist survivors. One such incident was when U-boat 156, under the command of *Kapitänleutnant* Werner Hartenstein, sank the liner *Laconia*, not realising the vessel carried passengers including Italian prisoners of war. Hartenstein started a massive rescue, risked a radio message asking for help and was promptly attacked. Consequently, Dönitz issued what is known as his '*Laconia* Order' – an order not to stop and help survivors.

Interned U-boat commanders had sent an affidavit to Sir Geoffrey Lawrence, the British judge, stating Dönitz had never issued orders about killing survivors, and he

---

* This one verifiable incident of a U-boat commander firing on survivors related to a *Kapitänleutnant* Heinz Wilhelm Eck of U-boat 852 when he sank the Greek freighter SS *Peleus* in the South Atlantic. His excuse was that he did not want the enemy to find the debris and evidence of his whereabouts.

had the courtesy to let Dönitz know about this communication. A visiting American admiral had also conveyed his greetings to Dönitz during the trial and had left a message that he held the German admiral in the 'highest esteem'. He explained that if a U-boat were in any danger, it had a duty to leave the scene at once: it was no different from enemy submarine code of conduct.

Medical Mental Observations

It was interesting to note that when Dönitz met one of the psychiatrists, he proved to speak excellent English, and that he was 'polite, affable in a half-suspicious way … but must be given his own reins or he shuts up with this mouth firmly compressed'.[4] He was a man used to being in command and confused as to why he was indicted. He queried why the trial was trying to criminalise organisations which meant huge chunks of the population would become criminals. It was explained to him that the prosecutors were only after the leaders, but Dönitz had a valid point. He said he would retire and write a book to clarify to the German population how little the military leaders knew about Hitler and Himmler, a phenomenon he explained which was more possible in Germany than America.

The psychiatrist Goldensohn seemed to be able to converse with Dönitz with greater ease than the formal interrogator had done, as he talked of his early inexperience of U-boats. Later, he stated that he believed the Führer had selected him as commander of U-boats because he was a non-political person, which was the only reason he accepted the post. It was also evident that Dönitz had an aversion towards Austrians and Bavarians as they were more prone to be extremist. In a later conversation, he added that he had watched the various English people and noted that some were like north Germans and some like Bavarians. He was also averse to the Führer principle (*Führerprinzip*) on the grounds that every person needed some form of 'corrective'.

When asked about the future, he avoided the ever-emerging communist issue and spoke of a united Europe under British protection. This was a similar view to others such as Schacht and suggestive that it reflected times when the defendants had discussed such issues with one another. In the same vein, he blamed the Nazi rise to power on the Versailles Treaty and during the trials paid little heed to the atrocities on the grounds this was to do with the SS and not him. In a later interview with the psychiatrist, he stated that Soviet Russia was a criminal nation. Later, he pointed out that the Russians were taking some of his submarine designers, making it clear that he had no trust in the Soviet Union.

It was only during the proceedings that he claimed he had learnt of the persecution of the Jews. Like many, he may have heard rumours of the early concentration camps but as a totally dedicated naval man he was one of the few who may have possibly had some justification in a degree of ignorance. When pushed on the question of anti-Semitism, he pointed out that one of his vice-admirals called Bernhard Rogge was Jewish, along with many others. Rogge had written an affidavit on his behalf, and he claimed he had resisted calls from Hitler about having Jews in the navy.

Despite Airey Neave and many others finding him severe and somewhat forbidding, and Andrus thinking him 'imperious', the psychiatrist Dr Kelly reported he had a sense of humour and spent most of his time improving his English. He always declined to pass opinions on other defendants, claiming it was not his place to pass judgement, and each man must be responsible for his own past. All he wanted was to return to his wife, his daughter, and her three children, his two sons having been killed in naval actions.

Reactions during the Trial

Following the 29 November 1945 showing of the concentration camp documentary film, Dönitz was visibly shaken wondering how people had expected him to know such things. When Göring had been isolated from the others and Dönitz's lunch companions were the elderly conservative civilians, it was noted that the resistance to Göring was less obvious, although Dönitz being a military man was less affected. By the end of February 1946, it was clear to Gilbert that Göring's social absence was having a marked effect on Dönitz who was now admitting that after hearing the evidence of the atrocities, 'it was necessary to get to the bottom' of everything. During Keitel's trial, Dönitz held some hopes initially as Keitel explained his position as a military man, but when he creaked under Maxwell Fyfe's cross-examination Dönitz was annoyed at his weakness. During the Easter recess, Dönitz expressed the opinion that it was all very well for men like Schacht – who had openly called Göring a 'blustering windbag' – to be on 'their high-horses' as politicians, but they made the policies and soldiers and sailors had to do the fighting.

During the Frick trial, when Gisevius had given witness about Göring's involvement in all the dirty dealings (especially Generals Blomberg and Fritsch), Dönitz told Gilbert that the witness could keep talking because it 'showed how the politicians got themselves in a hole and then expected the generals to pull them out'.[5] It was becoming a major battle between the military and political defendants.

Dönitz took the stand on Wednesday 8 May 1946, the day of surrender a year before which led to a brief discussion between him and Gilbert who asked him what he had learnt during the year. Dönitz responded by saying he was 100,000 years wiser, but he could not have 'acted any differently' which was the basis of his defence.

Dönitz's Trial

When Dönitz and later Raeder appeared in the dock they always appeared well dressed and dignified compared to the other defendants. Dönitz's image was further enhanced by his counsel Otto Kranzbuehler equally well presented, often wearing his naval uniform as the German Navy was not yet dissolved for the practical reasons of mine-clearance. Kranzbuehler, one of the best counsels, was a naval lawyer and with Dönitz they were on firm grounds over naval technicalities, plans, and what had happened. He was also assisted by Hans Meckel who had been Dönitz's former Staff Officer Communications; of all the defences, this one was the most equipped with detailed technical knowledge. Kranzbuehler endeared himself to the Bench with his polite and discreet ways as well as the power of his arguments, basing all his requests on justified legal grounds. Kranzbuehler was also helped by the knowledge that the navy did not have the same reputation as the SS, the *Wehrmacht* and the *Luftwaffe*, and the courtroom had many Allied naval uniforms among the spectators interested in this case. Maxwell Fyfe, who later praised Kranzbuehler for his professionalism, knew he had to tread carefully in naval matters and being highly qualified himself, managed to conduct this part of the trial to everyone's admiration.

When Kranzbuehler asked him about Hitler and whether he considered disasso-ciating himself from the dictator, Dönitz promptly replied, 'I was strictly limited to my own department, since it was a peculiarity of the Führer to listen to a person only about matters which were that person's express concern'.[6] Dönitz's opening defence lines were based on the conduct of the U-boat warfare, orders he had received from Raeder, but the attack-without-warning orders were no different from those of the British. The major issues revolved around several critical themes, the first being the London Submarine Protocol of 1936 of not attacking until crew and passengers were safe. It was first clear the *Kriegsmarine* had broken the agreement but so had the British and Americans. Secondly, in terms of war, it was a nonsensical demand for submarines to surface and declare their intentions or for their own boat's safety. Earlier, in March, Kranzbuehler had sent the American Admiral Chester Nimitz an interrogation form, and later during Dönitz's trial, it was returned confirming that the Americans had deployed the same policy and it was well known the British had as well. It became an issue of *tu quoque* but Kranzbuehler with careful consideration based his defence on the ambiguity of the London Protocol. *Tu quoque* had never been an acceptable defence in court, but Dönitz's case was uncomfortable. Kranzbuehler avoided any unpleasant clashes by deliberately not using *tu quoque* but instead talked of the naval issues which faced both sides. There was a tussle between Kranzbuehler and Maxwell Fyfe on the documents which could be presented relating to the legal restraints appertaining to naval warfare. Kranzbuehler argued that the British, by demanding neutral ships to have 'navicerts' from a British consul to confirm what they were carrying, had introduced a 'new law', then raised the argument of American violations of neutrality before the USA declared war, which he claimed justified some German reactions. Dönitz also added that British merchant ships were radioing the whereabouts of U-boats. They were often armed and prepared to open fire, but further claimed they were only attacked when in the designated zones.

The second major issue was the supposed order to kill survivors. Two U-boat commanders had previously given evidence that Dönitz had given such orders. The first was Lieutenant Peter Heisig who had heard Dönitz lecture as a young man and probably had misunderstood what Dönitz was saying. The second was Captain Karl Moehle who was equally weak as a witness, because he had been captured and accused of issuing the *Laconia* Order; he was regarded as 'saving his own neck' and not reliable. Dönitz said in court that he 'regretted that Moehle did not find occasion to clarify these doubts immediately'.[7]*

After the *Laconia* incident mentioned above, when Hartenstein had surfaced to help survivors and had been attacked by American bombers, Dönitz sent the message that 'no attempt of any kind must be made at rescuing members of ships sunk … rescue runs counter to the elementary demands of warfare for the destruction of enemy ships and crews'.[8] The prosecution used this last sentence as proof which Dönitz quite understandably claimed was a misreading. There was a general impression that Dönitz was sincere concerning the *Laconia* incident and had supported the U-boat's humane efforts.[9] There had been only the one established case of a U-boat committing the crime of firing on survivors (mentioned above, namely *Kapitänleutnant* Heinz Wilhelm Eck of U-boat 852), and the main perpetrators were executed by the Allies. Later, post-war historical investigation produced many examples of U-boats surfacing when safe to give any support they could for men swimming for their lives, and in this court, one of the witnesses (see below) pointed out times when a U-boat had motored towards the sinking vessel to offer aid only for the vessel to fire upon the U-boat.

Dönitz was challenged on the number of times he met Hitler, intimating he was closer to the Führer than he pretended. He rebutted this by pointing out that the claimed 120 times he had met Hitler was due to naval conferences which would be normal for him to attend, as in any other country. He said he was a patriot and a sailor, and he had always refused to hand over seditious sailors to the People's Court, indicating he considered himself non-political. Whether he was non-political or not could be regarded as an ongoing debate, with some claiming he was disingenuous, others he was politically naïve, and some accepting his claim.

In another session, Dönitz described Germany as surrounded by enemies and noted that anyone attempting a coup in wartime would be a traitorous act, which was a dig at Schacht, pleasing Göring, and worrying Speer. He continued his theme that his U-boat warfare was no different from the enemy, which was basically true. During his cross-examination by Maxwell Fyfe, Dönitz made it clear he was not interested whether foreign labour built his U-boats or not; all he needed were as many as possible. When questioned on whether he agreed with shooting prisoners, Dönitz answered he did not 'agree now' but was somewhat evasive on this issue.

---

* Moehle was sentenced to five years for passing on the *Laconia* Order; he died in 1996.

In the next session, Maxwell Fyfe pinned him down on the requisitioning of some 12,000 concentration camp victims as part of his workforce. Maxwell Fyfe spent considerable time on the Führer Conferences, seeking an opening that proved Dönitz was more involved in the government than he had previously intimated. The British prosecutor returned with more success to the use of concentration camp labour, raising the issue of a dockyard strike in Copenhagen where Dönitz had transmitted Hitler's message to 'deal with terror by terror' over which Dönitz was somewhat evasive if not confused. In terms of the *Athenia* (the British passenger liner sunk by Fritz Julius Lemp in U-boat 30 on 3 September 1939), Dönitz acknowledged there had been a cover-up but by a higher authority.

Kranzbuehler summoned three other naval witnesses who were called to question the validity of the two U-boat commanders who had 'misread' Dönitz's orders following the *Laconia* debacle. There were lengthy discussions on this subject, not helped by the confusion of dates and timings. In the final analysis, the prosecution case was weakened by relying on the one case of the bungling U-boat *Kapitänleutnant* Eck of U-boat 852 who had ordered survivors to be shot. It was also helpful for Dönitz when Admiral Nimitz's reply was entered into the proceedings albeit late in the day, which gave Dönitz a real sense of hope.

The witnesses Admirals Gerhardt Wagner and Eberhard Godt gave support, and even Dönitz's son-in-law, Captain Günter Hessler, explained the training naval officers received in terms of measuring whether a ship should be attacked. It was Hessler who pointed out that a sinking ship often fired on a U-boat as it was coming to help (mentioned above). Everyone knew that the British Admiralty was unhappy about the case against Dönitz, who also received the stunning support of Admiral Nimitz thanks to the interrogatory form sent to him by Kranzbuehler.

One accusation levelled against Dönitz was when Hitler had designated him as head of state but the war continued. Following a discussion with Jodl, he explained why it was necessary to delay surrender, stating that had they capitulated too early, 'two million soldiers in the East would have fallen into Russian hands'.[10] Given the developing friction with Stalin's regime, this must have rung bells that some two million men would have been at the mercy of the Russians; 'having saved life of this scale it made Dunkirk look a very minor achievement'.[11] As a general impression, most of the prosecution charges in naval matters were well defended as was Dönitz's continuation of the war for the safety of German troops. There were, however, difficult questions about the use of slave labour and the shooting of prisoners of war which were not easily resolved and thus cast a shadow.

After Taking the Stand

Dönitz was pleased that Allied naval officers, including Admiral Nimitz, had shown him support, and some were in attendance during his trial. He also argued that he favoured the western side by moving the fleet in their direction. He warned Gilbert that the Russians were busy seeking Germany's latest U-boat technology, especially their development of a submarine which did not have to surface, being equipped with an extended pipe which could draw down sufficient oxygen for its batteries; it was fast and was known as the X U-boat. He was playing on the fear of Russian dominance which was emerging as the Cold War.

It was clear during Raeder's trial that there was no love lost between Dönitz and Raeder, but try as he may Gilbert could gather no reaction on this aspect of their lives. Dönitz explained somewhat lamely that he and Raeder were not friends because Raeder was some 16 years older, and he was more interested in talking about Admiral Nimitz's support. He was deep down smarting at a reference in Raeder's trial referring to him 'as Hitler's boy', especially when he had become head of state for a few days.

During the Schirach trial, Dönitz pointed out the anti-Church policy of the Hitler Youth. But he had brought up his children as Christians and they had joined the Hitler Youth; his two sons were killed in battle as good soldiers and Christians. He then launched his habitual attack on Frick and the politicians.

Summation, Final Statements, and Verdicts

Kranzbuehler on behalf of Dönitz pointed out that in naval matters, there were two issues: the unlawful sinking of ships and the killing of survivors. He skilfully summarised the main arguments covered in the defence and made much of Nimitz's support of Dönitz. He also emphasised that during the early years, Dönitz held a junior rank and had a limited range of authority.

The prosecution summation addressed Dönitz as the 'legatee of defeat' and allowed his U-boat commanders the freedom to act as if they were in the jungle.[12] Shawcross was especially vitriolic, referring to the sinking of the *Laconia* as brutal, even though the attacking U-boat had spent two days rescuing survivors and had been attacked during these efforts.

In his final words to the court, Dönitz not only denied any criminality or that he had made any mistakes, but also stated that he would 'have done the same all over again'. He repeated his main themes that the German U-boat warfare had been honourable, that the conspiracy charge was mere political dogma, and as the last technical head of state, he took full responsibility.

Dönitz had been charged under counts one, two, and three but was only convicted under counts two and three. He had received support both from the British Admiralty and the Americans, the British seeing the German naval war as almost chivalrous. Count one was put aside as he had not been privy to the higher-level discussions relating to any conspiracy to wage aggressive war. As such, count two was something of a surprise in being active in waging aggressive war, because on these grounds all senior military officers could be convicted for following their duties. Behind the scenes, there was considerable debate regarding Dönitz, and at one stage Biddle wanted him acquitted, but there was formidable opposition to this view.

In the verdicts, Dönitz was given 10 years which was the lightest sentence, with many thinking he should have been acquitted. Later, he was puzzled by the sentence, reminding others that he had received the support of the British Admiralty and the American navy. In his appeal against the sentence, Kranzbuehler pointed out that Dönitz had not been found guilty of planning aggressive war, nor crimes at sea, and asking what merited 10 years in prison.

Post-war

Having been sentenced to 10 years, he tended to mix with Neurath and Schirach in Spandau Prison, remaining hostile towards Raeder after his reported pronouncements in Moscow about Dönitz. His wife Ingeborg complained of poverty as Dönitz's pension was set at pre-Hitler appointment levels, though this was later restored.[13] She had been working as a nursing sister in a Hamburg hospital. He was released on 1 October 1956 and retired to Aumühle (north-west Germany) where he worked on two books, his *Memoirs: Ten Years and Twenty Days*, and another *My Ever-Changing Life* dealing with his times before 1934. He was helped by his son-in-law, Günter Hessler, who had access to archives held by the British.

The discussion on the *Laconia* incident continued, and on 13 February 1959, a Captain Stephen Roskill wrote that in this affair, 'Dönitz and his crews were doubtless largely in the right'.[14] For his part, Dönitz argued that the trial should have been a German affair, but the post-Great War trials at Leipzig had not given much confidence in repeating this effort because they had proved to be an international catastrophe. The ex-navy and BBC commentator Ludovic Kennedy interviewed him, recalling his first impression as 'how small he was, in repose like a wizened nut, in conversation like a virile old ferret'.[15]

In May 1962, the same month in which he had lost his two sons, Ingeborg died, by which time Dönitz had become a convinced Christian. He died in 1980, and many attended his funeral (6 January 1981). The new German government allowed no military honours, no uniforms, but in attendance were over 100 holders of the 'Knight's Cross of the Iron Cross'.

Final Notes

Many have often queried as to whether the charge on count two was right in the first place. Telford Taylor and many others at the time and since have wondered whether he should have been acquitted.[16] Even in 1946 it was regarded by many as a matter of naval honour and after the trial Dönitz and Raeder had a hundred or more British and American naval officers deploring their verdicts.[17] The view that Dönitz was a gentlemanly naval officer was, according to Neave, 'ingenuous'.[18] Not everyone disagreed, but in the words of one of his biographers, 'It is extremely difficult, if not impossible, to discover from the language on what grounds these guilty verdicts were brought', with which this writer tends to concur given the universal brutality of submarine warfare and Dönitz's support of helping the *Laconia* survivors.[19] However, it also seemed clear that he had been content to use slave labour and concentration camp victims in building U-boats, albeit that he was not involved in the extermination policy and deplored this action.

Erich Raeder 1876–1960

Background

Erich Raeder joined the Imperial Navy in 1894 (making him the second oldest defendant) and rose rapidly in rank becoming chief of staff to Admiral Franz von Hipper in 1912. He married his first wife Augusta in 1903. They had three children, but the relationship was strained, and they divorced in 1919. He tended to be puritanical and felt ashamed by this domestic discord, but married Erika in 1920, and had one daughter. Erika died in 1959, a year before Raeder.

Raeder. (Photographer Ernst Sandau Jr, Bundesarchiv 146-1980-128-63, Licence CC-BY-SA 3.0)

He was fluent in Russian and was sent to the Far East to observe the Russo-Japanese War of 1904–05. While staying as Hipper's chief of staff, he had combat experience at the battle of Dogger Bank (1915) and the battle of Jutland (1916), and near the end of the war received a major promotion as deputy to Admiral Paul Behncke, playing a major role in trying to suppress the German naval revolt. Following the failure of the Kapp *putsch* (an attempt to overthrow the fledgling Weimar Republic), he worked in the archives where he helped in writing the German naval history during the Great War, including a book entitled *Cruiser warfare in foreign waters*. Thereafter, his rise continued and was appointed a vice admiral in 1925. As a point of interest, it was Raeder who cashiered Heydrich for having an affair with a young woman.

Hitler had assured Raeder there would be no war until 1944 and Raeder had hoped to construct a fleet able to take on the Royal Navy. But with the speed of events, this was unattainable. Nevertheless, he was promoted to grand admiral. Without a major fleet, he had to resort to stop-gap measures and short-term policies, and his policy of attacking British merchant fleet routes was initially regarded as successful. He needed airpower but there was constant rivalry between Raeder and Göring which meant there was no progress in this vital area. With the sinking of the German battleship the *Bismarck*, Hitler seemed to lose his nerve at the embarrassment of losing major battleships. When the pocket battleship *Lützow* and the cruiser *Admiral Hipper* failed to destroy a convoy in December 1942, Hitler wanted the major surface ships decommissioned. Raeder resigned (or perhaps was resigned) and given the post as the navy's inspector general. His parting words to Hitler were, 'protect the interests of the navy, and my successor against Göring'. He was correct in this acerbic comment because it was rapidly becoming recognised that ships needed aerial support.

The interrogators and medical interviewers found him somewhat difficult and uncooperative, Gilbert finding him removed and difficult in conversation. Raeder was unused to being questioned, was detached, and at times aloof, not wanting to discuss any matter. Raeder was hardly recorded by the various observers during the trial, but he was noted for his incredulity in Kaltenbrunner's defence of not knowing about the massacres and not being responsible for any participation in crimes.

Raeder's Trial

Raeder's counsel was Dr Walter Siemers, and because Dönitz's lawyer had dealt with the issue of sinking ships without warning, this was not discussed, although Raeder was equally guilty under this specific but questionable charge. Some may have thought Raeder's case could be dealt with more swiftly, but this was not the case because Raeder had held a top military post over a long period of time, and his lawyer, unaccustomed to the Anglo-American legal system, tended to offer too many explanations while the elderly Raeder tended to 'ramble'. Raeder admitted that in the early stages he had been impressed by Hitler as had other officers in the light of the hated Versailles restrictions. He also acknowledged he was aware of Hitler's aggressive attitude but added in defence that he had been unaware of his intentions of planning war. He had also accepted Hitler's statement there would be no war with Britain, which Hitler may have hoped for as well. Raeder also claimed with some justification that he had opposed the war against Soviet Russia.

The case against Raeder was conducted by prosecutor Elwyn Jones using captured German documents which testified that Raeder had persuaded Hitler to give the orders to attack Norway to expand the German coastal area, establishing his culpability under counts one and two. Raeder's defence was that the Germans were only trying to beat the British to Norway. This was challenged as patently false, but it was embarrassing, as the German defence knew that some venture of this nature was planned, and although denied by the British, they had considered, not so much invading Norway, but had mined their waters and considered possible strategies for occupying their ports. The Norwegians had been justifiably concerned about German intentions, but they were equally concerned that Britain's interference would increase their dilemma, provoking the very war they feared. When the German invasion eventually happened in April 1940, 'the King of Norway when told asked "who was invading?"'[1] Naturally, the British Foreign Office was reluctant to release documents on this issue, but Raeder was convinced that through the 'offices of Admiral Canaris that the British intended to occupy bases in Norway' with some justification in this information.[2] The defence posed the vexed question as to whether this was a preventative war to stop the British. Documents proved that Britain had looked to occupy ports and even airports, but the Tribunal saw no evidence of British occupying troops, and 'that the expectations of Germany at the time of launching the invasion did not as a matter of fact include a belief that Britain was about to launch troops into Norway'.[3] The German claim was made that Norway was a preventative measure, but it was countered by the observation that 'it must be remembered that preventative action in foreign territory is justified, only in the case of instant and overwhelming necessity for self-defence'.[4] It was not recalled that during the Phoney War Britain and France were desperate to enter neutral Belgium but resisted until invited and when it was too late.

Raeder's defence (Wednesday 15 May 1946) started with the effort to build up the navy because of the threat from Poland and arming merchantmen. In his next session, Raeder claimed Hitler did not want to compete with the British naval rearmament, thereby the Naval Pact of 1935 which preserved the three-to-one ratio, which was a breach of the Versailles Treaty by both sides. He raised the Hossbach Memorandum having been present on the occasion but denied its aggressive intentions. On the Friday morning session, Raeder described the plans for attacking Czechoslovakia and Poland as mere security measures. When the sinking of the liner *Athenia* was raised, he admitted that it had been a mistake, and he had been annoyed at the cover-up, especially the claim that Churchill had organised it for propaganda purposes. He explained how Fritzsche had informed him that Hitler had ordered the news of the sinking to appear in the paper *Völkischer Beobachter* and concluded that Hitler had lied about Churchill using it as propaganda. Schacht cleverly summarised Raeder's defence by stating that 'he disapproved of aggressive war and was deceived by Hitler, but he planned and began the aggressive war just the same—that's a militarist for you'.[5]

On the morning session of Saturday 18 May, Raeder explained how he and Hitler had advised the Japanese to attack Singapore to keep America out of the war but had known nothing about Pearl Harbor. He then described the breakdown in his relationship with Hitler and his resignation, not least because he considered Hitler unreasonable, to which Dönitz was heard exclaiming 'crap'.

The evidence on war crimes was scanty but Maxwell Fyfe disclosed that Raeder had passed on the Commando Order – authorising the execution of Allied commandoes, even in uniform – to naval headquarters without questioning its validity. When his two witnesses from the late 1920s were called, they were not helpful as under cross-examination they both stated that as soon as Hitler came to power, they knew it meant aggressive war, thereby implying Raeder should have had the same perception.

Maxwell Fyfe raised the embarrassing statements Raeder had made to the Russians during his interrogations about Göring concerning the Blomberg and Fritsch affairs, which confirmed the witness statements by Gisevius, and caused Raeder more embarrassment that he had been aware in his senior position of this 'frame-up'. His open statements to the Russians about fellow defendants caused problems, not least with Dönitz. Those who had found themselves in Russian captivity had been more prepared to disclose the details of the past with the image of the Lubyanka being as sinister as Gestapo headquarters in Berlin. Maxwell Fyfe also challenged him on the Hossbach Memorandum suggesting Raeder must have been aware of Hitler's intentions, causing Dönitz to 'look at the clock as though hoping to be saved by the bell'.[6] Raeder came across as a major player on the scene but not as implicated as some others in the barbarities.

After Taking the Stand

Gilbert found Raeder 'overstimulated' by the cross-examination but relieved it was over, and for the first time he talked a little more to his visitor. He explained that in Moscow he had been promised that if he gave the facts, he would not be tried as a war criminal and thinking the Russians as 'fine people' would not lie out of political reasons. He felt assured that he would not have to confront the 'others' as a war criminal. He described the Russians as friendly but warned they wanted to control Europe having sacrificed so much during the war, with Gilbert noting how popular the game of playing the West against the East had become. Raeder concluded this conversation by stating that he knew he would be executed but hoped it would be by shooting and not hanging.

Gilbert managed to obtain a copy of Raeder's Moscow confession which had been refused admission in court, but it was read by many of the defendants and, according to Gilbert, strained many of the military relationships.[7] Dönitz said little but was obviously annoyed, as was Keitel.

Summation, Final Statements, and Verdicts

Raeder's counsel Dr Siemers appeared to lack the presentation skills of Dönitz's counsel, and his summation was a recount of the main defence deployed by

Raeder – the British intentions in the Norway question. He never mentioned that Raeder had approached Hitler because of his wishes of extending Germany's coastal facilities. He also omitted any reference to the Danish occupation which held no British interests at the time. He avoided dealing with the issue of the Commando Order where British prisoners had been executed in the port of Bordeaux. He used the same dubious defence that Hitler made all the orders and finished by asking that his client be acquitted on all the charges.

Raeder was referred to as the 'political animal' in the prosecution summation who in defiance of the Versailles Treaty built up the German Navy and used it in aggressive war.[8] In his final statement, Raeder could add little as Dönitz's defence had done the task well, and he ignored the Norwegian issue. He stated that if he had incurred any guilt this was mainly 'in the sense that in spite of my purely military position I should perhaps have been not only a soldier, but also up to a certain point a politician, which, however, was in contradiction to my entire career and the tradition of the German armed forces'.[9] During the quiet period of September, Raeder was visited by his son and daughter, but his wife could not visit because she was still in Russian confinement. Despite pleas to Rudenko, she was not allowed to visit.

When it came to the final judgement, although he had disagreed with Hitler, he was found guilty on counts one and two and because of the British commandoes shot in Bordeaux under the Commando Order, he was also found guilty under count three. In the verdict, Raeder escaped execution and was given a life sentence, but made it clear he preferred death and had expected execution.

Post-war

His wife was assisted by veterans to have him freed, but it took ill-health for this to happen on 26 September 1955. He wrote his post-war autobiography (*Mein Leben*) using a ghostwriter, and it has since been produced in English.[10] It was in this book that he announced that he had first heard of Nazi atrocities when he had visited an old colleague who had been disfigured after a short spell in a concentration camp. He also claimed that he had shown his protest by not wearing the Nazi Golden Party Badge, which by any account, sounds weak and dubious. He died in Kiel on 6 November 1960, a year after his second wife, and was buried in the North Cemetery of Kiel.

Final Notes

Erich Raeder belonged to the old Imperial Germany and to all appearances accepted the changes of government 'as one of those things'. Because of his prominent position, he would have been aware of the planned impending war and looking for a return to the Imperial Germany of military success. With his maritime responsibility, he was undoubtedly interested in the long Norwegian coastline if he was going to have any success against his old adversary, the British Navy. Although he was not at all involved in the barbarity of the extermination camps, he probably knew something about their cruelty as he later hinted in his memoirs and was well aware of the Commando Order. Like his army colleagues, he regarded his life as one of duty and following orders. He did, however, have the good fortune to fall out with Hitler, leading to his dismissal. He was the oldest defendant, belonging to the traditional imperial class and thereby lacked a degree of independent thinking, but he must have been aware of the Nazi regime's immoral behaviour. A sentence of imprisonment was more justified than hanging, but many believe, probably rightly, that a life sentence was too harsh.

Baldur von Schirach 1907–76

Hitler, Bormann, Göring and Schirach at Obersalzberg, 1936 (*Bundesarchiv* B 145: F051620-0043, Licence CC-BY-SA 3.0)

Background

Baldur von Schirach was educated in Weimar and was attracted to the Nazi Party as early as 1924. He claimed he developed his anti-Semitism by listening to men like Streicher, Rosenberg, and Sauckel, but later said this bigotry was based on Henry Ford's book *My Life and Work*, which was unlikely. He joined the Nazi Student League and attracted Hitler's attention, and in 1931 he was made Reich Youth Leader and then elevated in 1933 to the head of the *Hitler-Jugend* (Hitler Youth), becoming a minor government official. Other youth organisations were encouraged to join, otherwise they were dissolved or abolished, and by 1939, membership was compulsory. Affiliation to the Hitler Youth started at the age of 10, known as *Pimpf*, and at 14 years they became full members, the *Jungfolk*.

He was close to Hitler in the early days and with his wife Henriette (the daughter of Hitler's official photographer) was often a guest of Hitler. They had four children, but she divorced him during his later imprisonment in Spandau. He was for a brief time elected to the Reichstag and on being made head of the Hitler Youth took the rank of SA *Gruppenführer* and made a 'secretary' in 1936. He served in the army during the invasion of France, was promoted to lieutenant and awarded for his bravery. On 8 August 1940 he succeeded Josef Bürckel as *Gauleiter* in Vienna until the end of the war where he lived in luxury with nearly 20 servants. His notoriety increased as he was held responsible for deporting Jews from Vienna to the eastern camps. It is known, however, that Richard Strauss, with his son and family, moved to Vienna to seek Schirach's protection. It is also known that he protested at the treatment of the Jews and clashed with Hitler in 1943 but remained in post. His wife had also spoken to Hitler about the treatment of the Jews which was courageous. It was his deportation of the Jews on which his main prosecution dwelt, but initially his name had been included on the grounds of his 'vicious indoctrination of the young'.[1]

After the war, it was believed he was dead, and he heard this on a BBC report while pretending to be a novelist called Richard Falk. Later, on hearing of the arrest of Hitler Youth leaders, he decided to give himself up, which at first was difficult because until he appeared in person it was considered a poor joke.[2] In Nuremberg, he had sat in the dock for five months before his case was heard and he tended to be regarded as a person of minimal interest. His early adoration of Göring and the Nazi system fluctuated wildly, seemingly treating Göring as a hero. However, once Göring was separated from the rest because of his bullying attitude, Speer exercised some influence over Schirach and he slowly moved toward denouncing Hitler, though he tended to be swept by the tide or moved by the latest events or words, deemed by most observers to be malleable. Airey Neave wrote that he looked 'bi-sexual and soft with *thé-dansant* eyes. He looked a man who might be dangerous to small boys'. He saw him as a pampered boy from the upper-middle class and was the 'original Nazi', once with a 'fat eunuch's face', clearly indicating Neave's immediate distaste for this defendant.[3] Neave met him several times and always found him repellent and full of 'pampered self-assurance'.

Medical Mental Observations

Goldensohn, on the other hand, described Schirach as 'bright, self-effacing, very courteous, and friendly. He takes himself rather seriously, as is obvious and can be gleaned from his general demeanour and words'.[4] This insight was reflected again in a 1967 interview looked at later in this text. Like other defendants, he was unhappy about prosecuting various organisations, arguing that the whole group could become 'legendary'. He admitted there had been a degree of anti-Semitism in so far that the Jews should have no power, but it was, he argued, taken too far, and when Himmler and Hitler mentioned it was necessary to extinguish the Jews, 'the German tendencies to perfectionism and exaggeration' were taken literally. He then attacked Bolshevism based on conversations he had with Germans who had been to Russia, asking the same question as Schacht as to whether Europe would become Bolshevist or remain 'European'.

He claimed he was widely read and spoke of his days as head of the national youth. He explained that it was run on democratic lines because the young leaders would be brought together for discussion, and he insisted it should not be regarded as merely part of Nazism. When Goldensohn pushed him on this matter, asking him whether the Hitler Youth would have made Germany more democratic if Germany had won the war, he was promptly rebuffed by Schirach stating that it was absurd to think Germany could ever have won the war, stating that he hoped for peace through Britain and America at the very least, and that attacking Russia had been ridiculous.

When Goldensohn raised the arguments of Oswald Pohl of obeying orders in terms of the extermination plans, Schirach 'made a wry face and said "horrible"', making it clear he did not want to discuss such people. He was also convinced that Bormann would eventually turn up and was probably in the hands of the Russians or Germans and gave his opinions about him. He said Bormann was not well educated but was industrious, and when made head of the party, despite his minor role, Bormann 'virtually became Hess's boss'.

In court, Schirach had called Hitler a 'million times murderer' and condemned the 'wrongness of anti-Semitism'. He told Goldensohn that in the Hitler Youth they had free discussions and based on this he concluded that to put power in the hands of one person or a small group of people was a mistake, because power corrupts, and 'authoritarianism is a system which destroys man's morality'. As Goldensohn approached the matter of removing Jews from Vienna, he described Schirach as 'smooth and rationalising' as ever, as Schirach pointed out that the process had been in hand before he arrived; some 130,000 Jews had already left and only 60,000 'under my aegis'. He added that he thought the further away the Jews moved from Goebbels, the safer they would be, and the whole process was carried out through Heydrich's SS processes. He explained what a difficult task it had been in Austria following the *Anschluss*, and the cultural differences between north Germans and Austrians, but he had been under the impression that once in Poland the Jews could live like any other human beings. He admitted that with the information which had now been disclosed he felt guilty for the part he had played. Goldensohn asked Schirach if there were others apart from Jews who suffered, such as opponents to the regime.

Schirach gave a somewhat lame answer saying that when he walked through factories where some political opponents were working, he 'was not attacked' because they recognised him as a 'good socialist', seemingly never crossing his mind that any attack on him, verbal or otherwise, would result in their instant death. He thought Hitler's policy was to keep Austria dominated by ruling it in districts, and that the idea of making the provincial city of Linz the capital 'was ridiculous'. He concluded this conversation by reminiscing that he should have listened to his wife when she had recognised 'Hitler's abnormality and cruel nature years before' it had dawned on him.[5] He told Gilbert that his wife had been distressed watching Jews being dragged into the streets, which was an interesting comment given the ignorance assumed by many Germans when the persecution was so obviously public.

Schirach confessed to Gilbert that he had come under the influence of Streicher who was able to dress anti-Semitism in 'pseudo-scientific garb', explaining to Gilbert he felt betrayed because 'the elders' had never explained the *Protocols of the Elders of Zion* were a forgery and Ford had repudiated *The International Jew*.[*] He claimed to Goldensohn that he had protested to Hitler, and added that it was the breaking of promises at Munich which had first drawn his attention to Hitler's failings, and he later thought him insane.

Reactions during the Trial

On 21 November 1945, when Jackson had opened on the Jewish persecution and Gilbert found Schirach in his cell deeply troubled, it was enough for Colonel Andrus to have him checked for safety reasons. Schirach had been deeply upset that he was in court because Himmler's murder machine had trapped him, even though he had 'tried to check it'.[6] Gilbert calmed him down by telling him he would have an opportunity to put his case which seemed to give him some relief, having evidently not understood the Anglo-American legal adversarial system.

On Friday December 14, when Poland and the associated atrocities were raised, Schirach mentioned *en passant* to Gilbert that he doubted a German woman would buy lampshades from human skin. But when Gilbert suggested that if such a gift were given by a German man, she would accept it as a matter of course, Schirach slumped back looking despondent, with Keitel who overheard the conversation mumbling 'terrible'.

It was clear that Schirach was all but frightened by Göring and his outbursts, and his own views were becoming subdued causing Gilbert to write, 'the essential moral

---

* The anti-Semitic articles which made up *The International Jew*, attributed to Henry Ford, were translated into German in 1922. Following a lawsuit in 1927, Ford closed his paper *The Dearborn Independent*, stating that he had been unaware of the shocking content. Ford was the only American to be mentioned by Hitler in *Mein Kampf*.

weakness of this narcissist has been clearly shown in the manner' he had allowed Göring to influence him.[7] Schirach was further unsettled when he heard his family had been arrested with Gilbert placating him by pointing out that the Americans would not treat them as the Gestapo would have done. The discussion moved onto Ribbentrop with Gilbert probing, and Schirach explaining with some pleasure that the German royal aspect of the 'von' was not really part of Ribbentrop's background. Following his visits during the Easter recess, Gilbert concluded that being separated from Göring, Schirach had returned to his 'more repentant attitude', especially after hearing Frank's open confession. Part of his defence would be how he was deceived by Streicher and the Nazi leadership with Gilbert detecting an 'element of exhibitionism' entering his thinking.

Schirach had always regarded Göring in a heroic light and was concerned when he was 'unmasked' by Frick's witness Gisevius, causing him to become defensive, claiming that his adoration for Göring had stemmed from his immature youth. Later, Schirach avoided the subject of his lost hero who had been exposed as a lying self-seeking tyrant. Gilbert dropped heavy hints that it would be more acceptable 'for a person' to demonstrate that they had been deluded into anti-Semitism and then realised the immorality of racial prejudice.

Schirach's Trial

As Schirach's trial opened, there was a degree of moodiness in the court as there had been considerable repetition of information, answers were too long, and a sense of tedium was becoming the prominent feeling within the court. When he appeared in the witness box, William Shirer described him 'looking like a contrite college boy'.[8] Schirach's case did little to help as he expounded on his thinking and his past, deviating to grow his image, and several times Lawrence had to intervene threatening to stop him unless he 'stuck to the point'. He dragged out his background, his father as an army officer, his four children, and was especially keen to expound on Weimar, the native city of all Germans. In the first lunchtime break, the judges discussed how they might 'stop all the hogwash'.[9] Those who endured the case were not impressed by Schirach either as a person or in his views and the way he expressed them.

He claimed that as head of the Hitler Youth, he never held a major post and had nothing to do with the military plans. Schirach had started his defence (23 May 1946) with a degree of cultural exhibitionism by assuming full responsibility for educating German youth not just for National Socialism. He had expanded on Goethe whom he loved and German culture. He compared the *Hitler-Jugend* to a boy scout organisation, and he had stopped them joining in the 1938 Jewish pogrom. He admitted, though, he had become anti-Semitic because of Ford's book *The International Jew*, which was somewhat cunning. In the next day's session, Schirach expounded on this issue further claiming that he had anticipated a 'peaceful solution' to the Jewish issue, poured scorn on Streicher's *Der Stürmer*, and said the 1938 pogrom was a disgrace. His counsel was Dr Sauter who encouraged him in questions about the Hitler Youth, tempting him to distance this movement from military activities, claiming the gun clubs were only 'fun marksmanship' tests. It was easy for the prosecution to prove otherwise and that Schirach was producing the next generation of Nazi soldiers. It was argued, though, that as in other countries, individual scout leaders differed vastly in their objectives, and that Schirach himself was not guilty of any criminal acts.

Judge Biddle felt obliged to intervene as Sauter was spending far too much time on the perceived innocence of the Hitler Youth. The prosecution had already cited a Hitler Youth song entitled 'We are the soldiers of the future', and Schirach could not deny that he was training the youth for total obedience to Hitler. Schirach had also prepared for recitation a special grace before the evening meal:

> Führer, my Führer, given me by God,
> Protect and preserve my life for long,
> You rescued Germany from its deepest need
> I thank you for my daily bread.

The case took a more sinister twist when it turned to examine Schirach's time as *Gauleiter* in Vienna at the time when Jews in the city were being moved east. He said it was a time when he had no control over the situation, and he was probably correct in so far that the SS under Anton Brunner (a subordinate of Adolf Eichmann) was in charge and it was above Schirach's pay scale. Various authorities and papers differ over the precise number of those Jews moved, ranging from 60,000 to 185,000, demonstrating not only the ignorance of the day but the general mayhem as it is difficult to pinpoint a verifiable number. He had to admit that when he was in Vienna, he had backed up the deportation of the Jews with a speech (15 September 1942) and added that it was a 'false loyalty' to the Führer. He described his break with Hitler as stemming from this issue and cultural clashes. He tried to explain that the Jews were being deported for their own safety. The prosecution produced a speech he had made in 1942 during which he said, 'every Jew who operates in Europe is a danger to European culture', to which his only defence was that it was misplaced loyalty to Hitler.[10]

When Sauter asked him about Auschwitz he then denounced Hitler, expressing the view that Höss had only been the executioner at Auschwitz on orders from Hitler.[11] He took, he said, 'full responsibility' and it was a guilt he would carry before God that he had raised the Hitler Youth for a person he had once considered an 'impeccable leader'. He said Auschwitz had signified 'the end of racial politics and anti-Semitism', not that it did, sadly. At this stage, it was observed that Fritzsche and Speer were pleased with the way Schirach was being so open and honest, which was regarded as a victory over Göring's cynicism.

The prosecutor Captain Drexel Sprecher demonstrated that many in the Hitler Youth were encouraged to join the SS, but this proved difficult to explain, and he made more progress as he turned to Schirach's time in Vienna. Nor could Schirach claim total ignorance of the extermination policy, because earlier, at the start of January 1946, the witness Alois Hoellreigel, an SS NCO who had been a guard at Mauthausen, stated that Kaltenbrunner and Schirach had visited the camp in 1942 and saw SS officers killing prisoners by having them pushed off a cliff.[12]

He looked to the defence that Hitler was complaining that he was too lenient, that he alone bore responsibility for training young men to be loyal to the Führer whom he had once believed to be above criticism, and that the extermination of the Jews was 'a racial policy which led to disaster for five million Jews and all Germans'. *The Times* commented that Schirach's remarks had been expressed 'in the bitterest terms the court had yet heard'.[13]

Prosecutor Dodd informed his listeners that Schirach had good reasons for being repentant, but he had not mentioned everything, not least educating German youth to become patriotic warriors with the gun clubs and glider piloting. This sense of repentance Schirach displayed was soon dashed by inept witnesses and Dodd's attack. Dodd produced evidence that Schirach and Himmler had agreed to recruit members of the youth organisation for *Totenkopf* ('skull', 'death's head') units mainly used in concentration camps, and that in 1937 some 10,000 rifles were given as a gift by the *Wehrmacht* to the Hitler Youth, as were plenty of Nazi songs from the various handbooks. This attack pleased his critics among the defendants.

Dodd produced documentation indicating that Schirach had attended a small meeting with Hitler when he had made clear his intentions of exterminating the 'Polish intelligentsia' which Dodd proposed had not weakened Schirach's admiration for the dictator. On Monday 27 May, Dodd caused Schirach some embarrassment when he was obliged to admit that he had suggested to Bormann that in retaliation for the death of Heydrich, the *Luftwaffe* should bomb a selected English cultural town. He pinned him down over the evacuation of Jews from Vienna, as well as the question of importing 10- to 14-year-olds from occupied countries for exploitation.

Despite some signs of repentance, possibly brought on by revelations in the proceedings, the influence of Speer, the fluctuating Schirach could not avoid a degree of serious involvement in the criminal activities of the Nazi regime.

After Taking the Stand

After taking the stand, Gilbert found Schirach satisfied with the impression he had made, and especially the underlining of his break from the dead Hitler. He then turned the discussion onto the subject of Hitler and his relationship with women. Schirach suggested Hitler did not know how to behave with them socially, sometimes showing 'inordinate politeness' by kissing their hands, that he probably kept Eva

Braun just as 'a pet', and it was not a normal male-female relationship. When Dodd cross-examined Schirach he was more ill at ease, pleasing some of the loyal Nazis, with Frank pointing out that Schirach was 'trying to simplify things too much with his grand confession' which despite its venom may have had a ring of truth. Dönitz also expressed the opinion that Schirach was attempting to cover up too many things. Speer remained happy because Schirach had denounced Hitler, but Fritzsche was upset when he discovered how tied up Schirach had been in criminal activities.

Summation, Final Statements, and Verdicts

Schirach's lawyer Dr Sauter emphasised Schirach's renunciation of Nazism and anti-Semitism which meant Schirach had to be careful with whom he mixed with among the defendants to stay comfortable, as this was an area of internal contention. He claimed that it was a misunderstanding to regard the Hitler Youth as a 'prep-school for the *Wehrmacht*', that the Vienna appointment could not be refused, and he had committed 'no punishable act'. The prosecution summation called him the 'poisoner of a generation' training them for the SS and the *Wehrmacht*.[14] This stung Schirach, and in his final statement he concentrated on the Hitler Youth, never mentioning his time in Vienna. He expressed his anger at being described as 'the corrupter of young people', and countered it by defending German youth, asking they be freed from 'hatred and revenge'.

Schirach had been charged under counts one and four, but count one was quickly dismissed as the Hitler Youth had not been involved in planning war. His time in Vienna and the deportation of the Jews found him convicted by the judges on count four. When the verdict of a 20-year sentence was pronounced, Schirach did not flinch, probably grateful to have escaped hanging.

Post-war

He was released from Spandau Prison on 30 September 1966 and retired to south Germany, living in Munich with his son Robert. In 1967 he appeared on British television in an interview with David Frost following the publication of his memoirs *Ich glaubte an Hitler* (I Believed in Hitler) the same year. It was a curious interview in which Schirach presented as a kind, old, reflective gentleman admitting a degree of guilt but maintaining an overall innocence and presenting himself as more sinned against than sinning.[15] Schirach reminded his listeners he had an American mother, and when questioned about the early Hitler, said he was witty, loved jokes, and was opposed to smoking. Throughout his interview, Schirach constantly smoked a variety of pipes, as if making a point. He said Hitler opposed hunting animals with guns, and Frost later responded with the cynical note that Hitler may have loved animals, but he killed millions of people. Frost asked Schirach if he thought Hitler was mad to which Schirach responded affirmatively, saying he could date the moment when he thought it was confirmed. He claimed he challenged Hitler over invading Poland saying it would involve the USA, and after Stalingrad had suggested to Hitler that he replace Ribbentrop only to be told again that Ribbentrop was 'another Bismarck'. It can never be certain, indeed it is unlikely, that Schirach confronted Hitler with such questions, and he was clearly making a laborious effort to exonerate himself. When asked to define Hitler, Schirach said he was a man of great gifts, in some ways a genius, but he 'was a man without measure' which was the root of the problem. He pointed out that it was Hitler who had given the unemployed work with bread and butter following the disaster of the Treaty of Versailles.

Frost asked him about the Jesuit claim 'give us a child until seven and we will give you the man', and whether that was what Schirach intended with the Hitler Youth. Schirach promptly said, 'Yes', and told Frost he loved the kids and 'they loved me'.

When asked about the Jewish persecution, Schirach also claimed he had challenged Hitler somewhere in the period 1933–35, and that he was not anti-Semitic adding the somewhat lame note that his parents had many Jewish friends. He admitted that 'we got the Jewish business wrong', but he never heard Hitler mention the Final Solution which was all to do with Himmler, Hitler, and Bormann, implying that he was not involved. Frost persisted in telling Schirach that he knew his mother had received a copy of *Time* magazine which laid bare the facts, but Schirach said they took it to be propaganda. When he took charge of Vienna, he was told the SS had already started to move the Jews east and it should not concern him. He said he had asked about their welfare, only to be told it was safer for them to have their own area than be killed by the local population, claiming the SS were always so 'sweet' when answering his questions. Frost pushed him again when there was a tinge of anger from Schirach who said, 'human beings are not brave, and we sometimes close our eyes'. Frost sympathised with this, returning Schirach to his charming self again, as Schirach admitted that standing up against the Nazi regime demanded special courage, which was of course true except for a few brave souls. How far Schirach knew about the Final Solution cannot be fathomed from this conversation, but there may have been a hint in this final part of the interview that for reasons of either self-defence or shame, he knew more than he wanted to know.

Final Notes

Schirach died aged 67 on 8 August 1974. He was constantly in a state of defence, explaining his role under Hitler to his death.[16] He was the youngest defendant, had been easily influenced by Hitler, and was undoubtedly delighted at his appointments and rise in prominence. He was only 24 years old when he was given his first opportunity as Hitler spotted a young man who obviously admired him and who would be obedient. He was evidently taken in by his own self-importance and despite later protestations took everything without question because of his immaturity and ambition. He knew enough by the Nuremberg Trial to be evasive and painted an idyllic boy-scout image of the *Hitler-Jugend*. He underplayed his role in Vienna, and probably for safety reasons turned against his hero Hitler, but remained conscious of Göring's bearing. From his interview with David Frost and his memoirs, it was clear that from 1945 onwards his life was a matter of self-justification. In watching the interview, and trying to be as objective as possible, he struck the writer as distasteful, still self-important, but without any justification. The case against him with the Hitler Youth was one thing, but his awareness and involvement in exterminating Jewish people remains unforgivable.

Fritz Sauckel 1894–1946

A worried Sauckel arrested by American soldiers. (Bundesarchiv, 146-1991-033-00, Licence CC-BY-SA 3.0)

Background

Fritz Sauckel, who appeared 'small and inoffensive', was prosecuted for overseeing forced labour. He had started life as a seaman, had been shipwrecked off the Scottish coastline when on a trip to Australia, and was interned by the French during the Great War. In post-war Germany, he became entangled in politics, regarding the

NSDAP as the way forward and was the *Gauleiter* for Thuringia from 1927. He married in 1923 and had ten children, one later killed as a fighter pilot and another somewhere in an American prisoner-of-war camp. He had been low on Gilbert's IQ listings but had proved to be good at giving speeches and had published many articles and two books. He was a family man, and his hobby was stamp collecting.

As the war started in September 1939, he became Reich Defence Commissioner in his military area involving control over civil defence. He had been associated with the SS since 1934, and in January 1942 on Bormann's recommendation, he was appointed General Plenipotentiary for Labour Development working under Göring's Four-Year Planning office. He was both an SS and SA general in an honorary sense. Labour was critical and not enough volunteers were available forcing a demand for more labour. Much of this came from Poland and Soviet areas press-ganged by the military. When Speer took over from Todt, the new efficiency demanded more labour, providing Sauckel with his defence that he had been made responsible by Speer's demands for armaments. The labour came from all over occupied Europe, with Italians and French and others from the western zones, a mixture of volunteer and forced workers, and their conditions were known to be brutal with untold numbers dying. Sauckel wrote a letter to Rosenberg (20 April 1942) with a report on the labour development stating that 'all the men must be fed, sheltered, and treated in such a way as to exploit them to the highest conceivable degree of expenditure'.[1] Sauckel may have evaded the dock had his letter used the word 'encourage' rather than 'exploit', because long before the war ended it was widely known that forced labour for prisoners of war and civilians alike was simply brutal and life-threatening. He was eventually unmasked after the war by a young Austrian, and Edgar Snow, an American journalist, met and described him as 'a dark little man, sullen and suspicious', which is reflected in the photograph.[2] When Airey Neave first met him, he had been anticipating a formidable type of character, but found 'a little bald man with a feeble Charlie Chaplin moustache and stupid brown eyes'.[3]

Medical Mental Observations

Goldensohn described Sauckel as a short man, less than six foot, balding, and wearing a 'small Charlie Chaplin/Hitler-type moustache. He appeared tense but controlled, smiled often and nervously', with many of his responses sounding automatic.[4] His basic thinking tended to revolve around four major points. The first was that the NSDAP had done a good job for Germany until recent years, and the second, as usual, was that the atrocities and exterminations were unknown to honourable men like himself. Thirdly, the cause of the war could be found in the terms of the Versailles Treaty, and finally, and in line with most of the defendants, the argument that anti-Semitism had nothing to do with his department. He added that there had been too many Jews in Germany, but they had not been persecuted until late in the war, which was either a downright lie or he had been living on another planet. He also argued that two fifths of his five million labourers had been volunteers and that Vichy France had sent workers to Germany. He further argued they had been treated well with the same benefits as German workers.

He pointed out that his sister-in-law had emigrated to America (as did many Germans), but he would not do the same because in his position it would have felt more like desertion. He raised the subject of Marxism and explained he had rejected it for three reasons: the first, his religious upbringing, the second, he did not regard owning property as theft, and finally, he objected to the thesis of a 'class-struggle', preferring the Nazi theme of national unity. Looking back, he often wondered how he had entered politics. He would rather have stayed a seaman, but that employment was diminished, and he was struck by the size of the unemployment which attracted him to help. He persisted in trying to emphasise that his intentions were good, and he made a point that when he became governor of Thuringia, it had been Hindenburg's respectable signature on the document, though it was known that he had been a Hitler appointment. He claimed at the outbreak of war he had volunteered for the navy, but his request was denied.

Goldensohn asked him directly how much he knew about the rounding up of slave labour and the separating of families. He evaded a direct answer by asking, 'What would you do if your country's welfare depended on labour?' He recalled that as a child he had never been conscious of anti-Semitism, and it was the Nazis who took the general social bigotry against Jews and raised it to extreme hatred. He claimed there were no Jewish persecutions in Thuringia while he was there, and he knew nothing about the extermination processes. All he wanted was to work to the highest ideals and unify German life, proudly claiming that he owned no property, no large amounts of savings, and had a blind loyalty to Hitler which still seemed to persist. As with many others, he shifted the blame of events onto Himmler, Bormann, and Goebbels, even blaming the Nazi estrangement from Christianity on Bormann. When questioned on this issue, he admitted he left the church but remained religious 'at home', trying to present himself in the best possible light. It was ironic that when he surrendered to the Americans, he did it through the offices of a Catholic chaplain. He insisted that 'he had personally done nothing to be ashamed of', and having taken office, did his best to get food and billets for Russian prisoners of war.[5] He was the only defendant to think he was totally innocent; he argued he may have erred, but he 'was well intentioned'. When confronted by Göring's claim to have built concentration camps for communists, Sauckel claimed they were only for those who opposed the state. He said he had many communist and social democrat friends who accepted the rightful government, and in the next breath said the churches had financial state support. Either Sauckel was totally gullible or thought his American conversationalist was naïve. Sauckel may not have been astute, and in his adoration of Hitler he had taken everything at face value without question. Nevertheless, his belief and pride in nationalistic Germany remained immense and major question marks were posed over how much he knew. He must have known the circumstances of the forced labour over which he had control. Schacht had described Sauckel as a 'poorly educated man of poor descent', which was a condescending viewpoint, but there was a distinct impression that Sauckel was out of his depth.

Reactions during the Trial

Following the 29 November showing of the concentration camp film, Sauckel was back in his cell trembling and shaking at what he had seen, claiming it was a disgrace and he had nothing to do with such acts. He remained in this state for most of the time, always ill at ease as if any visitor were about to torture him. He protested that in providing labour he was like a man who provided crew members for a ship but could not be held responsible as the land agent for things which happened at sea. Gilbert did not ask him the question as to whether it would be different had he heard evil rumours about the ship he supplied.

As the trial continued, Gilbert found Sauckel always anxious and 'tremorous', continuing his defence that he had looked after the foreign workers, that he had only done his duty, and that the 'foreign-Bolshevistic-Jewish-capitalistic world had forced war on Germany'. Dönitz told the story that, overwhelmed with his responsibilities, Sauckel had once stowed away on a U-boat and had to be sent back.[6] Whether this was true or not is questionable, but it underlined his unpopular reputation.

Sauckel's Trial

He was charged under all four indictments, but he had no military or diplomatic connections which tended to rule out the first two counts, begging the question as to why they were raised in the first place. The main thrust of Sauckel's trial revolved around his time in office as Plenipotentiary General for the allocation of labour. The Hague Convention of 1907 permitted employment of local labourers for the needs of the occupying army, but not to involve them in war operations against their own country.[7] Nazi Germany employed or rather ruthlessly deployed millions as slaves and moved them from country to country.

Sauckel's defence counsel Dr Robert Servatius* painted his client as a man of the labouring class, an unpretentious party man looking to promote the collective utility of the working classes, implying that Speer's demands and pressures bore the major responsibility. This defence tended to fail on the grounds that Speer had many areas of responsibility, but forced labour was solely Sauckel's area. Servatius did his job well but was not helped by Sauckel who according to Telford Taylor seemed to

---

* Dr Servatius later represented Eichmann in his Jerusalem trial in 1962.

pause at each word before considering the next. Sauckel came from the traditional working class and spoke with a dialect some of the defendants mocked. He always managed to skirt the major issue of the brutality experienced by the workers of which he was evidently aware.

Permeating this case was this clash between Sauckel's account of the past and colliding with Speer, both accusing the other of manipulating the forced labour. Years later when Speer wrote his memoirs, he recorded that 'during the early weeks of our association we [Sauckel and Speer] cooperated smoothly', but a paragraph later claimed Sauckel was not meeting his commitments.[8] During the trial, Sauckel explained he had been given the post on Speer's suggestion but in his memoirs, Speer was insistent it was all down to Bormann. Had it just been volunteers, there would have been no case to answer, but Sauckel was reminded of the minutes of a Central Planning Board meeting where he said that 'out of the five million foreign workers who arrived in Germany, not even 200,000 came voluntarily'.[9]

The French prosecutor Jacques Herzog obliged him to admit he had utilised the army and the SD to find and bind (literally in some cases) the required labourers, and he had used the Gestapo to track down escapees and evaders. He would often shout his replies and speak too much, but Biddle subdued this tendency by simply raising his hand. Despite Sauckel's continuous plea that he had done his best to look after the workers, which sounded genuine, Dodd presented incontestable evidence of brutality and deprivation. There was widespread information about the treatment of workers, and even Mussolini instructed his ambassador in Berlin Dino Alfieri to protest to Ribbentrop but with 'moderation'.[10] Their treatment was widespread and not hidden away as with some concentration camps. Under these circumstances, Servatius was reduced to trying the defence of shifting the blame elsewhere by emphasising that Sauckel's role was not that important. It was no easy task as there was a record of when Sauckel had summoned no less than 800 officials in Weimar (6 January 1943) and told them 'we are going to discard the last remnant of our soft talk about humanitarian ideas'.[11] Sauckel's witnesses were of little help apart from the last one who claimed Sauckel had tried to make conditions better, but such was the amount of incrimination this evidence failed to assist. Another witness was a Wilhelm Jaeger, a doctor at Krupp's industry in Essen, and he drew attention to the appalling conditions under which the labourers worked. Sauckel concluded that given the nature of the war situation, he had to do his best and 'considered it justified', which was a frank answer but not helpful to his cause, already damaged by the accumulated written evidence.

Summation, Final Statements, and Verdicts

Sauckel's defence lawyer Servatius began by arguing that there were no clear guidelines in either the London Charter of 1899 or the Hague Convention on Land Warfare of 1907 about the nature and legitimacy of forced labour in war, which were the main foundations of the charges against his client. It was well presented, and he concluded by emphasising Sauckel's 'good intentions'.

The prosecution through Jackson described Sauckel as the 'greatest and cruellest slaver since the Pharaohs of Egypt' driving foreign peoples into bondage.[12] It was agreed by some observers that Sauckel's final statement was well presented, but somewhat long as he described himself as a humble family man obedient to Church and state. He concluded that his actions in finding forced labour was because of the emergency of the war.

When it came to the Tribunal's decision, Sauckel who had been charged on all four counts found the Tribunal had quickly dismissed the first two for lack of evidence, but he was found guilty under three and four because of his work in the forced labour drive. He was condemned to death by hanging and unlike most of the others showed great signs of his inner distress, and down in the cells he cried.

Final Notes

He was described as the 'greatest slaver' of all times, but Speer with his demands was perhaps a stronger candidate. It seems Sauckel had no real authority, and some have questioned whether he deserved to hang. Neave always thought the sentence on Sauckel was wrong.[13] As Schirach's youthful immaturity had lured him into Nazi prominence, it appears that Sauckel's humble working-class background had the same effect. His working-class dialect derided by Schacht had not stopped his rise to power. He may have pretended that he had no idea of the brutality of the extermination camps, but the forced labour was not only repulsive but led to countless deaths through hunger, overwork, and non-existent living conditions which Sauckel, Speer, and many others must have been aware of. Whether hanging for a such a man was justified raises some questions, but perhaps another question hovers over why Sauckel was hanged and Speer imprisoned.

Alfred Jodl 1890–1946

Background

Generaloberst Alfred Jodl was a high-ranking general just a step below that of field marshal and came from a family whose background was military with a tradition of looking down at politicians. His father had been in the 2nd Bavarian Field Artillery Regiment, and he had uncles of some importance in the military and academic world.

Between 1914 and 1916, he served first on the Western Front and was awarded the Iron Cross 2nd class for bravery, then on the Eastern Front before returning to the west where he received the Iron Cross 1st class. Oddly, given his character, it was known that he was critical of the Kaiser's leadership. As with other selected and often gifted officers, he served post-war in the *Reichswehr*, serving in the General Staff (*Truppenamt*) forbidden by the Versailles Treaty. He married Irma, Countess von

Alfred Jodl. (Bundesarchiv 146-1971-033-01, Licence CC-BY-SA 3.0)

Bullion, in 1913 but she died near the end of World War II and he married Luise von Benda in 1944. She helped him in Nuremberg and was much admired not least for her pretty looks. It is generally understood that Jodl had little time for Hitler or any politicians, but once Hitler became head of government his background Prussian influence was ignited and obedience was demanded which explained why Hitler had so many loyal military officers. Like many such men, Jodl hoped that Hitler might restore some of Germany's lost military pride.

In August 1939, Hitler selected him as Chief of Operations Staff for the OKW and following the occupation of Poland and Norway and the defeat of France he was optimistic, thinking England's collapse 'was only a matter of time'. Of all the defendants he spoke the most often with Hitler, although he did not meet him until 1939, but it was mainly concerning technical and organisational matters. From his discovered notes with its many sentences of praise for the Führer in the early days, it clearly indicated he thought highly of Hitler, but as the war progressed, the relationship became somewhat more difficult. The belief and charge that he had assisted the Nazi rise to power and planned for wars of aggression was tenuous.

Jodl had signed some of the notorious orders such as the Commissar Order (6 June 1941) for shooting Soviet political commissars, as well as the Commando Order (28 October 1942) which authorised the execution of Allied commandoes even in uniform, as well as partisans. Nevertheless, Jodl had argued with Hitler over the correctness of the Commando Order, and it was generally known that he was courageous enough to question and even challenge the dictator. In August 1942, he was sent by Hitler to demand some action from Field Marshal Wilhelm List in Russia, only to return informing Hitler that List's evaluation of the military situation was correct, and Hitler's directions could not be carried through. This led to a furious row with Hitler refusing to shake hands with him or eat at the same table. There was chatter about Jodl being replaced by Paulus after the anticipated capture of Stalingrad, and it was known that Jodl had made many requests to be transferred to frontline duties.

He spent most of his time in the vicinity of Hitler, especially at the Wolf's Lair (the forward command post in deep woods near Rastenburg, Prussia), and was promoted to *Generaloberst* (Colonel General). He was slightly injured in the 20 July 1944 Plot and, being Jodl, was furious that fellow officers had made this attempt on the Führer's life. It was Jodl who signed the German surrender in Reims on 7 May 1945 and a few days later 'was belatedly and by now somewhat pointlessly awarded the Oak leaves to go with his Knight's Cross'.[1]

Many thought that with Keitel in the dock as the administrator of the *Wehrmacht*, Jodl as the technical assistant was unnecessary. Like most others he was anti-Semitic, believing that Germany had to free itself from Jewish influence and domination, and although he may have been against the liquidation of the Jews, he persistently supported the Nazi regime until his death. It is claimed that he always behaved correctly and politely towards individual Jews, and during his trial, a Jewish woman by the name of Moskovitch offered to give evidence that Jodl and his wife had tried to help her leave Germany. When in Nuremberg Prison, he was known by his American guards as 'Happy Hooligan' after some strip cartoon character, but Andrus liked him because he kept his cell in meticulous tidiness.[2] In a secretly taped conversation in England, it came to light through an *Oberst* (Colonel) Walter Köhn that many people regarded Jodl as simply ambitious, and in another conversation, he was regarded as lacking moral courage.[3]

Interrogations

Alfred Jodl, as Chief of Operations, was questioned about his area of responsibility and was closely interviewed about his views of the previous years. He described the various 'conferences' as they were called, mainly army, but the *Luftwaffe* and *Kriegsmarine* were often called in, and they generally started at midday and continued into the late afternoon. This was of immediate interest, but Jodl had no idea where the records of such meetings were kept. It was only after 1942 that a stenographer was used, and it was about this time, Jodl stated, that he had a major disagreement with Hitler in August 1942. He was not explicit about the row, but it appeared that Hitler was prone to give orders and then become angry if they had gone wrong when carried out. Jodl thought it necessary to record decision making, thus the stenographer. As with many defendants, Jodl was happy to blame Bormann for controlling the whereabouts of such meeting notes.

He also explained that it was Hitler who made all the decisions, and when asked if they were good, he refused to generalise. He praised Hitler for the decision to invade Norway, for the attack plan on France, and stopping the retreat in Russia in November 1941. He felt Hitler's initial successes, which had been against the advice of his military officers, indicated, as Speer also intimated, some sense of genius at work, and that Hitler was a 'great military leader'; Jodl compared him to Hannibal. Again, like Speer, he felt that after 1942 the decisions were not so good, acknowledging that his trench warfare had taught Hitler much, but he was no expert on mobile warfare and did not have the necessary military training.

He was questioned over the air-warfare and had decided that the Western Allied control of the air had been a deciding factor in the final victory. He interestingly mentioned that the attacks on German cities were the most worrying, as news of these raids unsettled the soldiers at the front when they realised their families at home were being obliterated. They continued to fight but lost some of 'their enthusiasm'. The bombing had destroyed necessary supplies and the ability to transport them; artillery shells and motor vehicles were especially in short supply. He talked of the *Luftwaffe*'s inability to fight the modern Allied planes and their lack of technical advancements. He commented on the seriousness of the loss of pilots, especially on the Russian Front, which meant that pilot training officers had to be used in emergencies, thereby making training new pilots difficult.

These perceptions were similar to those Speer had offered, but with additional insights into the way killing the soldiers' families had unsettled fighting soldiers, and the technical failures of *Luftwaffe* development. His praise of Hitler's attack on Norway and France placed him within the charges of waging aggressive war as did his uncompromising albeit critical support of Hitler. Very much like Keitel, despite the claimed disagreement with Hitler in August 1942, he was another form of 'yes-man', although the general impression indicated he was not quite as tethered as Keitel.

One of the military's main defences was based on an interview with General Heinz Guderian (the famous tank commander and later army chief of staff) who argued that German soldiers fought the war according to the laws of war and it was the SS who carried out the atrocities. This was seized upon for many years, especially by the German public with its thousands of ex-*Wehrmacht* soldiers, assisted to a degree by the Allies in the light of the Cold War and keeping West Germany on side. It was historians like Omer Bartov who later challenged this myth by exposing that the *Wehrmacht* was a deeply Nazi institution which played a key role in Nazi barbarity, causing considerable public debate in the late 20th century. Guderian had told his interrogators that he had refused to pass on some orders from General Walther von Brauchitsch at OKH because they would encourage excess and possible criminality among his troops and disrupt military discipline. He insisted they followed the Geneva Convention and had two soldiers executed for violating the law.[4] In this testimony, Guderian's type of defence was used across the *Wehrmacht*, but it was personal to Guderian who was eventually released without trial in 1948, which was unusual. With reference to Jodl, he informed his interrogators that Jodl was a conscientious, hard-working general staff officer, but 'he was also very strongly under the influence of Hitler. He would maintain his own views and oppose Hitler only on rare occasions'.[5]

Medical Mental Observations

Goldensohn noted that Jodl:

> … was a colourless fellow who requires slow, careful study. He gives the impression of competence, coolness, and oxlike stubbornness and obsessiveness, which may be incorrect, but which is suggested by his bearing, detachment and also the remark on my entering his cell concerning the infrequency of my visits as compared to my visiting some of the other defendants. He has apparently noted this.[6]

Goldensohn made light of Jodl's inference that he had not been visited claiming he did not think Jodl needed a psychiatrist, which Jodl acknowledged as true. Jodl was proud of his family background, that his uncle had been a professor of philosophy, and he took after him. His second wife, Jodl proudly explained, was helping in his defence along with two professors of law, one of whom knew his uncle. He was not bothered by incarceration as he felt 'an inner sense of innocence'.

Jodl was described by Gilbert as even more Prussian than Keitel, Jodl stating that 'the indictment knocked me on the head' as he had no idea about 90 per cent of the accusations but adding that a soldier obeyed orders.[7] He then returned with the barbed comments that the Russians had no right to sit in judgement because of their behaviour, telling Gilbert that cruelty was an Asiatic characteristic, not German; Russian behaviour had been dubious but the racist slur must have made Gilbert think.

Reactions during the Trial

When Airey Neave presented him with the indictment, he noted that Jodl was transfixed by his polished Sam Browne belt and displayed no emotion. He threw the British officer with his question as to whether he needed a criminal or international lawyer, and by requesting that he needed paper and pencils to prepare his defence. When on 26 November 1945 the Hossbach Memorandum was raised, Jodl mentioned it at lunchtime because he had never heard of it, but he had observed in the papers that it had 'overestimated Italy's importance'. Göring said it was nothing, and the Americans had done the same by 'grabbing Texas and California'. Following the 29 November film of the concentration camp, Keitel, Dönitz, and Raeder found it shocking, but Jodl was the calmest commenting on how so many young people had joined the party with idealistic motives. The next day, he was shocked, as were Keitel and Ribbentrop, when the witness General Lahousen testified about the resistance within the *Abwehr*, and hearing a fellow general denounce Hitler's aggressive war plans. Gilbert noticed at one stage that Jodl had left Keitel's canteen table as he was finding, Gilbert speculated, the company distasteful because Jodl believed he had been working to defend his country, not to plan aggressive wars. When on Friday 14 December the razing of Warsaw to the ground and extermination of the Jews was raised, Jodl furiously shouted out 'the dirty arrogant SS swine'.

He gave a similar heated reaction on 4 January 1946 when the case against the General Staff was presented. He appeared 'red with rage', telling his counsel to remind the 'squealing generals' they were only trying to save their own necks. When Keitel took the stand, Jodl was 'moved' to see the Chief of the OKW having to do this in a military tribunal of this type. Jodl was annoyed at the killing of the RAF prisoners of war and claimed that as from that moment, he knew 'what kind of man Hitler was'. When asked how he explained Göring's loyalty, Jodl explained that he was 'in deep' and a party member, but most of the true officer class were not pro-Nazi but had to 'play-along because he was the legally chosen Reich Chancellor'.

Jodl was prone to sudden outbursts of anger, and when a General Adolf Westhoff was giving evidence on the abuse of Russian prisoners, Jodl jumped to his feet shouting that the eastern war had been barbaric on both sides. During the Easter recess, Gilbert visited Jodl and found him wondering about Frank's confession and whether he was genuine, pointing out that in the past he had behaved like 'a little king' with all his demands. He smiled when Gilbert mentioned Frank's jibe at the 'looting Göring' but was concerned that he gathered from Höss that the orders for extermination had started as early as 1941. Gilbert challenged him asking whether, if he had known about the orders, he would have continued or revolted. Jodl paused, claiming he would have had no idea if it would happen or not.

Jodl had another outburst during Frick's trial when the Röhm death and the Night of the Long Knives was raised, causing Jodl to yell out at lunchtime that one pigsty was as bad as the other. He was amused later by Streicher starting his time in the witness box by denouncing his own counsel. Jodl was certainly cynical when reflecting on Schacht's trial, explaining he might have withdrawn his loyalty on moral grounds but not on stock-market trends.

During a discussion with Gilbert, Jodl explained that at the signing of the surrender he had asked for delays, not to prolong the war, but to give time for Germans to seek safety by retreating from the Eastern Front. He believed by doing this he saved some 700,000 men. After the Raeder trial, Gilbert showed Jodl a copy of the *Stars and Stripes* containing an article on the massacre at Malmedy where some 84 Americans were shot by the Sixth Panzer Army. Jodl point-blank refused to believe that Sepp Dietrich was responsible because he and Rundstedt were honourable soldiers.[*]

Jodl's Trial

Jodl's defence team were Professor Dr Hermann Jahrreis and Professor Franz Exner who were highly professional and well equipped for their role. Jodl had asked for some 19 witnesses but only four were granted; it was not a concern about timing, but 'that the evidence given by a witness should neither be cumulative nor irrelevant; exactly the same rule had been applied to the prosecution'.[8] Jodl had always been reticent with other people while in prison, often standing apart, but having watched the film on concentration camps, he poured out his feelings to his wife, stating, 'I would not have tolerated such wrong doing for a single day'.[9] She was the only person to whom he expressed his emotions; his wife was attractive and managed to stay during the trial by acting as an assistant to the defence team. When Jodl entered the witness box, he found on the ledge a small bunch of flowers with a note from his wife telling him to remain calm, another time a watercolour of his favourite Bavarian mountains with the same instruction.

Jodl took the stand on Monday 3 June 1946 charged on all four counts. He claimed he was a professional soldier by blood and not a politician. He explained he had been sceptical about Hitler during the Munich *Putsch*, but any misgivings about Hitler had been 'quieted' by men like Papen and Neurath, which was a further 'dig' at those he placed among the political breeds. Jodl had expressed anger at Gisevius's assertion that he had withheld news from Hitler and claimed he had promptly reported the Malmedy massacre. Jodl explained he would like to have told Hitler more, but the dictator relied too much on more dubious sources outside the military. Jodl rapidly moved on to attack those who prepared coups while soldiers

---

[*]   Later, 73 SS men stood trial and 43 death sentences were given. None of them were executed because there was evidence that some confessions had been beaten out of the defendants and Senator Joseph McCarthy objected because he had many German constituents; the first reason was more reasonable.

were fighting. He frequently lost his temper in court, but it was known he had temper attacks with Hitler according to many sources including Kesselring. He also pointed out that he was one of the few who tried to defy Hitler and challenge him. Later, during Speer's trial when his counsel said Speer was the only man to stand up to Hitler, Speer later wrote, 'I interposed, saying that Guderian, Jodl, and many of the commanders of army groups had also defied Hitler'.[10]

In terms of his knowledge of Hitler's plans, his counsel asked him when he first met Hitler to which Jodl said he had been presented by Keitel on 3 September 1939 and 'at any rate that was the day I first exchanged words with him'. He later added that 'discussion of political questions was generally not admissible'.[11] Two days later, Jodl explained that the first time he heard about 'Russia being hostile was 29 July 1940 at the Berghof', giving Jodl the impression, he claimed, that the attack on Germany was a preventative war.[12]

He tried to describe the German dictator but was interrupted and rapidly moved on to state that following the murder of the escaped RAF prisoners of war, he realised Hitler had no concept of human rights.* He said it was a slander to suggest that military officers had enriched themselves, for which the other military defendants (except for Göring) indicated some appreciation. He was 'hunted' by the British prosecutor Geoffrey Dorling 'Khaki' Roberts (an international rugby player) over the RAF killings because one of those killed was a Roger Bushell, a friend and barrister in his chambers.

The Commissar Order, instructing that all Soviet political commissars should be shot, was also raised and Exner claimed Jodl had written a note in the order's margin that it should be withdrawn. His team then referred to how Jodl had refused to carry out Hitler's order to shoot commandoes. Hitler sent the order directly and without Hitler or Keitel knowing, Jodl sent another order saying commandoes should be treated as prisoners of war; Jodl explained he was never sure of the legality of the order. When Exner turned to the Jewish extermination policy, Jodl claimed he had no idea what Himmler was doing in the concentration camps, had not been concerned about the Jews escaping from Denmark which was a political matter, and only had a hint of Himmler's behaviour when he heard during the trial about the destruction of the Warsaw ghetto.†

During the afternoon session, he stated that he felt Germany was unprepared for war and it was a mystery to him why the British and French had not attacked during the Phoney War because they would probably have been successful given the number of troops available. He further described the occupation of the Rhineland as

---

*   Gilbert later asked him what he would have said about Hitler had he not been interrupted and Jodl told him that his feelings towards Hitler fluctuated between admiration and hatred.

†   Most of the Jewish population had escaped to Sweden with Danish help; only about 200 had stayed and were trapped.

a gamble, that the occupation of Austria was improvised, and the Sudetenland was a 'gift of the Munich Pact'. He was taken by surprise when the rest of Czechoslovakia was occupied and had no idea of the impending attack on Poland, but in his diary described the Czechs 'as the real villains'. None of this was believed by the prosecution. In his position, he had met Hitler for the first time in September 1939 and suggested he was in the dark, especially over SS functionary Alfred Naujocks's statement on how prisoners known as 'canned goods' had been killed in the supposed Polish border raid at Gleiwitz.[13]

The next day (5 June), Jodl explained that taking Norway was simply to beat England arriving there first, and the Low Countries were overwhelmed to prevent France invading. The Norwegian issue was an embarrassment the British Foreign Office wanted kept under wraps for fear of *tu quoque* arguments. He concluded the session by stating the principles of military obedience and the prosecution should thank their own obedient soldiers for placing them in a position so that they could prosecute. It appeared according to Jodl that all these wars were defensive, and he thought war was good for mankind. When challenged on his views and reactions, he replied, 'I must say it was obedience – for obedience is really the ethical basis of the military profession'.[14]

Jodl testified how Hitler had spoken to him about Operation *Barbarossa* in July 1940 and ordered troops into Romania to protect the oil supplies. Jodl claimed he never thought Hitler would attack Russia except out of necessity making it in his opinion once again a defensive war. In the witness box, Jodl had support from Göring and Dönitz, but Schacht and Papen grumbled about him. Jodl renounced the concept of a conspiracy, claiming it was only Poland that Hitler was after, and the subsequent wars were brought about by necessity. He also indicated that Rommel and Rundstedt had advised Hitler as early as 1944 that the war was lost, but he refused 'to budge' until the bitter end.

In his cross-examination, Mr 'Khaki' Roberts questioned Jodl's sense of honour as Jodl desperately tried to control his anger. He then admitted he had discussed the prepared incidents at the Polish border but never thought them necessary. Jodl evaded the mixed messages and conduct relating to the Low Countries and their invasion by arguing it was a political matter. During the afternoon, the cross-examination became more rancorous, with Jodl having to defend the bombing of Rotterdam in 1940, which he countered by saying it was not as bad as the bombing of Leipzig in 1943 by the Allies when the war was all but won. He consistently blamed the politicians and accepted that the rightness of the attack on Russia would have to wait until Russian intentions were clear. Jodl supported the suppression of partisans, but was against killing saboteurs, and he considered the killing of the escaped RAF personnel as outright murder. When asked if breaking promises was against an officer's honour, Jodl agreed but cynically noted it was another matter with politicians.

Exner pointed out that Jodl had the time to burn all his documents before he surrendered, but he handed them over to the victors, as he was convinced that the campaigns which he had worked for were justified and they had been fighting a preventative war against Russia. Jodl concluded his defence by stating, 'it is not the task of a soldier to be the judge of his commander-in-chief. May history or the Almighty do that'.[15] History did pass judgement but not to everyone's agreement, and the Almighty's verdict cannot be known.

After Taking the Stand

When asked by Gilbert why he so strongly denounced those who were trying to remove Hitler, Jodl replied that he had always disliked National Socialism, but he obeyed the head of state chosen by politicians, and when they realised that they had made a mistake they expected the *Wehrmacht* to 'get rid of him'; it was the 'double-dealing' which disgusted him as a soldier. Later, Jodl claimed none of the generals wanted a war – they had already had a 'belly-full' from the first one. When Gilbert asked him if it was Hitler alone who caused the war, Jodl paused and then confirmed that thought, saying it was all 'Hitler's will-power' and he had 'his mind set on it'. Following his cross-examination, Jodl thought he had done well and impressed the judges and had controlled his temper. He had no doubt that Hitler had started the war, he had no love for the assassins of the 20 July Plot, and apart from a few who were idealists, others had climbed on board because the 'wind was blowing the other way'.

Summation, Final Statements, and Verdicts

On behalf of Jodl, Dr Exner stressed Jodl's insecure arguments that Germany's wars were defensive, attacking the Low Countries because they had not stopped British planes flying over them (in those days to drop propaganda leaflets) and finished by telling the Tribunal that he had warned Jodl of his own lack of legal court experience, drawing the response from Jodl that 'if I felt a spark of guilt within me, I would not have chosen you as my defence counsel'.[16]

Jodl was described as the 'betrayer of the traditions of his profession', violating its code to pursue the barbarous aims of the Nazis, to which Jodl, being Jodl, exhibited his fury.[17] In his final remarks, Jodl stated that as a *Wehrmacht* leader he had not served the powers of hell and had not served a criminal but acted for the people and the fatherland, and that had been the 'guiding principle' of all his actions. He told the court he would leave the room with his head held high just as he had entered it months before. Many people thought Keitel's final statement was much superior. Jodl had always believed he would be found innocent, but in the judgement, he was found guilty on all four counts as he was deeply immersed in high command

and followed criminal orders. The verdict was announced as death by hanging, which, like Keitel and Göring, he found wrong by their traditions, and according to Telford Taylor he 'stiffened' and turned his eyes towards him. In the cells, he was bitterly angry over the fact that he was to hang and not be shot as a soldier. As Jodl became progressively angrier, his wife wrote to all the Allied generals of note and to the national leaders begging for his life, but to no avail.

Final Notes

Whether he was guilty or not and whether hanging was right is still debated. Had the trial taken place a year or so later, as with Field Marshals von Manstein and Kesselring, he may have been given a prison sentence and later released as the Cold War impacted. Kesselring, known as one of the best commanders, was condemned for allowing the execution of prisoners of war, was sentenced to death, later commuted to a life sentence, and freed a few years later. In 1953 legal proceedings in Munich declared Jodl not guilty and the French judge Professor Henri Donnedieu de Vabres in 1949 claimed the verdict had been a mistake.[18] Perhaps it should have been noted that Jodl was overworked, he had one period of leave during the whole war, and 60,000 messages a year crossed his desk.[19] In this writer's opinion, a prison sentence would have been more appropriate as the first two counts appear weak, and he had tried to stop Hitler on the Commando Order. He had exhibited more moral fibre than Keitel and there is a possibility he had been somewhat oblivious to the extermination policies because of his fixation on military concerns.

Arthur Seyss-Inquart 1892–1946

Background

Arthur Seyss-Inquart fought for the Austro-Hungarian Army during the Great War with some distinction and afterwards trained as a successful lawyer. He married in 1916 and had three children. He worked for the Austrian chancellors Engelbert Dollfuss and Kurt Schuschnigg, and when the latter resigned in 1938 in the face of the Nazi threat, Seyss-Inquart was promptly appointed his successor. He only lasted two days as Hitler had considered making Austria a puppet state. Such was the Austrian response, it has been argued that Hitler opted for the 'full *Anschluss*', and Austria was incorporated into the Third Reich as the province of *Ostmark*. Seyss-Inquart had not only joined the Austrian Nazi Party but drafted the necessary legislation, signing it into law. As such, he was appointed Governor (*Reichsstatthalter*) of *Ostmark* making him Hitler's personal representative.

Seyss-Inquart. (Netherlands National Archives)

After the invasion of Poland in September 1939, Seyss-Inquart was nominated a chief of civil administration for southern Poland, but the General Government was quickly declared, and he became deputy to Governor-General Hans Frank. He supported Frank in what was known to be a heavy-handed approach including the persecution of the Jews. He admitted later that in the interbellum years he believed the Jews and Slavs in the Austro-Hungarian Empire had betrayed the German nation. He held the honorary rank of SS general and stayed in touch with the higher echelons of the SS command structure.

Following the fall of the Low Countries, he was made *Reichskommissar* (Reich Commissioner) of the Netherlands (May 1940) and thereafter was associated with a reign of terror in that country. His task was to direct the civil administration, the economic collaboration with Germany, and to defend the interests of the Reich. He was fierce in tackling any resistance, introducing special summary court-martials, imposing heavy collective fines, and ordered probably more than a thousand executions. As a fierce anti-Semitic, he created a ghetto in Amsterdam and organised for the Jews to be sent to the camps, and it has been estimated that of the 140,000 registered Jews in the Netherlands, only 30,000 survived the war. These figures vary according to numerous sources, but at least 80 per cent of Dutch Jews were killed. He wrote to Bormann and seemed pleased with the amount of money he made for the Reich by taking property, businesses, and wealth from the Dutch Jews, and remained unrepentant of these actions. Later, he would claim that he kept the number of hostages killed to human proportions as prescribed by international law, and he had followed Speer's views and resisted Hitler's scorched earth policy by not flooding the Netherlands.

Under the Dönitz government, he was to replace Ribbentrop as foreign minister but was arrested on the Elbe Bridge in Hamburg by a Royal Welsh Fusilier called Norman Miller. Miller's original name had been Norbet Mueller, ironically a German Jew from Nuremberg who through the *Kindertransport* (Children's Transport (1938–40)) had been sent to Britain as a child to avoid the persecution.

Telford Taylor described Seyss-Inquart as 'limping slightly and peering through thick spectacles ... he was the least scrutable of the defendants',[1] although those sitting next to him often found him amusing and good company, with Papen describing him as a typical Austrian, 'cheerful, relaxed, often telling Viennese stories'. However, those who wanted to interview him for information on events, or the psychologists filling their information sheets by making conversation, found it impossible to gain any sense of response.

Medical Mental Observations

Airey Neave who had spent the last part of the war fighting in the Netherlands and had seen the suffering expected to find a limping monster. However, as a Colonel Dunn, one of the psychiatrists, had noted, Seyss-Inquart 'was not sullen but gives the impression of being cool and distant', and as a fervent Catholic was inscrutable and 'his own man'. His involvement in the *Anschluss*, which he minimised, meant he could be viewed either as a traitor to his own country of birth or simply as an Austrian who preferred the Nazi Party, as did many other Austrians who welcomed the German takeover.

Reactions during the Trial

Seyss-Inquart took as low a profile as he could, emerging from his silent background during Göring's trial on hearing Dahlerus give evidence, wondering how the British took the witness so seriously, especially Lord Halifax, who was known to be a man desperate to resolve the issue of war before it was too late, turning over any stone to succeed in gaining peace.

During the Easter recess, Gilbert raised the question of anti-Semitism, but he did not raise Streicher because he thought that Seyss-Inquart's intellectual depth might lead to sensible discussion. When asked by Gilbert how he accounted for the American tolerance and sense of peace, Seyss-Inquart responded that Germany and the USA were two quite different countries. He pointed out that America had started with an influx of peoples from different countries. Gilbert had to accept this but argued that Dönitz and Göring had pointed to the different temperaments of north and south Germany which Seyss-Inquart accepted, pointing out that the Prussian north never thought of racial and political theories and that the Prussian tradition was to obey orders. Gilbert found Seyss-Inquart 'cagey' about expressing opinions about other defendants.

Seyss-Inquart's Trial

Seyss-Inquart was charged under all four counts having been a member of the Austrian Nazi Party since 1931. His lawyer was Dr Gustav Steinbauer appeared somewhat helpless when Seyss-Inquart was under pressure. The *Anschluss* was of special interest but of little consequence because it was only a treaty violation not coming under any of the indictments, and there was no evidence that Seyss-Inquart wanted war. When Hitler appointed him governor in Austria, he was soon replaced by a hard-line Nazi called Josef Bürckel, but when questioned, Seyss-Inquart made no attempt to shift the blame onto Bürckel, accepting that as head of the civilian administration he had issued the necessary decrees for the treatment of the Austrian Jews. When Seyss-Inquart had been transferred to Poland as Frank's deputy he made a tour of inspection including Warsaw and Lublin. Evidence was produced to show he told his colleagues that 'independent political thought' was no longer permissible, and everything must be done 'in the interests of the Reich'. He witnessed the devastating scene of Jews trapped between the frontiers of Poland and Russia and showed no signs of disenchantment with the way the Nazi regime was conducting its policies.

It was noted that his testimony had not left a good impression and 'Schacht called it clumsy, and it is surprising that an intelligent man and a trained lawyer to boot could not make a better job of it'.[2] His only excuse for the execution of hostages was blamed on Himmler, and the theme of his defence was simply 'matters could have been worse'. However, there were no indications that Seyss-Inquart was a personally brutal man and had probably been pleased when he was transferred as Reich Commissioner to the Netherlands, because the Dutch were regarded in a different light to the east European Poles. In Norway, the Nazi Quisling had been given some authority, but Seyss-Inquart virtually ignored the Nazi Dutch leader Anton Mussert. When he was asked by Steinbauer how he handled the Jewish situation, Seyss-Inquart was frank, replying that, 'I will state quite openly that since the First World War and the post-war period, I was an anti-Semitic and went to Holland as such', viewing the Jews as being 'against National Socialist Germany' and there 'was no discussion of the question of guilt as far as I was concerned'.[3] He explained he had been visited by Reinhard Heydrich and this had been followed by Hitler's orders to evacuate Dutch Jews. He started to do this by collecting them in Westerborg concentration camp prior to transporting them east, with Seyss-Inquart adding that the German people were in a life-and-death struggle. Given what was happening to the Jewish victims, this must have raised a few eyebrows in the court. He was then questioned about forced labour and was again frank, saying, 'I believe I enrolled some 250,000 Dutch people to work in Germany, and I testified to that yesterday', reminding his prosecutor he should have been listening.

Finally, he was asked about the end days, when he had travelled by sea to Kiel to secure Dönitz's cancellation of Hitler's scorched earth policy and returned to the Netherlands by land when he was captured. When asked in court why he risked the journey back, he explained he wanted to take care of his co-workers, and he had held the opinion 'that since we had been out front in the hour of triumph, we could lay claim to being out in front in the hour of disaster as well'.[4] His witnesses brought little relief to what was regarded as an honest admission to his involvement, but one Dutch witness described his efforts to ease the pressures of occupation. Hitler appeared to think highly of him as he had proposed Seyss-Inquart to replace Ribbentrop in Dönitz's new government. In his later memoirs, Speer noted that 'by lucky chance, a few days after the testimony which sealed his death sentence, he received the first good news about his son, who up to this time had been missing in Russia'.[5] Speer was right – Seyss-Inquart had been open and frank in his answers even though it meant condemnation of his actions.

Summation, Final Statements, and Verdicts

During this period, Gilbert talked to Seyss-Inquart about anti-Semitism in Poland. Frank had just attributed it to the 'passionate prejudices of the Polish people', but Seyss-Inquart argued that it was a 'left-over' from the Middle Ages and a Christian superstition of 'save the faith and kill a Jew'. It was clear that his counsel Dr Steinbauer had a difficult hill to climb, not least because Seyss-Inquart refused to denounce Hitler and all Steinbauer could do was search for some form of mitigation. He explained that his client's involvement in the *Anschluss* and Poland involved no criminality, although evidence had previously been given of his anti-Semitic statements and his reputation was well known. His conduct in the Netherlands proved more difficult but which he countered by evidence that Seyss-Inquart had tried to stop the flooding of that country under Hitler's scorched earth policy. Jackson referred to his time in the Netherlands as pillaging 'for the benefit of the German juggernaut'.[6]

Seyss-Inquart's final statement was more of an apologia as he attacked the prosecution effort trying to implicate him in planning aggressive wars. He argued that had the Danube remained a unity as in the Austro-Hungarian days there would have been peace, and that when war broke out, he recognised it as a life-and-death struggle which meant unconditional service to Germany. Regarding his time in the Netherlands, he claimed he was no hangman, that the Dutch liked Germany, but he had stopped the flooding of their territory. At one stage, the Tribunal had to encourage his counsel to omit pages on the contribution of Beethoven to the cultural life of Vienna. He concluded by referring to Hitler with a degree of reverence and esteem, bravely announcing that he could not shout out '"crucify him", as yesterday I cried "Hosanna"'. As with many of the defendants, there were attempts to introduce the *tu quoque* argument but rarely a mention of any admission to personal guilt.

Seyss-Inquart out of all the defendants had made the least effort to defend himself and had been indicted on all four counts. Having made no effort to denounce Hitler or Nazism, he had coloured the waters against himself. The general impression was he was not by nature a brutal man and was acquitted on count one but found guilty on the three remaining counts. He remained calm even as the death sentence was passed upon him. Down in the cells, he told Gilbert that he had expected the sentence and asked if they would still receive their tobacco ration; he then apologised for being so trivial.

Final Notes

A few commentators have since questioned whether he should have received a life sentence and whether he should ever have been charged on count one. Many, including his son Richard Seyss-Inquart, expressed this opinion to a British newspaper and pointed out that his father was 'no more guilty for things that happened in the war than any other German, or any Englishman or Dutchman for that matter'.[7] The counterargument under the feelings of the day were strong, especially his anti-Semitism and transporting Jews to their death, and his often-quoted brutal conduct in the Netherlands. He never denied Hitler, was an ardent nationalist and was one of the few defendants who stood by his original views. This writer spent some time in the Netherlands and Belgium as a young boy in the 1950s, and although more interested in fun and seeing new places, can still recall his hosts talking about the fear and dread of living under German occupation. At least Seyss-Inquart stopped the Netherlands being flooded and was not evasive or lying about his activities. But his adherence to Hitler and the Nazi regime was the reason why so many died and others suffered in the Netherlands, and his anti-Semitism added yet more brutality to his personal record of immoral behaviour.

Franz von Papen 1879–1969

Background

Franz von Papen was a Prussian nobleman who trained as a General Staff officer and served as chancellor of Germany in 1932 and then as vice-chancellor under Hitler from 1932 to 1934. When questioned in court about his life, he explained he came from 'the soil which has been in the possession of my family for 900 years', implying nobility, and it was known he had married into money. Whilst in the role of staff officer, he had been appointed (1913) as military attaché in Washington where his activities – allegedly planning to blow up bridges and railway lines – annoyed the American government, and by 1915 he was declared a *persona non grata*. He was purported to have been a spymaster but bungled too many things despite his smooth ways (he was known as the 'Silver Fox' at Nuremberg). During the

Franz von Papen. (Bibliothèque nationale de France, Photographer, R.Sennecke)

Great War, the *New York World* had placed some of his secret reports on its front pages. In America with him was a naval intelligence officer called Franz von Rintelen who described Papen as a 'foolish and stupid intriguer'.[1] He returned to serve in Europe where he made further blunders such as leaving some secret documents in frontline headquarters while on leave which were overrun by the British who discovered them.

After the war, he was elected to a seat in the Prussian state parliament, and at this stage was considered a witty companion in social circles but of little political significance. The Catholic Party rejected him as leader a few weeks before he was due to be chancellor for a short duration and he was soon defeated by a vote of censure. He had tried to create a new state somewhere between democracy and totalitarianism and was unsuccessful. He and Hindenburg had failed to see the changing times as they swerved towards a pact with the Devil, as Papen suggested Hitler as chancellor and himself as vice-chancellor. Papen was the extreme collaborationist believing he would be able to control Hitler about which he tried to convince his readers in his memoirs.[2]

He believed that by supporting and controlling Hitler, he could return to power. He later told the Nuremberg Tribunal he had no idea why Hindenburg had selected Hitler, but historically it has been suggested that it was because he was deemed to be a malleable type of person. The French Ambassador to Germany André François-Poncet at that time summarised Papen by writing 'that if he succeeds in an undertaking, he is very pleased; if he fails it does not bother him'.[3]

During the Night of the Long Knives, he was arrested at home by the SS, had his telephone lines blocked, and some of his associate staff were murdered. He thought he had been released with Göring's help, but later in an interview he added that it was because Göring was concerned about bad publicity. It was probably that Hitler did not want a well-known man in his position murdered on the world stage. He told Hitler he could no longer serve under him and did not attend another cabinet meeting, yet he accepted the post of Ambassador Extraordinary in Austria. Papen stood beside Hitler as German troops moved into Vienna, personally accepted the Golden Party Badge from Hitler, and later was ambassador in Turkey. He objected to Hitler's methods but never joined the German resistance who would probably have worried about his reliability. Airey Neave made the comment in his memoirs that on meeting Papen he would never have trusted him.[4]

He was found after World War II by an American platoon in Westphalia. He had been on the run since finding his way out of Turkey, but he was more worried about the Gestapo.

Interrogations

Papen, as with the other traditionally conservative-minded defendants, argued he was able to operate a moderating influence over the regime. He was a deeply conservative aristocrat of the old order who like Neurath hated the Weimar Republic, and he was by now infamous as being instrumental in Hitler's appointment as chancellor in 1933. He was not a major component in terms of the various indictments, but the Allies regarded him as a possible Nazi collaborator by assisting Hitler's ascendancy, even though in his interviews and more pertinently elsewhere he had exposed his hatred for the Nazi regime. He especially resented Nazi attitudes towards the churches and the Jews, but he stayed in office which puzzled Dodd who took a special interest in this defendant. Papen had resigned in 1934 but unlike others offered no resistance to the regime on the grounds that he might still be able to exert some influence by taking ambassadorial roles in Austria and Turkey, which understandably perplexed Dodd who interviewed him several times. For the Americans it was a simple black and white situation, not understanding Nazi Germany with its threats, the sinister implications, and the unknown future.

There were several lengthy interviews assisted by Papen's excellent English, and his background as a civilised, educated, committed Catholic projected him as a point of interest, and hopefully some form or explanation for others of this social class who had seemingly supported Hitler. A previous chancellor Heinrich Brüning had left Nazi Germany in disgust and settled in America, and another, General Kurt von Schleicher, had withdrawn and was later killed on the Night of the Long Knives. Dodd was curious as to why Papen had continued to work with the Nazis, why he had supported them even in ambassadorial roles even though he had made it apparent he objected to their conduct.

By way of explanation, Papen explained that the Weimar Republic's democratic system had trouble forming a reliable government under the strains of the economic duress of those days. The SPD was failing, the communists (KPD) were slowly increasing and only the NSDAP seemed to hold them back as the SPD declined in public support. It was generally understood that President Hindenburg was opposed to Hitler, denigrating him as the 'little corporal', but knew that a government had to be formed, if only to keep the communists out. Papen was elusive on the part he played in convincing Hindenburg of appointing Hitler as chancellor, arguing that the Nazi vote was increasing and could not be ignored. He agreed that Hindenburg regarded Hitler as a 'nobody' but intimated that the choices were limited with Germany's need for stability. Dodd pressed Papen as to how far he was responsible in changing Hindenburg's mind which he evaded. It was seemingly impossible to establish how far Papen had influenced Hindenburg, with Papen constantly claiming that both men were only looking for a way to take Germany 'out of this mess'. Papen pointed out that the Nazis were gathering popular support especially among the growing unemployed and the young with Hitler's promises of a better future. He claimed his only intention was to stabilise Germany and for that country to lead a normal life. He admitted he admired the way the Nazis had promised a classless society and urged the need to fight Bolshevism.

When questioned about being a prominent figure who had made no attempt to stop Hitler, even when his evil intentions were becoming openly exposed, was a question Dodd relentlessly pursued. Papen had shared the belief the communists had started the Reichstag fire, and had not opposed the Enabling Act even though it meant thereafter that it was impossible to exercise any control, influence, or restraint on Hitler. Papen pointed out that after the Night of the Long Knives, he had protested at the excesses, later leading to his resignation, which after Hindenburg's death meant there were no traditional conservative influences left. Nevertheless, Dodd pointed out that he continued to serve Nazi Germany in Austria and Turkey at the ambassadorial level. He argued with Papen that it would have been better to have opposed Hitler or even have left the country in disgust. Papen continued to argue that he had hoped to offer some restraining influence or moderation, but Dodd countered by stating it needed more than this hope. When Dodd compared the situation with similar events in America, Papen, probably rightly, pointed out that the two countries could not be compared. The Night of the Long Knives had been a clear indicator of the disabling terror regarding Nazi recrimination, which induced a sense of apprehension and even dread in those who considered opposing Hitler. The 20 July 1944 Plot and many other incidents confirmed that such fears were justified and demanded incredible courage from any opposition. Papen recognised that he 'could have done that', but he had hoped as a prominent figure he could have brought some restraint and moderation. He pointed out that following the Munich Agreement, Hitler seemed to change direction and tactics, and he had hoped that at best he could save Germany from conflict, from a war which 'disgusted' him. He suggested he had thought of returning to the army (in which he had served in the Great War) or staying in post to use other influences. He even quoted his son who had been in Argentina and who knew what was happening but returned to risk his life for his country.* Papen demanded that Dodd should speak to other foreign diplomats with whom he had worked as they would explain exactly what he thought of the Nazi regime.

When asked about the concentration camps from 1934 onwards, Papen replied, 'I don't think anybody hasn't had an idea what was going on. We knew of the [early] concentration camps, but we always believed that the people were treated honestly there, kept in prisonship, [sic] yes, but well treated'.[5] When questioned about later revelations of the brutality of these early camps, let alone the later extermination sites, Papen had said he had found it hard to believe that such things could happen. Later, he stated he felt a guilt about the situation because he had played a part in bringing Hitler to power. Dodd had interviewed Papen rather than interrogated him, and there was a general impression that although Dodd was puzzled by Papen's reasons for assisting Hitler to the chancellorship and continuing to work for the Nazi regime having resigned from the government, there was a small degree of empathy for Papen's situation. Dodd seemed to have little idea about life in the Hitler regime and seeking comparisons with America would have raised Papen's eyebrows.

Medical Mental Observations

When Goldensohn met Papen during the trial proceedings, he described him as a 'very alert, smiling man, is polite, exerts a definite personality and charm of the

---

*   His son survived the war and assisted his father during the trials.

old school'.[6] During Hess's time in court, Papen was bemoaning the ignorance of the Foreign Office, and Hess about life outside Germany. Papen then latched onto Himmler and the way he was constantly watched and under suspicion, especially because of his leaning towards the Catholic Church. He described the time when Engelbert Dollfuss was killed and two SS men came to the door, which his son and he approached armed, for fear of being assassinated. As it transpired, all they wanted was to instruct him to phone Hitler who needed him to go to Vienna to handle matters. He knew nothing about the *Anschluss* and was moved from Vienna before it occurred because he had told Hitler that although it was good to have a union with Austria, it should not be by force.

Gilbert asked him whether he believed Hitler at this stage and Papen 'sighed and said yes'. He was assigned to Turkey as ambassador and Goldensohn asked why he agreed if he was so disapproving of the Nazi regime. Papen replied it was for the sake of peace and he did not want Germany surrounded by enemies. Goldensohn questioned the logic of this with Papen responding that at that time he believed Hitler would not start a war if Germany was not threatened by encirclement. However, in March 1942, Papen had held a discussion with the diplomat Hassell who was a member of the resistance and who recorded in his diary that Papen had explained that 'he believes he can bring about Turkey's entry into the war on Germany's side'.[7] Meeting Hassell was dangerous, and it was fortunate for Papen that Hassell's diaries did not come to light in 1945–46, not just for safety from the Gestapo, but otherwise the prosecution would have been further armed. He changed the subject back to Himmler who had warned him about too much Catholicism; Papen informed Himmler that Turkey was an Islamic country. He also noted that when he returned after the 20 July Plot 1944, Hitler had changed.

In another meeting, he talked to Goldensohn about Germany's history, the problem of federal states, the achievements of Otto von Bismarck in 1871 founding the Reich, and relating some of the problems experienced during the Weimar Republic days. There had been a time when Papen wanted to be prime minister of Prussia but Göring had proved the more popular choice, which he accepted if only because there had to be an agreement on the 'main points of national policy'. He explained that the British and Americans would find this difficult to understand but given Germany's history it needed an agreed direction and not the turmoil of the recent past. It was necessary to have a workable majority and Hitler gained the votes because he had made promises to the millions of unemployed, and the NSDAP's form of socialism was superior to that of the communists whose activities had been suppressed; he had made the same point to Dodd during the interviews.

When questioned about anti-Semitism, he pointed to his 1931 speech in Gleiwitz on the Polish–German border where he said there was nothing wrong in stressing the good points of a certain race, but this did not make it better than others. It was a moot point which Goldensohn did not challenge, because if it is argued a 'certain race' has good points, it infers that it is lacking in others. He later pointed out that he had argued that Jews who had been in Germany since 1914 should be allowed to stay, mentioning that in 1918 Germany had a massive influx of Jews from the east which had to 'be corrected'. Goldensohn noted that the Papen reminiscences 'sounded well-rehearsed, given in a studied manner, without much emotional tone or feeling'. From Papen's point of view, he was innocent, had been chancellor of Germany, and was now answering questions from an American psychiatrist inside a cell. He had been a strong conservative, patriotic if not a nationalistic politician, and had blundered in thinking Hitler could be controlled. His anti-Semitism seemed to be more of the general social bigotry type and not the evil policy of the leading Nazis.

Gilbert described Papen as 'the soul of politeness and courtesy except when some slight irritation revealed the irritability of his 70 years'.[8] Gilbert noted that Papen could never fully explain why he kept working for Hitler when he had described him as a 'pathological liar' and had tried to explain to Hitler why his anti-Semitic policies were wrong. He agreed that Hitler's breaking of the Munich Agreement had been wrong, but asked Gilbert what he could have done, since he hoped to do some good which would not have been the case had he fled.

Reactions during the Trial

When Airey Neave delivered the indictment, he found Papen wearing a blue pinstripe suit as if about to go to his gentlemen's club, self-possessed, and speaking with what he described as an 'Etonian blend' of English. Gilbert also described Papen as looking debonair with his white handkerchief in his pocket looking incongruous with the shirts and pants which he wore at the weekends.[9] Neave and Papen talked about Hitler during a weekend recess (12–13 January 1946) with Papen explaining how he and Schacht had agreed that in the early days it was possible to persuade Hitler one way or the other and neither had the impression that he was a madman. However, it had soon dawned on them that it was impossible to reason with Hitler, quoting the time they had tried to stop him leaving the League of Nations, which although he listened, he point-blank refused to heed their advice. Gilbert asked him whether he had read *Mein Kampf* to which Papen responded that it had been written for political reasons and no one took it seriously. This was probably true of many others on the international stage, but in hindsight was a mistake. Papen claimed he had his differences with Hitler, but he never thought he would wage war until the breaking of the Munich Agreement. When challenged as to why he stayed working, as Goldensohn and Dodd had also questioned, he gave the same answer asking what else he could have done, and at least as ambassador he had managed to keep Turkey neutral and 'keep that corner of Europe at peace'. Given there is no reason to doubt Hassell's diary above, Papen was lying but this could not be proved in the courtroom.

At the end of February, Papen managed to obtain a copy of the Evening Post in which he read an article on militarism, causing him to expound on the subject and claiming that it needed a German to explain this to the German people. He said he would like to raise this at his trial but understood it would be regarded as an irrelevancy. He also asked why they could not see more of the daily press, so Gilbert brought him a copy of the Soviet *Pravda* in which there was an attack on the Pope. Papen responded by pointing out that the main resister to Nazism was the Catholic Church rather than the Protestants (who he explained had been too divided). He was staunchly Catholic and conservative, a man of the last generation who expressed his disappointment in Göring because he had come from a respected family background.

Following Schacht's trial, Papen was astute in claiming that Schacht had been something 'of an opportunist' looking for a place to do business but 'who had bet on the wrong horse'.[10] After Jodl's defence and just before Papen's trial there was a sharp interchange between Papen and Göring. Göring had reminded Papen that Hitler was once chief of state, to which Papen angrily retorted Hitler was a Nazi chief of state who murdered six million people.

Papen's Trial

Papen's counsel was Dr Egon Kubuschok and was assisted by Papen's son Friedrich. Apart from the political reasons to assist Hitler to the chancellorship, there were no obvious reasons as to why he should be charged even under the question that he promoted the Nazi accession to power. Papen later wrote that 'I had no archives or documents at my disposal', and 'I have referred more than once to our unfamiliarity with the procedure adopted by the court', but given he was the 18th defendant in a row, he must have had some knowledge by this stage.[11]

As with Hess and Schacht, he was not accused under counts three and four. The prosecution claimed he had supported Hitler politically and in public, even though it was well known that his Marburg University speech in June 1934 calling for reform had been suppressed by the Nazis, and during the Röhm purge he had been held under arrest and two of his working associates had been killed. Despite this, he had worked for the Nazi regime as ambassador first to Austria and then Turkey. During his defence presentation, he and his team did their best to make him as innocent as possible.

Papen started (Friday 14 June) by portraying himself as religiously inclined, a traditional conservative coming from a historical family. There was a general impression that Papen 'was always too complacent and self-righteous to regret anything', and his script was overwritten with 'too many references to the aristocracy'.[12] It was used against him with remarks that as an aristocratic Catholic he had used this reputation in favour of the Nazi Party, but he must have been aware that the Vatican had complained about the Nazi regime.

He explained that in the Great War he had travelled to the USA looking for war materials, not spying, which had been a popular accusation for a time when he had been called 'the devil in a top hat'. He described his membership of the Catholic Centre Party trying to amalgamate the many political segments in the confusion of post-1918. He defended Hindenburg and the Weimar Republic (though deplored it later), claiming he worked to reduce unemployment, control inflation, and tried to correct the injustices of the Versailles Treaty but had not succeeded. The other nations had failed to listen, and the Nazis were growing in power to such an extent Hindenburg was obliged to appoint Hitler to the chancellorship as he alone could provide a viable party to govern.

After the weekend, Papen explained how Hitler arrived in power because of the political difficulties and a civilised if not Christian approach was anticipated. He mentioned the Concordat with the Vatican of July 1933, but Hitler had merely regarded it as a piece of paper. Papen also claimed he had been tricked by Hitler and Goebbels into believing the Jewish problem would have a peaceful solution. In the afternoon, he explained how the Nazi Party became a dictatorship and not a coalition, which prompted him to give his Marburg University address during which he denounced all that was happening with the restrictions on free speech, religion, and human rights. Goebbels had blocked the publication of the speech and Papen had offered his resignation which Hitler refused.

He described his arrest during the Röhm slaughter, when under Göring's orders he was detained at home without radio or telephone. When two of his assistants were shot dead and others sent to concentration camps, he had accepted Göring's explanation they were involved in a plot, and how after his release he had again offered his resignation to Hitler who asked him to postpone it until the agitation died away. He turned down the offer to be ambassador to the Vatican, but just prior to the murder of Dollfuss, he accepted the ambassadorial role in Vienna, claiming it as a matter of duty and conscience.

Hitler had given him the Nazi Golden Party Badge simply to camouflage their differences. He had accepted the ambassador's role in Turkey to avoid a 'hostile encirclement' of Germany but was astounded when he heard of the outbreak of war describing it as a crime, as he did with the war on Russia. He claimed that by taking the role in Turkey he was trying to establish peace, though Jodl quietly whispered that the German Embassy in Ankara had been used by the *Abwehr* for espionage work. His counsel produced an affidavit which indicated that the 20 July 1944 plotters had considered Papen as their foreign minister.

Papen was embarrassed by Maxwell Fyfe who quoted some of Papen's pro-Hitler speeches, not least when he referred to Hitler as 'heaven sent' to the German people. Maxwell Fyfe, despite Papen's attempts at explanation, continued to provide documentary evidence that he had willingly collaborated. One observer noted that Papen was 'drawn down from the Olympian heights to political murder and violence which had surrounded his career'.[13]

Maxwell Fyfe demanded from Papen what the Church had expected from the Concordat with Papen weakly explaining that he had assumed Hitler would support religion. A few days later, Maxwell Fyfe demonstrated that Papen had written to Hitler congratulating him with the words 'the clever hand which eliminates political Catholicism without touching the Christian foundations of Germany', which pleased Göring as Papen evaded the issue.[14]

Maxwell Fyfe then challenged Papen as to why, after the Röhm purge and the murder of his assistant, he kept working for Hitler by accepting another post. This purge and the *Anschluss* were raised again by the British prosecutor with the constant demand for Papen to explain why he kept supporting Hitler by accepting new roles, and whether he was just looking after his sense of dignity; Papen could only answer by claiming it was his sense of duty. Maxwell Fyfe finished by directly asking the embarrassing question as to how Papen could continue working for the Nazis when they murdered his own assistants, to which Papen responded that it was his sense of patriotism and he could only answer to his own conscience. Chief Justice Lawrence also created further embarrassment when he asked Papen whether his claim he had saved 10,000 Turkish Jews conflicted with his claim that he knew nothing of the extermination policy, which Papen could not explain.

Maxwell Fyfe did his best to unravel this scenario of innocence during his cross-examination, and although it was generally acknowledged as a masterly demonstration of a barrister's skills, it could not undo the presented evidence. He had to prove that Papen had promoted a war of aggression for which there was no evidence. Maxwell Fyfe focused his attack on Papen's seeming support of Hitler until the Röhm purge, that he had supported Hitler over the *Anschluss*, which may have cast Papen in a poor light but failed to pinpoint him as a component in seeking an aggressive war. It was becoming abundantly clear that under the indictments Papen could not be pursued. Maxwell Fyfe even accused Papen of cowardice, which may have been true, but this only caused Papen embarrassment, and as Telford Taylor noted, 'Papen might well have responded to Fyfe that it is easy for A to tell B that B ought to have been a hero'.[15]

Maxwell Fyfe cornered Papen on his claim he knew little of the brutality, referring to his friend Herr Fritz von Tschirschsky who had sent Papen a detailed account of his time in Gestapo hands when he witnessed the barbarity of the cells, addressing Papen with the accusation that 'you had a pretty good idea of SS and Gestapo methods', yet Papen continued to work for Hitler.[16] Papen could only reply that the major powers had tried to work with Nazi Germany and all he was doing was trying to serve his country.

After Taking the Stand

During the trial Papen, having raised the question of the Church, provoked considerable discussion among the defendants with Rosenberg claiming that most priests, especially Polish ones, were basically anti-Semitic, with Frick throwing in the Spanish Inquisition, enabling Frank to tell Gilbert that 'the beast in man keeps coming out again and again'.[17] Schacht raised the question as to why Papen had returned to work for the Nazis, a question raised in cross-examination, while Göring, sat in the dock, called him a scared rabbit and a traitor. Frick and Frank observed that Papen was trying to avoid the fact that 'he played along with the party'. Papen himself had been taken by surprise by Maxwell Fyfe's tough cross-examination and when talking with Gilbert tried to explain how useless other alternatives were. He said he had saved 10,000 Jews in France because they were Turkish nationals. The final questions by Maxwell Fyfe and even Judge Lawrence had, according to Gilbert, upset Papen who thought his image had been marred.

Summation, Final Statements, and Verdicts

Papen's counsel gave him a good brief, asking for nothing but the obvious fact that Papen was not guilty. Jackson's summation of the prosecution described Papen as the 'pious agent of an infidel regime, who held the stirrup while Hitler vaunted into the saddle'; he assisted the *Anschluss* and helped the Nazis as a diplomat.[18] Jackson described him as 'the old-school diplomat, who cast the pearls of his experience before the Nazis' as their guide.[19]

Papen was beside himself with fury and could hardly believe such a personal attack had been made. He was angry, and after Göring had made his final statement Papen attacked him for being the main cause of all the suffering and the problems.

Papen described Shawcross and Jackson as wrong for treating him so disdainfully, for showing indifference to the other defendants, and concluded by saying, 'when I examine my conscience, I do not find any guilt where the prosecution has looked for it and claims to have found it. But where is the man without guilt and without fault?' Papen had been indicted on counts one and two and when it came to the judgement, on a two-to-two vote he became the second defendant to be acquitted.

Post-war

Franz von Papen was one of the three defendants who were acquitted. He had blundered in helping Hitler to power, acknowledged this but had not been involved under any of the Tribunal's indictments. However, in 1947 he passed through a denazification court and was given an eight-year prison sentence of hard labour but was released in 1949. In 1952 and 1953 he published his memoirs, and with these and many papers continued to defend himself against the charge he had helped Hitler to power, which led to some heated debate within West Germany. He published his *Memoirs* in English in 1953.[20] He died in Obersasbach, West Germany on 2 May 1969 aged 89.

Final Notes

Throughout the trial notes, it is possible to detect that Papen was always scared for his life acknowledging 'that if he had said publicly that he was finished with the whole rotten regime he would have disappeared as did my associates'.[21] This cannot involve some comfortable moral judgement because few people can know for certain how they would react under the fear of something like the Nazi regime. He made a political misjudgement in believing Hitler could be controlled and for not perceiving the true nature of the dictator, but many politicians have made similar errors. He was generally known from his time in America for making blunders, but the unseemly side appeared in his continuing to work in ambassadorial roles which gave him a status he always sought whatever the cost. It was seeking status that prompted him to help make Hitler chancellor, and status which probably encouraged him to be an ambassador because his claim that he could exercise any influence at this stage was pure nonsense, and he must have known this. He was not guilty of the charges and rightly set free, and his imprisonment by the German courts was probably based on his initial support of Hitler. Nevertheless, he left a general feeling of weakness and distaste.

Albert Speer 1905–81

Speer at the Atlantic Wall. (Bundesarchiv, 183-J14294, Licence CC-BY-SA 3.0)

Background

Albert Speer came from a well-established middle-class background whose mother at first rejected his proposed wife on social snobbery grounds. Nevertheless, he married Margarete Weber in August 1928 and they had six children, but they grew apart from 1933 and never returned to family closeness. Speer joined the Nazi Party in 1931 and because of his architectural skills, he drew close to Hitler and thereby was prominent among party members. In 1937 he was appointed Inspector General with

Hitler designating him as the architect for the rebuilding of a victorious Berlin and Germany. Hitler's frustrated wishes as a young man in art and architecture, along with Speer's charming and accommodating personality made him easily acceptable to Hitler. Hitler's megalomaniac ambitions could find light in the overly grand buildings he and Speer planned. Speer was also behind the layout of the stadium at Nuremberg providing an outstanding public platform for Nazism producing 'a pioneer version of *son et lumière*'.[1]

Following Operation *Barbarossa*, he turned to military construction led by Dr Fritz Todt but following Todt's death in a plane crash (8 February 1942), Speer was appointed Reich Minister of Armaments and War Production (War Production was added on 2 September 1943) at the age of 36; this work involved him in the issue of forced labour. He oversaw army armaments but, according to some, coveted control of the *Kriegsmarine* and *Luftwaffe* resources. He took over the air-armaments from Göring on 1 August 1944 assuming total control of all production with a labour force of some 14 million. He had political protection because of his closeness with Hitler, and Dönitz once referred to him as Europe's economic dictator. He was regarded as one of the major defendants even though it was only the last three years which were of interest to the court. Airey Neave found that it was Speer's smoothness which repelled him, and thought that it was his social charm which had made Nazism feel acceptable to the arts and science. This was a sweeping judgement of Speer but with a degree of validity.

Interrogations

If Hess offered nothing of value with his amnesia, tactic or otherwise, Albert Speer was frank and open with the Western interrogators. He started the proceedings by offering the information that he had seriously considered assassinating Hitler the minute he realised that the Führer intended to initiate a scorch-earth policy as Germany was being overrun. It was late in the day when he came to this decision as he was intelligent enough to see they had lost the war and looked to a future for post-war Germany. He explained he was supported to a degree in this claim of killing Hitler by Dietrich Stahl who had been an armaments ministry official. There had been discussion between them about using gas in the bunker, but this proved difficult. Stahl mentioned that Speer even planned to assassinate Hitler along with Himmler and Goebbels which Speer never mentioned and seemed, given Speer's character, somewhat unlikely. Up to this point, Speer had never been actively involved with any form of resistance to Hitler, but according to most available sources, Speer was believed on the 'gassing Hitler project', writing it into his own memoirs. However, there must have been some questions that Stahl and Speer had concocted this concept if only to ingratiate themselves with the incoming enemy forces, a cunning plan, or that the two had simply played with the idea in those moments of depression as the inevitable end was in sight.

As noted above, Speer had originally come to Hitler's attention because he was an architect whom Hitler wished to utilise in his grand building scheme of the successful Third Reich; they were in the early stages almost friends, as far as Hitler was capable of personal friendships. Speer having joined the Nazi Party rose somewhat rapidly in the regime when he helped build models of Hitler's dream cities and enhanced the Nuremberg rallies with the use of searchlights. In February 1942, such was Hitler's trust that Speer was appointed armaments minister having benefitted from the death of Fritz Todt whose death drew the usual conspiracy theories. There is no question that he was good at his job, and in the short-lived government of Dönitz in May 1945, Speer was appointed as economics minister in this bizarre Alice in Wonderland scenario. His relationship with Hitler by his own and other accounts had deteriorated, as he came to realise (especially after the virtual destruction of Hamburg) that Hitler needed to come to terms with reality. Hitler saw less of him preferring his advisers to be more optimistic and never doubting or questioning him. Speer believed that Hitler had to understand that the economic war was lost, and any reasonable defence demanded resources. He worked behind the scenes to try and hinder the scorched earth scheme, and even talked to Field Marshal Albert Kesselring and others about the sheer negativity of such a policy. Hitler had decided in his usual obstinate way that the Germans had not risen to the occasion and deserved their ghastly future. From what could be gleaned, it appeared that Speer made many efforts to resist the policy, but Hitler remained obdurate as always and was still feared.

In the end days when still at Flensburg, Speer was visited by American officers from their bomber command investigating the effects of the bombing raids on Germany. It was immediately clear that he had much to offer and was willing to do so which made him a candidate of immediate interest. Three days after this interview, the Flensburg government was surrounded by British troops, Speer was arrested and flown to the Ashcan, then on to Paris, and after further interrogation was sent to the Dustbin camp. He became a serious focus of interest, not just for his informed and intelligent approach to the effects of the bombing strategy deployed against Germany, but also in connection with the military weapon developmental advances where it was acknowledged the Germans had made significant advances. He was interviewed and interrogated more than the other defendants as he was prepared to be open, and he had inside knowledge, both personal and technical. He was able to explain how despite the bombing of German industry, it was still able to maintain a reasonable output.

His sound control of English and his general demeanour with his pleasant and frank approach meant he was treated well and was seemingly valued, much more than many of the other defendants; even the critical and somewhat cynical Airey Neave appreciated some of his characteristics. It was also believed that he could shed some interesting light on the nature of the Nazi regime and Hitler himself. It was discovered that the carpet bombing had not been that effective in terms of Germany's war effort, and especially that of the British who bombed at night. The more specific targets selected by the Americans had not been according to Speer the best, stating that they should have attacked the armament plants, especially electricity generation targets which would have had a major effect on the war factories. Speer's technical knowledge and position as armaments minister gave the Allies invaluable insights, and such was the relationship Speer was probably surprised when he was indicted as a war criminal. The central charge was the brutal exploitation of enforced labour which he tried to blame on Fritz Sauckel who had already maintained that he had followed Speer's demands. As regards the exploitation of Jews, Speer blamed Himmler and Goebbels, and when asked about the conditions of the labour force, he simply stated that he knew nothing about the conditions, and it was not his area of responsibility.

He tried to challenge the need to place him in the dock by appealing to the fact he had been so totally cooperative and had tried to kill Hitler. He was permitted to prepare a submission for Jackson to review the case as Speer perceived it to be. There was also his fear and implied threat that he should not share his information with the Soviets.

The Soviets wanted Speer dead because of his proximity to Hitler and based their reasoning on the abuse of forced labour, especially the Russians. Speer was interrogated by the Soviets led by a Colonel Rosenblit who questioned his affiliation to the Nazi Party, queried whether he had read *Mein Kampf*, wanted to know about Hitler, but concentrated on their main prosecution case namely Russian prisoners of war used as labour. In short, they refused to accept his version of events, stating, 'I am not satisfied with this reply. Do you have nothing else to say about this … it seems to me that your explanations avoid the subject'.[2]

Perhaps one of the most interesting insights Speer provided was during an interview by the American interrogator Captain Otto Hoeffding in October 1945 when he was questioned about Hitler.[3] Such was the information Speer provided, it generated extended discussions on Hitler, mainly because most trial defendants were not much questioned over Hitler, being more inclined to blame Himmler.[*] None of them stated Hitler was mad, and Speer's insights were received with interest. It did not take long after the war before many biographies were written about the German dictator,

---

[*]   In his diaries, Victor Klemperer, the German Jewish scholar, referred to Himmler as the 'the party's most notorious bloodhound' which was close to the truth as even Göring was worried about him and saw him as a potential enemy. See Victor Klemperer, *To the Bitter End: The Diaries of Victor Klemperer* (London: Weidenfeld & Nicolson, 1999), 244.

but in 1945 information about Hitler as a person was scarce. Speer was especially interesting in his views on Hitler as the war turned against Germany and its effects on the Führer. The way the Germans had fought right up to the centre of Berlin when the odds were so severely stacked against them was almost mind-defying with major loss of life and destruction, and how and why this happened was believed to rest in the singular nature of the dictator.

Speer admitted that until 1942 the German achievements had surprised everyone, and even their ability to resist thereafter was a factor which could not be ignored, even if, as Speer admitted, it was an error. The driving force behind the initial success and the determination to defend had its focus in Hitler. The idea that one man alone could be so powerful prompted the interviewer to ask how Hitler chose his advisers or rather 'principal collaborators'. Speer pointed out that Hitler's initial propensity was to surround himself with old party members, but many of whom became not just aged but indulged in lives of luxury, Göring being a prime example. Speer pointed out a parallel with Napoleon, and he indicated Hitler who relied on intuition could be unpredictable and later chose 'outsiders'. This was the way Speer admitted he had been chosen because he happened to be at Hitler's headquarters when Todt's death was announced. Hitler knew and liked Speer and selected him even though he had little experience for his new post. According to Speer, Hitler exercised 'unnatural power of personality on all those around him', 'his subordinates fed him what he wanted to hear', and during the war there was 'the rigid line he took in his decisions and the obstinacy with which he followed it'.[4] Those around Hitler were, according to Speer and many others, under his spell. Speer felt that following Hitler's success between 1933 and 1941 many believed in his 'greatness and mission' implying a historical significance and demanding a sense of reverence. Hitler also surprised Speer and many people with his ability in memory recall of facts, figures, and technical knowledge. If he ever called any form of conference, it was only to announce his recent plans or thinking, rarely to confer. Stalin had a similar attitude, but Churchill was moderated by his chiefs of staff and answerable to parliament; dictators were not hampered in this way.

One of the aspects Speer admired about Hitler was his ability to stay calm, even when receiving bad news, as when Italian General Pietro Badoglio's defection was announced while Speer was present. Not everyone would have agreed with this view, as when Hitler was informed Mussolini had been deposed, he had been in a conference. He demanded of Himmler, who had brought the news, to find out whether Mussolini was still alive and where he 'was holed up'.[5] Many of those present claimed he was in deep distress and virtually threw a tantrum.[6]

Later, Speer would claim people like Bormann influenced Hitler against him and he was certainly not around too much during the end days, so these observations by Speer are more reliable when referring to the earlier days of Hitler's reign. Speer intimated there was no clear methodology applied by Hitler in selecting his associates, that he preferred 'yes-men', and they attracted behind them similar types of people with the developing situation of a dictator surrounded by a weak system. This led, as Speer noted, to Hitler's propensity of 'divide and rule' made much easier by the choice of his minions. Some dared question Hitler, which he took as challenging him, and they were soon side-lined or given another posting. Speer claimed Hitler was too trustworthy with his political colleagues and never trusted the military who soon became critical as Germany's survival became doubtful. As Speer admitted, he had the impression that Hitler was not a good judge of people. He would only listen to acknowledged experts in their given fields, but he made all the major decisions, first, Speer stated, on intuition, later with attempted reasoning, and finally on the whimsical belief that providence was looking after him. This was reinforced with the failure of the 20 July 1944 Plot, which also sapped any remaining courage from military leaders who knew that he was making serious military errors. Hitler, according to Speer, always thought that he knew better than his generals because he had experienced trench warfare, and no one wanted the fate of facing the people's court. According to Speer, Hitler's sole interest had always tended to be foreign policy and military matters and he knew little of the internal state of Germany. He never visited a bombed area, was always surrounded by guards, and was not seen mixing with the public as in the 1930s. Later in his interview, Speer stated that 'a useful gift was his ability to talk with the man in the street and to draw him out'. This must have been rare; there are films and pictures of Hitler in the 1930s greeting adulatory crowds, talking to children, receiving applause, but speaking to the 'man in the street' may have been his one gift in the 1920s.

Before the war, it appeared to most people, including Speer, that Hitler had plenty of time on his hands, pondering on building in Linz where he wanted to retire and dreaming of times when he could live in a large house and away from politicians whom he told Speer he disliked.[*] An ironical comment in many ways because he was the major sole political figure in his totalitarian society. Life changed for him as he became immersed in the war, Speer thinking he was a genius but quickly adding the traditional caveat that genius and insanity were 'closely related'. Speer said he lost his sense of intuitive thinking and made blunders. When questioned on this, Speer explained that he thought a more generous approach in Russia might have helped. Historically, he may have been more correct had he specified the Ukraine who generally despised Stalin, but under the barbaric Nazi misrule the Soviets became the preferred rulers.

There was no question that Speer was correct in his assessment that Hitler needed considerable self-assurance to control the situation, which with his popularity in the 1930s under Goebbels's propaganda was always assured. In war, he was self-isolated,

---

[*] According to Speer, Hitler loved the classical style of Paris which he anticipated creating in Linz.

nearly always in the company of military men, overworked, suffering mental tiredness, watching fewer films, and kept going by his personal doctors, Karl Brandt and Theodor Morell. In the end days, Speer even noted that 'he often reminded me of a senile man'. Some military men talked of a 'leadership crisis', but after the 20 July 1944 Plot it would be dangerous to make such statements. The only social gatherings Hitler enjoyed were in the evenings when he entertained his associates with long, boring monologues on his past or his views or listening to his favourite music. The Italian foreign minister Galeazzo Ciano wrote in his diary:

> Hitler spoke for nearly two hours without a pause, and Mussolini kept looking at his wristwatch, Cavallero pretended 'he was in ecstasy', Jodl, after an epic struggle fell asleep on his sofa, and Keitel, uncomfortably close to Hitler, was reeling but managed to stay awake.[7]

According to Speer, the one person Hitler could rely on was Eva Braun who, as is well known, seemed to love him and died with him in a joint suicide pact. But by 1944 even the strongest personalities were frightened in his presence. According to Speer, the early military commanders such as Fritsch were self-confident, and so they had to go; the new ones received massive financial gifts from Hitler to ensure their loyalty. He promoted 'yes-men' such as Keitel, and after the 20 July 1944 Plot it was a matter of blind obedience so military commanders, like many others, jumped on Hitler's orders and directives without question. These gifts, according to a report by Hans Lammers, had been a tradition in Germany before Hitler, and they were meant to ensure the top men were not hindered by financial worries.* Such were the amounts, the gifts had to be more than financial relief and tended to reflect a form of feudalism.

The military was, according to Speer, hindered by the head of state being their commander-in-chief. Hitler and his senior officers believed they could run the war using maps from the safety of their various headquarters. Hitler was ignorant of the realities of the frontline and its conditions.

Speer concluded by observing that Himmler's SS took all the finest young men, potential officer material for the *Wehrmacht*, and simply squandered their lives, as Hitler had done by insisting on continuing to fight a lost war. He finished this interview by expressing the hope that the rule of one man 'surrounded by weaklings' should be prevented ever occurring again. Speer provided a frank inside knowledge of Hitler the man.

When Speer was interviewed on matters of foreign policy, he confirmed what many had already suggested, that Hitler made all the decisions. He would sometimes tussle as to where he stood, whether to support Mussolini over the invasion of Ethiopia or the British who opposed the Italian dictator. Speer was asked for Hitler's views on Stalin's purges and show-trials. Hitler initially thought they had been staged,

---

*   Hans Lammers was a bureaucrat and chief of staff in the Reich Chancellery.

which was not unreasonable, but later concluded that it made sense cleaning out the old guard and restoring new and more active military leaders. This probably reflected more Hitler's views on his own military commanders. Speer claimed that Hitler really did not want to start a war again in the west. Hitler believed that the German reoccupation of the Rhineland was the riskiest moment, and its peaceful resolution was down to the influence of King Edward VIII on whom he had placed many hopes. Speer intimated that Hitler's main interest in supporting Franco was to avoid being surrounded by communists, and that although the Germans had been impressed by the Italian navy and air-force, 'not enough attention was paid to the fact that the Italians were not soldiers'. This was a patent myth and Speer missed the point that unlike Germany many Italian people had no trust in the war or Germany, and they did not revere Mussolini as the Germans did with Hitler. He admitted that Hitler put much store in his relationship with Mussolini and was grateful for his silence over the *Anschluss*.

In terms of his plans and intentions in 1938–39 Speer drew his observations from side-comments by Hitler when discussing the architecture for a future Germany. Hitler wanted a grand façade to impress the 'little nations' which Speer saw as Hitler's dream of power politics with Germany as the central power. Hitler made similar comments when Speer described designing the stadium at Nuremberg which was now only a place of curiosity for off-duty Allied soldiers. When asked if Hitler had intended to start a world war, Speer replied that he did not think that was his intention but added the caveat that everyone in the inner circle was prone to lying or smoke-screening. Speer admitted that 1939 was the best time because Germany was ahead in military logistics and preparation, but at this stage Speer was more Hitler's architect friend and not part of the military-party inner circle, so this could only have been speculation. Speer made one important observation drawn out by being asked about America, and that was that Hitler and his henchmen had never travelled globally; Hitler had visited Italy and occupied countries, but never America or Britain. Hitler thought the Americans would make weak soldiers, Ribbentrop that they would stay isolationist, and Göring and Goebbels that they only made kitchenware and razorblades.

Medical Mental Observations

Goldensohn took few serious observational notes on Speer, and Gilbert wrote he was the most realistic of all the defendants. Speer was not shocked at the indictment, claiming that history demanded such a trial, which would have been music to Gilbert's ears.[8] He claimed he knew nothing of the extermination programme any more than other ministers knew about the V-2 rockets. This was a peculiar note because the 'wonder-weapon' was common gossip, and perhaps the rockets and

Jewish persecution were widely known but not the details. Gilbert concluded that on re-examining the nature of the Nazi leadership, it 'had apparently shattered the illusions of the architect Speer'. There are to this day varying opinions on Speer, but he was able to win over many people to his seeming innocence during this time.

Reactions during the Trial

Gilbert found Speer on a pre-Christmas visit as 'calm and responsible as ever' who when questioned about Hitler explained that he saw him as 'a selfish destructive force that had no consideration for the German people'.[9] Like many others, he had been astonished at the evidence that Hitler had started the Polish conflict with provocation provided by the SS.

On Thursday 3 January 1946 at the restart of the trial, the SD chief Ohlendorf described in detail the orders from Himmler for exterminating 90,000 Jews, thereby on behalf of Hitler. This caused Göring to refer to Ohlendorf as a swine and traitor, not so much because of his actions but by announcing it in court. Speer created a sensation by asking his counsel to ask Ohlendorf whether he had been aware of Speer's attempts to kill Hitler and even capture Himmler. Everyone was shocked by this public announcement and during lunch Göring attacked Speer only to be stunned by Speer who 'virtually told him to go to hell'. That evening in his cell, Speer appeared to Gilbert to be somewhat nervous but smiling at his revelations and how other defendants, even his friend Dönitz, were avoiding him. A few days later during a weekend cell-visit by Gilbert, Speer claimed that the other defendants were 'coming around and accepting the fact he had made an assassination attempt' on Hitler. Speer claimed they all had to pretend to be faithful to the Führer which was probably due to the pressure applied by Göring. He said they 'did not have the guts' to tell the truth. He acknowledged that he felt a responsibility in belonging to the party leadership.

Speer was happy with the return to isolation following Göring's overbearing influence, having already expressed his feelings that Göring was dominating everyone. Later, Gilbert sat with Speer and had a talk about Göring, agreeing that Göring terrified the others, even making Papen tremble. Even Speer admitted he would be less reluctant to express what he wanted to say. Later, in early April, Gilbert found Speer depressed because he thought that men like Göring and Keitel in their defence arguments were 'getting away' with their pleas of loyalty, and they were not being 'unmasked'. He did admit after Keitel's trial that the field marshal had been more honest than Göring. Like Schacht, Speer was delighted when the witness Gisevius exposed Göring's questionable machinations on the political side. This had unsettled his friend Schirach, and Speer spent some time trying to draw him away from the 'Hitler line', succeeding to a degree.

Speer's Trial

Speer came to his trial well prepared with his memory fresh and helped by the many interrogations which he had conducted in such an open way as to encourage one interview after another by all interested parties, from military to industry. He was charged on all four counts, but the first two were weak given his late rise to power in the regime. His lawyer was Dr Hans Flächsner and Speer's initial testimony demanded a full day. Flächsner quoted facts and figures to the sheer boredom of many, some suspecting he was explaining what a competent job Speer thought he had done.[10]

Speer was little better than his counsel, informing the Tribunal (Thursday 20 June 1946) of how he had taken over the role of war production and of his work between 1942 and 1944, listing facts and figures. This proved as boring as his counsel had been, and he seemed to be 'putting on record his outstanding competence ... some might think he was attempting to dazzle with the brilliance of his achievement so as to be blind as to its cost'.[11] He had some 14 million workers and admitted some were prisoners of war, others foreign labour, and a few from concentration camps. He claimed that they amounted to only one per cent but that it was against the Geneva Convention which meant he had often been at odds with Sauckel over the nature of their procurement. He also expressed the opinion that he had not been in favour of bringing the workers to Germany on the grounds they could have done this work in the occupied countries. He was somewhat arrogant if not casual in his explanation:

> I had no influence on the methods by which workers were recruited. If the workers were brought to Germany against their will that means, as I see it, that they were obliged by law to work for Germany. Whether the laws were justified or not, that was a matter I did not check at the time. Besides, this was no concern of mine.[12]

Nevertheless, as the prosecution was quick to point out, Speer applied pressure on Sauckel to produce more workers. When Speer turned to the effects of the bombing on Germany over which he had been interviewed many times, it was of no relevance to the court, but they listened as it was of considerable interest. Moving away from the hitherto milder approach, Jackson cross-examined him aggressively the next day, especially on the use of forced labour and deploying concentration camp victims, speaking of a deal Speer had arranged that in exchange for the camp-inmates, Himmler would receive five per cent of the arms. Jackson was not so much accusing Speer of the brutality but obliging him to admit that he was aware of the situation. At one stage, Speer claimed he thought Mauthausen was a model of cleanliness and the camps had been established to save the workers the strain of travel. He stated he had not realised the cruelty of the camps which may have taken place in Himmler's factories which were beyond his sphere.

It was clear that the first two counts had little application to Speer, but the use of forced labour clearly brought him within counts three and four. After this part of the courtroom drama, Speer turned to his so-called planned attack on Hitler which was to have taken place near the end of the war when defeat appeared inevitable. He admitted he was guilty, accepted what he called 'common responsibility', and the trial was right in seeking the truth. According to some reporters, he was so open and frank that it sounded like King's evidence (giving evidence for the crown in return for a reduced sentence).[13] He accused Hitler of avoiding responsibility by killing himself, and 'I, as an important member of the leadership of the Reich, therefore, share in the total responsibility, beginning in 1942'.[14]

He claimed that Hitler's scorched earth policy clearly indicated that Hitler had identified the German people with his own fate, and he denounced the Führer with some passion.[15] He said that in his opinion the war had been lost in 1943 from the military point of view but by January 1945 from the industrial production perspective. Hitler was determined to fight on despite the hopeless situation which Speer saw as a betrayal of the German people. He explained how General Guderian had explained this to Ribbentrop who returned from Hitler stating that this attitude would be regarded as an act of treason, and later that Hitler claimed the German people were not fit or worthy to survive. This prompted Flächsner to ask Speer about his hopes of assassinating Hitler using gas and other ideas he had purportedly conceived based on the grounds that it was an act of loyalty to the German people. Telford Taylor described Speer's story as 'more psychodrama than melodrama' as Speer pondered killing the man who had done so much for him.

Speer also revealed that Hitler had considered gas warfare, but the military was against this for fear of retaliation. He also referred to Hitler's views of Göring which sent the subject in the dock into a state of 'squirming', especially when he mentioned that Göring had forbidden General Adolf Galland of the *Luftwaffe* to tell the truth about the enemy's fighter power.

Earlier in the case, Flächsner had questioned Speer on his relationship with Hitler. He explained his association with the Führer became formal after the outbreak of war, and deployed Dönitz's argument, namely 'Hitler knew how to confine every man to his own speciality', indicating how the defendants listened to previous arguments which might bolster their arguments.[16]

Flächsner did not call any witnesses but entered some interrogation reports from some of Speer's associates. Later, Judge Biddle asked Speer to clarify what he meant by 'common responsibility', to which Speer responded by stating that all members of the (so-called) government were responsible for the broad general policy and for their actions at the beginning and end of the war. Speer left a good impression from his time in court, with his denunciation of Hitler and his explanations of the system, with Biddle regarding him as 'the most humane and decent of the defendants'.

However, his knowledge of the barbaric use of forced labour and his apparent stance that it was not his concern was somewhat denying any chance of acquittal, and he would have realised this situation. He was obliged to admit he knew about the deportation of 100,000 Hungarian Jews, and that he had threatened reluctant or tardy labourers with concentration camps and was quizzed by the prosecution on the way they were treated.[17] He had to accept the evidence but tried to modify it by claiming he had not realised the true nature of the atrocities in the camps. On reading the trial transcripts, it appears that Speer had his own motives in his open admissions and frankness. He never denounced the Hitler of the early days and his aggressive wars, claimed he knew nothing of the extermination processes, and only turned, he purported, to plan Hitler's death at the last moments of the war. If true, it gave the sense that Speer was the only one to keep his sanity which is what he tried to convey. Whether he had experienced a moral transformation is an impossible question to answer, and Jackson's probing of slave labour and Speer's evasive defence left doubts in this area. His lack of response to questions about forced labour conditions, the use of Russian prisoners of war and the concentration camps simply seemed unbelievable. When Jackson questioned him about the production of steel whips at Krupp's for controlling the workers, Speer explained they were simply to replace truncheons.[18] When the Russian prosecutor Maxim Raginsky pressed him on the matter of *Mein Kampf* which revealed Hitler's aggressive intentions, Speer confessed that despite previous claims he had lied and had not read the whole of the book.[19] To anyone who has tried to read Hitler's literary effort, this would have rung some bells both then and now as it is relentlessly boring and rambling.

Speer's ability to project himself in a better light than most was his main feature, and the current writer can recall reading Speer's book *Inside the Third Reich*, in 1982 and being somewhat impressed by the conveyed image. But on more mature reflection, it is easy to gain the impression he admitted the truth when it reflected well on him, but he pretended ignorance when it did not.

After Taking the Stand

During the trial, Sauckel was evidently angry at Speer shifting the blame in his direction, and Keitel expressed the opinion that Speer was the one man who could have stopped the war by telling Hitler they had run out of ammunition and armaments. Naturally, when Speer mentioned assassination it aroused considerable debate among the divided defendants. Göring had to exercise some control on himself, but made it clear he would 'get even' with Speer, making sinister threats over which Speer expressed some concern. Speer recognised that he had deepened the divides among the defendants causing a high degree of consternation. He had been unprepared for Judge Biddle's question about 'common responsibility', and he wondered whether he should write a letter explaining more precisely what he meant. Speer realised he had lit a fuse and told Gilbert that the defendants' nerves were at breaking point, and that Gilbert could expect the 'polite masks' to be removed.

Summation, Final Statements, and Verdicts

Speer's counsel as with those of Sauckel and Seyss-Inquart spent part of his summation time challenging the Hague Convention on matters of forced labour. It was soon clear that the court was not finding Flächsner's arguments viable. His defence counsel then turned to Speer's efforts to counter Hitler's end-day policies of destruction, making a plea for mercy because Speer had to make the choice between betraying Hitler or remain loyal to the German people. If Jackson had any empathy with any of the defendants it may have been Speer, but in his sarcastic way noted that Speer had secretly 'marshalled the entire economy for armament, but he had no idea it had anything to do with war'.

Speer was probably the one man for whom the court may have felt a slight degree of sympathy, but his involvement in forced labour amounted to serious criminality against which it was difficult to argue. In his final statement, he dwelt on his defiance of Hitler over the scorched earth policy in the end days, and then gave a lecture on the advances of military technology concluding that the goal of the Tribunal was preventing 'degenerate wars in the future'. Although Speer had been indicted on all four counts, the first two made little sense as he had only been a background friend of Hitler so he was acquitted of these charges. However, there was no avoiding the issue of the use of forced labour and he was found guilty on the last two counts, with Biddle noting in the report he read that 'in mitigation, it must be recognised that … he was one of the few men who had the courage to tell Hitler that the war was lost'.[20] The Russians demanded the death sentence, but his efforts with the West at least gave him imprisonment for 20 years. In the filming of the sentences, the official camera focused on the various defendants as their verdicts were announced. When Speer's turn came, and a 20-year imprisonment was announced, he blew his cheeks out in relief that it was not death.

Post-war

When he was released from Spandau Prison in October 1966, he was greeted by massive media interest but saved his major comments for *Der Spiegel* in November 1966. His views were widely welcomed as words of comfort because he seemed to whitewash the older Germans. This was especially true for those of Speer's middle-class background who could claim they were so busy doing their jobs and duties they had little opportunity to know what was going on. When he left Spandau, he donated his *Chronicle* to the German Federal Archives; it was later edited and noted there was no mention of the Jews. He tried to return to architecture but failed. He published two autobiographical accounts, both written whilst he was in Spandau, entitled *Inside the Third Reich* and *Spandau: The Secret Diaries*. During the 1980s, some of his reputation as a brilliant technocrat suffered as did his claim that he knew nothing about the Holocaust.

He made himself available for historians and in October 1973 made his first flight to Britain for a BBC interview; a few days later, he appeared on the programme *World at War*. He returned in 1981 to appear on *Newsnight* but died from a stroke on 1 September.

Final Notes

During captivity, Speer had been full of candour, admitting his loyalty to Hitler but prepared to denounce him, but this did not obscure his guilt. There is a sense over the years that there was something of a cunning fox in Speer who used his intelligence and social skills to successfully engage himself with the new political masters. Many have rightly asked whether he deserved a lesser sentence than Sauckel, or whether Sauckel should have been hanged if Speer received a prison sentence. He had 'escaped a death sentence by presenting a subtle and sophisticated mixture of self-exculpation and self-blame. He had not known about Auschwitz, he said, a palpable untruth, but he should have done'.[21] It could be noted with a degree of appropriate cynicism that compared with Sauckel and Streicher he came from a better social stratum and had more appeal to the Western judges.

In Nuremberg, Speer successfully started his variation of a story of a man dedicated to his technical work, at which he was supposedly excellent, and repentant that he had been too busy to realise the enormity of the Nazi barbarism. His daughter Margret Nissen wrote in her memoirs of 2005 that her father had spent all his remaining time constructing the 'Speer myth'.[22] He took the myth building of his past to a new level, using every resource in the modern media and with the aid of some historians. He was the picture of the apolitical technocrat who regretted his failure to see the crimes of the regime. The British historian Hugh Trevor-Roper saw him as a person who only cared for his projects, clever at administration, but failed to see the evil of Nazism.[23] This was probably too kind an evaluation. In a recent book by Getta Sereny she summarised the human side of Speer, basically stating he was a flawed man seduced by power.

In preparing such a myth, it was not just a matter of Speer painting colours in different shades, or making slight adjustments to given perspectives, but he simply must have recognised the conditions of enforced labour, and he would have known about the concentration camps and the extermination of the Jews. A man in his political position could hardly have known otherwise, and there seems little doubt that at the trial and afterwards he lied. The German historian Matthias Schmidt wrote that Speer had ordered the eviction of the Jews from their Berlin homes.[24] He knew what was happening with extant photographs of him at Mauthausen and Gusen concentration camps. It is now dawning on most historians that Speer had lied and did so until his death. He was undoubtedly quite unscrupulous, and this raised the question of whether the plan to gas Hitler was fabricated. His memoirs were less than honest, embellished, and the truth edited.

Constantin von Neurath 1873–1956

Background

Baron Constantin von Neurath studied law as a young man and joined the civil service following a brief time in a local law firm. In May 1901 he married Marie von Filseck and had a son and daughter. He arose from minor Swabian nobility of the Protestant variation, serving as a diplomat. Between 1903 and 1908 he had been vice-consul in London, then spent time back in the German Foreign Office before being posted to Turkey in 1914. During the Great War, he was awarded an Iron Cross First Class and was wounded. In 1919 he was appointed ambassador to Denmark, then to Italy (1921–30), and then spent two years in London as ambassador to Great Britain. In 1932 he was appointed foreign minister by Franz von Papen, holding the post under Hitler. He had asked Hindenburg if he

Constantin von Neurath. (Bibliothèque nationale de France)

could continue to be ambassador in London because the king of England had asked for his return, but he was instructed to accept the new appointment.[1] He was by nature right-wing and unhappy about the Versailles Treaty, but concerned about Hitler's expansionist policies, prompting him to resign and Hitler to replace him with the more compliant Ribbentrop in 1938. He was appointed as Reich Protector of Bohemia and Moravia, although from 1941 to 1943 this was only a nominal post. Hitler appeared to want to keep the man for his international reputation and appointed him as minister without portfolio and to the cabinet, which was more a paper exercise than an important body, and which, according to Göring, never actually met. Hitler may have selected Neurath in the forlorn hope it might calm international outrage over the occupation of Czechoslovakia. Neurath arrived at Prague Castle and inaugurated a press censorship, banned trade unions and political parties, sent some protesting students to concentration camps, and followed the Nuremberg Laws regarding the Jews. Nevertheless, the Nazi regime considered him too lenient, and Heydrich was named his deputy and held the real power. Neurath's position was in name only and he tried to resign in 1941 but it was not accepted until August 1943. There were some hints that he had been involved in a plot to overthrow the Nazi regime but there was nothing substantial in this claim.[2] He was eventually captured by the French who had a few issues they wished to discuss with him.

Interrogations

As with the other more conservative-minded defendants, Constantin von Neurath argued he was able to operate a moderating influence over the regime. As with Schacht and Papen and many of the military commanders, Neurath had little liking for the Weimar Republic, disliked the new politics, hated communism, and resented the results of the Versailles Treaty. The conservative elements thought they had seen in Hitler a way forward and had been early collaborationists under the general and misguided view that they could exercise some control over the regime, a mistake for which they were now held accountable. For Neurath, Papen, and Schacht, their relationship with Hitler was strained when he started to plan for aggressive expansionism. All these three men fell within the prosecution's orbit under criminal conspiracy because they had voluntarily opted to work alongside Hitler and had to answer for their actions. When asked why they had not withdrawn, probably from discussions with one another they all claimed they stayed to try and attempt damage control. Neurath always argued that after his resignation as foreign minister he had taken on the post of Reich Protector to restrain the extremists, to try and uphold Christian principles. Neurath, like the other traditional conservatives, had tendencies for loyalty, patriotism, right-wing to their very roots, and considered resignation almost as desertion. None of them associated themselves with the resistance against Hitler such as the ex-German ambassador Hassell who paid the penalty following the pseudo-legalistic trials following the 20 July 1944 Plot, though there may be evidence that Neurath may have made some contact later in the war.

Medical Mental Observations

Goldensohn found Neurath spoke English but not fluently and described him as 'an old man' in dark clothes 'sitting on his cot'. He asked Neurath about his hometown of Kleingladbach and his family background, and his regret at having no grandchildren as his only son had married a widow. Neurath took control of the conversation asking Goldensohn what he thought about the trial, voicing his own opinion that the prosecution of organisations was 'poor'.

He described his first clash with Hitler in 1935 when he opposed Ribbentrop's appointment as 'ambassador at large in London', which was to be the first of many confrontations with Hitler which he lost. Even Göring acknowledged to Gilbert that Neurath was 'a man of standing and insight, he would contradict Hitler on occasions and reason with him'.[3] Neurath described it as Hitler's 'power politics', and it was an early indicator that it would be difficult for Germany's traditional conservative right wing to control the dictator. Neurath had already expressed doubts over the ways the Nazis had conducted the elections. He had been surprised when asked to be the Protector of Bohemia and Moravia and asked Hitler about the French and British reactions. He was told that it was necessary because Emil Hácha had asked for German protection, and Hitler explained that Neurath had been asked because it was known he was a moderate man.

Hitler may have been correct in his belief that Neurath was a reasonable person, but Karl Frank, Neurath's secretary of state, whom Neurath described as a 'bad man', represented Himmler over whom Neurath had no control. When Hitler told Neurath he was too mild he resigned, which was not accepted, but he never returned to his post, and his resignation was not recognised until 1943. Neurath fell into that category of men like Papen who had once been powerful and influential and believed they could control Hitler. They were on trial because in their ambitious hopes that they could control Hitler they had played a part in his rise to total dictatorship.

Reactions during the Trial

When Airey Neave presented the indictment, he noted that Neurath shivered which caused him to reflect it was little wonder Neurath always deferred to Hitler, and never challenged him. On a pre-Christmas visit, Neurath explained to Gilbert that 'Hitler was a liar' which he had failed to recognise in the early stages, and Hitler had fooled people. Gilbert gave him two cigars for his birthday and as he smoked one in his cell, he explained to Gilbert his defence, especially in terms of the Hossbach Memorandum and his disagreement with Hitler over that speech, and the part he played in the Munich Agreement. He was not foreign minister at the time but 'forced' his way into Hitler's presence to express Mussolini's views. He also pointed out Daladier's hard-nosed attitude that the Czechs had to live with the decisions. When he did exercise some power, it was interesting to note that when in 1937 Britain's Pell Commission had opted for a Jewish state in Palestine, Neurath sent diplomatic guidelines to oppose the idea.[4]

Just before Dönitz's trial started, Neurath and Papen talked about America sharing some of the guilt on the grounds they had not joined the League of Nations. America after the Great War had entered a state of isolationism, but Neurath and Papen being diplomats were desperately reaching for slender excuses to explain Hitler's rise to power, over which they alleged that they had no influence.

Neurath's Trial

Neurath's counsel was Dr Otto Freiherr von Lüdinghausen who provided Neurath with written questions and answers. He spent far too much time on Neurath's early life which had nothing to do with the trial, and the Versailles Treaty problems which had already been ruled out as unnecessary and needlessly repetitive. He talked of Neurath's 'noble Swabian family', his Christian way of life, but the judges became increasingly irritated by this approach wondering when Lüdinghausen or Neurath would arrive at the critical year of 1933; both Lüdinghausen and Neurath were too verbose.

Neurath had approved of the early Hitler, and even accepted Hitler's explanations of the Röhm purge. When Neurath was questioned about anti-Semitism, he referred to the 'Jewish problem' not the Jews. Neurath responded by explaining his Christian upbringing and humanitarian convictions stopped him being anti-Semitic, but he conceded he had been concerned about the massive Jewish influence on German life. This long opening cast considerable light on Neurath but barely touched upon the question of the indictments. He appeared to have no knowledge of Hitler's aggressive military intentions until a meeting on 5 November 1937 (Hossbach Conference) when Göring and Raeder were also present. He explained he could not accept this policy and offered his resignation which was not accepted until 4 February 1938 when he was replaced as foreign minister by Ribbentrop. He helped draft a reply to the British objection to the *Anschluss* because Ribbentrop was still in London, but explained it was done under Hitler's direction. There was a serious clash within his own evidence because earlier he had objected to the Hossbach Conference but when asked again claimed there was no talk of aggressive plans, indicating a degree of expediency. He then retired to his home but was soon called back to help in the Munich Conference, later accepting the appointment of Reich Protector of Bohemia and Moravia. He explained that he had been informed that it was a Czech request for him to be involved, which may have been a falsehood by him or others. It was clear that Neurath had not been so shocked by the Nazis as 'to lend his name to Hitler's regime by taking on purely titular posts'.[5]

Karl Frank was installed as Neurath's secretary of state and along with Himmler dictated what would happen in Neurath's area which meant an abundance of anti-Semitic measures. It was clear Neurath made no initial attempt to resign, but claimed he made some effort to curtail these activities by Himmler. He was summoned by Hitler and told he 'was too mild with the Czechs' and so he offered his resignation, but Hitler refused it. He was told to take leave and in October 1943 Hitler accepted the resignation.

Maxwell Fyfe's cross-examination was tough, and he started by exposing that Neurath's claim of not being anti-Semitic was doubtful, quoting Neurath from a statement he made to the *Völkischer Beobachter* (17 September 1933):

> The Minister [Neurath] had no doubt that the stupid talk abroad about purely German affairs, as for example the Jewish problem, will quickly be silenced if one realises that the necessary cleaning up of public life must temporarily entail *individual cases of personal hardship* but that nevertheless it served only to establish all the more firmly the authority of justice and law in Germany.[6]

None of this helped Neurath when Maxwell Fyfe gave evidence that Neurath had purchased his Berlin home at a low price because the previous owner's wife had been Jewish. It was proposed to Neurath that he had a realistic sense of what Himmler and his policies were, long before he accepted the post in Prague. The Russian judge Nikitchenko trapped Neurath by exposing that although he had opposed Hitler and had agreed that Hitler 'made short work of any opponents', nothing had happened to him, to which Neurath could only reply that he always 'expected it'. Had Neurath not accepted the post in Prague and stayed retired, he would not have been in the court; there is the prevailing sense that pride in position was important to the Swabian of noble birth.

Summation, Final Statements, and Verdict

Neurath's defence summation was the longest of them all and according to Telford Taylor the 'most tedious'. It was simply a repetition of all that had been said in the main defence. The prosecution against him was tough based on his long service to the regime. His was the briefest of all the final statements informing the court he stood before them with a clear conscience. Neurath was indicted and found guilty on all four counts which raised a few eyebrows of those listening, but in mitigation the judges recalled that he had interfered with the security police and arranged the release of many arrested Czechs. This helped because he was sentenced to 15 years, but he was still upset that it was so long. However, late observers might note that he was convicted on all four counts but given only 15 years, which made a strange contrast to Dönitz. He was released from Spandau Prison on health grounds following a suspected heart attack in 1954 and retired to his family estate where he died two years later.

Final Notes

Neurath had belonged more to the old Imperial Germany, he had been distrustful of the ideals and behaviour of the Weimar Republic, and he had acted as a bridge between the old Germany and the Nazis. In doing so, he had fallen into the trap of failing to understand the demonic elements within Hitler. This happened to many people, but it was less of an excuse for a man of Neurath's education and background, although again he was not alone here. Hassell knew Neurath and reported him as lazy, somewhat insignificant, and when he gave 'magnificent hunting parties', he was 'no more than an extra'.[7] It is easy to glean from these remarks and other insights that Neurath was a lowly, below the parapet figure, and had he not become involved as the protector in Bohemia and Moravia, he could have faded into the background and would have been of little interest to the outside world. Like many, he was anti-Semitic but not an extremist of the Nazi variation. However, as Maxwell Fyfe had suggested during his trial, he must have been aware of Himmler's intentions and what was happening in the so-called Final Solution. He was hardly a major figure, and his sentence may be questionable, but Maxwell Fyfe made many pertinent points, and he was found guilty more because of his attitudes than his deeds.

Hans Fritzsche 1900–53

Background

Hans Fritzsche was slight in build and appeared young. He had served as a 17-year-old soldier in the Great War, although as Telford Taylor noted, there was 'nothing martial about him'. His wife was a dentist and they had one daughter, but he remarried following his release in 1950 to a Hildegard Springer. He was the one defendant who exhibited the most shock at the films of the atrocities, at one time bursting into tears. He had been to university but never graduated, and in 1923 he started life in an editorial position but soon became a well-known broadcaster working for Goebbels's Ministry of Public Enlightenment and Propaganda. He had joined the Nazi Party between 1929 and 1933 and was a member of the SA. At the time, he worked for the wireless news service which became part of Goebbels's realm. During his 12 years of rule, Goebbels changed his chief of the

Hans Fritzsche. (State Treasury of Poland, Photographer Beiber)

radio division no less than five times. Hans Fritzsche was his last appointment in 1942, and he was to be a familiar voice on the airwaves. He became known as 'his master's voice' with his introductory sentence of 'Hans Fritzsche speaks'. Goebbels was constantly in disagreement with Fritzsche which typified the personal animosities that were characteristic of the regime, copying Hitler who based his usual strategy on 'divide and conquer'.[1]

In May 1942 he clashed with his boss Dietrich and joined the propaganda party attached to an infantry division in General Paulus's Sixth Army near Stalingrad. Fritzsche never met Hitler but strangely he was in the bunker in the last days and crossed the lines to offer Berlin's surrender to the Red Army. He was imprisoned in the Lubyanka and according to Fritzsche the Russians tore three gold teeth from his mouth, he was placed in a coffin-type cell where he could not sleep, and understandably signed all the confessions demanded from him. While there, he met a Russian general, who had been in prison for four years, isolated and without any news. He wrote an account of these experiences when on trial at Nuremberg.

He was politically and militarily insignificant compared to most of the other defendants, but he was charged with conspiracy to commit crimes against peace, war crimes, and crimes against humanity, brought about by his propaganda efforts as a radio broadcaster. He was never part of the policy-making process, and Shirer wrote that 'no one in the courtroom, including Fritzsche, seemed to know why he was there – he was too small a fry – unless it were a ghost for Goebbels'.[2] Shirer's cynicism was probably correct. It has also been suggested that Fritzsche was only added to 'caress' the ego of Soviet Russia who had taken him prisoner.

Medical Mental Observations

The main interrogators and official interviewers had little interest in a broadcaster, but his personality and thinking processes emerged more in the various psychiatrist reports, where he was described as youthful even though he was 45 years old and had a sickly upbringing. In his initial conversation with Goldensohn, he explained how he had graduated with a thesis entitled 'Humanity, Our Eternal Desire', how some of his closest friends had been Jewish, how he had helped free a Jew from a concentration camp, and how he respected 'individual rights'. How far any of this was true is questionable. Throughout these various conversations, he consistently referred to the five million murdered Jews and how shocked he had been at the news. In a later interview, Goldensohn found him busy working on his defence trying to understand how his work could have had so many people killed. He pointed out that because of these dreadful deeds by the Nazi hierarchy there were now fifty million Germans living on the breadline. Goldensohn asked if he was implying that the blame for the starvation levels should be placed on the five million Jews to which he responded 'No, no, no, a thousand times. The German people must now bear the accusation of these murders and rightfully'.[3] He then returned to his theme of how he had helped Jewish people and some letters which had arrived thanking him. He explained that Himmler had once asked him if he would like to join the SS which he had declined, and how Goebbels had summoned him for defying Himmler. He alleged he had also fired people when he discovered they were working for the Gestapo, pointing out that those still living could justify his claims.

He was desperate to demonstrate that although he had been used as a tool by the Nazi regime, he had played no conscious part in their evil plans.

He explained that in propaganda it was a matter of drawing the attention of people to one side and away from the other, which both sides did, and demonstrated his point by a box of matches which had the slogan 'Crush the Axis'. He further argued that during the Great War the Allies had used propaganda showing German soldiers chopping off the hands of children. This deceitful use of propaganda had caused a degree of cynicism among many people, and which had often thrown doubt on the possibility of the rumour that the extermination of the Jewish race was underway. There was, Fritzsche argued, poor conduct in terms of propaganda and behaviour by both sides. Despite the various theories he propounded, he kept returning to the slaughter of the concentration camps and felt that all the legal niceties could be cast aside, and judgement made on this sole issue. He argued that he had denounced Streicher's publication *Der Stürmer*, and he acknowledged that the *Protocols of the Elders of Zion* was a 'stupid invention', although he blamed Hitler more than Streicher whom he regarded as simply 'stupid'. At times, he was evidently lost in his own arguments, stating that *Der Stürmer* was taken more seriously abroad than at home, then saying that in fact it had a 'tremendous influence'.

In between these recurring themes, he tended to speak of his early life as a journalist, his family, especially his mother and his wife (who had never been a party member). Trained as a dentist, she was not allowed to practise probably because she had been married to him. He like many others had a mistress and felt torn in loyalty, but he appeared genuinely worried about his wife and daughter living on the breadline in Hamburg with the threat of being made homeless.

Another of his favourite conversational lines was that the Germans mainly fought a 'clean war', and it was not only the Germans who committed atrocities. He was especially vociferous about the Russians, but also the Western Allies. He had not been overly impressed by Hitler and explained his rise to power by pointing out that the Weimar Republic had 36 political parties, and Hitler was the only means to form a government, which historically underlined one of the weaknesses of the early German democratic system.

He was asked for and offered opinions on the other defendants and Goebbels, pointing out that his mother had not liked Goebbels when she once met him, although his boss was charming to her. He later said that Goebbels was aware of the extermination of the Jews which he kept hidden from him. He complained that Göring had led a life of luxury and collected art, Frank was a liar and knew precisely what was happening within his area of responsibility, and criticised Schacht for continuing to work for Hitler when he knew the facts, implying that he himself did not. He accused Raeder of lying over the sinking of the liner *Athenia* and blamed him for the incident. He later added that Rosenberg had a 'one-track mind', and Fritzsche was opposed, he claimed, to the Führer principle of total obedience.

He often gave the appearance of trying to show he was a good citizen totally unaware of the Nazi atrocities which had taken him by surprise. He referred to the occupation of France as 'peaceful', arguing that it became more turbulent as resistance movements started, even claiming that 'not more than ten wristwatches were looted by our troops in the whole of France' which defies belief.[4] Goldensohn noted that there was a sense of 'pathos and bathos' emerging in Fritzsche as he struggled with his circumstances. The general impression was that Fritzsche was struggling with his past when confronted by the statistics of death. He was finding himself as a mere pawn on a chess board among the same ranks and diagonals as the major pieces.

Reactions during the Trial

Fritzsche later wrote that as he entered the courtroom, he scanned the press gallery and recognised many who would once have been 'glad enough to catch my eye, were now studiously looking in the opposite direction'.[5] Fritzsche was out of place when compared to the other defendants, but Speer found in him about the only person who shared his new views.[6] When on Tuesday 19 February 1946 the Russians showed their film on the atrocities, Gilbert noticed that Fritzsche was trying not to cry and had put dark glasses on to hide this from the others. Gilbert even offered him the possibility of returning to his cell fearing he was not well, but Fritzsche refused on the grounds it would attract more attention. Back in the cell, he explained to Gilbert, 'That was the last straw. I have had the feeling – of getting buried in a growing pile of filth – piling up week after week – up to my neck in it – and now – I am choking in it'.[7] It was obviously serious because Gilbert organised for him to have sleeping pills, and he promised to suggest to Goldensohn that he be excused the next day. During Rosenberg's trial, Fritzsche fastened onto the idea that some German people should be included among those passing judgement on their own leaders. During Frank's trial, Fritzsche was unhappy that Frank had identified the whole German people with crime.

Fritzsche's Trial

Fritzsche's trial was the last individual trial, and he was at the 'rough end' of a court tired and exasperated with repetition. By the end of Fritzsche's short trial, the proceedings had lasted 166 days, with nearly 100 witnesses, and 143 interrogatories for the defence. There had been some discussion whether Fritzsche had a case to answer, but his previous captors the Russians were insistent. Although Fritzsche was a section head in the propaganda ministry, he was a low-level defendant, only known because of his broadcasting of 'Hans Fritzsche speaks' with most Germans being familiar with his voice. He was popular as a broadcaster because of his chatty style, often sounding reasonable and not screaming instructions and demands down the microphone. His programmes rejoiced in the victories and denounced the Jews, but it was not a strong case. He was accused of having used his post to disseminate the Nazi doctrines, the anti-Semitic policies, the forced labour, and to foment aggressive war. All this, although he had never met Hitler and previously only four of the other defendants.

Such were the indictments laid against him he was convinced he would be hanged as Goebbels's representative. His counsel was Dr Heinz Fritz who unlike many others presented a smooth defence. Fritz was able to claim he had never heard anyone speak of aggressive war and he had no idea about the plans and intentions. He further claimed that what he said on the radio was not determined by him but by the organisation under Goebbels; 'As with Streicher they had to face the fact that it was extraordinarily difficult to prove the connection between one man's words and another's deeds'.[8] It was already understood that the evidence available was short and held remarkably little against him.

He had realised that sometimes the news he was given was entirely false and referred to the time that the Germans had claimed that Churchill had organised the sinking of the liner *Athenia*. His defence became more problematic on war crimes where he was accused of having incited hatred through his radio speeches, quoted as broadcasting that 'Even worse than the marks of the mental, economic, and social terror exercised by the Jewish commissars were those of physical terror which the German army encountered along the roads of victory'.[9] He tried to counter this by claiming that he was only attacking the Soviet system, not the people, and referred to the 'absolute cleanliness and honesty of the whole German conduct of the war', which struck his listeners like a thunderbolt having by this time heard the exposures of the military and civil atrocities. Fritzsche either indicated a deep ignorance of the realities, or a belligerence aimed at the Soviets who had captured him and kept him in solitary confinement.

During his short time with General Paulus's army, mentioned earlier, he had received the instruction to kill Jews and any Ukrainian intelligentsia, and was aware of the *Einsatzgruppen* activities. He declared like most he was anti-Semitic but only in so far that he wanted to reduce their influence. The Soviets who had captured him and wanted him in the dock never handled the court system well, often shouting accusations and not overly concerned about any replies. When Rudenko asked him if he knew about the invasion of Poland, Fritzsche took the opportunity to respond by pointing out the Russian joint action at the time. While in Russian captivity, he had refused to sign depositions against other defendants and signed only one against himself for safety, but he protested that the one in court had alterations and it was not his signature. He was generally believed.

The lawyers from the other delegations were not interested in asking more of Fritzsche, and it occurred to Telford Taylor that 'Fritzsche did not emerge from his ordeal as young and innocent as when he began, and he knew much more about

German atrocities than he let on'.[10] He never denied any direct knowledge of the atrocities which he picked up from rumours. He declared himself gullible when he passed them on to his seniors, as he had believed their explanations. Some may have thought he was lying to protect himself, and as an ex-broadcaster he did not perform well in the box. There was little press response about this trial, but he did stand out by blaming the Nazi regime as well as himself.

Summation, Final Statements, and Verdicts

On behalf of Fritzsche, his counsel Dr Fritz gave a professional address to a court already inclined to find the defendant not seriously guilty in terms of the indictments. Fritzsche had admitted broadcasting, but despite the prosecution's claims, this did not make him a party to the conspirators and waging aggressive war. Fritz also pointed out to the Tribunal that in German law, even if Fritzsche was regarded as 'an accomplice', he should be punished less severely than the perpetrators. He told the Tribunal that he was not pretending that Fritzsche was 'whiter than snow', but he was not guilty in terms of the indictments. The prosecution conveyed the image of a corrupter of the German public, but Fritz accused the Tribunal that through its evidence of selected films and witnesses, it had portrayed Germany as a 'den of iniquity'. Fritz said that the world would avoid suffering if the Tribunal could 'separate German crime from German idealism'. Jackson stated that Fritzsche on the radio had 'anaesthetised the independent judgement of the population so they did without question their master's bidding'.[11] In his final statement, Fritzsche admitted he believed in 'Hitler's assurances of a sincere desire for peace' which is why 'I strengthened the trust of the German people' and he had believed in the denials of atrocities, 'that is my guilt, no more, no less'.[12]

After Fritzsche, the court was adjourned to consider its judgements. The new psychiatrist Dr Dunn was somewhat concerned about Fritzsche and wondered whether he was a suicide risk as Fritzsche was worried that he would be executed as the sacrificial lamb for the deceased Goebbels, the vicarious victim, or that he might possibly be handed back to the Russians.

When the Tribunal returned a month later, Fritzsche, who had been indicted on counts one, three, and four, was acquitted. Fritzsche was so taken aback by the verdict he collapsed back on his seat with the shock of relief. The missing Bormann was found guilty under counts three and four and sentenced to death if found, and the session was closed.

Post-war

He was surprised and relieved to be discharged, but then had to face the reality of the German courts. Later, in a denazification trial he was condemned as a major offender and given the maximum imprisonment of eight years, but he was pardoned in 1950 on the condition he should not speak or write a book, which he did. The book was described on the title page as having been told to Hildegard Springer (a former colleague) whom he married (1950) after his release.[13] He even attempted whitewashing Funk by suggesting the films of gold teeth were lies. He died three years after his second marriage, in 1953.

Final Notes

Fritzsche was of minor significance both in terms of the trial and the life of the Nazi regime. He had been one of many broadcasters and in terms of being charged under count one, it was evidently ridiculous. It struck the medical observers that Fritzsche was genuinely shaken by the news of the atrocities and to all appearances Fritzsche was not a perpetrator, but he probably knew more than he pretended. News broadcasters, especially those working in propaganda, by the nature of their work had to be informed and were more than prone to the gossip and rumours of the day. However, knowing something and not being able to do anything about it may be considered by some as morally questionable. In his minor position, protests would have been futile or fatal, but whilst this was immoral it had not been illegal. The court was undoubtedly correct in finding him innocent of the charges, and the suggestion he was standing in for Goebbels may have held some truth. There would have been hundreds of thousands of people who would have been like Fritzsche, aware of much, hearing the rumours, seeing the signs, and doing nothing, but it takes real courage to be a 'Good Samaritan'.

Robert Ley 1890–1945

Background

On 10 May 1933 Hitler appointed Robert Ley head of the newly founded German Labour Front, often known as DAF (*Deutsche Arbeitsfront*) which superseded the Nazi trade union formation. Ley was not the best of administrators and much of the work was done by Reinhold Muchow. Ley was more the upfront man who escorted the Duke of Windsor (formerly King Edward VIII) and his wife Wallis on a tour of Germany in 1937, during which his love of alcohol became clear as he crashed the Duke's car into some gates. It was widely known that Ley 'was drinking himself to death'.

As a means of encouraging workers or avoiding their dissatisfaction, he established the much-vaunted 'Strength through Joy' (*Kraft durch Freude*, KdF) offering benefits and promises to the

Robert Ley. (Public Domain)

workers and their families. These included holidays, involving two purpose-built cruise-liners, and the promise of family cars. He appeared in Italy on occasions and was remembered as an organiser of the Nazi Party and an SA general, describing Hitler in 1938 'as the only human being who never made a mistake'. He remained totally loyal to Hitler attending his last birthday party on 20 April 1945. He left for Bavaria thinking this would be the last stand, the 'National Redoubt', but was captured by the Americans while still in his pyjamas, trying unsuccessfully to confuse them with the wrong name.

Interrogations

Robert Ley argued he was only an administrative agent and had nothing to do with criminal acts. He had been severely distressed by his imprisonment and the charges. It was noted that he had a weak character, had consumed too much alcohol, was overly fond of women, and had sustained a head injury in a plane crash in 1917. He denied drinking, claiming he had been a teetotaller for many years, he only looked to women after his wife's death, and had a mistress before being taken captive. His reputation was otherwise, and for 'many years Ley had been an oafish womaniser, but he had been much disturbed by the recent death of his wife, and despair now lent him ingenuity'.[1] His interviews and notes which he wrote in his cell indicated he had some form of psychosis, and he had been appalled at the way he was treated, hated being locked in a cell, and wrote letters to his wife Inge who had killed herself three years earlier as if she were still alive.

Few others within the Nazi structure liked him, but he had been loyal to Hitler and rewarded by his position as head of the German Labour Front. He was medically examined with the conclusion that the plane crash and subsequent events had not impaired his reasoning ability or intellect, but they may have left him emotionally unstable. In his conversation and notes, he would often refer to God, and even proposed a world conference between anti-Semitic Germans and Jewish leaders. Another idea of his was that Germany and America should unite under a National Socialist policy, and he wrote a letter (undelivered) to Sir (sic) Henry Ford that in his car building, he was no different from the American car producer. It was clear that he was becoming more deluded, and although a cause of concern the charges still stood. For many, he appeared to live in his own world of fantasy.

Following the line of Hitler and Goebbels, he left his own written political testimony addressed to 'my German people'. Much of the content dwelt on his views of God, Hitler, and his anti-Semitism. He admitted that his will power was broken, and he now awaited to commit himself 'unconditionally' into the hands of God who had 'led me to Adolf Hitler'. It had been God who helped him achieve so much on the German Labour Front, his campaign for 'Strength through Joy', and God had been his inspiration. He decided that Germany had deserted God who now deserted Germany. He praised National Socialism but proposed that the sheer anti-Semitism had been a mistake, although he still claimed that the initial form of stopping Jews flooding into the country was right. He wrote that this was no criticism 'of my dead Führer', because he was 'too great and too noble to be tainted by a passing mistake'.[2]

The only admission of guilt he was prepared to make was admitting that his anti-Semitism had been wrong, but he instantly added that this did not make him a criminal. He projected the future as being one of reconciliation between

Jew and German. He also wrote that 'the Jew' must learn from this, and that it was not just Germany which was anti-Semitic. He was of course correct in this observation to the shame of all gentiles, but Nazi anti-Semitism had advanced from ridiculous social snobbery to extermination. He believed that almost all Jews spoke German, and he challenged America to come to the front as 'the age of nationalities is past, the age of races begins', and asked God to help him and deliver his plans of racial unity.

His frantic appeals to God would give most theologians serious indigestion, psychologists reams of research papers, but to most people it was clear that his attempts at self-justification were the rantings of a man caught between the thorns of humiliation, conscience, self-justification, wild apologia with no idea which way to turn. As mentioned above, his wife Inga had shot herself (29 December 1942) after drinking too much in a domestic argument. According to various sources, she was depressed after a complicated childbirth and was drug dependent. Ley continued to write letters to the deceased Inga asking her if she knew whether the Führer was dead and so forth. This was interpreted as another sign of Ley's sheer madness, but this could be a mistake. Many priests and others know that the bereaved often express their sadness through talking and writing to their loved ones to express or even expunge their grief. When Galeazzo Ciano lost his father, he wrote in his diary of his childhood days asking his father if 'he could recall them', and he cried on seeing flags at half-mast.[3]

When presented with the indictment Ley challenged it on jurisprudential grounds, rejecting the legal basis for the trial, revealing a sharper mind than hitherto suspected; Ley remained totally confident in his innocence. He challenged the question of retrospective law, pointing out that God gave the Ten Commandments, appointed judges in Israel, but noted that:

> The Inter-Allied Powers are violating those principles of law by not setting up a law until 8 August 1945, that is after all the crimes mentioned in the indictment, which they wish to judge, had been committed, in making the Tribunal itself the legislator, they are again fundamentally violating the principles of law which have been handed down.[4]

He studied the indictment clause by clause, not he claimed for fear of being shot, but because he was not a criminal. He worked for a legitimate government and never ever took part in any discussions relating to foreign policy. This was probably true, but he had arrived ostensibly for a holiday in Italy when Hitler was applying pressure on Mussolini and was soon in the *Duce*'s office. He took Mussolini into his confidence and, according to Ciano, dropped major hints about Hitler's aggressive plans.

He rebutted the crimes against humanity, and although he confessed to be a repentant anti-Semitic, he noted that the war against the Allies was because it was believed they were the tools of international Jewry. In his arguments, he referred to

St Paul as the greatest Jew, forgetting that Christ was Jewish, and later argued that Christ was anti-Semitic!

He referred to the indictment against himself on recruiting foreign labour, pointing out that he simply chaired the committee for 'the welfare of foreign workers', stating he improved their food rations, billets, clothing, and gave them professional training and looked after their interests. He was at times alert when looking at the details of the indictment, but his general lack of mental balance was self-evident to observers at the time.

Despite these mental issues, Ley wrote a report for his captors on the rebuilding of Germany, as did Schacht. Ley concentrated his work on his own experience of rebuilding homes from the all-pervading rubble. The British and Americans were already feeling concern about the future of Germany, especially in the light of the growing friction with the Soviet Union. It appeared to be a comprehensive report, looking to the rebuilding of cities, towns, communication lines, and estimating the sort of money required. He noted it had to have a capitalistic basis, had to be a nationally based effort, employing new methods, machines, even examining the problems of utilising the rubble, and looking to the essential nature of villages, farms, and the agricultural side of life. He could not help himself, referring in the final part of his report to how good National Socialism had been at these issues, despite its later mistakes, and how impressive his work on labour had been.

Medical Mental Observations

He told Gilbert, who had been testing him in prison, 'Stand us against a wall and shoot us, well and good, you are the victors. But why should I be brought before a tribunal like a c-c-c', being unable to produce the word 'common criminal'. As he did this, he placed himself against the walls with arms spread out in a crucified position.[5] When Airey Neave presented him with the indictment, Ley stared at him with bloodshot eyes and asked how he could prepare a defence shouting, 'Am I supposed to defend myself against all these crimes which I knew nothing about?'[6] In his report to the Tribunal on 24 October 1945, Neave referred to Ley's unstable mental condition, but too late.

Within hours, Ley managed to evade the trial by unpicking a towel, making a noose from the threads, and managing to hang himself. From this point on, an angry Colonel Andrus changed the prisoners' routines, and a guard was posted at every cell door each minute of the day. Of the various defences of amnesia, denial, suicide was the most effective, but it was a personal escape and did not wipe out the charges. He was not the first suicide, because earlier in the same month a Reich Health Minister, Dr Leonardo Conti, associated with the euthanasia of the mentally ill, had hanged himself. With depression widely ranging from cell to cell,

Hess's unbalanced state of mind, and Frank's previous attempt, it was little wonder that Andrus had to take extreme measures in watching the inmates.

Gilbert was with Göring when the news circulated about Ley's suicide, with Göring claiming it was just as well, wondering how Ley would have behaved at the trial and describing him as 'scattered brained' and 'he would have made a spectacle of himself'. Some of the other defendants expressed similar views.

Reflections

Some Legal Issues

Nations going to war has been a human trait from the beginning of recorded history. It 'was forecast at the opening of *The Iliad* when European armies first attacked Troy', and the Old Testament endorsed this human feature.[1] The Kellogg–Briand Pact of Paris (1928) between 62 countries tried to outlaw war and failed, but long before this and since, international efforts have attempted to formulate guidelines as to how war should be conducted. Many have regarded the IMT as a major step forward in this process of controlling conduct, but the issue of 'victor's justice' and the legality of the process remains an issue of debate, some seeing it as a device to demonstrate that the victorious powers were now masters. Therefore, some critics regard it as political justice, the legal basis often laid at the feet of countries founded on liberal, Western concepts.

It is generally understood that legal procedures must never involve politics, but when international war trials threaten post-war relationships between states, it has proved impossible to keep politics out of the scene. So, for example, the USA, despite protests from its Allies, would not allow the Japanese emperor to stand trial on the grounds of post-war reconstruction, despite the argument that justice cannot be served if politics intrude.[2] There is also the problem of valid jurisdiction, though it has been argued that by May 1945 the prosecuting states were the only legitimate authorities in Germany and the IMT was a legitimate extension of that fact. At the time and since, the IMT has had its critics both for and against.

Those supporting the IMT claim that with the volumes of recorded evidence there was plenty of historical and educational value accumulated on the origins of the war and the Nazi regime. It is further claimed that in practice it was a fair trial and encouraged the concept of a wider jurisdiction for issues beyond a national scope. Critics fall into two broad cases of those who objected to the decisions and sentences, and those who objected to the law. The latter point dealing with legal issues tends to focus on the claim the IMT had no jurisdiction as mentioned above, and it tended to apply *ex post facto* law, that it was one-sided, and the trial was politically expedient as all sides were guilty in one way or another, and it may reduce the unity of the state given that 'sovereign states cannot be subjected to foreign jurisdiction without their concern, but no such principle applies to individuals'.[3] It has also been argued that to be effective, sanctions must be placed on individuals and not states, and not make inroads into national sovereignty, and there should be no law against states preparing for a preventative war.

However, as noted above, by May 1945 there was no German government, just a land mass occupied by the four Allied powers who had assumed the sovereignty including all administration, justice, with absolute control over Germany. It has been argued that the Germans had signed the Kellogg–Briand Pact of Paris and as such had broken the international agreement so the well-known *nullum crimen sine lege* (no crime without law) had been observed.

It has been further argued that the Nazi regime and its actions were immoral, but not all moral laws are necessarily illegal, for breaking a moral norm to be regarded as a criminal act other matters must be added to the equation. In the past, norms of behaviour in war had tried to be established in The Hague and Geneva Conventions but not all states ratified them, but there must be just standards of due process at all times. The issue of *mens rea* (intention) and *actus reus* (the guilty act) must be established, as well as the link between criminal responsibility and criminal liability. Did the commander order the criminal acts in war or did some soldiers away from his command perpetrate the action? How far a commander was responsible demands substantial evidence. It was fortunate for the IMT that the meticulous way Germans recorded everything meant this was not a difficult task.[4] The constant human anomaly is that although rules of war and law may be given, once the battle starts it is always a time of brutality which is why Shakespeare referred to the 'dogs of war'.

The IMT had to link two principles, first, that individuals ought to be judged on their behaviour and not claim obedience to superior orders as justification, and secondly, that having participated in the Nazi regime was not in itself necessarily a criminal act. It was, once again, a matter of establishing the necessary *mens rea* and *actus reus* mentioned above.

The IMT at Nuremberg was a 'stripped down version of domestic British or American trials', but it was not a 'naked exercise of state power' as the defendants 'faced full-blown Western legalism as in its domestic context'.[5] Conspiring to plan aggressive war and war crimes can be related to many nations, but the planned annihilation of European Jews and unrestrained massacres was for many the focus of these trials, though not seemingly at the time. The legal arguments are complex and will long be discussed, but not at length here because the focus of this study is on the human element of the defendants.

Personal Anger in the Trials

Many wanted revenge and retribution and a trial seemed the most civilised way forward. The war had generated considerable hatred, anger, and human reactions were heated. When Airey Neave watched Dönitz, he could not help recalling that he had known a young officer with his wife and child who died on the *Laconia*, and was unforgiving of the German admiral.[6] The British prosecutor 'Khaki' Roberts relentlessly pursued the case of the executed RAF prisoners because one of those killed was a Roger Bushell, a friend and barrister in his chambers. The personal side of the finished conflict would take years if not generations to subside. The world, and Europe especially, was in a state of total chaos – friends and families had been lost or killed and the news of the atrocities was almost unbelievable, which should be remembered by students of this subject in the comfort and safety of their studies a generation later. Human reaction is not always justified, not always morally right, and revenge and retribution are powerful factors of human nature, but apart from a few saints is a common feature of human life.

Criticisms of the Trial

There were those critical of the trial taking place, many at first concerned about creating martyrs or even giving Nazism a platform, but this never happened. The Roman Catholic and Protestant Churches led a protest at 'the legitimacy of the United States war crimes adjudications' before 1948.[7] As early as 1946, Clemens August Graf von Galen, Bishop of Münster, who had bravely opposed the Nazis giving him the right to speak, denounced the IMT, calling it a show-trial. There was also a prominent American bishop Aloisius Joseph Muench in North Dakota, later the Vatican representative in occupied Germany (1946–59), who compared the Nazi and Allied crimes by pointing to the atomic bombs dropped on Japan.[8] One Chief Justice in America accused Jackson of conducting a high-grade lynching party, and another claimed it was the usual victor's justice of crimes being defined after they had been committed and substituting power for principle. The legal value was scrutinised, and the value of the trial was criticised because there had been no total agreement, Germany had not given its consent, and the crimes against humanity were *ex post facto*.

The Church protests were easier to understand because they were seeking peace and reconciliation rather than revenge and retribution. How crimes against humanity were *ex post facto* is difficult to comprehend. Torturing, starving, beating, and killing people goes back to Cain and Abel, always regarded as a crime, and the only difference is that in the Biblical image there was one Abel, but during the Nazi regime there were millions. The American Republican Senator Robert A. Taft regarded the trials more as 'an instrument of government policy, determined months before at

Yalta and Teheran'.[9] Some of the military commanders were critical, especially over placing Dönitz in the same dock as Nazi leaders, and others realised that it could act as a condemnation of the Allied military alliance which had not been immune from acts of atrocity.

There were some legal points which were more substantial, especially when the Soviets produced false documents relating to the Katyń massacre as they tried to blame the Germans. It has been claimed that Jodl's wife, who had cunningly worked her way into the trial by assisting the defence counsel, later made the pertinent point that the prosecution made charges against her husband based on documents which they refused to share. Whether this was true or not, Jodl was able to refute most charges, but with the thousands of documents and the translation problems there were undoubtedly errors. However, it is widely accepted that the President Judge Lawrence ensured a fair hearing for the defence.

Hypocrisy of the Trial

The claim of hypocrisy has often been levelled at the Nuremberg Trial both at the time and since, some based on moral grounds. The Scottish historian Niall Ferguson wrote that 'they were accused, firstly, of the planning, preparation, initiation, or waging of a war of aggression, or war in violation of international treaties' and so forth.[10] He then supported his argument by pointing out the moral problems of the Soviet Union's behaviour and then underlined the bombing raids on Germany and Japan, the suffering of the fleeing Germans relating to the Soviet sinking of the German ship *Wilhelm Gustloff* with more than 6,000 helpless refugees on board, and the behaviour of Russian troops raping women and young girls. Moral arguments could not be disregarded by the IMT – it was the bedrock of many of their arguments – but they could not ignore the 'beam in our own eye' and the accusations of hypocrisy cannot be ignored.

To defeat the menace of Nazism, the democracies had aligned themselves with the Soviet Union which was virtually under the rule of the totalitarian Stalin, whose prison camps although not extermination centres were as equally brutal and larger than the Nazi camps. Stalin's show-trials had been well broadcast, he had joined the Nazis in invading Poland, started an aggressive war against Finland, occupied the Baltic States and it was generally known, without being said, that it was his orders which had prompted the massacre at Katyń, and despite all this, Russian judges at his command sat in judgement. The West and the Soviet Union had been a marriage of necessary convenience for both sides, with the Russian loss of some 20 million lives blurring the landscape in popular judgement. It was probably not until the famous novelist and Soviet dissident Aleksandr Solzhenitsyn published his books in the 1960s and *Glasnost* appeared in the 1980s that the Western public became aware that Stalin had been a monster. When the infamous show-trial judge Andrei

Vyshinsky appeared and proposed 'a toast at a Nuremberg reception of "Death to the Defendants", as usual his Western partners did not understand Russian. They drank the toast without hesitation, then asked what it meant afterwards'.[11] Some knew the truth of the Soviet behaviour but most regarded the Russians as a good, friendly force fighting Nazism. However, from what is now well known, the old 'USSR must be classed as a criminal regime before the war began, and it continued to commit mass crimes both during and after the war'.[12] Just before Streicher was executed, he shouted, 'the Bolsheviks will hang you one day'; many of those listening had become aware of the growing tensions between the Western Allies and the Soviets.

There were other elements within the trial which hinted at hypocrisy, often made impossible by legal rules objecting to *tu quoque* arguments, but which were adroitly circumnavigated by Dönitz's lawyer. British and French plans to mine Norwegian waters and even occupy coastal areas were kept low-key, as were submarine warfare and strategic (carpet) bombing, and even when the Russians raised Katyń, they were advised against doing so. They later held their own trial over the supposed perpetrators of Katyń and hanged some eight German prisoners of war for the part they were purported to have played, which was unbelievably immoral.[13]

Telford Taylor later expressed the view that in such trials the rules should apply to all sides: 'I am still of that opinion. The laws of war do not apply only to the suspected criminals of vanquished nations. There is no moral or legal basis for immunising victorious nations from scrutiny. The laws of war are not a one-way street'.[14] Telford Taylor spoke with a sense of idealism and morality, but when Lieutenant William Calley was convicted of the infamous My Lai massacre in Vietnam, he was given a life sentence, but after public protests was placed under house arrest and then released. This illustrated 'the selfishness of state, even those of liberal ones. We put our own citizens first—by an amazing degree'.[15] There were similar incidents of massacres by American soldiers at No Gun Ri in Korea and Thanh Phong in Vietnam, often accompanied by excuses such as 'no one intended to commit them ... but the politics of memory are precisely about contesting and confusing' that which is embarrassingly known to be true.[16]

The same sense of leniency had been experienced in Germany after the Great War when the Germans took over the court cases. Rebecca West wrote that 'it has to prove that victors can so rise above the ordinary limitations of human nature as to be able to try fairly the foes they vanquished, by submitting themselves to the restraints of law ... it will also warn future war-mongers that law can at last pursue them into peace and thus give humanity a new defence against them'.[17] There is a place for noble action which can be found in words written and spoken, but whether in human action is another problem. As the American historian Richard Raiber, who researched the crimes of Field Marshal Kesselring, wrote, 'Unpalatable thought it might be to many ... the twin doctrines of military necessity and national sovereignty will continue to erase all potential laws of war'.[18]

The hypocrisy of human nature is unquestionable, and the Tribunal ruled that it could not judge those deeds done in the heat of battle; instantaneous reaction in a bloody conflict could not be part of their calculations. Any soldier when caught in fierce combat and seeing friends killed or maimed without time for thought will often react in ways which he would normally have found immoral. The question at Nuremberg was not the role of the combatant in conflict, but those who gave the illegal or immoral orders, and those who had time to think and still obeyed them. The Nuremberg Trial looked at those who set the scene, both politician and soldier. Keitel and Jodl were executed, and after the trials many other generals found themselves indicted.

Once again, some have levelled the hypocrisy charge. When in Sicily some out-of-control American soldiers murdered Italian prisoners of war in cold blood, they were not prosecuted but 'let off the hook' by General George S. Patton. As British historian Max Hastings wrote, 'Patton, whose military ethic mirrored that of many Nazi commanders' claimed these killings had been thoroughly justified.[19] Later, when just inside Germany, Patton was informed his son-in-law, a Colonel John Waters, was being held at a prisoner-of-war camp near Hammelburg (*Oflag* XIII-B). Patton behaved recklessly and immorally, sending a task force into enemy-held territory for a family member. It was a total fiasco, and all but a few of the three hundred men sent were killed, wounded, or captured.* There was no serious investigation into why so many men died on the orders of a senior general.

There may be some truth in these various accusations but on a scale of some 50–60 million dead, individual judgements can only be left in the hands of personal conscience. In human terms, there was a genuine desire that at the end of the war people wanted peace, Maxwell Fyfe noting that 'most men at the close of the war wanted a better world'.[20]

The initial trial was looking beyond the gun smoke to those who started the war and their servants who ordered some of the most atrocious barbarity ever known in human history. It was a German philosopher Georg Hegel who once said, 'the only thing that we learn from history is that we learn nothing from history'.

Outcome of Trial

Historians, legal experts, and many others have written considerable tomes on the outcome of the trials, questioning the reasons, the course of the trials, and the ramifications. The trials continued with what was called the Subsequent Nuremberg Proceedings (SNP) until 1949, conducted by the Americans. The British held some further trials and across the world there were many others as the attacked and

---

* Only 15 survived without injury or capture according to Alex Kershaw, *The Liberator* (London: Hutchinson, 2012), 236.

dismembered countries sought some form of retribution. In this initial major trial explored above, the question of organised conspiracy and waging aggressive war had caused the most debate but there was a hope that it would set a legal precedent for the future; whether this was achieved or not is a major question. More pertinently, it was hoped that the exposure of the downright evil of the Nazi regime would be instructive in helping the German public realise the true nature of the Nazi regime, a form of education. How much the German public knew about the atrocities remained a contentious issue, but in late 1945 they were shown a newsreel film *Die Todesmühle* ('The Mill of Death'), where most sat in silence 'without visible emotion. Some women wept; others laughed hysterically, then burst into tears, men were seen sitting with bowed heads, covering their faces with their hands'.[21]

Vexed questions as to whether the hub of the problem was political or military have been explored but with no conclusive results because it was about human nature, whether in suits or uniforms. It did establish one major factor, that crimes were committed by men such as some of them in the dock, and not by some abstract or vague entity in the background forcing their hands. For generations, criminals have been forced to stand trial for crimes committed; for most people, many of the defendants had acted on or given criminal orders and were as guilty as the murderer and thief standing trial in ordinary life.

Nearly a century later, we now know that the horrors displayed at Nuremberg and the legal precedents established for the trial have marked delineations of behaviour, but it has not changed human conduct. Since 1945 there have been wars of aggression, genocide, and countless crimes against humanity. The Vietnam War was arguably an act of aggression by America and there were notable war crimes committed by both sides. There have been conflicts in Korea, Afghanistan, Iraq, Kuwait to name but a few, and from Yugoslavia to Africa to the Far East there have been acts of genocide; war and atrocity appear inherent to human nature. Jodl wrote that 'the preservation of the state and people and the assurance of its historical future … give war its total character and ethical justification' if the word 'ethical' can be associated with this human conduct.[22] Telford Taylor counterclaimed when he wrote, 'It was high time that such antediluvian and essentially murderous paeans to the morality of war be buried'.[23]

Whether the claim that the trial was meant to educate the German public was valid is a complex matter. In the late 1940s the German public was as torn apart and bewildered as the rest of Europe, divided between the four powers, starving, homeless, anxious about Soviet occupation, humiliated, and the lessons of Nuremberg were for many something happening on another planet. To stay safe, it was critical for individuals and families to distance themselves from any Nazi past and simply survive. The IMT had clearly outlined the Nazi crimes in occupied countries as well as many in Germany, but when in 1995 German research clearly indicated that the *Wehrmacht* (some 20 million members) had been involved in many atrocities, it came as a shock despite the Nuremberg findings. There grew the belief that the German public 'remained largely unaware of the killing of civilians in territories occupied by Germany during World War II'.[24] This debate was amplified by the major agitation if not outcry when an exhibition entitled 'War of Annihilation: Crimes of the *Wehrmacht* 1941–44' was mounted by the Hamburg Institute for Social Research 1995–99 which remains controversial. After the war, members of the German Army were divided as some had been fanatical Nazis and others less so, and some were anti-Hitler and anti-Nazi. In his post-war memoirs, General Frido von Senger und Etterlin had made this clear while in a prison camp in Wales.[25]

Nevertheless, on the wider scale, the Nuremberg Trial set a pattern for the future. It was used as a basis for the Eichmann trial, and for international courts at The Hague when dealing with the Balkan Wars, and at Arusha for the genocide in Rwanda. It helped develop international law and was the precursor of the 1948 Genocide Convention, the Universal Declaration of Human Rights 1948, the Nuremberg Principles 1950, the Convention on the Abolition of the Statute of Limitations on War Crimes and Crimes against Humanity 1968, and the Geneva Convention on the Laws and Customs of War 1949 with its supplementary protocols of 1977. The Nuremberg Trial helped establish a permanent international court by being the first one of any substance.

The trial made an extensive effort to disclose the recent past, examining the war in detail with documentary evidence, witnesses, films, confessions, and diaries, leaving no doubt as to what happened, which makes a nonsense of those misguided people or politically corrupt individuals known as Holocaust deniers. In many ways, the trial was politically necessary to show the dangers of authoritarian rule leading to the lowering of moral standards as epitomised by the Nazi regime. It even made the victorious Western Allies reconsider some of their own rules – the American field manual was changed about taking hostages, and it was stipulated that American and British soldiers should only obey lawful orders.[26] The British manual at paragraph 454 had stated that 'Reprisals are an extreme measure because in most cases they inflict suffering upon innocent persons. In this, however, their coercive force exists, and they are indispensable as a last resort'.[27] Nuremberg's revelation of atrocities against civilians caused the democracies to rethink their military policies.

However, since the last war, the public has remained somewhat ambivalent about the purpose of war crimes, treating 'justice' as synonymous with 'punishment', and often glibly referring to 'victor's justice'. Much can disappear from the collective memory and be retrospectively reinterpreted as victor's justice which needs no preceding crimes. This issue raised the phenomenon of *Vergangenheitspolitik* – the politics of memory, a word coined by German historian Norbert Frei. As the friction increased between America and the Soviets there was a shift in balance identifiable from about 1949, but with murmurings much earlier. The British and Americans deliberately started to refer to the 'image of a clean *Wehrmacht*' as it dawned on them that West Germany was a possible ally at best, or a buffer state between the Soviet world and the democracies. As later trials continued with senior men such as Kesselring and Manstein, it dawned on the Allies that it would 'not help their cause if respected German military commanders were under death sentences or interned. Very soon after the major trial, the Western powers 'colluded in the fiction of a decent but simple soldiery led astray by Nazi ideologies. This reflected sheer ignorance and wishful thinking, particularly in the cases of officers like Manstein and Kesselring', but compelled by the sudden need to bring West Germany into the new NATO alliance.[28] Thus, despite the Tribunal not finding the OKW a criminal organisation, in 1946 Eisenhower often stated the *Wehrmacht* and especially the officers corps had identified with Hitler. However, six years later he wrote that 'the German soldier as such had not lost his honour' and the despicable acts had been committed by a few; the effects of the Cold War were mounting.[29]

Despite the immediate Allied injunction against Germany ever possessing arms, 'the mounting fear and hostility towards the Soviets convinced Western Powers of the Federal Republic's strategic importance as a military force on the European continent'.[30] Further, 'The need to retain Germany as a frontline state in the Cold War conflict against the Soviet empire, meant that few of the many thousand convicted Nazis, including those responsible for acts of genocide, were still in prison after 1953. Once again, highly contingent imperatives of political expediency clashed and overcame the supposed 'independence' and 'universality' of liberal standards of law and justice'.[31] It was not just West Germany though. Truman never changed his mind about Franco, the despised Spanish dictator, but his military men, especially General Omar Bradley, were now showing considerable interest in Spain, and this included Eisenhower, the NATO commander-in-chief.* In June 1951 they made contact with Franco with a view to using Spain for military bases. The Americans were continuously aware of the European distaste for Franco 'and concluded that military necessity outweighed political sentiment'.[32]

By 1949 a new era was marked by the occupying powers with the establishment of the Federal Republic of Germany, with America wanting to contain the Soviet Union. Attention turned towards those field marshals such as Kesselring and Manstein and others still in custody. There were pressures applied for a reappraisal from many directions. B. H. Liddell Hart's book *The Other Side of the Hill* gave a positive image of German leadership, even suggesting that Hitler's planned invasion of England, according to the trial, had almost obligated him against his wishes to invade Norway, and that he 'did not want to conquer England'.[33] Liddell Hart wrote claiming Norway had not been premeditated by Hitler who 'was led into it

---

* Omar Bradley saw the peninsula as 'the last foothold in continental Europe'. See Stanley Payne and Jesús Palacios, *Franco: A Personal and Political Biography* (London: University of Wisconsin Press, 2014), 311.

more by fear than desire'.[34] There was also political support from such men as Lord Hankey. In effect, the changing political scene of the 'West German State created a new constellation'.[35] Although the SS, SD, and Nazi Party were all denounced as criminal, the *Wehrmacht* had the myth of *die saubere Wehrmacht* (the upstanding *Wehrmacht*) which exonerated the soldiers and provided an alibi for the nation. Officials stopped referring to war criminals and the Americans did not publish the trial in German. By 1958 all were released from the subsequent proceedings (SNP).

A new identity emerged from the ashes. Its premise was that the Germans were victims of a criminal regime, of disastrous defeat, national division, and of arbitrary Allied policies. Their relationship with the past was much more ambiguous.

Final Thoughts

Overview of Defendants

When exploring the conduct and reactions of the defendants, the dangers of the totalitarian system became evident. This form of government control produces unchallengeable figures such as Hitler, Stalin, Franco, Mao Zedong, with whom life can be under constant threat and this must be kept in mind. Few were brave enough to challenge these ruthless dictators, and most people would do their best to keep their heads below the parapets. The defendants at the Nuremberg Trial had been charged on four counts, more appropriate for Hitler who was missing, but these men had been his servants or henchmen. For many people, the main charge was the massacre of millions of totally innocent people, notably the Holocaust, as well as the slaughter of others including Slavs, Russian prisoners of war, and Roma and Sinti. The Russians wanted all the defendants to hang. They disagreed that those who were guilty on counts one and two were not necessarily to be hanged, since the starting of the war was for them the supreme national crime; notably, only those who also faced charges of brutality were hanged.[1] Having the enemy sitting in judgement, especially the Soviets, would have increased the sense of fear and all the basic human instincts of personal survival soon emerged.

They behaved as most people do when on trial, whether guilty, partially guilty or not guilty; 'they slithered away from the specific and hid in euphemisms, cloaking facts in vagueness ... and avoided nasty words'.[2] Some blamed others, some accepted limited liability, some forgot, presenting a scenario of 'enormous crimes but without criminals'. Most of them had played a part within the regime, some more than others, but they were all standing in for the missing Hitler. For a few of them, he became the central focus of blame, shared to a certain extent with Himmler and Bormann. For others, they stood by the dictator, refusing to denounce him.

Since the conclusion of the trial in 1946, some observers have questioned the justification of some of the sentences. Streicher was the most repellent and repulsive of all the defendants and this probably did not help him when it came to committing him to the gallows. He was charged under count one which was ridiculous but found not guilty, but he was sentenced to death on count four which was somewhat dubious. There is no evidence that he killed anyone, or was involved directly in mass murder, and was hanged on the grounds that he incited racial hatred. This was questionable because if criminalised for this offence millions could suffer the same fate. He was a hate-filled bigot of the worst possible type but life in a psychiatric prison may have been more effective, not only from the moral point of view but for understanding the nature of the anti-Semitic driving forces and racism in general.

The working-class Sauckel was hanged for his abuse of foreign labour, but the beguiling middle-class Speer was imprisoned for the same offence, presenting an awkward anomaly. There have been many other questions raised over some of the sentences such as that of Jodl who was later cleared by a German court but who, had he been tried a few years later as with Manstein and Kesselring, would have survived to write his memoirs. Although Dönitz received the lightest sentence, and his lawyer was clever using the essence of the banned *tu quoque* argument without obviously deploying it, many still feel that Dönitz was innocent. These are a few question marks which still hang over some of the decisions.

Some of the defendants had anticipated they would face a death sentence. Göring felt this because he was Hitler's number two and expected to be shot but would leave a heroic image for posterity. Others felt that their past deeds merited such a sentence, such as the repentant Frank. Understandably, most wanted to avoid the gallows, though Raeder claimed he would rather die than have a life sentence, and Fritzsche had convinced himself that he was regarded as Goebbels's stand-in and was surprised when declared innocent. Most of them would do and say anything to avoid an organised death.

A few turned to God, notably Frank who reconverted to his Catholic faith and used that as his mainstay to the bitter end. Robert Ley in his desperate hours wrote about God and the necessity of racial peace being carefully organised at an international level. Most went to chapel if only to have a change of atmosphere from the solitary life in the cell as once explained by Göring, but Hess, Rosenberg, and Streicher always refused. Yet Hess's final words were 'I shall someday stand before the judgment seat of the Eternal. I shall answer to him, and I know he will judge me innocent'.[3] Ribbentrop whispered, 'I'll see you again' to the Lutheran chaplain Pastor Gerecke. Keitel, before his execution, received the sacraments and Göring asked to receive them before he died, but the Lutheran chaplain denied his request. In Shakespeare's play *The Tempest* (Act 1 Scene 1), the vessel is sinking and the crew shout 'All is lost! To prayers, All lost', and even the headstrong Göring turned to a belief in God just in case he had been wrong about His existence. Frank had committed many immoral acts but took comfort in his conversion and confession, and he seems to have been genuine in this act of repentance.

The Various Defences

Different excuses or explanations were deployed. The most common was the belief in **obeying orders** which was widely utilised for years to come by both the minor and most senior figures in the regime, especially Jodl and Keitel as military men. Obeying orders was a strong feature of Prussian military discipline, but soldiers were expected to obey orders whether German, Russian, British, or American. As mentioned in the previous chapter, it did lead to some revision of military rules in the Allied camp which clarified the law that orders had to be legal, and the Americans and British also had to rethink their military field manuals about hostages. If a soldier is ordered to barbeque a baby because it was Jewish, the order is so evidently immoral and obscene that any normal, level-headed soldier would disobey. However, babies, women, children, helpless old people were killed by their millions in this war, many by bombs, but doing such a thing in a 'hands-on' situation displayed something 'deeply rotten' in the state of Nazi Germany and any regime of that type.

Hitler was regarded as the key, and many of the defendants after deploying the defence of obeying orders turned to admitting that they had come under **Hitler's influence**. Ribbentrop used this to the point of being subservient, Keitel, the 'office manager', did what he was told, and even the older men such as Papen and Neurath displayed a degree of fear and obeyed against their better traditional instincts. Hitler demanded total loyalty, and it came, as the defendants showed, in different varieties. Some gave their allegiance out of a sense of duty such as Jodl and Keitel, some because they liked power such as Göring and probably Ribbentrop, some out of friendship such as Streicher and Hess, and some out of pure fear.

Most were subservient to one degree or another, but also claimed **innocence** and non-involvement. The classic example was Schacht, and although presenting as an arrogant old man, he may have been closer to the truth than most. Funk claimed the same and may have escaped sentence had it not been for the question of gold teeth over which there had been some debate. Dönitz, who did not meet Hitler face to face until early September 1939, claimed he was not involved in any of the counts, as did Schirach, Sauckel, and Fritzsche, all with some question marks over their claims. They may have known what was happening, but they were not all part of the decision making. Schacht was the most indignant about being on trial, constantly pointing out that he had opposed Hitler and landed up in a concentration camp, which had more reasoning behind its claim than most, especially Speer whose only real claim was that he had tried to stop Hitler's scorched earth policy at the last moment; innocence has many faces.

The next recourse they had was to **blame others**, Hitler first, but if nervous of doing so then Himmler and Bormann received condemnation as part of their defence. Even Göring became duplicitous and blamed Hitler and Himmler regarding the Holocaust for which there were no counterarguments. Kaltenbrunner blamed Heydrich and even the so-called philosophical Rosenberg resorted to the 'blame-game'. The repentant Frank was vitriolic about Hitler, as was Schirach. Sauckel, possibly with some justification, blamed Speer for forced labour, and Himmler and Bormann for the Holocaust. Seyss-Inquart accused Himmler of the atrocities in Poland, and Speer blamed everyone with Fritzsche saying the same thing hoping that the German people would not be condemned. They were mere human beings trying to avoid anything which may raise suspicion and take them to the gallows. Ribbentrop, Schirach, Speer, and later Fritzsche denounced Hitler, but Göring, Hess, Jodl, Rosenberg, and Seyss-Inquart tended to stand by their dead dictator, the cause of some division among the defendants as noted in the text.

The defendants, like many examined in the witness box, tried other methods in their defence. Hess is still widely known for his **amnesia** which the British had detected when he was their prisoner, only to have him announce it was a ploy, then to become immersed in his amnesic condition again. His mental problems were a constant source of discussion by the bench and the legal teams, and a matter of bemusement for observers. There is a tendency by some to think Hess was being clever, and by others that his mental ill-health was genuine. Below the level of amnesia is **forgetfulness** used by many under scrutiny, and along with being **evasive**, Ribbentrop was the most annoying and best at this form of self-defence. Funk deployed forgetfulness and being evasive but not as cunningly as Ribbentrop. Schirach was evasive over the motivations behind the *Hitler-Jugend* as he painted it as a benign, non-political and non-military boy scout movement. Sauckel was evasive over workers' conditions, Papen over his early support for Hitler.

It was also clear that for many, **lying and offering misrepresentations** was necessary, but this type of defence fell easy prey to the Anglo-Saxon method of cross-examination, especially with the reams of gathered documents and witnesses. When Kaltenbrunner took the stand, even the other defendants did not believe him. Ribbentrop, along with being evasive, also lied, and there is the possibility that Speer may have lied about his plans to kill Hitler. Even the repentant Frank was accused of not telling the truth. On the other hand, others argued their actions were totally **justified**, with Göring being the most forthright. Hess when occasionally 'on the ball' was similar, Frick claimed he always followed German law, Streicher never deviated from the belief he was right, Dönitz and Jodl used duty as their reason, and Sauckel, Papen, Neurath, and Fritzsche claimed they had done nothing wrong. Their final device was the **warning** that the Western Allies would regret what was happening because of the Soviet threat. Kaltenbrunner especially used this as a last-ditch argument, and Streicher bellowed out this warning seconds before he died on the gallows.

Facing the Final Solution

As the memory of the 1939–45 conflict fades, some battles remain well known mainly because of popular films and documentaries. Leading figures also remain widely known – among the defendants, Göring – but the horrors of the concentration and extermination camps still mark the memories of most people. They revealed the essence of Nazi Germany and many of the defendants had authorised, participated, and known about 'the slaughter and barbarism that ordinary Germans were willing to perpetrate in order to save Germany and the German people from the ultimate danger—THE JUDE'.[4] This highly contentious area which would later be known as the Holocaust, along with other massacres in the concentration camps, had been made manifest during the trial with so much undeniable evidence in film and witnesses that everyone was understandably shocked. Mere words such as Final Solution, extermination, and numbers even of five to six million were for some vague concepts reflecting general policies, but when exposed to the films of individuals suffering horrific torture and death the reality was sharply brought home. The shockwaves from these revelations were immense and caused more consternation among the defendants than the other charges.

This issue raised an essential element not only for the defendants but for the overall structure of the trial. The well-known *tu quoque* argument had long been banned, as mentioned, because using another person's behaviour as an excuse cannot be legally or indeed morally justified. However, the judges represented their four nations all of which had histories of planning aggressive war, conspiracy to accomplish making war, going to war, committing war crimes, and it was not only part of their history but as mentioned in the text has not stopped since the IMT. Crimes against civilians took place before and have taken place since the 1939–45 conflict, but where the *tu quoque* argument fell short was over the brutal reality of the Holocaust. The Russians who claimed they had lost some 25 million people did not think the elimination of Jews worth emphasising against their losses, and anti-Semitism right across Europe had been prevalent in one form or another and was now suddenly an embarrassment. It is unquestionable that political and social bigotry was evident. However, the elimination of a whole race, which the historians Manvell and Fraenkel described as *The Incomparable Crime*, stood free from the *tu quoque* issue. Despite many cases of notorious massacres, even attempted genocide, before and since, what made the 'Jewish Holocaust so unparalleled in history was the industrialised manner in which the deed was carried out'.[5] Modern Germany has felt the guilt of the past, but it belongs also to the whole of mankind with the responsibility of making it open to history. The defendants to a man felt the impact with the films exposing the brutal and unforgivable reality of this issue as they tried to extricate themselves, having in common the outright denial that they had been aware. Had the trial consisted only of passing judgement on the Holocaust and the enormous massacres of others, it may have avoided many of the legal criticisms mentioned above.

Göring knew all about the policy – the evidence for this at the time and since has proved overwhelming – and yet he brushed it aside as pretending that he thought the Final Solution had not meant vicious deaths. He lied because even he recognised the evil of the policy, as it was evident that he had signed orders with Himmler for Heydrich to draw up the Final Solution plan.[6] Some even claimed that Göring had a humane side to his character, but this was totally misleading. Having a social fun-side concealed his lack of humanity. Ribbentrop lied, having been exposed as demanding Italian, Hungarian, and French Jews be shipped east. He pretended along with Speer that he knew nothing of the policy of extermination. He had urged the Italians that 'the anti-Jewish measures from the Reich Security Head Office ... must not be sabotaged any further'.[7] When Admiral Horthy asked Ribbentrop what to do about the Jews since he could not kill them all, Ribbentrop responded, 'quite unequivocally that they must be either exterminated or taken to concentration camps' where it would be done for him.[8] Frick claimed he had no idea, shifting the blame onto Himmler not so much for the policy but for keeping it secret. However, Frick and Schacht had planned to constrain the economic position of Jews in the early 1930s.

Funk, Schirach, Sauckel, Schacht, Papen, Neurath, and Fritzsche all expressed sheer shock and claimed **they knew nothing** of the policy or what was happening. This was the same line of defence used by the four military leaders on trial, proving more successful for the naval men than the army officers. There were over a thousand camps spread across Europe, not all extermination centres but all extraordinarily brutal, and it was simply inconceivable that those in the upper echelons of the Nazi regime could be any more ignorant than the nearby neighbours of such camps. Many of the nearby civilians were obligated to go and see the death and destruction and facing it first-hand came as a devastating shock as it had to the defendants on seeing the films. It was so brutally ghastly that Frank was the only one to change his mind and accept the shame. Other excuses unfolded such as quibbling over the **semantics** of the word 'extermination' and the phrase 'Final Solution'. But for most of them, especially Ribbentrop, Schirach, and Sauckel, it slowly dawned on them that this was the singular issue that placed their feet on the rungs of the gallows.

Of all the four counts, it was the fourth on crimes against humanity, especially the annihilation of European Jews, that every defendant realised was the one they had to deny simply because it was unbelievably immoral and downright evil. Even Göring, so normally accepting and defensive of Nazi conduct, tried to evade the issue.

Göring in Life and Death

These three photographs of Göring, in resplendent power, in prison clothes, and then his dead body, provide a sharp reminder that the defendants were not some extra-terrestrial beings dreamed up by a filmmaker but human beings with many of the traits and behavioural patterns which can still be seen in ourselves and our

In power. (Public Domain)

In court. (Italian Harvard Law School)

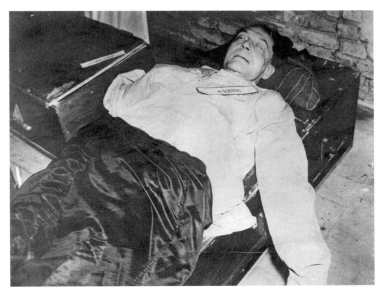

In death. (US Federal Government)

neighbours. The IMT may have tried to draw a curtain over the war years and seek a signature to end it all, it may have sought an instructive, educational element into the dangers of this type of regime, and it may have attempted to underline the importance of international law and rules in conducting war, but human beings sadly do not seem to change. This exploration has been about the human element of the defendants, who are now all dead by execution or old age, but their human characteristics survive to this day. There seems little point in listing these features such as the need for power, greed, racism, a blind eye to suffering in others, rampant nationalism, self-importance, and many others because they are all too human and belong to the Christian theology of 'original sin'. The major lesson for this writer is to be found in the need to be aware of the political dangers of any form of totalitarian power or any form of government in which these human traits are utilised and over which there is no form of check or counterbalance. The understanding that international co-operation is of prime importance, while a person's race, religious faith, and colour is irrelevant. If the need for international cooperation as hoped for by the IMT is not understood, then peace will be evasive as already proven, and the need to address climatic change might be too late.

Glossary

Abwehr	German Military Intelligence
Anschluss	Annexation of Austria 1938
COMINTERN	Communist International for world communism
DAF	*Deutsche Arbeitsfront*, German Labour Front
Einsatzkommando and *Einsatzgruppen*	Task Forces (for killing)
Führerprinzip	Leader principle, implying obedience to *leader*
Freikorps	(Free Corps) Irregular German paramilitary units
Gauleiter	Political officer in charge of an area
Gestapo	(*Geheime Staatspolizei*) Secret Police
Glasnost	Policy of open government in USSR
IMT	International Military Tribunal.
KdF	*Kraft durch Freude*, Strength through Joy, see DAF
KPD	German Communist Party
Kriegsmarine	German navy from 1935 to 1945
Kripo	German Criminal Police
Lebensraum	Territory (space) needed for natural development
NCO	Non-Commissioned Officer
NSDAP	National Socialist German Workers Party (Nazi Party)
Oflag	Prison Camp for Officers
OKH	*Oberkommando des Heeres*, High Command of Nazi German Army
OKW	*Oberkommando der Wehrmacht* (High Command)
OSS	Office of Strategic Services, US Intelligence organisation
Putsch	German word for a coup
Reichkommissare	Reich Commissar usually official in public office
Reichsleiter	Second highest rank in Nazi Party
Reichsmarine	German navy name during Weimar Republic
Reichswehr	Official name of German armed forces 1919–1935
RSHA	The Reich Main Security Office
SA	*Sturmabteilung*, Storm Detachment, Nazi paramilitary wing
SD	*Sicherheitsdienst*, Security Service

SNP   Subsequent Nuremberg Proceedings

SPD   Social Democrat Party

SS   *Schutzstaffel*, 'hall security' grew to powerful military wing

UNWCC   UN War Crimes Commission

USAAF   United States Army Air Force

Wehrmacht   Unified armed forces of Nazi Germany, often associated with the army

Appendix: Survey of Charges and Sentences

This list surveys who was charged under the four counts (X) followed by the sentences of Guilty (G) or Not Guilty (NG) and the verdicts.

COUNTS	1	2	3	4	1	2	3	4	Verdict
Göring	X	X	X	X	G	G	G	G	Death
Hess	X	X	X	X	G	G	NG	NG	Life
Ribbentrop	X	X	X	X	G	G	G	G	Death
Keitel	X	X	X	X	G	G	G	G	Death
Kaltenbrunner	X		X	X	NG		G	G	Death
Rosenberg	X	X	X	X	G	G	G	G	Death
Frank	X		X	X	NG		G	G	Death
Frick	X	X	X	X	NG	G	G	G	Death
Streicher	X			X	NG			G	Death
Funk	X	X	X	X	NG	G	G	G	Life
Sauckel	X	X	X	X	NG	NG	G	G	Death
Jodl	X	X	X	X	G	G	G	G	Death
Seyss-Inquart	X	X	X	X	NG	G	G	G	Death
Speer	X	X	X	X	NG	NG	G	G	20 yrs.
Neurath	X	X	X	X	G	G	G	G	15 yrs.
Bormann	X		X	X	NG		G	G	Death
Schirach	X			X	NG			G	20 yrs.
Raeder	X	X	X		G	G	G		Life
Donitz	X	X	X		NG	G	G		10 yrs.
Schacht	X	X			NG	NG			Freed
Papen	X	X			NG	NG			Freed
Fritzsche	X		X	X	NG		NG	NG	Freed
Ley – suicide									n/a

Endnotes

Preface

1   Trial Papers, 17 January 1946.

Introduction

1   Mary Fulbrook (ed.), *Twentieth-Century Germany: Politics, Culture, and Society 1918–1990* (London: Hodder Headline Group, 2001), 23.
2   Frank B. Tipton, *A History of Modern Germany since 1815* (London: Continuum, 2003), 329.
3   Michael Howard, *The Invention of Peace & the Reinvention of War* (London: Profile Books, 2001), 62.
4   Eric Weitz, *Weimar Germany: Promise and Tragedy* (Woodstock: Princeton University Press, 2007), 144.
5   Richard Overy, *Interrogations: The Nazi Elite in Allied Hands, 1945* (London: Penguin Books, 2002), 7.
6   Ibid., 8.
7   John Colville, *The Fringes of Power: Downing Street Diaries 1939–1955* (London: Hodder and Stoughton, 1985), 26.
8   Ann Tusa and John Tusa, *The Nuremberg Trial* (London: BBC Books, 1995), 10.
9   Quoted in Tom Bower, *Blind Eye to Murder: Britain, America and the Purging of Nazi Germany* (London: Warner Books, 1995), 21.
10 See Bower, *Blind Eye to Murder*, 26.
11 Ibid., 102.
12 James Owen, *Nuremberg: Evil on Trial* (London: Headline, 2007), 179.
13 Leon Goldensohn, edited by Robert Gellately, *The Nuremberg Interviews* (London: Pimlico, 2007), xii.
14 Telford Taylor, *The Anatomy of the Nuremberg Trials: A Personal Memoir* (New York: Alfred Knopf, 1992), 4.
15 Janet Flanner, *Janet Flanner's World: Uncollected Writings, 1932–1975* (London: Harcourt Brace Jovanovich, 1979), 101.
16 See Overy, *Interrogations*, 48.
17 Bower, *Blind Eye to Murder*, 98.
18 Taylor, *The Anatomy of the Nuremberg Trials*, 252.
19 Trial Papers, 26 November 1945.
20 Tusa and Tusa, *The Nuremberg Trial*, 101.
21 Overy, *Interrogations*, 30.
22 Bower, *Blind Eye to Murder*, 3.

23 Airey Neave, *Nuremberg* (London: Biteback Publishing, 2021), 16.
24 See Taylor, *The Anatomy of the Nuremberg Trials*, 228.

Two Critical Issues

1   Overy, *Interrogations*, p.158.
2   See for example Christopher Browning, *Ordinary Men: Reserve Police Battalion 101 and the Final Solution in Poland* (London: Penguin Books, 2001).
3   For an excellent article on the Holocaust see Fulbrook, *Twentieth-Century Germany*, 149–73.
4   Trial Papers, 3 January 1946.
5   From Interrogation Papers by Lieutenant-Colonel Smith W. Brookhart and Mr Sender Jaari, 15 November 1945, quoted in Overy, *Interrogations*, 356.
6   Trial Papers, 25 January 1946.
7   Ibid., 20 December 1945; see also Trial Papers, 11 January 1946.
8   Lawrence Freedman (ed.), article by Arendt, *War* (Oxford: OUP, 1994), 175.
9   See Browning, *Ordinary Men*.
10 Ibid., 221.
11 Stanley Milgram, *Obedience to Authority: An Experimental View* (New York: Harper and Row, 1974).
12 Owen, *Nuremberg*, 84.

Procedures

1   Overy, *Interrogations*, 61–2.
2   See Lt. Col. A. P. Scotland, *The London Cage* (London: Landsborough Publications, 1959).
3   Owen, *Nuremberg*, 195.
4   Tusa and Tusa, *The Nuremberg Trial*, 121.
5   William Shirer, *The Rise and Fall of the Third Reich: A History of Nazi Germany* (London: Mandarin, 1997), 1142.
6   Trial Papers, 21 November 1945.
7   Owen, *Nuremberg*, 320.
8   Trial Papers 28 January 1946 and 19 February 1946.

Hermann Göring, 1893–1946

1   Erich Gritzbach, *Hermann Goering: The Man and His Work* (Georgia: Historical Review Press, Third Impression, 1980), 9.
2   Ibid., 14.
3   Richard Overy, *Goering: Hitler's Iron Knight* (London: I. B. Tauris, 2012), 76.
4   Ulrich von Hassell, *The Ulrich von Hassell Diaries, 1938–1944* (London: Frontline Books, 2011), 39 and 145.
5   Neave, *Nuremberg*, 53.
6   Ibid., 64.
7   Overy, *Interrogations*, 295.
8   See Leonard Mosley, *The Reich Marshal: A Biography of Hermann Goering* (New York: Doubleday, 1974), 289.
9   See Lynn Nicholas, *The Rape of Europa* (London: Papermac, 1995), 343.

10 Goldensohn, *The Nuremberg Interviews*, 108.
11 Overy, *Interrogations*, 312.
12 Goldensohn, *The Nuremberg Interviews*, 101.
13 Neave, *Nuremberg*, 60.
14 Flanner, *Janet Flanner's World*, 98.
15 Albert Speer, *Inside the Third Reich* (London: Weidenfeld & Nicolson, 1995), 681.
16 Ibid., 682.
17 G. M. Gilbert, *Nuremberg Diary*, (New York: Da Capo Press, 1995) 49.
18 Tusa and Tusa, *The Nuremberg Trial*, 423.
19 Gilbert, *Nuremberg Diary*, 79.
20 Trial Papers, 7 January 1946.
21 Overy, *Goering*, 229.
22 Flanner, *Janet Flanner's World*, 109.
23 Gilbert, *Nuremberg Diary*, 252.
24 Tusa and Tusa, *The Nuremberg Trial*, 269.
25 Flanner, *Janet Flanner's World*, 113.
26 Taylor, *The Anatomy of the Nuremberg Trials*, 329–30.
27 Flanner, *Janet Flanner's World*, 116.
28 Trial Papers, 14 March 1946.
29 Ibid., 19 March 1946.
30 Taylor, *The Anatomy of the Nuremberg Trials*, 336.
31 Rebecca West, *A Train of Powder* (Chicago: Ivan R Dee, 1955), 17.
32 Trial Papers, 18 March 1946.
33 Tusa and Tusa, *The Nuremberg Trial*, 269 and 285.
34 Trial Papers, 20 March 1946.
35 Quoted in Tusa and Tusa, *The Nuremberg Trial*, 269 and 292.
36 Michael Salter, *Nazi War Crimes: US Intelligence and Selective Prosecution at Nuremberg* (Abingdon: Routledge Cavendish, 2007), 297.
37 Gilbert, *Nuremberg Diary*, 278.
38 Hassell, *The Ulrich von Hassell Diaries, 9138–1944*, 187.
39 Gilbert, *Nuremberg Diary*, 415.
40 Neave, *Nuremberg*, 57.
41 Trial Papers, 31 August 1946.
42 Taylor, *The Anatomy of the Nuremberg Trials*, 535.
43 Ibid., 588.
44 See Owen, *Nuremberg*, 78, and Burton Andrus, *I was the Nuremberg Jailer* (New York: Coward, McCann & Geoghegan, 1969).
45 Overy, *Goering*, 21.
46 Max Hastings, *The Secret War: Spies, Codes and Guerrillas 1939–1945* (London: Collins 2015), 177.

Rudolf Hess, 1894–1987

1 Joseph Goebbels, edited by Fred Taylor, *The Goebbels Diaries, 1939–1941* (London: Hamish Hamilton, 1982), 363.
2 West, *A Train of Powder*, 5.
3 See Overy, *Interrogations*, 119.
4 Neave, *Nuremberg*, 70–1.

5   Trial Papers, 30 November 1945.
6   Tusa and Tusa, *The Nuremberg Trial*, 294.
7   See *Sunday Express* 24 March 1946.
8   West, *A Train of Powder*, 47.
9   Trial Papers, 26 July 1946.
10 Taylor, *The Anatomy of the Nuremberg Trials*, 536.
11 Trial Papers, 31 August 1946.

Joachim von Ribbentrop, 1893–1946

1   See Goebbels, *The Goebbels Diaries, 1939–1941*, 115, 176, and 422.
2   Hassell, *The Ulrich von Hassell Diaries, 1938–1944*, 12 and 196.
3   Neave, *Nuremberg*, 77.
4   See Overy, *Interrogations*, 162.
5   Ciano, Galeazzo, edited by Renzo De Felice, *Ciano's Diary 1937–1943* (London: Phoenix Press, 2002), entry 7 December 1941.
6   Goldensohn, *The Nuremberg Interviews*, 184 and 185.
7   Gilbert, *Nuremberg Diary*, 16.
8   Shirer, *The Rise and Fall of the Third Reich*, 1142.
9   Gilbert, *Nuremberg Diary*, 43.
10 Trial Papers, 30 November 1945.
11 Ibid., 3 January 1945.
12 Gilbert, *Nuremberg Diary*, 151.
13 Ibid., 169.
14 Flanner, *Janet Flanner's World*, 106.
15 Tusa and Tusa, *The Nuremberg Trial*, 253–4.
16 Ibid., 300.
17 Trial Papers, 2 April 1946.
18 Taylor, *The Anatomy of the Nuremberg Trials*, 353.
19 Paul Schmidt, *Hitler's Interpreter: The Memoirs of Paul Schmidt* (Cheltenham: The History Press, 2016), 94.
20 Tusa and Tusa, *The Nuremberg Trial*, 306.
21 Trial Papers, 2 April 1946.
22 Gilbert, *Nuremberg Diary*, 339.
23 Trial Papers, 26 July 1946.
24 Owen, *Nuremberg*, 330.

Wilhelm Keitel, 1892–1946

1   O. Bartov, A. Grossmann, and A. Nolan, *Crimes of War: Guilt and Denial in the Twentieth Century* (New York: The New Press, 2002), 36.
2   Ian Kershaw, *The End: Hitler's Germany 1944–45* (London: Penguin Books, 2012), 338.
3   Kershaw, *The End*, 380.
4   Overy, *Interrogations*, 533.
5   Goldensohn, *The Nuremberg Interviews*, 158.
6   Ibid., 160.
7   Gilbert, *Nuremberg Diary*, 25.

8   Neave, *Nuremberg*, 209.
9   Taylor, *The Anatomy of the Nuremberg Trials*, 25.
10   Ibid., 353–4
11   Tusa and Tusa, *The Nuremberg Trial*, 307.
12   West, *A Train of Powder*, 48.
13   Tusa and Tusa, *The Nuremberg Trial*, 310.
14   Trial Papers, 6 April 1946.
15   Sönke Neitzel (ed.), *Tapping Hitler's Generals: Transcripts of Secret Conversations 1942–45* (Barnsley, Frontline Books, 2007), 42, 79, 81, and 124.
16   Hassell, *The Ulrich von Hassell Diaries, 1938–1944*, 4.
17   Tusa and Tusa, *The Nuremberg Trial*, 413.
18   Trial Papers, 26 July 1946.
19   Walter Gorlitz (ed.), *The Memoirs of Field Marshal Wilhelm Keitel: Chief of the German High Command, 1938–1945* (London: Cooper Press, 2000) and see Taylor, *The Anatomy of the Nuremberg Trials*, 607–8.
20   Neave, *Nuremberg*, 213.
21   Peter Longerich, *Holocaust: The Nazi Persecution and Murder of the Jews* (Oxford: OUP, 2012), 146.
22   Trial Papers, 3 April 1946.

Ernst Kaltenbrunner, 1903–46

1   Kershaw, *The End*, 227 and 230.
2   West, *A Train of Powder*, 59.
3   Neave, *Nuremberg*, 129.
4   Goldensohn, *The Nuremberg Interviews*, 140.
5   Ibid., 156.
6   Gilbert, *Nuremberg Diary*, 64.
7   Taylor, *The Anatomy of the Nuremberg Trials*, 249.
8   Tusa and Tusa, *The Nuremberg Trial*, 316.
9   *Daily Telegraph*, 11 April 1946.
10   Trial Papers, 12 April 1946.
11   Flanner, *Janet Flanner's World*, 110.
12   Taylor, *The Anatomy of the Nuremberg Trials*, 361.
13   Ibid., 362.
14   Trial Papers, 15 April 1946.
15   Ibid., 26 July 1946.
16   Bartov *et al.*, *Crimes of War*, 12.

Alfred Rosenberg, 1893–1946

1   Longerich, *Holocaust*, 289.
2   Neave, *Nuremberg*, 107.
3   See Goldensohn, *The Nuremberg Interviews*, xvii.
4   See Ibid., 197.
5   Ibid., 199.
6   Gilbert, *Nuremberg Diary*, 63.

7   Taylor, *The Anatomy of the Nuremberg Trials*, 366.
8   Trial Papers, 17 April 1946.
9   Longerich, *Holocaust*, 289.
10 Trial Papers, 26 July 1946.
11 Taylor, *The Anatomy of the Nuremberg Trials*, 538.

Hans Frank, 1900–46

1   Richard Evans, *The Coming of the Third Reich* (London: Penguin Press, 2004), 179.
2   Shirer, *The Rise and Fall of the Third Reich*, 661.
3   Goldensohn, *The Nuremberg Interviews*, 18.
4   Gilbert, *Nuremberg Diary*, 20.
5   Trial Papers, 14 December 1945.
6   See Taylor, *The Anatomy of the Nuremberg Trials*, 201.
7   Ibid., 368.
8   Tusa and Tusa, *The Nuremberg Trial*, 322.
9   Ibid., 26 July 1946.
10 Niklas Frank, *In the Shadow of the Reich* (London: Alfred Knopf, 1991).
11 Hassell, *The Ulrich von Hassell Diaries, 1938–1944*, 34 and 128.
12 Ibid., 157 and 169.
13 St Paul's letter to the Romans, chapter 7 v19 (King James Bible).

Wilhelm Frick, 1877–1946

1   Taylor, *The Anatomy of the Nuremberg Trials*, 267.
2   Overy, *Interrogations*, 354
3   Goldensohn, *The Nuremberg Interviews*, 40.
4   Owen, *Nuremberg*, 33.
5   Hans Gisevius, *To the Bitter End* (New York: Da Capo Press, 1998).
6   Tusa and Tusa, *The Nuremberg Trial*, 333.
7   Gilbert, *Nuremberg Diary*, 295
8   Trial Papers, 26 July 1946.
9   Ibid., 31 August 1946.

Julius Streicher, 1885–1946

1   Evans, *The Coming of the Third Reich*, 188.
2   Shirer, *The Rise and Fall of the Third Reich*, 1142.
3   Norman Davies, *Europe: A History* (London: Pimlico 1977), 1051.
4   Taylor, *The Anatomy of the Nuremberg Trials*, 159.
5   West, *A Train of Powder*, 5.
6   Goldensohn, *The Nuremberg Interviews*, 252.
7   Ibid., 262.
8   Gilbert, *Nuremberg Diary*, 9.
9   Ibid., 73.
10 Ibid., 125–6.

11 Ibid., 301.
12 Taylor, *The Anatomy of the Nuremberg Trials*, 379.
13 See Tusa and Tusa, *The Nuremberg Trial*, 336.
14 Trial Papers, 24 April 1946.
15 Ibid.
16 Ibid., 26 July 1946.
17 Taylor, *The Anatomy of the Nuremberg Trials*, 493.
18 Ibid., 539–40.
19 Tusa and Tusa, *The Nuremberg Trial*, 453.
20 See Ibid., 333–4.
21 Taylor, *The Anatomy of the Nuremberg Trials*, 590.
22 Ibid., 631.

Hjalmar Schacht, 1877–1970

1 Alan Bullock, *Hitler: A Study in Tyranny* (London: Penguins Books, 1962), 174.
2 Amos Simpson, *Hjalmar Schacht in Perspective* (Paris: Mouton Group, 1969), 179.
3 See Shirer, *The Rise and Fall of the Third Reich*, 907.
4 Overy, *Interrogations*, 96.
5 Goldensohn, *The Nuremberg Interviews*, 218.
6 Gilbert, *Nuremberg Diary*, 19.
7 Colonel Burton Andrus, *The Infamous of Nuremberg* (London: Leslie Frewin, 1969), 166.
8 Neave, *Nuremberg*, 183.
9 Taylor, *The Anatomy of the Nuremberg Trials*, 386.
10 Tusa and Tusa, *The Nuremberg Trial*, 338.
11 Trial Papers, 2 May 1946.
12 Ibid.
13 Ibid.
14 *Daily Telegraph*, 3 May 1946.
15 Hassell, *The Ulrich von Hassell Diaries, 1938–1944*, 6.
16 Ibid., 72 and 140.
17 Ibid., 67 and 222.
18 Trial Papers, 26 July 1946.

Walther Funk, 1890–1960

1 Shirer, *The Rise and Fall of the Third Reich*, 143.
2 Tusa and Tusa, *The Nuremberg Trial*, 35.
3 Goldensohn, *The Nuremberg Interviews*, 76.
4 Neave, *Nuremberg*, 118.
5 Gilbert, *Nuremberg Diary*, 206.
6 Tusa and Tusa, *The Nuremberg Trial*, 347.
7 Taylor, *The Anatomy of the Nuremberg Trials*, 394.
8 Trial Papers, 7 May 1946.
9 See Taylor, *The Anatomy of the Nuremberg Trials*, 5.
10 Trial Papers, 15 April 1946.
11 Ibid., 26 July 1946.

12 Taylor, *The Anatomy of the Nuremberg Trials*, 591.
13 See West, *A Train of Powder*, 236.

Karl Dönitz, 1891–1980

1   Quoted in Neave, *Nuremberg*, 223.
2   Taylor, *The Anatomy of the Nuremberg Trials*, 86.
3   Neitzel, *Tapping Hitler's Generals*, 153–8.
4   Goldensohn, *The Nuremberg Interviews*, 3.
5   Gilbert, *Nuremberg Diary*, 296.
6   Trial Papers, 9 May 1946.
7   Ibid.
8   Taylor, *The Anatomy of the Nuremberg Trials*, 403.
9   Tusa and Tusa, *The Nuremberg Trial*, 357.
10 Trial Papers, 9 May 1946.
11 Tusa and Tusa, *The Nuremberg Trial*, 353.
12 Trial Papers, 26 July 1946.
13 Paddy Padfield, *Dönitz: The Last Führer* (London: Harper & Row, 1984), 471.
14 *Sunday Times*, 13 February 1959.
15 Padfield, *Dönitz*, 487.
16 Taylor, *The Anatomy of the Nuremberg Trials*, 631.
17 Neave, *Nuremberg*, 221.
18 Ibid., 224.
19 Padfield, *Dönitz*, 467.

Erich Raeder, 1876–1960

1   Andrew Sangster, *The Diarists of 1940: An Annus Mirabilis* (Newcastle: Cambridge Scholars, 2020), 118.
2   Trial Papers, 17 May 1946.
3   David Kinsella and Craig L. Carr (eds), *The Morality of War: A Reader* (London: Lynne Rienner, 2007), 115.
4   Ibid, 333.
5   Gilbert, *Nuremberg Diary*, 336.
6   Ibid., 338.
7   See Ibid., 341–2.
8   Trial Papers, 26 July 1946.
9   Taylor, *The Anatomy of the Nuremberg Trials*, 541.
10 See Erich Raeder, *My Life* (Naval Institute Press, 1960).

Baldur von Schirach, 1907–76

1   Taylor, *The Anatomy of the Nuremberg Trials*, 86.
2   See Tusa and Tusa, *The Nuremberg Trial*, 40.
3   Neave, *Nuremberg*, 95.
4   Goldensohn, *The Nuremberg Interviews*, 237.

5 Ibid., 250.
6 Gilbert, *Nuremberg Diary*, 40.
7 Ibid., 139.
8 Shirer, *The Rise and Fall of the Third Reich*, 1142.
9 See Tusa and Tusa, *The Nuremberg Trial*, 374.
10 Ibid., 375.
11 Trial Papers, 24 May 1946.
12 Taylor, *The Anatomy of the Nuremberg Trials*, 249.
13 *The Times*, 24 May 1946.
14 Trial Papers, 26 July 1946.
15 See David Frost interview of Baldur von Schirach.
16 Neave, *Nuremberg*, 99.

Fritz Sauckel, 1894–1946

1 *Trials of War Criminals Before the Nuremberg Military Tribunals. II.* Washington: United States Government Printing Office, 1950, 407 (doc. 016-PS). Online edition. Internet Archive.
2 See Tusa and Tusa, *The Nuremberg Trial*, 38.
3 Neave, *Nuremberg*, 140.
4 Goldensohn, *The Nuremberg Interviews*, 204.
5 Ibid., 211.
6 Neave, *Nuremberg*, 140.
7 See Tusa and Tusa, *The Nuremberg Trial*, 378.
8 Speer, *Inside the Third Reich*, 307.
9 Taylor, *The Anatomy of the Nuremberg Trials*, 429.
10 See Ciano, *Ciano's Diary 1937–1943*, 496.
11 Taylor, *The Anatomy of the Nuremberg Trials*, 430.
12 Trial Papers, 26 July 1946.
13 Neave, *Nuremberg*, 356.

Alfred Jodl, 1890–1946

1 Kershaw, *The End*, 377.
2 Neave, *Nuremberg*, 193.
3 Neitzel, *Tapping Hitler's Generals*, 89 and 265.
4 Overy, *Interrogations*, 529.
5 Ibid., 533.
6 Goldensohn, *The Nuremberg Interviews*, 138.
7 Gilbert, *Nuremberg Diary*, 28.
8 Tusa and Tusa, *The Nuremberg Trial*, 253.
9 Ibid., 382.
10 Speer, *Inside the Third Reich*, 690.
11 Trial Papers, 3 June 1946.
12 Ibid., 5 June 1946.
13 Ibid., 20 December 1945.
14 Taylor, *The Anatomy of the Nuremberg Trials*, 437.
15 Ibid., 439.

16 Ibid., 486.
17 Trial Papers, 26 July 1946.
18 Neave, *Nuremberg*, 206.
19 Ibid.

Arthur Seyss-Inquart, 1892–1946

1 Taylor, *The Anatomy of the Nuremberg Trials*, 438.
2 Tusa and Tusa, *The Nuremberg Trial*, 387.
3 Taylor, *The Anatomy of the Nuremberg Trials*, 442.
4 Ibid., 444.
5 Speer, *Inside the Third Reich*, 687.
6 Trial Papers, 26 July 1946.
7 Ann Leslie, *Daily Mail*, 15 June 1973.

Franz von Papen, 1879–1969

1 See Captain von Rintelen, *The Dark Invader* (London: Penguin Books, 1938).
2 See Franz von Papen, *Memoirs* (reprint edition) (London: Ams Pr Incp, 1953).
3 See André François-Poncet, *The Fateful Years: Memoirs of a French Ambassador in Berlin 1931–38* (London: Victor Gollancz, 1949).
4 Neave, *Nuremberg*, 170.
5 Interrogation Papers taken by Thomas Dodd, 12 October 1945, 12–17, and quoted in Overy, *Interrogations*, 431.
6 Goldensohn, *The Nuremberg Interviews*, 174.
7 Hassell, *The Ulrich von Hassell Diaries, 1938–1944*, 160.
8 Gilbert, *Nuremberg Diary*, 29.
9 Ibid., 119.
10 Ibid., 321.
11 See Owen, *Nuremberg*, 24–5.
12 Tusa and Tusa, *The Nuremberg Trial*, 389.
13 Ibid., 391.
14 Gilbert, *Nuremberg Diary*, 392.
15 Taylor, *The Anatomy of the Nuremberg Trials*, 447.
16 Trial Papers, 19 June 1946.
17 Gilbert, *Nuremberg Diary*, 383.
18 Trial Papers, 26 July 1946.
19 Ibid.
20 See Franz von Papen, *Memoirs* (London: Dutton, 1953).
21 Tusa and Tusa, *The Nuremberg Trial*, 392 and Trial Papers, 19 June 1946.

Albert Speer, 1905–81

1 Tusa and Tusa, *The Nuremberg Trial*, 394.
2 Quoted in Overy, *Interrogations*, 475–6.
3 FIAT Intelligence Report, EF/Min/3, 19 October 1945 which can be found in Overy, *Interrogations*, 215–57.

4   Overy, *Interrogations*, 105.
5   Henrik Eberle and Matthias Uhl (eds), *The Hitler Book: The Secret Dossier Prepared for Stalin* (London: John Murray, 2005), 124.
6   Nicholas Farrell, *Mussolini: A New Life* (London: Sharpe Books, 2018), 532.
7   Ciano, *Ciano's Diary 1937–1943*, 515–6.
8   Gilbert, *Nuremberg Diary*, 24.
9   Ibid., 74.
10 Trial Papers, 20 June 1946.
11 Tusa and Tusa, *The Nuremberg Trial*, 395.
12 Taylor, *The Anatomy of the Nuremberg Trials*, 451.
13 *The Times*, 21 June 1946.
14 Trial Papers, 20 June 1946.
15 See Ibid.
16 Ibid.
17 Ibid., 21 June 1946.
18 Ibid., 21 June 1946.
19 Ibid., 21 June 1946
20 Taylor, *The Anatomy of the Nuremberg Trials*, 596.
21 Richard Evans, *The Third Reich at War 1939–1945* (London: Allen Lane, 2008), 742.
22 See Michael Kitchen, *Speer: Hitler's Architect* (Yale: Yale University Press, 2015), 343.
23 See Hugh Trevor-Roper, *The Last Days of Hitler* (7th edition) (London: Pan Books, 1947), 68–70 and 214–5.
24 See Matthias Schmidt, *Albert Speer: The End of a Myth* (New York: St Martin's Press, 1984), 186.

Constantin von Neurath, 1873–1956

1   Goldensohn, *The Nuremberg Interviews*, 171.
2   See Shirer, *The Rise and Fall of the Third Reich*, 1032.
3   Gilbert, *Nuremberg Diary*, 13.
4   Longerich, *Holocaust*, 67.
5   Tusa and Tusa, *The Nuremberg Trial*, 402.
6   Taylor, *The Anatomy of the Nuremberg Trials*, 458.
7   Hassell, *The Ulrich von Hassell Diaries, 1938–1944*, 6, 14, and 66.

Hans Fritzsche, 1900–53

1   See Helmut Heiber, *Goebbels* (New York: Hawthorn Books, 1972), 146.
2   Shirer, *The Rise and Fall of the Third Reich*, 1143.
3   Goldensohn, *The Nuremberg Interviews*, 54.
4   Ibid., 66.
5   Owen, *Nuremberg*, 32.
6   Speer, *Inside the Third Reich*, 681.
7   Gilbert, *Nuremberg Diary*, 164.
8   Tusa and Tusa, *The Nuremberg Trial*, 404.
9   Taylor, *The Anatomy of the Nuremberg Trials*, 461.
10 Ibid., 463.
11 Trial Papers, 26 July 1946.

12 Ibid., 31 August 1946.
13 Hans Fritzsche, *Es sprach Hans Fritzsche. Nach Gesprächen, Briefen, und Dokumenten (Hans Fritzsche spoke. After conversations, letters, and documents)* (Stuttgart: Thiele-Verlag KG, 1949).

Robert Ley, 1890–1945

1 Owen, *Nuremberg*, 76–7.
2 The Testament of Robert Ley, Justice Robert Jackson, Main File Box 3, document 27, August 1945 and quoted in Overy, *Interrogations*, 481.
3 Ciano, *Ciano's Diary*, entry 26 July 1939.
4 See Overy, *Interrogations*, 491.
5 Gilbert, *Nuremberg Diary*, 8.
6 Neave, *Nuremberg*, 137.

Reflections

1 Andrew Sinclair, *An Anatomy of Terror: A History of Terrorism* (London: Pan Books, 2004), 363.
2 Kinsella, *The Morality*, 345.
3 Ibid., 352.
4 See Kinsella and Carr, *The Morality of War*, 381.
5 Kinsella and Carr, *The Morality of War*, 352.
6 Neave, *Nuremberg*, 227.
7 Valerie Geneviève Hébert, *Hitler's Generals on Trial* (Kansas: University Press Kansas, 2010), 36.
8 Ibid., 43.
9 Davies, *Europe*, 1054–5.
10 Niall Ferguson, *The War of the World: Twentieth-Century Conflict and the Descent of the West* (London: Allen Lane, 2006), 579.
11 Davies, *Europe*, 1055.
12 Norman Davies, *No Simple Victory: World War II in Europe, 1939–1945* (London: Viking, 2007), 65.
13 See Michael Burleigh, *Moral Combat: Good and Evil in World War II* (London: Harper Press, 2010), 549.
14 Taylor, *The Anatomy of the Nuremberg Trials*, 641.
15 Kinsella and Carr, *The Morality of War*, 399.
16 Bartov *et al.*, *Crimes of War*, xxiii.
17 Rebecca West, *Daily Telegraph*, 26 September 1946.
18 Richard Raiber, *Anatomy of Perjury: Field Marshal Albert Kesselring, Via Rasella, and the Ginny Mansion* (Newark: University of Delaware Press, 2008), 184.
19 Max Hastings, *All Hell Let Loose: The World at War 1939–1945* (London: Harper, 2011), 445.
20 John Cameron, (ed.) *The Peleus Trial* (London: Hodge, 1948), xiii.
21 Roger Manvell and Heinrich Fraenkel, *The Incomparable Crime* (London: Heinemann, 1967), 244.
22 Taylor, *The Anatomy of the Nuremberg Trials*, 637.
23 Ibid.
24 Kerstin von Lingen, *Kesselring's Last Battle: War Crimes Trials and Cold War Politics, 1945–1960* (Kansas: University of Kansas Press, 2009), 7.

25   See General Frido von Senger und Etterlin, *Neither Fear Nor Hope: The Wartime Career of General Frido Von Senger und Etterlin, Defender of Cassino* (London: Macdonald, 1963), 347.

26   See Neave, *Nuremberg*, 372.

27   The UN War Crimes Commission, *Law Reports of Trials of War Criminals, Volume VIII* London; Volume VIII. Case No 47 (London: Law Reports of Trials of War Criminals, 1949), 12.

28   Burleigh, *Moral Combat*, 550.

29   Bartov *et al.*, *Crimes of War*, 171.

30   Hébert, *Hitler's Generals on Trial*, 4.

31   Salter, *Nazi War Crimes*, 7–8.

32   Paul Preston, *Franco* (London: Fontana Press, 1995), 612.

33   B. H. Liddell Hart, *The Other Side of the Hill* (London: Pan Books, 1999), 51 and 140.

34   B. H. Liddell Hart, *The German Generals Talk* (London: Harper, 2002), 36.

35   Lingen, *Kesselring's Last Battle*, 175.

Final Thoughts

1   See Kinsella and Carr, *The Morality of War*, 351.

2   Tusa and Tusa, *The Nuremberg Trial*, 236.

3   Taylor, *The Anatomy of the Nuremberg Trials*, 536.

4   Daniel Goldhagen, *Hitler's Willing Executioners* (London: Abacus, 1997), 461.

5   Guido Knopp, *Hitler's Holocaust* (Stroud: Sutton Publishing, 2001), xxx.

6   See Longerich, *Holocaust*, 175.

7   Ibid., 396.

8   Ibid., 405.

Bibliography

Books

Andrus, Burton. *I Was the Nuremberg Jailer*. New York: Coward, McCann & Geoghegan, 1969.

Andrus, Colonel Burton. *The Infamous of Nuremberg*. London: Leslie Frewin, 1969.

Bartov, O., Grossmann, A. and Nolan, A. (eds). *Crimes of War: Guilt and Denial in the Twentieth Century*. New York: The New Press, 2002.

Bower, Tom. *Blind Eye to Murder: Britain, America and the Purging of Nazi Germany*. London: Warner Books, 1995.

Browning, Christopher. *Ordinary Men: Reserve Police Battalion 101 and the Final Solution in Poland*. London: Penguin Books, 2001.

Bullock, Alan. *Hitler: A Study in Tyranny*. London: Penguins Books, 1962.

Burleigh, Michael. *Moral Combat: Good and Evil in World War II*. London: Harper Press, 2010.

Cameron, John (ed.), *The Peleus Trial*. London: Hodge, 1948.

Davies, Norman. *Europe: A History*. London: Pimlico 1977.

Davies, Norman. *No Simple Victory: World War II in Europe, 1939–1945*. London: Viking, 2007.

Eberle, Henrik and Matthias Uhl, (eds.) *The Hitler Book: The Secret Dossier Prepared for Stalin*. London: John Murray, 2005.

Evans, Richard. *The Coming of the Third Reich*. London: Penguin Press, 2004.

Evans, Richard. *The Third Reich at War, 1939–1945*. London: Allen Lane, 2008.

Farrell, Nicholas. *Mussolini: A New Life*. London: Sharpe Books, 2018.

Ferguson, Niall. *The War of the World: Twentieth-Century Conflict and the Descent of the West*. London: Allen Lane, 2006.

Flanner, Janet. *Janet Flanner's World: Uncollected Writings, 1932–1975*. London: Harcourt Brace Jovanovich, 1979.

François-Poncet, André. *The Fateful Years: Memoirs of a French Ambassador in Berlin 1931–38*. London: Victor Gollancz, 1949.

Frank, Niklas. *In the Shadow of the Reich*. London: Alfred Knopf, 1991.

Freedman, Lawrence (ed.), article by Arendt, *War*. Oxford: OUP, 1994.

Fritzsche, Hans. *Es sprach Hans Fritzsche. Nach Gesprächen, Briefen, und Dokumenten* (*Hans Fritzsche spoke. After conversations, letters, and documents*). Stuttgart: Thiele-Verlag KG, 1949.

Fulbrook, Mary (ed.) *Twentieth-Century Germany: Politics, Culture, and Society 1918–1990*. London: Hodder Headline Group, 2001.

Gilbert, G. M. *Nuremberg Diary*. New York: Da Capo Press, 1995.

Gisevius, Hans. *To the Bitter End*. New York: Da Capo Press, 1998.

Goldhagen, Daniel. *Hitler's Willing Executioners*. London: Abacus, 1997.

Goldensohn, Leon, edited by Robert Gellately. *The Nuremberg Interviews*. London: Pimlico, 2007.

Gorlitz, Walter. (ed.) *The Memoirs of Field Marshal Wilhelm Keitel: Chief of the German High Command, 1938–1945*. London: Cooper Press, 2000.

Gritzbach, Erich. *Hermann Goering: The Man and His Work*. Georgia: Historical Review Press, Third Impression, 1980.

Hastings, Max. *All Hell Let Loose: The World at War 1939–1945*. London: Harper, 2011.

Hastings, Max. *The Secret War: Spies, Codes and Guerrillas 1939–1945*. London: Collins 2015.

Hébert, Valerie Geneviève. *Hitler's Generals on Trial*. Kansas: University Press of Kansas, 2010.

Heiber, Helmut. *Goebbels*. New York: Hawthorn Books, 1972.

Howard, Michael. *The Invention of Peace & the Reinvention of War*. London: Profile Books, 2001.

Kershaw, Alex. *The Liberator*. London: Hutchinson, 2012.

Kershaw, Ian. *The End: Hitler's Germany 1944–45*. London: Penguin Books, 2012.

Kinsella, David and Craig L. Carr (eds). *The Morality of War: A Reader*. London: Lynne Rienner, 2007.

Kitchen, Michael. *Speer: Hitler's Architect*. Yale: Yale University Press, 2015.

Knopp, Guido. *Hitler's Holocaust*. Stroud: Sutton Publishing, 2001.

Liddell Hart, B. H. *The Other Side of the Hill*. London: Pan Books, 1999.

Liddell Hart, B. H. *The German Generals Talk*. London: Harper, 2002.

Lingen, Kerstin von. *Kesselring's Last Battle: War Crimes Trials and Cold War Politics, 1945–1960*. Kansas: University Press of Kansas, 2009.

Longerich, Peter. *Holocaust: The Nazi Persecution and Murder of the Jews*. Oxford: OUP, 2012.

Lucas, James. *Last Days of the Reich: The Collapse of Nazi Germany, May 1945*. London: Arms and Armour Press, 1986.

Manvell, Roger and Fraenkel, Heinrich. *The Incomparable Crime*. London: Heinemann, 1967.

Milgram, Stanley. *Obedience to Authority: An Experimental View*. New York: Harper and Row, 1974.

Mosley, Leonard. *The Reich Marshal: A Biography of Hermann Goering*. New York: Doubleday, 1974.

Neave, Airey. *Nuremberg*. London: Biteback Publishing, 2021.

Neitzel, Sönke (ed.). *Tapping Hitler's Generals: Transcripts of Secret Conversations 1942–45*. Barnsley, Frontline Books, 2007.

Nicholas, Lynn. *The Rape of Europa*. London: Papermac, 1995.

Overy, Richard. *Interrogations: The Nazi Elite in Allied Hands, 1945*. London: Penguin Books, 2002.

Overy, Richard. *Goering: Hitler's Iron Knight*. London: I. B. Tauris, 2012.

Owen, James. *Nuremberg: Evil on Trial*. London: Headline, 2007.

Padfield, Paddy. *Dönitz: The Last Führer*. London: Harper & Row, 1984.

Papen, Franz von. *Memoirs* (reprint edition). London: Ams Pr Incp, 1953.

Payne, Stanley G. and Palacios, Jesús. *Franco: A Personal and Political Biography*. London: University of Wisconsin Press, 2014.

Preston, Paul. *Franco*. London: Fontana Press, 1995.

Raeder, Erich. *My Life*. Naval Institute Press, 1960.

Raiber, Richard. *Anatomy of Perjury: Field Marshal Albert Kesselring, Via Rasella, and the Ginny Mansion*. Newark: University of Delaware Press, 2008.

Rintelen, Captain von. *The Dark Invader*. London: Penguin Books, 1938.

Salter, Michael. *Nazi War Crimes: US Intelligence and Selective Prosecution at Nuremberg*. Abingdon: Routledge Cavendish, 2007.

Sangster, Andrew. *The Diarists of 1940: An Annus Mirabilis*. Newcastle: Cambridge Scholars, 2020.

Schmidt, Matthias. *Albert Speer: The End of a Myth*. New York: St Martin's Press, 1984.

Schmidt, Paul. *Hitler's Interpreter: The Memoirs of Paul Schmidt*. Cheltenham: The History Press, 2016.

Scotland, Lt. Col. A. P. *The London Cage*. London: Landsborough Publications, 1959.

Senger und Etterlin, General Frido von. *Neither Fear Nor Hope: The Wartime Career of General Frido Von Senger und Etterlin, Defender of Cassino*. London: Macdonald, 1963.

Shirer, William. *The Rise and Fall of the Third Reich: A History of Nazi Germany*. London: Mandarin, 1997.

Simpson, Amos. *Hjalmar Schacht in Perspective*. Paris: Mouton Group, 1969.

Sinclair, Andrew. *An Anatomy of Terror: A History of Terrorism*. London: Pan Books, 2004.

Speer, Albert. *Inside the Third Reich*. London: Weidenfeld & Nicolson, 1995.

Taylor, Telford. *The Anatomy of the Nuremberg Trials: A Personal Memoir*. New York: Alfred Knopf, 1992.

Tipton, Frank B. *A History of Modern Germany Since 1815*. London: Continuum, 2003.

Toland, John. *The Last 100 Days: The Tumultuous and Controversial Story of the Final Days of World War II in Europe*. New York: The Modern Library, 1996.

Trevor-Roper, Hugh. *The Last Days of Hitler* (7th edition). London: Pan Books, 1947.

Tusa, Ann and John Tusa. *The Nuremberg Trial*. London: BBC Books, 1995.

Weitz, Eric. *Weimar Germany: Promise and Tragedy*. Woodstock: Princeton University Press, 2007.

West, Rebecca. *A Train of Powder*. Chicago: Ivan R Dee, 1955.

Westphal, General Siegfried. *The German Army in the West*. London: Cassell, 1951.

Diaries

Ciano, Galeazzo, edited by Renzo De Felice. *Ciano's Diary 1937–1943*. London: Phoenix Press, 2002.

Colville, John. *The Fringes of Power: Downing Street Diaries 1939–1955*. London: Hodder and Stoughton, 1985.

Goebbels, Joseph, edited by Fred Taylor. *The Goebbels Diaries, 1939–1941*. London: Hamish Hamilton, 1982.

Hassell, Ulrich von. *The Ulrich von Hassell Diaries, 1938–1944*. London: Frontline Books, 2011.

Klemperer, Victor. *To the Bitter End: The Diaries of Victor Klemperer*. London: Weidenfeld & Nicolson, 1999.

Online Archives

Trials of War Criminals Before the Nuremberg Military Tribunals. *II*. Washington: United States Government Printing Office, 1950, 407 (doc. 016-PS). Online edition. Internet Archive.

Papers, reports, and transcripts

Interrogation Papers by Lieutenant-Colonel Smith W. Brookhart and Mr Sender Jaari, 15 November 1945.

Interrogation Papers taken by Thomas Dodd, 12 October 1945, 12–17.

The Testament of Robert Ley, Justice Robert Jackson, Main File Box 3, document 27, August 1945.

Trial Papers, published in: The Trial of German Major War Criminals, *Proceedings of The International Military Tribunal sitting at Nuremberg, Part 5, 21 January to February 1946*. London: H.M. under authority of Attorney-General by HMSO, 1945–47.

The UN War Crimes Commission, *Law Reports of Trials of War Criminals, Volume VIII* London; Volume VIII Case No 47, London: Law Reports of Trials of War Criminals, 1949.

Video resources

David Frost interview of Baldur von Schirach, *Frost on Friday*. London Weekend Television, aired 13 September 1968. [YouTube].

Index

Author's note: *If Hitler and a few others are indexed every time their names occur the index would consume too many pages, therefore they are only indexed when significant.*

.